THE HISTORIOGRAPHY OF GLADSTONE AND DISRAELI

Anthem Perspectives in History

Titles in the Anthem Perspectives in History series combine a thematic overview with analyses of key areas, topics or personalities in history. The series is targeted at high-achieving A Level, International Baccalaureate and Advanced Placement pupils, first-year undergraduates and an intellectually curious audience.

A History of Ireland, 1800–1922
Theatres of Disorder?
Hilary Larkin

Britain in India, 1858–1947
Lionel Knight

Disraeli and the Art of Victorian Politics
Second Edition
Ian St John

Disraeli and the Art of Victorian Politics
Ian St John

Gladstone and the Logic of Victorian Politics
Ian St John

King John
An Underrated King
Graham E. Seel

The Creation of Modern China, 1894–2008
The Rise of a World Power
Iain Robertson Scott

THE HISTORIOGRAPHY OF GLADSTONE AND DISRAELI

Ian St John

ANTHEM PRESS

Anthem Press
An imprint of Wimbledon Publishing Company
www.anthempress.com

This edition first published in UK and USA 2016
by ANTHEM PRESS
75–76 Blackfriars Road, London SE1 8HA, UK
or PO Box 9779, London SW19 7ZG, UK
and
244 Madison Ave #116, New York, NY 10016, USA

British Library Cataloguing-in-Publication Data
A catalogue record for this book is available from the British Library.

Library of Congress Cataloging-in-Publication Data
Names: St John, Ian, 1965–
Title: The historiography of Gladstone and Disraeli / Ian St John.
Description: London : Anthem Press, 2016. | Series: Anthem perspectives in history; 1 |
Includes bibliographical references and index.
Identifiers: LCCN 2016020798 | ISBN 9781783085286 (paperback)
Subjects: LCSH: Great Britain—Politics and government—1837–1901. |
Great Britain—History—Victoria, 1837–1901—Historiography. |
Gladstone, W. E. (William Ewart), 1809–1898. |
Disraeli, Benjamin, 1804–1881. | Prime ministers—Great Britain—Biography. |
BISAC: HISTORY / Modern / 19th Century. |
HISTORY / Europe / Great Britain. | POLITICAL SCIENCE / History & Theory. |
Classification: LCC DA560 .S68 2016 | DDC 941.081092/2—dc23
LC record available at https://lccn.loc.gov/2016020798

ISBN-13: 978 1 7830 8528 6 (Pbk)
ISBN-10: 1 78308 528 2 (Pbk)

This title is also available as an e-book.

CONTENTS

PREFACE

It is the object of this book to trace the often sharply differing perspectives historians have formed with regard to the key incidents in the careers of the two foremost politicians of the Victorian age – William Gladstone and Benjamin Disraeli. As such, it is a work of synthesis. It seeks to juxtapose the various interpretations of events historians have advocated, rather than arrive at settled conclusions of its own. To aim for any kind of 'final verdict' upon the debates under review would not merely be presumptuous but also subvert the book's entire raison d'être. For it is the contention of this study, and of the wider series of which it forms part, that history is a continually evolving subject in which finality is not to be looked for. Every generation poses new questions, or reformulates answers to old ones, and there can be no end to this process. It is this very fluidity and contestability of key historical doctrines that gives the subject its perennial attraction and ensures that every student must confront the issues for themselves, and weigh up the sometimes bewildering array of theories and explanations, so as to come to their own conclusions: realizing, full well, that their own judgement can never be anything other than provisional and that new insights and discoveries will be made that will call for the matter to be re-evaluated by historians. If this book encourages the student to relish the interplay of argument and debate that makes up modern history, and helps them steer their way through the sometimes perplexing world of Victorian politics, then it will have achieved its purpose. To bring more forcibly before the reader the fact that written history is generated by actual historians operating within a particular social and intellectual context, a brief résumé of the career of the chief historians cited is included as an appendix.

Ian St John
Haberdashers' Aske's School, Elstree

Chapter 1

GLADSTONE AND DISRAELI TO 1851

Outline of Events

The opening of the 1840s saw William Gladstone and Benjamin Disraeli sitting together on the Tory benches and anticipating the fall of Lord Melbourne's Whig government. It was a brief moment of convergence. Their journeys to Westminster could not have been more different. Where Gladstone had left his mercantile home in Liverpool to attend Eton in 1821, proceeding from there to Oxford and then the House of Commons in 1833 at the age of 23, Disraeli, the baptized son of a literary Jew, had attended neither public school nor university, and had to struggle with debts and public disdain before finally securing a seat in 1837, at the age of 33. From 1841 their careers diverged again. While Gladstone became vice president of the Board of Trade in Robert Peel's Conservative administration, Disraeli languished sulkily on the backbenches. Momentous consequences followed from this. Gladstone, who in the 1830s had made his name as a High Church Anglican bent on raising the Christian tone of political life, now metamorphosed into an accomplished administrator, working closely with Peel to make Britain a land of free trade. Disraeli, by contrast, moved into a position of ever-more barbed criticism of Peelite Conservatism, which he branded an 'organised hypocrisy'. In 1845 these divergent trajectories collided with a crash that reverberated through the nineteenth century. As famine consumed Ireland, Peel decided to break with established Tory policy and scrap the duty on imported corn – the Corn Laws. Where Gladstone rallied to Peel's side, Disraeli launched a series of scathing attacks from the backbenches that have never been equalled in effectiveness. In 1846 Peel pushed through Corn Law repeal, but in so doing broke the unity of the Conservative Party. Peel, together with around one hundred Members of Parliament (MPs) (including Gladstone) who had supported Corn Law repeal, now broke away from the Conservatives, leaving

Disraeli as a prominent figure in the Protectionist Conservative rump. Never again would Gladstone and Disraeli serve in the same party. Here two controversies are considered: why did Gladstone abandon his inflexible High Tory politics for Peel's liberal reformism; and why did Disraeli denounce Peel so vehemently and champion opposition to Corn Law repeal?

1.1   Why Did Gladstone Go from High Tory to Reforming Peelite?

When it comes to Gladstone's early Toryism, nearly all historians take their lead from the characterization of him by his Whig opponent, Thomas Babbington Macaulay, as 'the rising hope of those stern unbending Tories'.[1] What distinguished Gladstone from his fellow Tories was the alacrity with which he articulated his conservative vision through a body of doctrine concerning the theology of politics so abstract as to be unique among British politicians. In his 1838 *The State in Its Relations with the Church*, Gladstone argued that the individual found the meaning of his life according to the place into which he was born in the God-ordained structure of society. He entered the world not with a set of rights or freedoms, but with a set of duties. The morality of British society was guaranteed by the teachings of the Church of England, and it was the government's duty to follow the guidance of the Church in its actions and privilege its members over those following other religious denominations and none.

But was Gladstone really as stern and unbending a Tory as it suited Macaulay to allege? Colin Matthew, the editor of Gladstone's diaries and, at the time of his death in 1999, the foremost interpreter of Gladstone's career, cautioned against making Gladstone 'too Tory'. He had always supported the right of Roman Catholics to become Members of Parliament, and he advocated strengthening institutions through moderate reform.[2] A bolder reassessment is provided by David Bebbington, a notable scholar both of Gladstone and the history of evangelicalism, who points out that besides obedience, Gladstone acknowledged self-government as a leading principle of the state, and that it only required 'a slight shift in the balance between self-government and obedience [...] to alter his political allegiance. Already the intellectual path was remarkably clear towards Liberalism'.[3] Such a path

---

[1] T. B. Macaulay, 'Gladstone on Church and State' (1839), in *Critical and Historical Essays Contributed to the* Edinburgh Review *by Lord Macaulay*, ed. F. C. Montague (1903), II, p. 331.

[2] H. C. G. Matthew, *Gladstone 1809–1898* (1997), p. 26.

[3] D. Bebbington, *The Mind of Gladstone* (2004), p. 41.

to Liberalism may have been apparent to Bebbington in 2004; however, the mere suggestion of it would have offended Gladstone and astonished contemporaries in 1838.

Whatever the initial rigidity of Gladstone's thinking, from the early 1840s he embarked upon a process of political re-evaluation that had led him, by 1851, to substitute for his formative High Toryism a style of politics that was more pragmatic, more reformist and more attuned to the doctrines of political economy than to the formulas of the Church Fathers.[4] Indeed for some, such as John Lawrence Hammond and Michael Richard Foot, he was already on his way toward Liberalism. Debate has centred upon the *motives* that led Gladstone to reconfigure his fundamental approach to politics. There are two main perspectives: first, that Gladstone abandoned his early views because of contradictions within his original theocratic position, and second, that what was important was Gladstone's experience of being confronted by realities his earlier ideas simply had not allowed for.

Church and state contradictions

Three problems associated with Gladstone's original project have been emphasized. First, there is the view that what primarily caused Gladstone to rethink his politics was the reaction to his book, which ran, even among Conservatives, from lukewarm to openly hostile. This was the reason stated by Gladstone himself, and endorsed in John Morley's official biography of the Liberal leader in 1903. Gladstone's State and Church book, writes John Morley, 'though exciting lively interest, was evidently destined to make no converts in theory and to be pretty promptly cast aside in practice'.[5] Erich Eyck, the German-liberal émigré historian, followed this interpretation in his 1938 *Gladstone*: 'shortly after the publication of his book, he had realised that he was a voice crying in the wilderness, "the last man on a sinking ship" [Gladstone] and that there was not a single politician who dreamed of making his axiom of the conscience of the State, and its duty of presenting the truth – the basis of a practical policy'.[6] Sydney Checkland similarly argues that the chief factor causing Gladstone to shift his political priorities was the unfavourable response to his book, including the disapproval of Peel. 'William's acceptance of the public reaction to his *State and Church* was the turning-point of his life. Rationality and a sense of the nature of the real

---

[4] Cf. E. F. Biagini, *Gladstone* (2000), p. 26.
[5] J. Morley, *Life of William Ewart Gladstone* (1903), I. p. 181.
[6] E. Eyck, *Gladstone* (1938), p. 45.

world, after a devastating struggle, overcame the system of thought that his emotional needs had imposed upon him.'[7]

However the idea that unfavourable responses to his book broke Gladstone's commitment to its doctrines is rejected by Perry Butler, whose *Gladstone: Church, State, and Tractarianism* (1982) is the most systematic investigation of the theological roots of Gladstone's early politics. According to Butler, in 1841 'the ecclesiastical bias of Gladstone's politics remained paramount [...] His response to criticism of his book had not been to retract his opinions nor modify the argument, but rather to publish, in April 1841, a revised and expanded edition'. At that time, notes Butler, he opposed a motion to allow Jews to hold government office and spoke in his diary of the importance of upholding 'the principle of National Religion (a principle, which is my bond to Parliamentary life)'.[8] Yet later in the same work Butler edges back to the more traditional Gladstone–Morley interpretation:

> The crisis of Gladstone's life was the fate of his book published in 1838. It was the realization that his ideal was no longer possible which, with the disintegration of the Tory party, forced him to seek a *modus vivendi* between the catholic tradition and the liberal principles of the nineteenth century.[9]

However the two most influential recent interpreters of Gladstone's career, Matthew and Richard Shannon, agree that it was not the *reaction* to the Church and State book that was decisive, but the discovery by Gladstone from 1841 that Conservative governments were unwilling to pursue theocratic dogmas, being as pragmatic in their politics as any Whig administration. The sustainability of Gladstone's system, believes Matthew, was heavily dependent upon the conduct of the Conservatives:

> The role of the Tory party was [...] crucial to the Gladstonian conception of State–Church politics [...] for if the Tories failed live up to their role, he would have to reconsider his own position and function in politics [...] The success of political Tractarianism had depended on infiltration and control of the Tory party. But it was soon clear that the Tory party in office [...] would fall far short of the high role accorded it by Gladstone.[10]

---

[7] S. G. Checkland, *The Gladstones: A Family Biography 1764–1851* (1971), p. 393.
[8] P. Butler, *Gladstone: Church, State, and Tractarianism* (1982), pp. 93–94.
[9] Ibid., pp. 233–34.
[10] Matthew, *Gladstone*, pp. 66–68.

By 1842 he was recognizing that it was no longer possible to bring the action of the state into conformity with the laws of the Church, a point made by Shannon, who observes that Gladstone was brought to accept that the forces animating government were not those of the Christian spirit.[11] Butler argues that, once within the Cabinet, Gladstone realized that

> the defence of the Church, was obviously neither properly understood nor even central to his colleagues' concerns. For a young man who had seen his political vocation in terms of "rescuing, rectifying and securing the institutions of the country" so that they could once more become the means of christianizing the social order, the whole drift of politics in the 1840s seemed alarming.[12]

A third development seen as compromising Gladstone's theocratic politics was the implosion of the Oxford Movement in the 1840s. Although Gladstone was never a Tractarian, and his book taught a doctrine at odds with the separation between Church and State Tractarians called for, the revitalization of Anglican doctrine initiated by John Henry Newman, Edward Pusey and John Keble at Oxford appeared to support Gladstone's ideas for it suggested that Anglican thinking was still a vital force, attracting the allegiance of the most talented young men of the universities and shaping the religious life of the nation. Hence Newman's 1845 conversion to Catholicism, followed by that of Gladstone's friends Henry Manning and James Hope, was a terrible challenge to Gladstone's vision of the future. Morley notes that the crisis of Peel's government coincided with that of the Oxford Movement.

> The fall of Peel and the break-up of his party in the state coincided pretty nearly with a hardly less memorable rupture in that rising party in the church, with which Mr. Gladstone had more or less associated himself almost from the beginning [...] two events so far-reaching as the secession of Newman and the fall of Sir Robert [...] brought Gladstone to an epoch in his life of extreme perturbation.[13]

Matthew concurs with the importance of this association: with the collapse of the Oxford Movement there 'could be no expectation of [...] that great burst of progress in English religion to which Gladstone looked to make his theory possible'.[14] Butler

---

[11] R. Shannon, *Gladstone: God and Politics* (2007), p. 46.
[12] Butler, *Gladstone*, p. 110.
[13] Morley, *Life of Gladstone*, I. p. 303.
[14] Matthew, *Gladstone*, p. 70.

agrees. 'The events of the early 1840s, culminating in Newman's conversion, were to shatter Gladstone's hope of a gradual and inevitable permeation of "Church Principles" and the creation of a national Catholic Church.'[15]

In fact, a number of writers including Butler, Bebbington, Peter Stansky, Jonathan Parry, and Checkland, regard the controversy generated by the Oxford Movement and the Gorham Judgement of 1851, when the Privy Council declared that it was permissible for members of the Church of England to deny the doctrine of baptismal regeneration (a central tenet of Gladstone's High Churchmanship), as being the precipitator of Gladstone's long-term evolution from Conservative to Liberal. If the state could not be relied upon to sustain authentic Church doctrine, then it was, contends Parry, better that the Church have the 'freedom to follow its teaching and its missionary work free from state interference. And if to secure this freedom it must relinquish its privileges, then it was right that it should do so.'[16] Gladstone began, says Stansky, to recognize the crucial importance of liberty of conscience. Once he recognized that the perfect union of Church and State could not be achieved, then 'there was no legitimate basis for discrimination: Catholics, Jews, Nonconformists – all were entitled to the aid and sustenance of the State.' By 1847 he was voting to admit Jews to parliament.[17] Gladstone 'made a fast but thorough transformation from a man who was practically a religious bigot to a man of tolerance'.[18] Butler calls this Gladstone's 'High Anglican road' to Liberalism:

> His Liberalism didn't emerge out of utilitarianism or secularism; it emerged out of a belief that the Church must be free from state interference so that it might preserve the purity of its doctrine and have the liberty to use its energies in its work. And if the Anglican Church was to have this freedom, all other religious denominations required it also.[19]

If, continues Butler, there was no longer a conscience in the state, there remained the conscience of the individual, and it was therefore vital that this be sustained.

> But this was impossible without liberty, religious liberty to choose Catholic truth, liberty in a more general sense to enhance the

---

[15] Butler, *Gladstone*, p. 103.

[16] J. Parry, *Democracy and Religion: Gladstone and the Liberal Party, 1867–1875* (1986), p. 159.

[17] P. Stansky, *Gladstone: A Progress in Politics*, p. 45.

[18] Ibid., pp. 46–47. Eyck shares this view. Cf. his *Gladstone*, p. 57.

[19] Butler, *Gladstone*, pp. 152–53.

consciousness of moral duty [...] If this was the kernel of 'Gladstonian Liberalism' then in a real sense its origin lay in the intellectual and religious crisis that followed the fate of his book.[20]

'There can be little doubt', writes Checkland, 'that the way in which religious argument was then conducted helped to push William toward political liberalism.'[21] This idea, that the concept of individual liberty that Gladstone always argued was central to his transition from Tory to Liberal lay in his re-evaluation of the importance of individual faith, is articulated by Bebbington:

> The politician may have learned the practice of economic liberalism from Peel, but the groundwork of his constitutional liberalism was laid in reflection on the best way to structure the church so as to stand up to the state. The value of freedom, the power of public opinion, and the need to extend the principle of participation all emerged from this phase in his thinking.[22]

The crucible of experience

Most historians have attributed Gladstone's changed political stance not to theological issues, but to his experiences as a politician in the 1840s. Crucial, it is argued, was his appointment to the Board of Trade in 1841 and his subsequent work with Peel in overhauling Britain's tariff system in the direction of free trade.

To begin with, it is suggested that only once he entered government did Gladstone confront a series of issues for which the speculations of Aristotle and Samuel Taylor Coleridge (whose reflections upon the ideal state had formed the staple of his reading in the 1830s) had little real relevance and it was now that his evolution into liberalism began. To quote Checkland,

> [a]t the Board of Trade he discovered how serious were the economic problems that now confronted Britain. Very quickly he came to the conclusion that the only way out was to continue the work of Huskisson, removing the remaining restraints on trade and industry imposed by the State and letting a further release of individual initiative relieve the

---

[20] Ibid., p. 150.
[21] Checkland, *The Gladstones*, p. 393.
[22] Bebbington, *Mind of Gladstone*, p. 111.

nation's economic difficulties [...]By the later 1840s William [...] was moving strongly in a liberal direction.[23]

Butler, although focusing upon Gladstone's religious dilemmas, acknowledges that a significant factor undermining his early approach to politics was 'the down to earth business of government he encountered at the Board of Trade'.[24] Though he regretted the curtailment of religious devotions that his work involved, 'he came to regard it as a necessary part of his vocation and in no way unworthy or second best'.[25] Above all, he became 'aware of the complexity of the social and political order. His analysis of the basis and function of government in the early 1830s had been, as he saw now, unrealistic and naïve'.[26] For Euginio Biagini, the Board of Trade provided 'an effective antidote to Gladstone's theocratic dreams and archaic Anglican idealism'.[27] T. A. Jenkins encapsulates the view that it was this induction into the problems of governance that was chiefly responsible for the abandonment of his Church and State vision:

> Experience as a minister in Peel's government soon demonstrated [...] that this theory was inapplicable to the complex reality of British society [...] and Gladstone was compelled to recognise that adaptability was a necessary part of the politician's craft. This liberation from the intellectual strait-jacket of his early years marked the beginning of that process of 'growth', which John Morley identified many years ago as the principal feature of Gladstone's political career.[28]

However, as Jenkins admits, while divesting himself of one 'intellectual strait-jacket', Gladstone quickly fastened himself in another: the theoretical suppositions of laissez-faire economics.[29] Gladstone was a born systematizer. He needed a body of doctrine that would make sense of the world – and he needed to believe that this system of thought was divinely inspired. Hence the attraction of the free market, which seemed to be a God-created order in which individuals made the best of themselves through hard work, and in which these individual actions were mediated through the competitive

---

[23] Checkland, *The Gladstones*, p. 394.
[24] Butler, *Gladstone*, p. 103.
[25] Ibid., p. 104.
[26] Ibid. Butler would here appear to be largely echoing the words of Matthew. Cf. *Gladstone*, p. 67.
[27] Biagini, *Gladstone*, p. 21.
[28] T. A. Jenkins, *Gladstone, Whiggery and the Liberal Party 1874–1886* (1988), pp. 19–20.
[29] Ibid., pp. 67–68.

system to bring the greatest prosperity for society and the greatest scope for moral choice in spending and saving decisions. It can thus be argued that Gladstone abandoned his State and Church doctrine because he had encountered a system of teaching which accorded far better with the world which he actually inhabited and yet which was infused by God's will. Matthew lends his authority to this interpretation. 'Gladstone more and more came to see free trade as an alternative, or at least a supplement, to the Church as the means by which the conscience of the State could be expressed and the relationships of an industrial society fairly adjusted.'[30] As his Church–State system collapsed in 1845, Gladstone, searching for a substitute, invested the concept of free trade 'with the moral role in the nation's ethical progress earlier attributed to the Established Church'. Thus,

> [t]he Aristotelian notion of a balanced society based on obligation and duty gave way [...] to a society in which the assertion of economic individualism gained predominance, conditioned though Gladstone hoped it would be by probity, self-control, and Christian morality.[31]

Shannon, too, observes how the principles of free trade, and their capacity to promote moral values such as individual responsibility and peace between nations, exerted a growing hold upon Gladstone: 'he was learning the great lesson of reconciling his preoccupation with the religious conscience of the State with a growing awareness of the moral dimension of political economy'.[32] There is, he writes, 'a convincing case to be made for Peel as the progenitor of Gladstone's Liberalism'.[33]

The continuing theological dimension to Gladstone's political practice is most forcefully expounded in Andrew Boyd Hilton's 1988 study *The Age of Atonement*. In explaining Gladstone's abandonment of his Church–State system, Hilton talks of his shift from a religious perspective based upon the revelation of Christ's message to one of God's will as revealed through nature – that is, a system of natural theology. Gladstone became increasingly preoccupied with the providential nature of existence, and this was reflected in the operation of the free market system, which displayed 'God's handiwork, his wise and moral economy of the world'.[34] Although Gladstone was already moving toward free trade, it was in 1845 that it became a 'burning moral

---

[30] Matthew, *Gladstone*, p. 75.
[31] Ibid., pp. 76–77.
[32] R. Shannon, *Gladstone: Peel's Inheritor* (1982), p. 125.
[33] Ibid., p. 166.
[34] A. Boyd Hilton, *The Age of Atonement* (1988), p. 351.

issue' with the Irish Famine, which he saw as a humiliating indictment of the Protectionist system. 'There is no doubt that for Gladstone [...] the repeal of the Corn Laws has to be regarded as an act of atonement.'[35]

A third encounter held to have shaped Gladstone's politics was his relationship with Peel. Gladstone, suggest the likes of Morley and Shannon, developed a tremendous admiration for Peel's administrative abilities and recognized that his reforms were really a form of ethical activity, deploying the power of the state to reform society in a way that made the Christian life more possible. Gladstone wanted to be an executive politician, and that meant being like Peel. Thus we find Morley arguing that

> [i]t was during these years of labour under Peel that he first acquired principles of administrative and parliamentary practice that afterwards stood him in good stead [...] We cannot forget that Peel and Mr. Gladstone were in the strict line of political succession [...] They [...] showed the same clear knowledge that it was not by its decorative parts [...] that the community derived its strength; but that it rested for its real foundations on its manufactures, its commerce, and its credit.[36]

'Gladstone's reverence for Peel', writes Eyck, 'increased with every day of service under him.'[37] Peel's 'pedagogic experiment' of sending a reluctant Gladstone to the Board of Trade in 1841 proved 'a brilliant success. The political bookworm had evolved into a practical politician of the first rank, who, instead of wasting his time on theologico-political tracts [...] promoted the business of the Government by writing reports on railways and commercial tariffs, and by mastering the concrete details of the national economy.'[38] Of recent historians, it is Shannon who has placed the greatest emphasis upon Peel's influence upon Gladstone, even subtitling the first volume of his biography of Gladstone *Peel's Inheritor*. For Shannon, Gladstone's encounter with Peel was the decisive event in his political career.

> Gladstone was by nature prone to be psychologically vulnerable to the kind of benignly authoritative herculean high-mindedness so completely incarnated by Peel [...] The sheer administrative grandeur of Peel's vision of the transmuting of economics into morals captivated Gladstone. It was from Peel, as of from some mighty alchemist of state,

---

[35] Ibid., pp. 351–52.
[36] Morley, *Life of Gladstone*, I. p. 269.
[37] Eyck, *Gladstone*, p. 22
[38] Ibid., pp. 43–44.

that Gladstone first learned the sublime art of turning the base metals of politics into gold.[39]

From Peel, Shannon later wrote, Gladstone 'learned the grand lesson that political party is a means to an end defined by executive necessity'.[40] Shannon's emphasis upon the Peelite origins of Gladstonian liberalism has, however, been questioned by Richard Gaunt, who argues that relations between the two men 'were characterised by a series of misunderstandings and, occasionally, incomprehension on both sides'.[41] Nothing, he writes, marked Gladstone out as Peel's 'inheritor' until the repeal of the Corn Laws, and even then the notion that Gladstone was the natural successor to Peel owed more to the early death of Peel's other colleagues and the fact that Gladstone deliberately capitalized upon Peel's reputation, so as to make 'the progression from Peelite Conservatism to Gladstonian liberalism look less incongruous than might otherwise have been the case'.[42] By the 1880s, continues Gaunt, Gladstone's liberal interpretation of Peel had become standard, not truly challenged until Norman Gash's biography of Peel in 1972 – and we are apt to forget 'how many of our views of Peel (and the Peelites) have been shaped by Gladstone himself'.[43]

Colonies and Italy

Some historians contend that, while it was an encounter with external realities that pushed Gladstone into revising his opinions, these realities were in the realm not of economic, but of foreign policy. It is argued, first, that it was during his time as colonial secretary between 1845 and 1846 that Gladstone was confronted with the fact that his belief that the government should only support the Church of England was not applicable to the colonies. Butler notes that the initial breach in his Church and State theory occurred over a proposal from the Canadian government to sell off land set aside for church building and divide the proceeds between the various Protestant churches. Although this meant the loss of any special status for the Church of England, Gladstone approved the measure, arguing that the colonies must be free to decide such matters for themselves. 'But [...] the settlement of the clergy reserves was yet another example of actual circumstances at odds

---

[39] Shannon, *Gladstone: Peel's Inheritor*, p. 121.

[40] Shannon, *Gladstone: God and Politics*, p. 51.

[41] R. A. Gaunt, 'Gladstone and Peel's Mantle', in *William Gladstone: New Studies and Perspectives* (2012), ed. R. Quinault, R. Swift and R. Clayton Windscheffel, p. 32.

[42] Ibid., p. 49.

[43] Ibid., p. 47.

with his theory.'[44] For other historians it was the politics of the colonial relationship that were crucial, opening, says Biagini, Gladstone's 'mind to Liberal opinions, especially as a consequence of his involvement with the drawing up of new constitutions for Canada and New Zealand [...] he became a strong advocate of colonial self-government and the establishment of representative assemblies'.[45] David Nicholls points out that Gladstone himself suggested that colonial subjects 'made a breach in my Toryism' as early as 1835, when he briefly served as undersecretary of state for war and the colonies. According to Nicholls, he quickly concluded that the British government 'should move in the direction of allowing as much freedom to its colonial subjects as it could within the limits of order'.[46] Checkland observes that '[e]xperience of colonial problems drove him in the direction of the reformers', while Matthew writes that his 'support for the idea of promoting self-governing English colonies around the world encouraged relations with radicals like Molesworth and Roebuck'.[47]

The second foreign policy issue impacting upon Gladstone arose from his encounter with prison conditions in Naples in the wake of the failed revolution of 1848. Though his initial break with Toryism, says Biagini, 'came over the question of free trade, the final steps had more to do with Italian than with British politics'.[48] Visiting several of his friends who had participated in the revolutionary government and were now incarcerated at the pleasure of King Ferdinand, Gladstone expressed his repulsion at what he saw in a *Letter to Lord Aberdeen* (1851). By thus openly condemning, says Morley, the kind of monarchical regime Conservatives generally supported, he was stepping outside the mainstream of European Conservatism, being drawn 'by the native ardour of his humanity, unconsciously and involuntarily, into that great European stream of liberalism which was destined to carry him so far'.[49] Several historians endorse this perspective. Gladstone's experience of events in Naples, writes Stansky, was 'a crucial one in moving him in the direction of Liberalism, a growing belief that certain minimum liberties, and self-determination, belonged to all'. Although his initial intention was conservative, to argue that moderate reform was the best way to avoid revolution, his argument

---

[44] Butler, *Gladstone*, p. 99.
[45] Biagini, *Gladstone*, p. 25.
[46] D. Nicholls, 'Gladstone on Liberty and Democracy', *Review of Politics*, Vol. 23 (1961), p. 402.
[47] Checkland, *The Gladstones*, p. 394; Matthew, *Gladstone*, p. 81.
[48] Biagini, *Gladstone*, p. 27.
[49] Morley, *Life of Gladstone*, I. p. 389.

'served him as part of his ultimate transition to Liberalism'. He 'was more of a Liberal upon his return from Naples than he was before'.[50] For Biagini, Gladstone was 'the hero of the Liberals, both at home and abroad', while Agatha Ramm notes that he had 'publicly and unmistakeably attached himself to a forward-looking, reforming Liberalism'.[51] Matthew is more cautious, recognizing that Gladstone had not deliberately embraced the Liberal cause. Even so, 'Conservative he might still feel himself, Liberal his language was certainly becoming'.[52]

Yet the idea that the Neapolitan controversy represented a turning point in Gladstone's politics has been criticized. Deryck Schreuder believes there 'was much truth in Gladstone's argument that his aim was conservative'.[53] Ferdinand's brutal misgovernment in Naples was fuelling radicalism by destabilizing society, and Gladstone feared that Ferdinand 'would destroy the established order itself'. The solution was to reform the administration of policing and justice: 'It was a simple creed, designed to preserve and not to change society.' Although Gladstone's arguments were misinterpreted as promoting liberalism, his involvement with Italian affairs represented an attempt to uphold the 'ancient order' of European society through 'enlightened conservatism'.[54] Shannon, too, believes that the 'Neapolitan lurch of 1850–51' has been accorded excessive importance owing to Gladstone's subsequent alliance with the Liberals in 1859. Gladstone was then 'running rather out of control', and 'the Neapolitan affair was random rather than purposeful, and certainly in no sense determinant. It was one lurch among several.'[55]

Church and state continuities

Uniting the above interpretations is the assumption that Gladstone's politics *did* undergo a transformation in the 1840s from an earlier preoccupation with the religious policy of the state to a more pragmatic reformism. Yet some historians, notably Richard Helmstadter, have challenged this, arguing that Gladstone's politics remained essentially theocratic. As Gladstone became more experienced as a politician he did become more flexible and willing to abandon positions taken up in 1838 as implications of his theory. However

---

[50] Stansky, *Gladstone*, pp. 61–62.
[51] Biagini, *Gladstone*, p. 28; A. Ramm, *William Ewart Gladstone* (1989), p. 25.
[52] Matthew, *Gladstone*, p. 81.
[53] D. M. Schreuder, 'Gladstone and Italian Unification, 1848–70: The Making of a Liberal?', *English Historical Review* Vol. 85 (1970), p. 480.
[54] Ibid., pp. 481, 483.
[55] Shannon, *Gladstone: Peel's Inheritor*, p. 242.

'he retained, at least as an ideal, the theory of church and state and unified society that he had developed in his first book'.[56] The idea of an essential conservatism running through Gladstone's politics is supported by Biagini. Although, he writes, Gladstone's shift towards free trade could later be seen as 'an important step towards liberalism', he was spurred on to embrace liberal causes for motivations which were intrinsically conservative. There was 'a long-term conservative strategy undergirding his views in both the fiscal and religious spheres'.[57] Rather than taking the first steps in a long walk to Liberalism, Gladstone, in the 1840s, was merely reassessing the means by which he could uphold his constant Tory ends of a stable hierarchical society.

The Maynooth issue of 1845 provides a test case for this debate. Gladstone had, in his Church–State book, criticized the parliamentary grant to the Catholic seminary of Maynooth in Ireland, arguing that the British state should only support Anglicanism. In 1845 Peel proposed to increase the Maynooth grant, hoping thereby to improve Anglo–Irish relations. Gladstone resigned from the Cabinet as a result – and then voted *for* the increase. Why did he act in such a contradictory manner? The conventional view is that Gladstone saw that Maynooth highlighted the impracticality of his earlier doctrines. He agreed that increased funding for Maynooth was politically justified, yet realized that this was a denial of his Church and State views. In resigning, Gladstone was signalling that he saw the contradiction, and in voting for the grant he was showing that he would no longer be held to his youthful Tory views. It was, according to Butler, 'a landmark in his political development', a 'cathartic experience' without which 'his subsequent development would have been impossible'.[58] Matthew provides the classic modern formulation of this viewpoint:

> The impracticality of Maynooth as a battle-cry was merely a measure of the impracticality of the theory it symbolized. With his recent training in Peelite techniques of administration Gladstone soon saw this. Principle rejected the Maynooth grant: good government demanded it. Thus Gladstone both resigned from the cabinet and voted for the grant [...] Idiosyncratic and perverse though Gladstone's action seemed to contemporaries, it was for him a pivotal and a purgative experience.

---

[56] R. J. Helmstadter, 'Conscience and Politics: Gladstone's First Book', in *The Gladstonian Turn of Mind*, ed. B. Kinzer (1985), p. 8.

[57] Biagini, *Gladstone*, pp. 24–25.

[58] Butler, *Gladstone*, pp. 95–96.

Never again [...] did he invest government or party with the high ethical status of *The State in its Relations with the Church*.[59]

While Morley and Eyck consider Gladstone's resignation as necessary to show that he was not voting for the grant in order to retain his Cabinet seat,[60] Matthew and others like Roy Jenkins and Stansky see it rather as a 'propitiatory act that allowed him to move on to new views and approaches'[61] – the discharge, in Jenkins's words, 'of a debt to the past, and maybe an expiration of what he was coming to see as the foolishness of *The State in its Relations with the Church*'.[62] As such, Gladstone's actions over Maynooth were largely symbolic, a point Shannon also emphasizes. Gladstone had already concluded that the State could not uphold high Anglican ideals. Maynooth merely forced Gladstone to acknowledge the contradiction and he had, in consistency, to resign. But this did not deflect his political trajectory – it just made manifest his willingness to seek for political remedies in the secular sphere. With Maynooth Gladstone publicly declared that the State could not be the agent of the Church's interest. 'Gladstone had reached the point of turning his original programme inside out.'[63] Butler summarizes the view that Maynooth represented 'the fatal blow to Gladstone's early political creed'.

> He had clung to the hope that the Conservative party would arrest the steady erosion of the State's confessional basis. His hope had been in vain [...] To look at the matter in a broader context, what Gladstone was being forced to recognize was the demise of the Confessional State and increasing political pluralism. This was what Maynooth really symbolised.[64]

Yet the idea that in voting for the Maynooth grant Gladstone was discarding his earlier Church and State doctrine is rejected by Helmstadter and Bebbington. Gladstone, writes Helmstadter, recognized that while the state's ultimate end was the good of its members, its immediate duty was to uphold social order. 'Gladstone reversed his position on the Maynooth grant in 1845 because he had become persuaded that social order in Ireland was in

[59] Matthew, *Gladstone*, p. 69.
[60] Morley, *Life of Gladstone*, 1: 278; Eyck, *Gladstone*, p. 46.
[61] Stansky, *Gladstone*, p. 113.
[62] R. Jenkins, *Gladstone* (1995), pp. 70–71.
[63] Shannon, *Gladstone: Peel's Inheritor*, p. 176.
[64] Butler, *Gladstone*, p. 121.

grave danger.'[65] Hence his support for the grant 'did not involve rejection of the principles and theories elaborated in his book'. In an ideal world, adds Bebbington, Gladstone still believed the state should 'uphold the teachings of the established Anglican Church'. But following Helmstadter, he argues that the state had first to be secure, and in Ireland 'the state could only be secure if it made concessions to different religions. Hence Gladstone amended the practice of his theory in the light of practical necessity.'[66]

Conclusion

While Helmstadter is right to say that at no point did Gladstone formally renounce the teachings of *The State in Its Relations with the Church*, there is a general consensus that in his political conduct from the early 1840s onwards he did not seek to realize its doctrines. His wholehearted support for Peel's economic liberalism, his acceptance of religious pluralism, his vote in favour of increased funding for the Catholic College of Maynooth, his revulsion at Ferdinand's suppression of constitutional movements in Naples and his personal shock at the implications of the Gorham Judgement, all suggest that his career was advancing to the beat of a very different drum. Where debate has been enjoined is over the motives and precise timing of this departure. True, Gladstone could not ignore the challenges posed to his theory by developments within the Church and the largely uncomprehending response of fellow Conservatives to his book. But as his subsequent career shows, he was more than able to justify apparently inconsistent positions when it suited him. In the 1840s it did not suit him. Gladstone, as Walter Bagehot later remarked, was someone highly receptive to the zeitgeist within which he found himself, and the fundamental change in Gladstone's circumstances during the 1840s was his assumption of office under Peel. The complexity of the economic issues he confronted and the example of Peel's executive brilliance supplied such a jolt to his world picture that the old Church–State road map had no relevance. Matthew and Hilton are surely correct to emphasize the appeal of the teachings of political economy on an ethical-cum-theocratic level, yet it is more plausible to see this new understanding of God's ways among men as a vindicator of Gladstone's adopted position, rather than as a motivator as such. In explaining Gladstone's shifting position the perspective provided by Morley and reiterated by Shannon still holds: namely, that it was Gladstone's encounter with the problems of modern government as viewed through the prism of Peelite reformism that was the

---

[65] Helmstadter, 'Conscience and Politics', pp. 33–34.
[66] Bebbington, *Mind of Gladstone*, p. 107.

key to his abandonment of his Tory Church–State theocratic system as a practical guide to action.

1.2   What Motivated Disraeli's Opposition to Peel in the 1840s?

From the early 1840s Disraeli waged a struggle for Tory supremacy against his Party leader, Sir Robert Peel, a struggle which eventuated in a fractured victory for Disraeli in 1846 as Peel's government collapsed and Disraeli emerged as a leading figure in the reduced ranks of the Conservative party. The matter of what motivated Disraeli in his pursuit of Peel is of considerable importance in assessing his political character: did he react against Peel out of an offended sense of what he was doing to the Tory tradition, or was he driven by a desire to advance his own career?

Disraeli is conventionally depicted as a supporter of Peel in 1841. He welcomed Peel's Tamworth Manifesto in 1834 and supported the government's initial liberalizing reforms, even proclaiming that free trade had all along been a Tory policy. John Vincent notes that even in his 1844 novel, *Coningsby*, Disraeli denounced the Toryism of exclusivity and commercial restriction: 'Certainly, in matters of trade Disraeli was an instinctive Peelite who associated fetters on commerce with the bad old days.'[67] Disraeli would thus have gladly accepted a place in Peel's 1841 government. However no such offer was forthcoming, and from this point Disraeli moved into a position of more open criticism of Peel's leadership, working in conjunction with the Young England group of Tory aristocrats to take issue with Peel on a succession of issues: Factory Reform, Sugar Duties, the Maynooth grant, and then, decisively, over Peel's attempt to repeal the Corn Laws in late 1845. On the latter question Disraeli's invective against Peel contributed to the collapse of Peel's administration, and when Peel left the Conservative party followed by around 100 MPs, Disraeli remained among the 200 Protectionist Conservative MPs who had opposed Corn Law repeal.

When considering the events of 1841–46, two questions claim our attention. First, what accounted for the estrangement between Disraeli and Peel, and second, why did Disraeli so vociferously oppose Peel's attempt to repeal the Corn Laws?

Explaining Disraeli's antagonism toward Peel

Disraeli presented his disillusionment with Peel as arising out of a deep-seated divergence in their conceptions of Conservatism. While

---

[67] J. Vincent, *Disraeli* (1990), pp. 89–90.

for Disraeli, Conservatism was about the importance of upholding an ordered society of classes integrated around the leadership of a territorial aristocracy, Peel had been seduced by the 'cosmopolitan' values of laissez-faire individualist economics and utilitarian reformism, the result being a government of 'Tory men and Whig measures' in the interests of the middle class. From this perspective, his clash with Peel was one of ideology. This understanding has found favour with a number of historians. James Anthony Froude, opinionated historian of the Tudor Reformation and disciple and biographer of Thomas Carlyle, was the author of one of the first serious studies of Disraeli's career in 1890. Carlyle had been a major contributor to the debate on the Condition of England Question of the 1840s, and Froude compared the responses of Peel and Disraeli to the challenges of that decade.[68] Disraeli, wrote Froude, was an unsparing critic of an economy given over to laissez-faire, with men linked by money alone and where the distance between rich and poor was so great as to make them 'two nations'. 'With the powerful Protectionist majority returned by the elections of 1841, Peel, in Disraeli's opinion, had an opportunity of bringing these demoralising tendencies under the authority of reason and conscience.' But Peel had no intention of doing this, being a practical politician who could deal only with immediate problems. 'Wages must be left to the market where he found them. All that he could do to help the people was to cheapen the food which was bought with them, to lay taxation on the shoulders of those best able to bear it, and by education and such other means as he could provide to enable the industrious and the thoughtful to raise themselves.'[69] In such a characterization it is not difficult to discern the influence of Carlyle's *Past and Present*, with Disraeli cast in the role of Carlyle's hero Abbot Samson, who had imposed good governance on the Abbey of St Edmunds.[70]

A more sustained attempt to develop the idea that Disraeli's rivalry with Peel emerged out of diverging responses to the social question of the 1840s was supplied in 1904 by Walter Sichel, an Oxford-educated lawyer, biographer and friend of Oscar Wilde. Disraeli's solution to the social problem was, he writes, the doctrines of Young England: a revival of national institutions; a reawakening of the sense of community, with the privileged classes taking an interest in the well-being of the poor; a

---

[68] The Condition of England question was a national debate that arose in the 1840s as to whether a society based on industry and mass urbanization was sustainable in the longrun.

[69] J. A. Froude, *Lord Beaconsfield* (1890), pp. 130–31.

[70] T. Carlyle, *Past and Present* (1843).

strengthened place for the Church and Monarchy in national life; and a strong government to lead the process of rebuilding reciprocal relations between the classes. Looking to Peel to provide such leadership, he was soon disabused as Peel promised to place the nation under the control of a narrow industrial class who saw labour as their enemies, not their allies. As a consequence 'Disraeli discerned that Peel's present "conservatism" was an "organised hypocrisy"; that [...] Peel's leading spirits were Manchester Radicals [...] that eventually the contest must lie between "national" Conservatism and international Liberalism'.[71] Harold Beeley concurs with this analysis. Like Karl Marx, says Beeley, Disraeli saw the danger of class war from the division between rich and poor, but unlike Marx he believed this division could be overcome by re-awakening traditional sentiments of loyalty and shared values, the onus for which fell to the younger generation of aristocrats who could win the loyalty of the lower classes. 'The key to the achievement of this was imaginative and charismatic leadership and it was this cohesive paternalistic leadership that Peel was failing to provide.'[72]

Although recent historians have been less inclined to depict the rivalry between Disraeli and Peel in ideological terms, this approach still occasionally finds favour. Thus for Sarah Bradford what was at stake in the 1840s was a battle for the soul of the Conservative party, with Disraeli 'staking his claim to be the ideologist of the Conservative party of the future, the guardian of the true spirit of Toryism; his underlying theme was an attack upon the soullessness of Peelite Conservatism'.[73] Similarly Edgar Feuchtwanger highlights the clash between the views of Peel and Disraeli:

> Peel wanted to fashion a moderate conservative block appealing to all the men of substance, the commercial middle classes as well as the territorial squirearchy and aristocracy [...] Disraeli envisaged a union between the landholding classes and the dispossessed masses held together by a bond of mutual obligation.[74]

Most recently, Douglas Hurd and Edward Young contend that while Disraeli needed to break Peel's hold on the Tory party if he were to advance his career, 'there was also a genuine intellectual difference between Disraeli and Peel'. Where Peel wanted to adapt the Tories to the 'spirit of the age', Disraeli wanted to resist the spirit of change and 'restore the old order based on

[71] W. Sichel, *The Life of Lord Beaconsfield* (1904), p. 72.
[72] H. Beeley, *Disraeli* (1936), p. 62.
[73] S. Bradford, *Disraeli* (1982), p. 137.
[74] E. Feuchtwanger, *Disraeli*, p. 37.

generous and stable relationships between classes'. Even so, Hurd and Young believe that such ideological differences cannot explain Disraeli's bitterness toward Peel, which they attribute, rather nebulously, to a personal revulsion against Peel's manner, speeches, pronunciation and vocabulary.[75]

However for most historians what was at stake in the 1840s was not the philosophy of Conservatism but Disraeli's political career. Disraeli, it is contended, was a man of disappointed ambition, his challenge to Peel arising out of his bitterness at being overlooked for office in 1841. Had he been a member of Peel's administration no comparable disagreements would have emerged.

The charge that Disraeli's conduct owed everything to ambition originated with the Peelites and remained a commonplace among political opponents. Thus T. Hayes, a vehement Liberal critic, wrote in 1878 that after having supported Peel and praising free trade, 'Disraeli, finding it hopeless to expect anything from Sir Robert Peel, changes his tactics and puts himself forward by degrees as one of the leaders of the Protectionist party'.[76] But it was not only his enemies who saw Disraeli's attacks as reflective more of ego than ideology. The Danish literary critic Georg Brandes remarked in 1880 that, as 'he could not get forward in company with Peel, he must try to do so as his opponent',[77] while in a 1891 book, his friend and former Conservative MP Sir William Fraser opined that Disraeli's criticisms of Peel were a product of frustrated ambition. 'My belief is that, had Disraeli been employed by Sir Robert Peel, he would never have betrayed him. I believe that he would have done his utmost to deserve the position, in which he had been placed [...] because he would have felt that, once in the groove of office, his fortune was made.' As it was he felt his 'great gifts were [...] utterly thrown away'.[78]

More significant was the weight William Monypenny and George Buckle lent to this interpretation in their *Life of Benjamin Disraeli* (1910–1920). Monypenny, the author of the first two volumes, argued that the significance of Young England to Disraeli's career had been overrated. 'Young England was, in fact, little more than a beautiful dream, and no dream could long detain a man like Disraeli from the world of reality.'[79] In his attack upon Peel ambition was the chief motive:

---

[75] D. Hurd and E. Young, *Disraeli or The Two Lives* (2013), pp. 84–85.

[76] T. T. Hayes, *Lord Beaconsfield: A Paper Read before the Members of the Leigh Liberal Club* (1878), p. 14. Hayes was the leader of the Liberal party in Leigh.

[77] G. Brandes, *Lord Beaconsfield: A Study* (1880), p. 150.

[78] W. Fraser, *Disraeli and His Day* (1891), p. 26.

[79] W. F. Monypenny and G. E. Buckle, *The Life of Benjamin Disraeli* (1929 edn), I. p. 701.

while it [Peel's ministry] stood his path was barred, and he now determined to advance to the assault upon it alone, to strike openly and persistently, and to extort by sheer aggression from a reluctant House of Commons the recognition which it had denied to his more persuasive methods [...] When his object was accomplished, the Government overthrown, the organised hypocrisy at length swept away, and a path cleared for his own ambition and the triumph of his ideas, he held his hand and struck no more.[80]

What makes this frank assessment of Disraeli's conduct so telling is that Monypenny had been commissioned by the *Times* to produce a sympathetic biography of the Conservative leader based upon privileged access to Disraeli's papers. Monypenny, himself a *Times* journalist and advocate of imperialism – he fought in the Boer War and later joined Lord Milner's staff in South Africa – proceeded to do just that, though he only carried Disraeli's career to 1846 at the time of his own death in 1912. Yet though supportive of Disraeli, the biography (which was completed by Buckle, a former editor of the *Times*) was still a major work of scholarship, and its interpretation of Disraeli's conduct in the 1840s as essentially motivated by ambition strongly influenced subsequent writing. Thus Ernest Llewellyn Woodward, in his 1938 contribution to the *Oxford History of England*, follows Monypenny and Buckle in seeing Disraeli's motives for joining with Young England as essentially instrumental:

> Peel paid heavily for his refusal to give him office. Disraeli gave the 'Young England' idealists the help of his debating powers. He was not likely to support them for long. He did not want to spend many more years out of office; these young men [...] were useful to him [...] They provided him with a platform from which he could make his attacks upon Peel.[81]

Writing 30 years later, Robert Blake made extensive use of Monypenny and Buckle's work for his highly respected *Disraeli*, similarly arguing that it 'is impossible to believe that he would have attacked Peel as he did, if he had been given the minor office which he wrongly expected in 1841'.[82] By 1845 'he realized [...] that all chance of preferment at Peel's hands

---

[80] Ibid., pp. 703, 806.
[81] E. L. Woodward, *The Age of Reform: 1815–1870* (1938), pp. 112–13.
[82] R. Blake, *Disraeli* (1966), p. 757.

had finally vanished, that [...] he had to stake his career upon the ruin of Peel's'.[83]

This remains the generally accepted interpretation of Disraeli's actions. Richard W. Davis, in a sceptical account of Disraeli's career, suggests that Disraeli's conduct from 1837 was essentially opportunistic. While not immediately setting out to destroy Peel after failing to secure office, 'he watched and waited for his opportunity. When it came he seized it'.[84] Paul Smith remarks that 'the philippics of 1844–6 owed as much to spleen at having been refused office by Peel in 1841, and to sheer ambition, as to divergence of political outlook. Disraeli's criticisms of Peel's Conservatism were rather nebulous, boiling down to the vague charge that it failed to assert genuine Tory principles.'[85] Ian Machin, the most critical of Disraeli's recent interpreters, agrees that it was frustrated ambition that led Disraeli to oppose Peel. His criticisms of Peel's liberal tendencies were 'spurious': '[h]e realised just as well as Peel the need to develop Conservatism in a liberal direction. Like Peel he abandoned the Protection which he had previously defended and he introduced further liberal elements into Conservative policy which Peel may not have contemplated.'[86] However, Machin suggests that Disraeli's initial objective in attacking the government was not to overthrow Peel but to 'get somewhere with them over the question of office'. Thus, in 1843 he approached ministers for a job for his brother, and it was their refusal that served as 'a launching pad for fiercer and deeper attacks on the ministry'. 'Disraeli came to believe more and more that [...] Peel was a vital obstruction to his ambition and must be removed.'[87]

Disraeli's opposition to Corn Law repeal 1845–46

While most historians have regarded Disraeli's criticisms of Peel as driven by a wish to undermine his leadership, they have, curiously, been more inclined to give credence to the arguments he advanced when challenging Peel's proposal to scrap the Corn Laws. He was not, declares Parry, some 'unprincipled charlatan'.[88] Three main grounds for Disraeli's opposition to Peel have been identified.

---

[83] Ibid., p. 183.
[84] R. W. Davis, *Disraeli* (c. 1976), p. 60.
[85] P. Smith, *Disraelian Conservatism and Social Reform* (1967), p. 23.
[86] I. Machin, *Disraeli* (1995), p. 41.
[87] Ibid., pp. 42–43.
[88] J. Parry, *Benjamin Disraeli* (2007), pp. 39–41.

First, it is argued that Disraeli's support for the Corn Laws reflected his recognition that the protection of agriculture was essential for the continuation of the territorial constitution he admired. Land was at the centre of society, politics and the Church, and if it was to sustain the burdens placed upon it then it required protection from cheap food imports. Monypenny and Buckle argue that Disraeli was never a dogmatist for protection or free trade, always seeking to ground his analysis in concrete realities, above all in its 'political bearings'. He knew that productive developments overseas would 'overwhelm our agriculture' and that it was the duty of a statesman to maintain a balance between agriculture and industry, especially given England's territorial constitution.[89] Free trade would break the prosperity of agriculture and with it the system of government based on the ownership of land, and it was against this ultimately political consequence of repeal which Disraeli protested. Blake follows Monypenny and Buckle in highlighting the importance Disraeli attached to the Corn Laws as underpinning a territorial constitution in which the burden of governance fell on the proprietors of land. Unless the agricultural sector was sustained, power would pass to the manufacturing interest.[90] Although he soon saw a return to protectionism was not feasible, this did not mean 'that he had been dishonest when he trounced Peel for abandoning it [...] There is no reason to doubt that at the time he genuinely believed what he said.'[91] Bradford, true to her belief in the integrity of Disraeli's Young England ideas, writes that there 'is little ground for thinking that he did not himself believe what he wrote and said; he had always been an opponent of liberal economics as a determining factor in policy, and [...] If one accepts this, then the central attitude of Peel's government offended against every canon of Disraeli's political belief.'[92] Parry likewise sees Disraeli's animosity toward Peel as reflecting his desire to defend 'aristocratic ideals in British politics' and uphold 'the territorial constitution'.[93]

The second reason cited for Disraeli's opposition to Corn Law repeal is that he believed that any tariff reductions should be reciprocal, advancing only insofar as other nations followed Britain's lead. Parry makes much of this aspect of Disraeli's thinking in his *Benjamin Disraeli* (2007). Commercial policy was a key element in the conduct of diplomacy, with countries making trade treaties as part of a process of building improved relations. So in the early

---

[89] Monypenny and Buckle, *Life of Benjamin Disraeli*, I. p. 766.
[90] Blake, *Disraeli*, p. 232.
[91] Ibid., p. 288.
[92] Bradford, *Disraeli*, p. 160.
[93] Parry, *Benjamin Disraeli*, pp. 39–41.

1840s Disraeli called for a commercial treaty with France to cultivate a new relationship with that country and even met with Louis Philippe to prepare the ground for it.[94] Monypenny and Buckle similarly highlight Disraeli's attachment to reciprocity. Such leading economic powers as France, the United States, and Prussia were all wedded to protectionist tariffs and would not reduce them if Britain threw open its ports.[95] The Conservative party had traditionally been committed to a policy of moderate tariffs, supplemented, since the time of William Pitt, by reciprocal tariff reductions through treaties, and there was no reason why it should depart from this. Smith endorses this interpretation, arguing that Disraeli showed a consistent attachment to a commercial policy of mutually advantageous reciprocity, rather than to protection as such.[96] Disraeli, agrees Feuchtwanger, 'had never been a dogmatic protectionist [...] Reciprocity was the principle he consistently advocated.'[97]

It has thirdly been contended that, while Disraeli did not see the Corn Laws as essential to the power of the aristocracy, he regarded any hasty capitulation to the middle-class Anti–Corn Law League as opening the way to further reform demands. The triumph of free trade would represent, write Monypenny and Buckle, what Richard Cobden boasted of: a transfer of power from the landed class to manufacturers. This 'thraldom' of capital would be an 'ignominious catastrophe'.[98] Sir Geoffrey Butler, in his 1914 *The Tory Tradition*, argued that Disraeli saw freetrade as essentially a means by which the Anti–Corn Law League hoped to attack the landed elite, since the 'ultimate aim [...] of the Free Trader, was to govern England in the interest of the Industrialist'.[99] The idea that it was less the fact of Corn Law reform to which Disraeli objected than the panicked manner by which Peel proceeded, was articulated by Froude. For Peel, as Disraeli argued in his biography of Lord George Bentinck, lacked imagination and hence prescience, and moved to total repeal with excessive haste.[100]

However plausible these arguments appear, they have not found general favour with historians, who see Disraeli as seizing upon the Corn Law issue as the one most likely to yield him victory in his contest with Peel. For most of the period after 1846 Disraeli's lack of principled attachment to the protectionist cause was held to be a mark of economic sagacity for the

[94] Ibid., p. 18.
[95] Monypenny and Buckle, *Life of Benjamin Disraeli*, I. pp. 761–62.
[96] P. Smith, *Disraeli: A Brief Life* (1996), p. 79.
[97] Feuchtwanger, *Disraeli*, p. 79.
[98] Monypenny and Buckle, *Life of Benjamin Disraeli*, I. pp. 766–67.
[99] G. G. Butler, *The Tory Tradition* (1909), pp. 58–59.
[100] Froude, *Lord Beaconsfield*, p. 131.

economic prosperity of the mid-Victorian years was widely attributed to the beneficial effects of free trade. Only in the troubled economic conditions of the interwar years, and the restoration of protective duties in 1933, did interest in the protectionist argument a century before revive. Symptomatic was the appearance in 1933 of Derek Walker-Smith's *The Protectionist Case in the 1840s*, which contained a preface by the Conservative MP and exemplar of the Disraelian 'One Nation' tradition, Harold Macmillan. But from this perspective Disraeli's performance in 1845–46 was distinctly underwhelming. As Walker-Smith showed, there was an argument to be made for Protectionism in 1845: only, Disraeli did not make it. None, he says, looked on Disraeli 'as a champion of Protection', adding that Disraeli's speech in answer to Peel's proposal to repeal the Corn Laws 'was concerned not with Protection, but with the constitutional issue and with what he viewed as Peel's treason to his party'.[101] In an earlier study, *Disraeli: The Alien Patriot*, E. T. Raymond lamented the fact that during the Corn Law debates Disraeli 'evaded, as far as possible, the main issue' – namely, whether Britain was to be primarily an industrial or rural society. He realized that consumers had little wish to pay higher food prices to profit the landowners, and neither did he want to antagonize the rising class of industrialists. Hence we 'seek in vain […] for the sort of insight and passion or the broad philosophic view which distinguished the novels'.[102] Raymond believed that Disraeli only wanted to overturn 'the leader who had neglected him'.[103]

The idea that Disraeli's conduct was primarily strategic is supported by T. A. Jenkins. Perceiving the widening gulf between Peel and the bulk of the Tory party, Disraeli realized this created opportunities for him to represent important sections of backbench opinion.[104] He did this over Maynooth in 1845, criticizing not the increased grant itself, but the immorality of the leader of the Protestant Tory party bringing in such a measure. This was the kernel of his argument over the Corn Laws. 'Disraeli's role during the crisis of 1846 was to act as the spokesman for the outraged country gentlemen by making a series of devastating attacks on Peel.'[105] Although Disraeli accused Peel of inconsistency and of sacrificing the interests of landed society to appease the middle class, he took up these arguments so that he could 'push himself forward into a prominent position, as there was a chronic shortage of debating talent

---

[101] D. Walker-Smith, *The Protectionist Case in the 1840s* (1933), pp. 2, 62.
[102] E. T. Raymond, *Disraeli: The Alien Patriot* (1925), pp. 142, 147.
[103] Ibid., p. 112.
[104] T. A. Jenkins, *Disraeli and Victorian Conservatism* (1998), p. 25.
[105] Ibid., p. 27.

within the protectionist ranks'.[106] Disraeli's subsequent eagerness to ditch protection betrays, says Jenkins, 'the fundamentally opportunistic nature of his attachment to the agriculturalists' cause in 1846'.[107]

This opportunity afforded by Peel's hasty move to repeal the Corn Laws is emphasized by several historians. Paul Smith observes that by 1844 Disraeli realized he was not going to be taken up by the middle-class meritocracy represented by Peel: 'His future in the Conservative party must depend on their displacement by other forces [...] The fulcrum from which to move them was supplied by Peel's decision at the end of 1845 to repeal the corn laws.'[108] Michael Bentley changes the metaphor but makes the same point: Disraeli, 'a climber disappointed by Peel's refusing him office in 1841 and latterly a spokesman of the jejune and ineffective Young England group, had at last found his vehicle, just as the body of confused mediocrity which populated the Tory benches had discovered an advocate of deadly brilliance'.[109] In a recent study of the parallel lives of Disraeli and Gladstone, Richard Aldous pulls few punches:

> For Disraeli, there was little or no principle involved at all. Later he would drop protectionism almost as quickly as he adopted it. His interest in 1845/6 was one of simple ambition. Here was an opportunity to confront a prime minister who would not promote him.[110]

Hurd and Young write that 'Disraeli had never been a serious Protectionist', and Machin concurs that Disraeli's calculus in 1846 was 'political rather than economic. He currently appeared a firm defender of Protection, but this matter was secondary to him whereas the removal of Peel was of primary importance. His later willingness, indeed eagerness, to abandon Protection testified to the absence of any decided and long-term commitment to it on his own part.'[111] Indeed, Machin dismisses Disraeli's entire anti-liberal Toryism of the early 1840s as a political posture which he recognized had little relevance to the emerging commercial society of Victorian England. Disraeli understood that only progressive politics capable of attracting a middle-class electorate were likely to get him a majority. He had usually been progressive before 1845, but had 'abandoned this tendency in order to win a great political triumph. He

---

[106] Ibid., p. 27–29.
[107] Ibid., p. 42.
[108] Smith, *Disraeli*, p. 80.
[109] M. Bentley, *Politics without Democracy 1815–1914* (1984), p. 122.
[110] R. Aldous, *The Lion and the Unicorn: Gladstone v. Disraeli* (2006), pp. 44–45.
[111] Hurd and Young, *Disraeli*, p. 88; Machin, *Disraeli*, p. 50.

had risen rapidly in 1845 and 1846 on the basis of policies which he could not realistically maintain. Therefore he had to return to progress.'[112]

Scepticism regarding Disraeli's commitment to agricultural protection finds support in his subsequent behaviour, when he saw, writes David Leslie Murray, that 'his first duty as Leader of the shattered Conservative party was to detach it from the lost cause of Protection'.[113] Even in the 1847 election he wanted the Tories to avoid references to the Corn Laws, and his 1852 budget made no attempt to restore a duty. Feuchtwanger, however, sees Disraeli's willingness to abandon protectionism not as a simple case of political arithmetic but as a response to the European revolutions of 1848. It was believed that a major reason Britain had escaped revolution was that Corn Law repeal introduced a sense of fairness into the policies of the state, and Disraeli feared that their restoration would carry a threat of social unrest.[114]

Disraeli himself always acknowledged that in his final assaults upon Peel he focused his attack, not upon Corn Law repeal as such, but the fact that Peel was betraying a core Conservative policy. As Brandes observes, Disraeli said little about the Corn Laws, his argument being that Peel had betrayed the Tories by taking over the ideas of its opponents. 'If the Corn Laws were to be abolished, it ought to be done by Cobden, not by a Minister like Peel, who was bound by previous pledges.'[115] Vincent concurs: in 1846, Disraeli 'attacked Peel not on grounds of economics [...] but on grounds of inconsistency and betrayal of pledges'.[116] The denunciation of Peel's propensity to rat on his own party (which he was held to have done over Catholic Emancipation and Maynooth) was always sure to evoke a cheer from the backbenchers, yet Disraeli tried to imbue the allegation with wider significance by arguing that the party system could only operate if political leaders conformed to party doctrine. If they did not, then Britain's representational system would collapse, as it would be factions, not the will of the electorate, that would settle policy. Some historians give credence to this argument. Smith believes Disraeli made an important constitutional point in arguing that in a parliamentary system leaders had to be true to the policies upon which they were elected, adding that, as a man without wealth or connections, 'he could look for advancement only as the servant of a party'.[117] This may be true, but it

---

[112] Ibid., p. 57.

[113] D. L. Murray, *Disraeli* (1927), p. 156.

[114] Feuchtwanger, *Disraeli*, p. 79.

[115] Brandes, *Lord Beaconsfield*, pp. 162–63.

[116] Vincent, *Disraeli*, p. 5. See also Jenkins, *Disraeli and Victorian Conservatism*, p. 42.

[117] Smith, *Disraeli*, p. 82.

is doubtful if Disraeli believed this: after contesting the 1852 election on the basis of the re-establishment of a measure of agricultural protection, Disraeli threw that policy overboard in his budget. Smith himself admits that it 'did not matter that he did not believe in protection. Party is the stirrup by which he must mount.'[118] Indeed, Davis suggests that the very idea that Disraeli was attacking, not Corn Law repeal but Peel's hypocrisy in undertaking it, was itself a perspective promoted by Disraeli to facilitate his own later abandonment of protection. While, says Davis, this might be a plausible distinction regarding his parliamentary speeches, there 'can be no doubt whatever [...] about the meaning of remarks he made at a series of Protectionist meetings around the country during the summer' when he created the impression that 'the leading Protectionist spokesman actually believed in protection'.[119]

Conclusion

Was there, then, any fundamental matter of principle at stake in Disraeli's opposition to Peel in the 1840s? Some historians, notably Sichel, Froude and Bradford, have contended that there was. Yet in doing so they have largely paraphrased the arguments advanced by Disraeli himself, forgetting that he had important reasons to justify his behaviour in this way. The idea that there were profound issues at stake is hard to square with Disraeli's actual conduct: his initial desire to join Peel's government; his breaking with Young England over Maynooth; his decision to attack Peel's proposal to repeal the Corn Laws on the grounds of betrayal rather than protectionist principle; and the speed with which he ditched protection as a Tory policy after 1847. Disraeli's motivation from 1841 was, it is agreed by a variety of historians ranging from the respectful Monypenny and Buckle via the authoritative Blake to the cynical Davis and Machin, driven essentially by personal ambition. Smarting at exclusion from office, Disraeli saw that so long as Peel retained his grip on the Tory party, his own prospects of advancement were feeble. For reasons of ambition, vanity and money, Disraeli needed office, and if Peel represented 'a vital obstruction to his ambition' then, says Machin, he 'must be removed'.[120] This is what Disraeli did in 1846, arguing not that the Corn Laws were essential to his vision of Britain, but that Peel was guilty of betraying Tory policy. His argument worked, and while the Corn Laws were thrown down, they took Peel with them, and when the dust settled Disraeli was left standing as one of the foremost men in the Conservative Party.

---

[118] Ibid.
[119] Davis, *Disraeli*, p. 79.
[120] Machin, *Disraeli*, p. 43.

Chapter 2

GLADSTONE AND DISRAELI TO 1865

Outline of Events

The years following 1846 were challenging for both William Gladstone and Benjamin Disraeli, and both experienced setbacks as well as achievements. On balance it was Gladstone who had the best of it. Although an admirer of Robert Peel, Gladstone dwelt in the shadow of the great man, and Peel's death in 1850 freed him to shape his own career. The problem was that, although propelled from the Tories over the issue of Protection, Gladstone retained many Conservative sympathies and still hankered after the liberal Conservatism of Peel's 1841 administration. He was not a Whig, was opposed to further parliamentary reform and had an active distaste for Lord Palmerston's populist and aggressive foreign policy. Rapprochement with a Conservative party on the basis of a shared commitment to free trade seemed the most likely outcome and on several occasions appeared in the offing. But each time something held Gladstone back. Why is not clear. Was it an eradicable aversion to Disraeli? A realization that the Tory backbenchers shared an equal aversion to him? A recognition that the Conservatives would be unlikely to command a majority? Or an instinctive awareness that he was evolving toward Liberalism? Gladstone's response to the uncertainty of his position was to capitalize on his one clear strength: his reputation as a great financier in the tradition of Peel. He had laid the basis for this reputation with his 1853 budget, and following the fall of the Peelite-Liberal coalition in 1855 he bided his time, awaiting the right moment to pledge his support to a government. This moment came in 1859 when Gladstone joined Palmerston's Liberal administration as chancellor of the exchequer. The decision was a happy one: chancellor during the boom years of the early 1860s, Gladstone had the fiscal scope to pursue his agenda of free trade and low taxation, and although his years at the Treasury were not an unblemished success, he established a reputation for financial acumen that has never been rivalled. With this achievement under his belt he was well placed to advance his career once Palmerston died in 1865.

For Disraeli, the middle years of his career were far less prosperous. Yes, he attained to successes that would have been unimaginable prior to the destruction of Peel: he led the Conservatives in the Commons and served as chancellor of the exchequer in two governments (1852 and 1858–59). But the overall theme was one of disappointed ambition. No matter how far he tried to tone down his idiosyncrasies and play the part of a Conservative statesman, he never commanded the respect of his own party. And no matter how hard he struggled to find vote-winning policies or attract parliamentary allies, the Conservatives remained locked into a minority position that seemed even more confirmed at the end of the period than it did at the beginning. Where Gladstone in 1865 could look back with satisfaction to the completion of his fiscal vocation and savour his rising popularity within the country, Disraeli, aged 61, had only the memories of two brief periods in office without power and the prospect of retirement when his chief and support, Lord Derby, quit the scene.

2.1   Why Did Gladstone Join Palmerston's Liberal Government in 1859?

From 1855 Gladstone conducted a bitter personal campaign against the political influence of Lord Palmerston and in 1859 sought to keep Palmerston out of office by voting for the Conservatives' 1859 Reform Bill. Yet when the Conservative government fell and Palmerston formed a Liberal administration, Gladstone agreed to serve as his chancellor of the exchequer – thereby cutting his remaining ties with the Conservatives. How have historians explained this apparent volte-face? Long-term answers make reference to Gladstone's evolving political philosophy and shifting position within Westminster politics, while short-term perspectives concentrate on Gladstone's actions in the years 1858–59.

1859 as the culmination of Gladstone's evolving politics

Gladstone argued that his decision to join with the Liberal party reflected 'the slow and resistless forces of conviction' (quoted in Jenkins, *Gladstone*, p. 261) operating since the 1840s and involving an ever-widening sympathy with Liberal policies – free trade, religious toleration, individual liberty, support for nationalist movements, meritocracy and a respect for the opinions of ordinary people. As Agatha Ramm remarks, in joining the Liberal government of

1859, Gladstone signalled that the 'Tory of 1833 had thus become a Liberal'.[1] F. W. Hirst agrees, stating that in 1859 Gladstone 'passed definitely from Conservatism to Liberalism'.[2] Justin McCarthy, a moderate Irish Home Rule MP who worked with Gladstone on Irish policy, elaborated this perspective in his sympathetic 1898 biography of Gladstone:

> Gladstone's mere acceptance of office under Lord Palmerston marked a new stage in his political career. He had definitely broken away from the Tory party [...] Now it was becoming every day more and more plain that Mr. Gladstone was growing out of the dusk of Toryism into the dawn of Liberalism.[3]

This portrayal of Gladstone's career as a pilgrimage out of the darkness of Tory intolerance into the sunny uplands of enlightened Liberalism is generally associated with Liberal-supporting writers of the late nineteenth century and has commanded little support among more recent historians. Still, a number of writers have utilized it to explain Gladstone's behaviour in 1859. Peter Stansky, for instance, believes that Gladstone's 'whole cast of mind and the general direction of his thought had predisposed him [...] to be more inclined toward Liberal thought', while Euginio Biagini notes that although he was 'personally closer to Derby than to Palmerston, his views were by now recognizably Liberal on certain important issues. These included colonial self-government, freedom of religion, and Italy.'[4]

However awkward objections have been raised to this comfortable account of Gladstone's ascent to Liberalism. Richard Shannon, for instance, rejects the entire premise of the argument: Gladstone, he declares, was never a Liberal at all – he was always a Peelite Conservative.

> Gladstone became a kind of Liberal without renouncing his Peelite inheritance: a Peelite, in short, in Liberal guise [...] It was a matter of adaptation not of conversion. He did not need Liberalism to teach him the merits of free trade. He did not need Liberalism to teach him the virtues of liberty [...] He did not need Liberalism to formulate for him the key to the politics of the future, the articulation between executive potency and responsive opinion.[5]

---

[1] Ramm, *William Ewart Gladstone*, p.33.
[2] F. W. Hirst, *Gladstone as Financier and Economist* (1931), p. 25.
[3] J. McCarthy, *The Story of Gladstone's Life* (1898), p. 224.
[4] Stansky, *Gladstone*, p. 81; Biagini, *Gladstone*, p. 38.
[5] Shannon, *Gladstone: Heroic Minister*, p. xv.

Gladstone had a political philosophy in 1859 – but 'the core of it was not a Liberal one'.[6] Theodore Hoppen concurs with this reading of Gladstone's politics: his decision to join Palmerston reflected not a reconfiguration of his political beliefs, but 'a conviction that the kind of reasoned and flexible conservatism which now constituted the kernel of Gladstone's politics – the belief in tradition tempered by reform, and the desire to harness forces of change to the maintenance of established society – would henceforth find a happier home among Liberals than Conservatives'.[7]

The idea that ideology played any part in Gladstone's decision of 1859 is similarly discounted by Perry Butler, for whom Gladstone's acceptance of office under Palmerston was 'not a decisive event in his political development', though it marked 'a definite change in his party allegiance'.[8] But where Shannon believes that Gladstone had not really become a Liberal by 1859, Butler holds the opposite view: he did not become a Liberal in 1859 because he already was one. Butler locates Gladstone's shift to Liberalism in the late 1840s and early 1850s and attributes it to his conversion to the principle of religious liberty over such issues as Maynooth and Jewish disabilities.[9] Jenkins similarly points to Gladstone's vehement opposition to Lord John Russell's 1851 Ecclesiastical Titles Bill as marking 'an important stage in his move toward liberalism, although not towards the leaders of the Whig party'.[10] Ironically, given the rigidity of his initial Church–State ideology, it was in the politics of religion that Gladstone's Liberalism was born.

Second, it is argued that even if Gladstone *had* evolved in a more liberal direction during the 1850s, this cannot explain his choice of party allegiance in 1859 since ideologically there were no real issues at stake between Liberals and Conservatives. The Conservatives had embraced free trade and moderate reform, and Derby was as much a liberal Conservative as Palmerston. This view was articulated by John Morley. As a liberal journalist owing his elevation to government office to Gladstone, Morley was only too happy to endorse the picture of Gladstone's political career as a progress toward Liberalism. However Morley believed that the ideological differences in 1859 were too slender to permit Gladstone's decision to join with Palmerston being accorded any particular significance:

---

[6] Shannon, *Gladstone: God and Politics*, p. 127.
[7] K. T. Hoppen, *The Mid-Victorian Generation 1846–1886* (1998), p. 210.
[8] Butler, *Gladstone*, p. 5.
[9] Ibid., 148–49.
[10] Jenkins, *Gladstone*, p. 133.

It seems a mistake to treat the acceptance of office under Lord Palmerston as a chief landmark in Mr. Gladstone's protracted journey from tory to liberal. The dilemma between joining Derby and joining Palmerston was no vital choice between two political creeds [...] To join the new administration, then, marked a party severance but no changed principles [...] it was not a conversion.[11]

Colin Matthew, who did nearly as much to define attitudes to Gladstone's career at the end of the century as Morley at the beginning, reaffirms that 'no great ideological difference separated Gladstone from the Palmerston government [...] except the character of its leader. On the other hand, no great question of policy seemed to bar his return to the Tory party.'[12] Thus, while Gladstone had, since the 1840s, 'travelled a very considerable distance in certain aspects of his thought towards a liberal position', his liberalism was, says Matthew, founded upon the doctrine of free trade, and this issue had ceased to define the difference between parties.[13] Given that Gladstone considered Palmerston's foreign policy immoral and his financial policy misguided, it is quite possible to conclude, as Shannon does, that

> [e]very argument of honour and consistency pointed to reunion with the Derbyites. Not only did protection not now stand in the way; on every great question of the hour, foreign policy, expenditure, taxation, the Peelites were 'in general agreement with Lord Derby & the bulk of his party'.[14]

Third, it is pointed out that explanations of Gladstone's behaviour founded upon the Liberal tendency of this thinking struggle to account for the events of 1857–59. During 1857 Gladstone had a succession of meetings with Lord Derby, who appeared keen to restore Gladstone to the Tory ranks. Following the 1857 election Gladstone's 'leaning towards the conservative party', writes Morley, 'seemed to become more decided rather than less [...] He saw nothing but evil in Lord Palmerston's supremacy.'[15] If, indeed, Gladstone had essentially become a Liberal, why, in 1857, did he join with Disraeli in a ferocious attack upon the Whig government's budget, lend his general support Derby's 1858–59 administration, accept from the Tory's the commissionership of the Ionian Islands and vote for the Conservatives' 1859 Reform Bill?

---

[11] Morley, *Life of Gladstone*, I. p. 631.
[12] Matthew, *Gladstone*, pp. 104–5.
[13] Ibid., p. 105.
[14] Shannon, *Gladstone: Peel's Inheritor*, p. 338.
[15] Morley, *Life of Gladstone*, I. p. 566.

Thus, recent writing suggests that Gladstone's shifting political allegiances must be explained with reference to something other than political ideology. For most historians this additional something was strategy. Gladstone was faced in 1859 with a problem of political decision-making and acted to maximize his likely benefits. In the late 1850s Gladstone was politically isolated. He had been out of government for four years, and for someone who relished executive action this was deeply frustrating. What Gladstone sought, writes Morley, was a party in conjunction with which he could realize the policy of Peel: 'of peace abroad, of economy, of financial equilibrium, of steady resistance to abuses, and promotion of practical improvements at home, with a disinclination to questions of reform, gratuitously raised'.[16] He was open to working with either party in this, and by joining the Liberals in 1859 he was signalling that it was they, and not the Tories, who would provide the fittest vehicle for his ambitions. Shannon endorses Morley's interpretation. For Gladstone the events of 1855 to 1859 showed that it was the Liberal party that would provide the surest foundation for the realization of his Peelite fiscal programme.[17] The 1857 general election was especially portentous, for after having been defeated in the Commons, Palmerston was returned to power by a clear majority, the Conservatives losing 50 seats. It was now obvious, writes Edgar Feuchtwanger, that the Conservatives had no foreseeable hope of a stable majority.[18] Thus while political logic pointed toward Tory reunion, one crucial fact, says Shannon, did not: Derby was much weaker than he was in 1852. 'Within the terms of Gladstone's new dual criterion for determining the optimum shape of future politics, that was a decisive verdict.'[19] Hence when, in February 1858, Derby invited Gladstone to join his Cabinet, Gladstone declined, and his 'refusal marked a stage in his emancipation from one of the main practical principles by which his political understanding had been anchored [...] He was never more studiously a Conservative than at the time of his coming to the conclusion that actually existing Conservatism would be most unlikely to be an adequate vehicle for his renewed vocation.'[20] Matthew endorses this analysis. Though Gladstone appreciated Derby's probity, the Tories 'offered no prospect of a satisfactory executive position'.[21] Parry puts the point more

---

[16] Ibid., p. 553.
[17] Shannon, *Gladstone: God and Politics*, p. 112.
[18] E. Feuchtwanger, *Gladstone* (1975), p. 101.
[19] Shannon, *Gladstone: Peel's Inheritor*, p. 339.
[20] Shannon, *Gladstone: God and Politics*, p. 115.
[21] Matthew, *Gladstone*, p. 106.

concisely: Gladstone 'was ambitious and realised that the Liberals had a natural majority and that the Conservatives did not'.[22]

Contributing to this strategic preference for the Liberals over the Tories was, says Shannon, Gladstone's conviction that the social and intellectual forces of the Victorian age pointed toward a liberal future and that it would be perverse to tie himself to a Conservative party set for secular decline. 'Aberdeen had already put his finger accurately on [the crucial consideration] with his simple doctrine that in this age of progress Liberalism must command politics.'[23]

The Disraeli factor

Another interpretation holds that what drove Gladstone toward the Liberals was his dislike of Disraeli. He had not forgiven Disraeli's role in the destruction of Peel and, writes Jonathan Parry, increasingly saw 'the Conservatives as irresponsible and willing to bribe sections of the House, mainly owing to Disraeli's lack of principle: Gladstone believed that, in 1846, in 1852 and in 1859 [...] Disraeli ruthlessly and recklessly demoralised and shamed the executive system, and in doing so destroyed the idea that the Conservatives were a disinterested party.'[24] Shannon pursues this theme in one of his characteristically grandiloquent passages:

> Indeed, if Gladstone needed for the reassembling of his vocation some kind of demon or devil-figure, Disraeli would be admirably adaptable for such a purpose: Peel's unkindest critic, an adventurer of dubious origins and dubious morals, an ex-dandy and rake of rather Mephistophelean appearance [...] Disraeli began to nestle in Gladstone's mind as possibly the focus of a kind of domestic version of the Neapolitan Horrors.[25]

The qualification 'if' should be noted here for, as we have seen, Shannon attributes Gladstone's conduct primarily to the Liberal's stronger parliamentary position. Biagini also emphasizes Disraeli's repellent effect upon Gladstone's political trajectory, quoting Edward Hamilton to the effect that Gladstone thought that Disraeli lacked character, treated politics as a game and could not be trusted. In addition 'both were bound to see each other as competitors for the same top jobs, especially for as long as the two men were rivals for the

---

[22] Parry, *Democracy and Religion*, p. 169.

[23] Shannon, *Gladstone: God and Politics*, p. 118.

[24] Parry, *Democracy and Religion*, p. 169.

[25] Shannon, *Gladstone: Peel's Inheritor*, p. 244.

leadership of the Conservative party'.[26] Here, for several authors, was the rub: to join a Conservative administration would mean sitting in the same Cabinet as Disraeli, with both being rivals to the chancellorship of the exchequer and the future leadership of the Conservative party. George Russell, a Liberal MP who served in Gladstone's 1880 and 1892 governments, suggested in an 1891 biography that the main factor determining his choice of party was Disraeli:

> Mr. Gladstone, if he became a Liberal, would [...] probably attain [...] the supreme place in Parliament. If he returned to the Tories, with Mr. Disraeli leading the House, he would be doomed to a position which, however high, was still less than the highest.[27]

Erich Eyck notes that, while Gladstone preferred Derby to Palmerston, what prevented his return to the Tories 'was the insoluble problem of Disraeli. Derby could neither drop Disraeli nor propose that Gladstone should serve under him.'[28] For Feuchtwanger, too, the 'position of Disraeli, more and more firmly entrenched, was certainly one important reason' why Gladstone declined reunion with the Conservatives.[29] Ramm goes further, suggesting that Gladstone's subsequent career was essentially his rivalry with Disraeli writ large: 'enormously ambitious', he was determined to avoid competing with Disraeli for position within the same party, preferring 'a greater battle – the battle before the country's electorate between himself, leader of one party, and Disraeli, leader of the other'.[30]

Michael Bentley, however, counters that to 'raise the spectre of Disraeli seems unnecessary in this context. He and Gladstone had already found themselves in the same lobby.'[31] Indeed, in the years 1857–59 Gladstone joined with Disraeli in attacking Cornewall Lewis's Whig budgets, and they voted together in 1857 to bring down Palmerston's government. While Gladstone disapproved of Disraeli, his dislike of Palmerston was equally intense. 'The importunate presence of Mr. Disraeli', observed Morley, 'was not any sharper obstacle to a definite junction with conservatives, than was the personality of Lord Palmerston to a junction with liberals.'[32] Matthew similarly reflects that '[t]o join with Disraeli was, in the Peelites' view, to place political morality at

---

[26] Biagini, *Gladstone*, pp. 29–31.
[27] G. W. E. Russell, *William Ewart Gladstone* (1891), p. 140.
[28] Eyck, *Gladstone*, p. 99.
[29] Feuchtwanger, *Gladstone*, p. 101.
[30] Ramm, *William Ewart Gladstone*, p. 34.
[31] Bentley, *Politics without Democracy*, pp. 138–39.
[32] Morley, *Life of Gladstone*, I. p. 553.

the service of chicanery, though in Gladstone's opinion Palmerston was not much better'.[33] Considerations of personality then, like ideology, seem not to have been sufficiently clearcut to account for the definiteness of Gladstone's political choice in 1859.

However, while Gladstone may have been comparatively indifferent to the rival personalities of Disraeli and Palmerston, this was not, as Morley and Matthew emphasize, true of the remaining Peelites, who generally did *not* wish to re-ally themselves with the Conservatives. This was important since Gladstone often spoke of being prepared to enter a Conservative Cabinet only alongside a wider body of Peelites, and the majority of his Peelite colleagues, writes Morley, were sceptical of a Gladstone reunion with the Tories – Sir James Graham arguing that Gladstone's politics were essentially progressive and therefore better realized in the Liberal ranks.[34] As a body, comments Matthew, the Peelites 'worked hard to push him away from Derby and appear on several occasions to have exercised at least a decisive negative influence upon him'.[35]

Parliamentary necessity

Angus Hawkins questions how far Gladstone truly had a choice with regard to party allegiance in 1859, for, whatever his preferences, the Conservatives were not keen to have him back. In the later 1850s Gladstone was, suggests Hawkins, seeking reconciliation with the Conservatives and using attacks upon the Whigs' fiscal policy as the basis for this. Derby and Disraeli were open to, but wary of, this adhesion of strength, realizing that Gladstone was extremely unpopular in Conservative ranks. 'Possible junction with Gladstone always raised the prospect of mutiny within the Conservative camp.'[36] Rank-and-file Conservatives resented his breaking with the party in 1846, disliked his self-righteous approach to politics and preferred Palmerston to Gladstone.[37] However much an alliance with Derby appeared tempting, Gladstone 'was subject to one determining circumstance. The Conservative party was more important to Gladstone than Gladstone was to the Conservative party.'[38] Thus, Derby's offer of a Cabinet place in 1858

---

[33] Matthew, *Gladstone*, p. 107

[34] Morley, *Life of Gladstone*, I. p. 556.

[35] Matthew, *Gladstone*, p. 107.

[36] A. B. Hawkins, *British Party Politics, 1852–1886* (1998), p. 61.

[37] A. B. Hawkins, *Parliament, Party and the Art of Politics in Britain, 1855–59* (1987), p. 41.

[38] Ibid.

was conveyed with 'little enthusiasm', and Gladstone, when declining, noted that there were many Conservatives who disapproved of him and as such he would weaken the government. Gladstone would probably have joined the Conservative government if he had been offered the leadership of the House of Commons over Disraeli, but Derby could not discard Disraeli, and on the Tory benches Gladstone was too unpopular to be given the lead.[39]

Why did Gladstone join a Liberal government in 1859?

Italian unification

When asked why he agreed in 1859 to serve under the hitherto reviled figure of Palmerston, Gladstone answered in one word: Italy. Here was a clear issue dividing the two parties, and it was one in which he was strongly on the Liberal side: for while the Whigs, like Gladstone, supported Italian independence from Austrian rule, the Conservatives preferred the maintenance of Austrian power. A number of historians have affirmed the central importance of the Italian issue in Gladstone's thinking. Most prominent are John Lawrence Hammond and Michael Richard Daniell Foot:

> Why did Gladstone take office under a statesman of whom he had been a most bitter and unsparing critic? Simply because the Italian issue had become the predominant one in the politics of western Europe. There had been little to distinguish Liberals from Conservatives in the fifties […] But with the war for the liberation of Italy an issue emerged on which public men were drawn by their sympathies into opposite camps. The Conservatives were Austrian in sympathy […] On the other hand, Palmerston, Russell, and Gladstone […] now found themselves in wholehearted agreement. For the sake of [the Italian cause] he was ready to put old prejudice aside.[40]

Hammond was a prominent Liberal who, in 1938, wrote an appreciative study of *Gladstone and the Irish Nation*. It might, therefore, be considered not unexpected that he should have seen Gladstone's conduct as being driven by progressive Liberal principles. The German Liberal Erich Eyck also highlighted

---

[39] Ibid., pp. 109–10.
[40] J. L. Hammond and M. R. D. Foot, *Gladstone and Liberalism* (1952), 79–80. Hammond died before completing the book, which was finished by a young Oxford graduate, M. R. D. Foot, who went on to attain an important place in Gladstonian scholarship, being the first editor of the Gladstone Diaries.

the role of the Italian question in Gladstone's decision, situating his behaviour within the wider context of his sympathy for Liberal nationalism.

> His whole heart was in the struggle of a long-oppressed people for liberty and unity. In his great speeches on matters of foreign politics he had spoken in support of the self-determination of even the weak nations [...] Now he saw that in Italy one of the great problems of the time was pressing for a solution [...] in the Liberal sense, and he was no less fervent in his support of this solution than were the Liberal leaders, Palmerston and Russell.[41]

In another 1930s study, Francis Birrell saw Italy as offering Gladstone a resolution of his political dilemmas of the later 1850s:

> A situation, which had been growing continually more strained, at last snapped, and the moment of its snapping was largely fortuitous. But the liberation of Italy offered a bridge between himself and Palmerston [...] The Italian question [...] enabled Gladstone to get on the right track at last.[42]

More recent historians have also pointed to the significance of Italy. Thus, Roy Jenkins writes that

> [t]here were broadly only two subjects on which Gladstone agreed with Palmerston. The first was Italy, and the second was their shared coolness [...] to an extension of the franchise. It was the prominence of these two issues, the first still more than the second, in the three months following Gladstone's return from Corfu which made Palmerston temporarily less repugnant to him than was Disraeli and led him to make a choice of direction which had the most momentous effects.[43]

Richard Aldous, like Birrell, sees Italian independence as a means to justify a step that would otherwise appear unprincipled. Though a 'gut-instinct' politician, Gladstone was unable to act without presenting a self-justificatory motive 'accompanied by credible public rationalisation'. Thus, if he were to

> abandon the Conservative party for the Liberals [...] he needed in his own mind and on the national stage a cast-iron explanation for his

---

[41] Eyck, *Gladstone*, pp. 110–11.
[42] F. Birrell, *Gladstone: Great Lives* (1933), p. 57.
[43] Jenkins, *Gladstone*, p. 199.

actions [...] The Italian Question [...] would quickly establish itself as one of the greatest and most contested ideological divides in nineteenth-century politics. This alone gave Gladstone a plausible reason to identify himself publicly with the pro-nationalist Liberal administration that took office in June 1859.[44]

Still, some historians have questioned how far Italy was a deal breaker in Gladstone's politics. Yes, it provided a justification for a decision that otherwise might seem too self-serving, but the real motivations lay elsewhere. Shannon remarks that, given Gladstone's preoccupation with fiscal reform in the later 1850s and his demand in 1859 that he serve at the Treasury, 'it is hard to see Italy as more than a convenient issue on which to combine with the Whigs on their own ground of foreign policy [...] he can hardly have seen Italy as the basis for a government'.[45] Jenkins, too, wonders why, if Italy was his dominating concern, 'he had insisted on being chancellor or nothing'.[46] The most respected survey of the impact of Italy on British politics in the period 1859–60 is by Derek Beales, a Cambridge historian whose work has greatly influenced several generations of historians of Victorian England. Beales suggests that Gladstone's emphasis upon Italy had a flavour of retrospective 'self-justification: Gladstone often wondered whether he had been wise to join a Government, many of whose policies he was to find disagreeable; and he looked on his efforts to "assist its Italian purposes" as a principal count in his vindication'.[47] Beales notes the other motives that affected Gladstone, notably his political isolation, dislike of Disraeli and, above all, his wish to 'have the opportunity to take part in a strong government [...] to carry through his great programme of reductions in [...] taxation'.[48] Given his past animosity toward Palmerston, it maybe, suggests Beales, that Gladstone needed 'a question of principle' that would justify his change of allegiance. 'This is the importance of the foreign-policy issue in Gladstone's case.'[49] This retrospective element in the assessments of 1859 is an important one. In 1859 Gladstone was only a supporter of Italian independence from foreign rule; he was not yet convinced of the case for Italian national unity. 'The implications of Gladstone's attitude to the

[44] Aldous, *The Lion and the Unicorn*, pp. 118–19.
[45] Matthew, *Gladstone*, p. 108.
[46] Jenkins, *Gladstone*, p. 208.
[47] D. E. D. Beales, *England and Italy 1859–60* (1961), p. 87.
[48] Ibid., p. 90.
[49] Ibid., p. 91. Garratt concurs with this rationalizing aspect. Cf. G. T. Garratt, *The Two Mr. Gladstones* (1936), pp. 69–70.

Italian question', remarks Shannon, 'were by no means as clearly "Liberal" in the 1850s as they came to seem later.'[50]

Parliamentary reform

But if it was not Italy that tipped the scales toward Palmerston, what did? Hawkins argues that the real issue at stake was parliamentary reform. Although Gladstone cited 'Italy' as his reason for joining the Liberals, his 'correspondence, statements, and speeches at the time [...] reveal the opposite of such a priority. It was reform and not Italy that decided his political course.'[51] Gladstone wanted to see the reform question settled quickly and moderately. He had hoped that Derby's Reform Bill of 1859 would succeed, and with its defeat he had looked to a centrist government of moderate Conservatives and Whigs to bring it about. Only when this scheme failed did he believe that Palmerston might effect such a settlement.[52] Of course, the problem with this argument was that Palmerston was notoriously cool toward electoral reform – and it was this shared scepticism toward the expediency of reform that was, according to Jenkins, one of the few issues upon which Gladstone agreed with the Whig leader.[53]

Hawkins also argues that by 1859 Gladstone had realized that fiscal policy no longer divided the parties as it had in the 1840s and Gladstone's position was weak as a result: he needed to swallow his pride and make a commitment. In support of this contention, Hawkins evokes the idea that 1857 constituted a 'profound personal crisis' for Gladstone with 'the repudiation of Gladstone's earlier vision of 1853 by fellow politicians' hostile intent, divergent expectation, and competitive political interests'. For in that year Gladstone had sought to coordinate with the Conservatives an attack upon Cornewall Lewis's budget. While the Conservative leadership agreed to this strategy, many backbench Conservatives disliked the vehemence of Gladstone's speeches and sympathized with Lewis's proposals, and the budget passed comfortably.[54] Thus by 1857 'Gladstone was forced to acknowledge the frightening reality of his individual dispensability [...] In political terms the strategy embodied in the 1853 settlement failed. Gladstone was not

---

[50] Shannon, *Gladstone: Peel's Inheritor*, p. 348.
[51] A. B. Hawkins, 'A Forgotten Crisis: Gladstone and the Politics of Finance During the 1850s', *Victorian Studies* Vol. 26 (1983), p. 318.
[52] Hawkins, *Parliament, Party and the Art of Politics*, p. 246.
[53] Jenkins, *Gladstone*, p. 199.
[54] Hawkins, 'A Forgotten Crisis', p. 312.

acknowledged as the authoritative arbiter of fiscal wisdom.'[55] His acceptance of office under Palmerston reflected this humbling lesson.

The 1859 election

Several historians contend that the 1859 election effectively resolved Gladstone's perplexities for him since it revealed, says Shannon, that

> in the series of general elections which had taken place since 1846 the Conservative party had failed conspicuously to recover the confidence of the electorate. It could not be the foundation of the kind of energetic government Gladstone was in quest of [...] From any point of view joining Palmerston was a better bet than joining the Conservatives, hopelessly in a permanent minority and with suspect Disraeli, only five years older than Gladstone, as their Leader in the Commons.[56]

And as Derby's star set, so Palmerston's had risen. Since the meeting at Willis's rooms (1859), Palmerston had emerged as the unquestioned leader of a reconstituted Liberal party with a clear majority. This was important, for it is generally agreed that what Gladstone most wished to see was a Derby–Palmerston coalition that would squeeze Disraeli to the margins.[57] But, writes Jenkins, 'that possibility disappeared at Willis's Rooms'.[58] If Gladstone held aloof now, he would be left an isolated figure clinging to a fiscal programme that was a fast-depreciating asset. Necessity not ideology drove his conduct – as Matthew emphasizes:

> Always reluctant to admit the role of ambition in politics, Gladstone was none the less aware of his abilities and their lack of application since 1855; his entry into Palmerston's Cabinet in 1859 thus involved no great moral choice [...] It was the hard-headed response of an able politician with a programme for action, invited to join a Cabinet at the outset of its formation.[59]

If, agrees Bentley, Derby's performance in the country had matched that at Westminster, then Gladstone would probably have joined his Cabinet. As

---

[55] Ibid., p. 320.
[56] Shannon, *Gladstone: Heroic Minister*, p. xv. See also Shannon, *Gladstone: Peel's Inheritor*, p. 335.
[57] Cf. Hawkins, *Parliament, Party and the Art of Politics*, pp. 246–47.
[58] Jenkins, *Gladstone*, p. 206.
[59] Matthew, *Gladstone*, p. 108.

it was, Derby's electoral weakness meant that to ally with the Conservatives would have meant 'sterility and attachment to a parliamentary party which held out hopes at best of minority power'.[60] We must not, reasons Bentley, infer from Gladstone's later Liberal career that opting for Palmerston in 1859 represented some existential act. 'Events, rather than class, ideology, upbringing or even self-interested strategy, had evolved a logic which pressed Gladstone into the deflection that was destined to harden into a lifelong commitment.'[61] Hoppen puts the point bluntly: Gladstone knew 'that this would be his last chance of leaving the wilderness'.[62] Feuchtwanger similarly believes that Gladstone was chiefly motivated by a desire to avoid being 'left out in the cold'. While he might have preferred to serve in a Derby–Palmerston government, if he turned down Palmerston's offer now, 'he would have been more isolated than ever'.[63]

Better prospects with Palmerston

But was the decision to opt for Palmerston merely an act of self-preservation? Was there nothing positive about it? Some historians think there was. Working with Palmerston had three distinct advantages. First, Palmerston was willing to offer Gladstone the chancellorship of the exchequer and the Conservatives were not. Ever since his assault on Disraeli's 1852 budget, Gladstone had defined himself through the fiscal principles he embodied, and he had spent the 1850s developing a programme of financial reform. To implement this it was vital that he return to his previous position as chancellor. But where Disraeli had a prior claim on the chancellorship within a Conservative government, Palmerston was willing to accede to Gladstone's terms, and serving under a prime minister whose chief interest was foreign policy could, says Matthew, 'have advantages for a Chancellor of the Exchequer with his own programme of legislation'.[64] Enhancing his confidence, says Ramm, was his knowledge 'that on finance he could argue Palmerston to a standstill. Nominally "under" the premier, he would actually be equal'.[65]

Second, Gladstone probably believed that Palmerston's advanced age meant he would soon quit the scene, leaving him with the Liberal inheritance. Hoppen places 'actuarial' considerations alongside those of Italy in explaining

[60] Bentley, *Politics without Democracy*, pp. 138–39.
[61] Ibid., pp. 168–69.
[62] Hoppen, *Mid-Victorian Generation*, p. 210.
[63] Feuchtwanger, *Gladstone*, p. 106. For a similar viewpoint, see Eyck, *Gladstone*, p. 112.
[64] Matthew, *Gladstone*, p. 109.
[65] Ramm, *William Ewart Gladstone*, p. 34.

Gladstone's decision: 'Palmerston was 74 and Russell 67, Disraeli however was 54', and this 'pointed strongly in a Liberal direction'.[66] Shannon similarly remarks that Gladstone had convinced himself that Palmerston, already 74, was a 'spent force' and that he was 'the destined heir of a post-Palmerston dispensation'.[67]

Ramm and Parry identify a third factor recommending Palmerston to Gladstone over Derby – namely his openness to public opinion. According to Parry, Gladstone was becoming increasingly preoccupied with the need 'to re-forge the bond between politics and public opinion; one of his most heartfelt complaints about the Conservative party was that Derby was unwilling to do this'.[68] Ramm similarly refers to 'Derby's indifference to opinion outside Parliament'. Gladstone was increasingly conscious of the need to engage with public opinion if the established institutions of governance were to survive. From this point of view, 'Derby's conservatism was too exclusively parliamentary ever fully to have engaged Gladstone'.[69]

Conclusion

The controversy regarding Gladstone's motives for joining in 1859 with his erstwhile enemy, Palmerston, goes to the root of the debate concerning his political conduct as such. Two narratives stand out, both reconcilable with events. On the one hand we have, in the writings of the likes of McCarthy and Hammond, Gladstone the man of principle – educating himself in the virtues of liberty and tolerance, for whom the Liberals offered a natural home. From this perspective it was only a matter of time before he overcame lingering Tory allegiances and joined a Liberal government. Italy was then the coping stone to a Liberal edifice he had been constructing since the 1840s – providing Gladstone with a clear-cut choice where moral commitment and ideology won over historic party connections.

Yet another narrative is presented in the pages of recent historians such as Hawkins, Shannon and Matthew, in which Gladstone was a frustrated man of government, searching for an administration in conformity with his political conscience but unable to find it in either the Whigs or Tories. He delayed making the final choice as long as possible, and it was only when, in 1859, the strength of the Liberal government persuaded him that his lingering hopes for

---

[66] Hoppen, *Mid-Victorian Generation*, p. 210.
[67] Shannon, *Gladstone: Peel's Inheritor*, pp. 358, 360. See also Shannon, *Gladstone: Heroic Minister*, p. xv and Birrell, *Gladstone*, p. 57.
[68] Parry, *Democracy and Religion*, p. 170.
[69] Ramm, *William Ewart Gladstone*, p. 34.

a centrist Whig–Conservative coalition were unobtainable that he overcame his distaste for Palmerston and joined with the Liberals. The year 1859 was not about ideology or Italy: it was about Gladstone.

What makes Gladstone so fascinating yet frustrating by turns is that it is impossible to resolve what truly guided his actions. It may even be wrong to assume that the two perspectives are mutually exclusive. Gladstone really did seem able to do the most self-interested things for the most exalted reasons. As the MP Henry Labouchere once remarked, 'I don't object to Gladstone always having the ace of trumps up his sleeve, but merely to his belief that the Almighty put it there.'[70]

2.2   How Effective a Chancellor of the Exchequer Was Gladstone?

Central to Gladstone's reputation as an executive politician was his performance as chancellor of the exchequer. Beginning with his work with Peel in overseeing moves toward free trade in the 1840s, he carried forward this project in the 1850s and 1860s through a series of budgets which not only did much to create the institutional framework of Victorian capitalism but also placed the office of chancellor at the centre of Gladstone's mission to elevate the Christian character of the nation. Hence Shannon sees financial reform as the second great 'vocation' in Gladstone's career: 'Gladstone was in need of a great new work to replace the abandoned State and Church cause. Everything pointed to finance as the appropriate core of such a work.'[71] Although Gladstone's basic achievements as chancellor have been little questioned, significant controversy surrounds details of his policies, their impact upon the economy and the degree to which reality conformed to Gladstone's ideal.[72]

Were Gladstone's economic principles appropriate and coherent?

Many historians praise the rationale of Gladstone's financial principles, which complemented an approach to economic policy based upon the free market economic institutions and minimalist state which economists from Adam Smith onwards had seen as necessary for maximizing the wealth of nations. These economic policies, contends Morley, promoted the well-being of the

---

[70] Cited in Eyck, *Gladstone*, p. 436.

[71] Shannon, *Gladstone: Peel's Inheritor*, p. 257.

[72] For a thorough defence at a time when Gladstonian financial dogmas were being questioned, see Hirst, *Gladstone as Financier and Economist*.

people, and thereby represented not merely an economic policy but also a social one.

> Tariff reform, adjustment of burdens, invincible repugnance to waste or profusion, accurate keeping and continuous scrutiny of accounts, substitution of a few good taxes for many bad ones, – all these were [...] directly associated in him with the amelioration of the hard lot of the toiling mass, and sprang from an ardent concern with improving human well-being, and raising the moral ideals of mankind.[73]

Matthew extended Morley's insight into the social dimension of Gladstone's policies to encompass their political significance. Gladstone placed fiscal policy at the centre of a mid-Victorian social compact designed to stabilize the political system by removing finance from the arena of political controversy. Free trade was one way to achieve this: once protective duties were discarded, interest groups would no longer lobby for preferential treatment.[74] Another was to make the tax system fair in its apportionment of direct and indirect taxes between different social classes – the so-called social contract of the Victorian state.[75] For example, in 1853 Gladstone brought the fiscal system into line with the franchise by reducing to £100 the income threshold for the payment of income tax, thereby ensuring that those who possessed the vote also paid income tax.[76] 'Income tax thus reminded the propertied class not merely of its fiscal but of its political responsibilities; it united the two factors which most Victorians regarded as cardinal to stability: fiscal and political probity.' These right financial relations contributed to the political stability of Victorian England: 'That finance as articulated in the budgets for the half-century after 1846 was more integrative than disruptive was a consequence partly of the compromise settlement of Gladstone.'[77]

Biagini similarly contends that the 'income tax and a more comprehensive succession duty were presented as twin pillars of a financial system through which social stability and economic growth would be achieved – aims which the propertied classes could see as more than compensating for the nuisance and expense of a moderate contribution to the Exchequer. To the artisans and consumers in general Gladstone offered a systematic reduction

---

[73] Morley, *Life of Gladstone*, II. pp. 56–57.

[74] Matthew, *Gladstone*, p. 115.

[75] H. C. G. Matthew, 'Disraeli, Gladstone, and the Politics of Mid-Victorian Budgets', *Historical Journal*, Vol. 22 (1979), p. 616.

[76] Ibid., p. 629.

[77] Ibid., pp. 630, 642.

or abolition of indirect taxes.'[78] This vision had two dimensions. On the practical level Gladstone wished, remarks Parry, to create a popular opinion in favour of cheap government and a passive foreign policy. This would not only entrench a bias in favour of a minimalist state but also it would cause the poor to press for lower taxation rather than a redistribution of wealth from the rich. But it also had a religious agenda. The more the working class regulated their own spending, the deeper would be their moral understanding, rendering them 'suspicious of demagogic politicians teaching class war and less hostile to the Church and better able to receive the consolations of religion'.[79] Biagini similarly notes that Gladstone regarded his fiscal policies 'as being the political and administrative expression of a comprehensive set of moral beliefs'.[80]

But were Gladstone's fiscal doctrines as righteous as this account suggests? It has been suggested that what Gladstone was really doing was justifying the interests of the propertied classes in a laissez-faire state at the expense of the kind of interventionist social investment that was needed if working-class conditions were to be elevated. Thus to Birrell, the friend of the economist John Maynard Keynes who, in the 1930s, was at the forefront of attempts to break the hold of Gladstonian finance on liberalism, Gladstone's financial theories appeared 'unadventurous and middle-class, the least interesting of his achievements'.[81] He stabilized 'laissez-faire beyond the point when laissez-faire was serviceable to the community'.[82] Ironically, given the centrality of middle-class opinion to the operation of the social contract, it was, as Biagini observes, at this point that the social compact began to unravel:

But while Gladstone's popularity amongst the working class increased, he met with growing resistance among the educated sections of society, who became unresponsive to calls for further retrenchment and who favoured increased defence spending for example. It was this that pushed Gladstone to consider the case for extending the electorate: if the existing voters weren't willing to back greater public economy then perhaps it was time to enfranchise the 'moral and responsible' working man.[83]

---

[78] Biagini, *Gladstone*, p. 32.
[79] Parry, *Democracy and Religion*, p. 172.
[80] Biagini, *Gladstone*, pp. 32–3.
[81] Birrell, *Gladstone*, p. 47.
[82] Ibid., p. 49.
[83] Biagini, *Gladstone*, p. 42.

In turning to franchise extension to preserve his social contract, Gladstone was acknowledging its failure – for it had been designed to *prevent* demands for further political reform.

How successful was Gladstone's handling of taxation?

Gladstone frequently spoke of his desire to abolish income tax. He objected to its intrusion into people's financial affairs, believing, remarked the Liberal MP Sydney Buxton in 1888, that its levy through self-assessment would always lead to 'fraud, inequality, and immorality, while it pressed too hard on intelligence and skill compared to property'.[84] More importantly, Gladstone believed that it generated revenue too readily, encouraging excessive government spending. He proposed, therefore, to phase out income tax and replace it with a combination of other direct taxes (notably on inheritance) and duties, which were to be reduced as low as possible and confined to a few key items. It was argued that, by lowering indirect taxes, trade would be encouraged and the remaining duties would generate all the finance required, while by placing taxes on only a few items of mass consumption, governments would find it politically impossible to raise taxes, thereby choking off increased government spending.

Gladstone's approach to fiscal policy has been praised. Despite ruthlessly cutting the number of goods subject to customs duties, 'within a few months, trade, consumption, and consequently revenue, were again making rapid progress'.[85] As the tax revenue yielded by the remaining duties increased, Gladstone was able to lower income tax until, in 1874, he promised to abolish it entirely. Jenkins summarizes Gladstone's achievement:

> As Chancellor of the Exchequer [...] Gladstone embarked upon a further extension of the principles of Free Trade, and within a few years the economy had grown so rapidly, and the government's revenue from the few remaining tariffs was so buoyant, that it became permissible for him to reduce the burden of income tax. By 1865 he had managed to lower the rate to just 4d. (less than 2p) in the pound.[86]

However these positive claims for Gladstonian finance have been disputed. There was, it is argued, a contradiction at the heart of Gladstone's approach. For, as Buxton observes, while he spoke of abolishing income tax, his

---

[84] S. Buxton, *Finance and Politics: An Historical Study 1783–1885* (1888), I. p. 113.
[85] Ibid., p. 261.
[86] Jenkins, *Disraeli*, pp. 66–7.

repeated use of surplus revenue to cut *indirect* taxes meant he never freed himself from the revenue income tax yielded. 'Mr Gladstone's dream has been to destroy the tax, his fiscal work has resulted in making it perpetual.'[87] Matthew likewise notes that by imposing indirect taxes on as few items as possible, he rendered the raising of revenue from indirect taxes less flexible, making it harder to abolish income tax.[88] Between 1844 and 1868 income tax always constituted at least 9 per cent of government income, and Matthew argues that Gladstone never seriously intended to abolish it. Since his basic object was to balance direct and indirect taxation, when surplus funds became available he did not simply use them to cut income tax, but to reduce indirect taxes as well. In 1860, he 'subordinated the abolition of income tax to the priority of a further round of tariff abolition and reconstruction and reduction of indirect taxation'.[89] There was thus an essential ambiguity in his approach to income tax. 'Gladstone mistrusted and feared the peacetime income tax', but it 'played too central a role in the great taxation compromise which legitimized the Liberal State in Britain'.[90] It was, in the words of Walter Bagehot, a 'tax *of all work*' to be used to fund any variations in revenue or spending.[91]

In an 1898 article F. W. Hirst defended the consistency of Gladstone's income tax policy. Although he did not like income tax, he saw free trade as vital to Britain's interests and consequently prioritized tariff reductions over income tax cuts. However by the 1870s Gladstone 'saw with consternation the income-tax which had been in the hands of [...] Peel and himself an indispensable weapon of commercial reform, perverted into an instrument for increasing the cost, the magnitude, and perhaps the corruption of our military and civil establishments', and this led him to attempt 'to get rid of it altogether'.[92]

Gladstone's assumption that income tax was a temporary imposition meant that he rejected calls to reform it, since to do so would imply, writes Matthew, its permanence.[93] Gladstone's authority, complained Buxton, ensured that schemes to reform the tax were not assessed during his lifetime,

[87] Buxton, *Finance and Politics*, I. p. 194.
[88] Matthew, 'Disraeli, Gladstone, and the Politics of Mid-Victorian Budgets', p. 617.
[89] Ibid., pp. 635–36.
[90] Matthew, *Gladstone*, p. 123.
[91] W. Bagehot, 'Mr. Gladstone' (1860), in St John-Stevas (ed.), *Collected Works of Walter Bagehot*, III. p. 432. Italics in the original.
[92] F. W. Hirst, 'Notes and Memoranda, Mr. Gladstone II', *Economic Journal*, Vol. 8 (1898), p. 534.
[93] Matthew, 'Disraeli, Gladstone, and the Politics of Mid-Victorian Budgets', p. 623.

meaning there was no 'attempt to establish the tax on a broader foundation and a juster basis'.[94] By this means income tax 'has crept into perpetuity [...] unawares, without system [...] with the result, that while the income tax is, as it should be, a permanent tax [...] it is a tax which [...] is in detail most faulty'.[95] Shannon, however, points out that Gladstone took some steps to refine the tax – for example, by introducing graduation in 1863 to ease the burden on payers in the £100–£200 bracket.[96]

Did Gladstone control government spending?

Reducing government spending was an absolute good in Gladstone's eyes, for government spending was wasteful, corrupting and reduced the freedom of people to decide how to spend their own money. It was also necessary if he were to abolish income tax and lower indirect taxes. 'Economy', says Shannon, 'was the "first and great article" of his fiscal creed.'[97] Hirst characterizes economy as the thread woven through the texture of his finance.

> If he learnt it originally from Peel, he proved himself not merely an apt pupil, but a master of surpassing power, zeal, industry and ingenuity in the art and science of impressing upon the nation [...] and our whole public service the supreme importance of preventing waste and suppressing all superfluity in the administration of public money.[98]

'The whole of his financial activities', agrees Eyck, 'were governed by the [...] greatest frugality to guard the national economy against the exaction of a shilling more than the State positively required for its just occasions.'[99]

Was Gladstone successful in reining back public spending? Matthew contends that he was. 'At a time when [...] the proportion of government spending to national wealth was rising rapidly in Continental nations, in Britain it remained both low [...] and fairly constant.'[100] Despite, says Morley, serving under Palmerston, who was a forceful advocate of increased defence spending,

---

[94] Buxton, *Finance and Politics*, I. p. 113.
[95] Ibid., p. 331.
[96] Shannon, *Gladstone: Peel's Inheritor*, p. 483.
[97] Ibid., 390.
[98] Hirst, *Gladstone as Financier*, p. 241.
[99] Eyck, *Gladstone*, p. 83.
[100] Matthew, *Gladstone*, p. 115.

he won no inconsiderable success. When 1866 came, and his financial administration ended, he had managed [...] to carry expenditure back to the level of 1857 [...] After half a dozen years of panic and extravagance, all sedulously fostered by a strong prime minister, that he should still have left the cost of government little higher than he found it was [...] an extremely satisfactory performance.[101]

In the period from 1860 to 1866, comments Stansky, 'the overall Budget was marked by a decrease of 7 per cent'.[102] And these reductions, remarks Parry, continued during Gladstone's first government: between 1868 and 1873, the overall Budget went down 6 per cent, with defence spending falling by £4m.[103] Hence Hoppen can conclude that Gladstone's objective of holding back the growth in government spending was achieved. 'Although total government spending did increase, it did so in line with rising population, so total government spending per person, which was £2 pa in 1846–50, stood at £2.4 in 1881–5.'[104]

Still, a number of historians have questioned how effectively Gladstone controlled public spending. When he first became chancellor in 1853 government spending was £55 million. When he next became chancellor, in 1859, it stood at £65 million, and when he quitted office in 1866 it had reached £67 million. Partly, says Hoppen, this reflected a doubling in civil spending between 1846–50 and 1881–5.[105] More important was Gladstone's failure to seriously curb military spending, which accounted for around 40 per cent of all government spending in the 1860s. There were, says Matthew, two main problems here. First, Gladstone never developed 'an effective critique of military expenditure'. Unable to accept the anti-colonialism of the Manchester school, he treated each imperial crisis on its own terms, and as each imperial action could be made to seem plausible, 'Gladstone, as Cobden often complained, found himself raising funds for imperialism as effectively as any Whig or Tory'.[106] As Buxton commented, although deploring public expenditure, 'he was ever ready [...] to propose the most enormous estimates to the House', and he was 'equally with his colleagues, morally and personally responsible for the enormous war expenditure which was incurred by the Government in time of peace'.[107] The second reason identified by Matthew

---

[101] Morley, *Life of Gladstone*, II. p. 51.
[102] Stansky, *Gladstone*, pp. 86–9.
[103] Parry, *Democracy and Religion*, p. 269.
[104] Hoppen, *Mid-Victorian Generation*, p. 121.
[105] Ibid.
[106] Matthew, *Gladstone*, p. 111.
[107] Buxton, *Finance and Politics*, I. p. 296.

for Gladstone's failure to cut defence spending was that whenever the military departments and the Treasury clashed over spending, the issue was taken before the Cabinet – which, under Palmerston's leadership, favoured the defence departments.[108] Hoppen follows Matthew's analysis, noting that 'a higher proportion of central government expenditure (39.4 per cent) was devoted to defence during the period 1861–5 than at any other time of peace during the whole of the nineteenth century'. Gladstone failed to develop an effective critique of defence spending and as a result was reduced to 'conducting a series of poorly co-ordinated retrenchment campaigns on disparate issues'.[109]

Buxton notes that during Gladstone's first four years as chancellor ordinary government spending rose from £34.75m in 1858 to £42m in 1862, largely due to a £6m rise in military spending.[110] 'This great and lavish expenditure had been entirely in accordance with public opinion.'[111] Indeed, according to Parry, Palmerston had 'an unanswerable case' for increasing defence spending in the context of fears of a rejuvenated France and more advanced military technologies.[112] Only after 1863, as the French threat receded, was Gladstone able to reduce government spending, which by 1865 was the lowest it had been since 1858. These developments highlight Gladstone's subordination to public opinion: when the public favoured increased military spending, he was compelled to provide the funds. Only when the context changed was Gladstone able to lower spending. And even then, in his 1865 Budget, Gladstone confessed, remarks Shannon, that government spending per annum was £10m higher than in 1853. 'That was the measure of his sense of what he had failed to achieve against Palmerston.'[113]

Gladstone's handling of the national debt has also been criticized. While Hirst praises the measures initiated in 1866 to reduce its size, these were, argues Buxton, too little and too late. Whenever Gladstone had surplus revenue, he nearly always used it to cut taxes and 'preserved no proportion at all between the specific reduction of debt and the actual remission of taxation'. Between 1859 and 1862 only £4.4m of debt were redeemed.[114] Matthew agrees that, although Gladstone warned in 'lurid terms' of the size of the debt, he took

---

[108] Matthew, *Gladstone*, p. 633.
[109] Hoppen, *Mid-Victorian Generation*, p. 214.
[110] Buxton, *Finance and Politics*, I. pp. 292–93.
[111] Ibid., p. 294.
[112] Parry, *Democracy and Religion*, p. 185.
[113] Shannon, *Gladstone: Peel's Inheritor*, p. 540.
[114] Buxton, *Finance and Politics*, I. pp. 216–17, 350.

few steps to reduce it. His chief weapon was to try to convert the debt into lower interest issues, but this had limited success.[115] Between 1859 and 1866 the national debt fell by only 3 per cent.

It is, finally, pointed out that Gladstone's determination to hold back government spending hindered necessary social investment. He was, for instance, keen to bear down on education spending: in the six years to 1859 government spending on education, art and science more than doubled; in the years 1859 to 1866 it increased by just 11 per cent. During his 1868 government Gladstone, says Shannon, similarly sought to 'rein back spending on education'.[116]

How successful were Gladstone's great budgets?

Gladstone's reputation as a great financier rests heavily upon his budgets of 1853 and 1860. His 1853 budget, in which he resumed moves toward free trade while outlining a programme to phase out income tax, has attracted extensive praise. 'The thoroughness and breadth of view displayed in the Budget of 1853', writes Buxton, 'raised Mr. Gladstone at once to the front rank of financiers as of orators.'[117] Barnett Smith, writing in 1880, said that the 'whole scheme' of the budget was regarded as 'the most able, far-sighted, and practicable of financial measures since Robert Peel's famous budget of 1844 [...] The scheme first astonished, and then pleased and satisfied the people.'[118] G. W. E. Russell also extolled Gladstone's achievement:

> Here indeed was an orator who could reconcile the spiritual and material interests of the age, and give a moral significance to dry details of finance and commerce. The scheme thus introduced astonished, interested, and attracted the country [...] The Budget demonstrated at once its author's absolute mastery over figures, the persuasive force of his expository gift, his strange power of clothing the dry bones of customs and tariffs with the flesh and blood of human interest.[119]

Notable are the quasi-religious qualities attributed to Gladstone's finance. Morley developed this theme, depicting Gladstone as a financial saviour

---

[115] Matthew, *Gladstone*, p. 634.
[116] Shannon, *Gladstone: Peel's Inheritor*, p. 390.
[117] Buxton, *Finance and Politics*, I. p. 108.
[118] G. B. Smith, *The Life of the Right Honourable William Ewart Gladstone* (1880), p. 149.
[119] Russell, *William Ewart Gladstone*, pp. 121–22.

whose budget brought justice to a land previously blighted by discord and special pleading:

> By 1851 [fiscal] floundering had a reached a climax [...] Every source of public income was the object of assault. Every indirect tax was to be reduced or swept away, and yet no two men appeared to agree upon the principles of the direct taxes that were to take their place [...] At last a statesman appeared [...] a financier endowed [...] with a combination of the spirit of vigorous analysis and the spirit of vigorous system, with the habit of unflagging toil, and above all, with the gift of indomitable courage.[120]

Morley refers to 'the extraordinarily far-reaching and comprehensive character' of the budget, which was 'one of the great parliamentary performances of the century'.[121] In his *Gladstone as Financier and Economist*, Hirst described the budget as 'perhaps the most brilliant of Gladstone's achievements [...] distinguished by the breadth and diversity of its aims, the boldness of its conception, and the immense benefits which it conferred on the nation'.[122] Gladstone's defence of his controversial decision to retain the income tax for seven years was 'one of the most wonderful passages of persuasive and successful reasoning in the records of parliament'.[123] 'Parliament and the nation', wrote Eyck, 'received the very definite impression that England had now a Chancellor of the Exchequer who had mastered the *whole* of the financial problem; who was working not for the moment only, but for time to come.'[124]

Historians continue to depict the 1853 budget as a grand achievement. For Matthew its significance lay in its establishment of the 'social contract of the Victorian state', as Gladstone balanced direct and indirect taxes and apportioned them between the various classes.[125] The income tax, which fell on the propertied, was maintained and extended as to the numbers who were subject to it. Indirect taxes, which fell more heavily on the working class, were reduced in level and number. The dividing line for income tax was made to follow that of the franchise – those who paid income tax had the vote, and this would encourage them to press for lower spending. Shannon declares

---

[120] Morley, *Life of Gladstone*, I. pp. 459–60.
[121] Ibid., pp. 461, 468–69.
[122] Hirst, *Gladstone as Financier*, p. 152.
[123] Ibid., p. 149.
[124] Eyck, *Gladstone*, pp. 82–83. Italics in original.
[125] Matthew, *Gladstone*, p. 123.

Gladstone's 1853 budget to have been 'brilliantly successful', launching his 'myth as the keeper of the Victorian financial conscience'.[126] Roy Jenkins, himself a Labour chancellor of the exchequer in the 1960s, is more than ready to endorse the myth of Gladstone's fiscal conscience.

> His need was not so much a budget for a year as a system of finance for the third quarter of the century. This he was held to have produced, and his achievement in this respect [...] laid the foundation of much of his subsequent reputation.[127]

Biagini, too, emphasizes the budget's impact upon the public imagination, remarking that Gladstone combined 'Peelite financial orthodoxy' with 'a moralist-populist appeal to public opinion as a direct source of political legitimacy'.[128]

However, in an insightful essay Hawkins presents the budget less as an inspired act of executive restitution, and more as a convenient solution to two converging sets of crises. First there was the personal crisis within Gladstone's politics created by the collapse of his Church and State vision: financial policy refounded his career on a far more secure elevation.[129] At the same time it solved a political crisis by stabilizing the Peelite-dominated Aberdeen coalition.

> The budget of 1853 [...] provided the new touchstone for political activity that parliamentary standing, private doubts, and party instability recommended [...] Gladstone [...] established the question of finance as a public issue of the greatest political moment. Strategy, principle, and manoeuvre coalesced in doctrinal statement, and Gladstone's oratory became the medium through which moral exegesis overlay administrative and political exigency.[130]

Yet Gladstone's 1853 budget has been held to have contained important flaws. While a brilliant *political* success, remarks Hoppen, 'it did not immediately establish Gladstone's reputation as a financial magus [...] Within twelve months worrying signs began to appear that not everything had been

---

[126] Shannon, *Gladstone: Peel's Inheritor*, pp. 271–72.
[127] Jenkins, *Gladstone*, p. 149.
[128] Biagini, *Gladstone*, pp. 32–33.
[129] Hawkins, 'A Forgotten Crisis: Gladstone and the Politics of Finance During the 1850s', *Victorian Studies* Vol. 26 (1983), p. 288.
[130] Ibid., pp. 287, 291.

competently done.'[131] Even the sympathetic Morley recognizes that the 'plans of 1853' were 'not without weak points'. The proposal to extend inheritance tax to personal property brought in only £0.6m of the £2m expected.[132] Gladstone's estimate of the return from legacy duty was wrong, says Ernest Woodward, 'because he allowed assessment to be made on the life interest of a holder, and did not take into account the extent to which real property was encumbered'.[133] Another disappointment was Gladstone's attempt to reduce the rate of interest paid on the national debt from 3 to 2.5 per cent. 'Although', comments Buxton, 'it was initially hoped to convert £490m of government stock to the 2.5 figure, in the event a bad harvest and a loss of investor confidence in the run up to the Crimean war, meant that hardly any stock was converted to the lower figure.'[134] Jenkins calls the debt refinance scheme a 'major misjudgement'.[135] 'All this', comments Morley, 'brought loudish complaints from the money market. The men at the clubs talked of the discredit into which Gladstone had fallen as a financier.'[136]

Paradoxically, the chief failing of the 1853 budget related to its most admired feature: the planned phasing out of income tax by 1860. When 1860 arrived there was a budget deficit of £10m and no question of discarding income tax. Why was this? Apologists for Gladstone point to the unforeseen shock of the Crimean War (1854–56). While, says Buxton, Gladstone was correct to assume that cutting tariffs would stimulate trade and raise total government revenues, the increase in expenditure of £13.25m between 1853 and 1860 due to the Crimean War 'entirely and unavoidably vitiated the elaborate calculations and brought to nought the scheme of 1853'.[137] However several historians observe that the Crimean War was not the only reason for the revenue undershoot by 1860. As Feuchtwanger notes, expenditure had been on a plateau of about £50 million. By 1860 it had risen to £70 million and did not come down again.[138]

Whereas the 1853 budget has often been regarded as a political success and an economic failure, Gladstone's 1860 budget has been seen as an economic success and a political failure. This budget contained three initiatives: the

---

[131] Hoppen, *Mid-Victorian Generation*, p. 152.
[132] Morley, *Gladstone*, I. pp. 513–14.
[133] Woodward, *Age of Reform*, p. 160.
[134] Buxton, *Finance and Politics*, I. p. 128.
[135] Jenkins, *Gladstone*, p. 156.
[136] Morley, *Life of Gladstone*, I. pp. 513–14.
[137] Buxton, *Finance and Politics*, I. p. 193.
[138] Feuchtwanger, *Gladstone*, p. 86. For further sceptical assessments, see Buxton, *Finance and Politics*, I. p. 215 and G. T. Garratt, *The Two Mr Gladstones* (1936), p. 71.

completion of the move to free trade; the tariff reduction treaty with France as a means to reducing Anglo-French tensions; and the proposal to satisfy radical demands for the abolition of the tax on paper. For Buxton, 1860 crowned 'the edifice of which his great master had laid the foundation stone', marking 'the final adoption of the Free Trade principle, that taxation should be levied for Revenue purposes alone'.[139] Of the 397 duties remaining, 259 were abolished. Rather than discontinue income tax, Gladstone raised it to 10 pence in the pound – a decision Buxton praises as it furnished 'the means whereby the tariff could be purged; and [...] would again do much to improve the trade and increase the wealth of the country'. 'The financial statement of 1860 was a masterly exposition of a masterly conception', superior to that of 1853, for it was 'in its results considerably the more successful of the two'.[140] Morley speaks of the Anglo-French tariff treaty as 'one of the boldest of all his achievements', and his budget speech 'was one of the most extraordinary triumphs ever witnessed in the House of Commons [...] Almost every section of the trading and political community looked with favour upon the budget as a whole.'[141] Eyck regards the budget of 1860 as 'Gladstone's fiscal masterpiece [...] it developed the principle of Free Trade to its last financial and political consequences'.[142] Shannon, too, describes the budget as another epic performance, repeating the tactics of 1853: 'The rhetoric [...] was of the same theatricalised politics and the same morality play of finance.' 'All immediate indications suggested that he had carried it off.'[143] Biagini sees the budget as representing a

> step forward in his strategy of 'politicization of the Exchequer': while previously Gladstone had used the budgets to shape a new social balance at home, from 1860 he tried to influence the Foreign Office and restrain the defence departments. He had not forgotten the lesson of the Crimean War – namely, that 'sound economy' at home could hardly be sustained without peace in Europe.[144]

Through his tariff treaty with France, Gladstone 'outmanoeuvred the "hawks" in a successful bid to divert public attention from coastal fortification and battleships to French claret and Parisian gloves'.[145]

---

[139] Buxton, *Finance and Politics*, I. p. 189, 195.
[140] Ibid., pp. 210–15.
[141] Morley, *Life of Gladstone*, II. pp. 24, 28.
[142] Eyck, *Gladstone*, pp. 120, 122.
[143] Shannon, *Gladstone: Peel's Inheritor*, pp. 408, 410.
[144] Biagini, *Gladstone*, p. 39.
[145] Ibid.

Ironically, given the budget's political dimension, it was on political grounds that it has been held to have failed. Roy Jenkins considers the budget to have been less successful than that of 1853. Gladstone's 'immediate post-budget prestige collapsed much more quickly than it had done in 1853, and he came to be widely regarded in both Cabinet and Parliament as hectoring and rather wild'.[146] Morley admits that once the initial euphoria had passed, 'a general atmosphere of doubt and unpopularity seemed suddenly to surround his name'.[147] 'Both the commercial treaty and the finance speedily proved to have made enemies.'[148] Gladstone's attempt to stand out against the war scare with France was quickly undone when France annexed Nice and Savoy. Fears of French expansionism, comments Shannon, caused 'demands for increased defence spending'. Criticism focused upon the proposal to scrap the tax on paper. This policy had never been popular with Conservatives and Whigs, who believed that the cost of newspapers and books should be kept high to discourage the dissemination of radical doctrines among the poor. With the revived French threat it was argued that the nation could not afford this loss of revenue. 'Gladstone', writes Shannon, 'was under pressure to postpone the abolition. He, as ever, retained his inflexibility of attitude and on 21 May the Paper Duties bill was rejected by the Lords.'[149] Buxton believed it was unjustified to impose another penny on income tax to cover the loss of revenue from the paper duty: 1860 was a year of great fiscal pressure and not the moment to place a greater burden on 'the already heavily mulcted income tax-payer'. By the time the Lords voted on the proposal, defence spending was rising due to an outbreak of hostilities in China. 'Taking all these circumstances into consideration, it must be confessed that financially the House of Lords were in the right [...] in rejecting the Paper Duty Abolition Bill.'[150]

How effective a war financier was Gladstone?

The carefully elaborated plans of 1853 were torn up in 1854 when Gladstone was called upon to fund the Crimean War, and the question of how effectively Gladstone oversaw the funding of the conflict has engaged commentators and historians. Typically Gladstone approached war finance with a clear principle: namely to meet the costs of war out of current

---

[146] Jenkins, *Gladstone*, p. 227.
[147] Morley, *Life of Gladstone*, II. p. 29.
[148] Ibid.
[149] Shannon, *Gladstone: Peel's Inheritor*, p. 446.
[150] Ibid., p. 212.

revenue. Besides wishing to avoid increasing the national debt, there was a political, even moral, rationale behind this rule. Gladstone believed that if a people wished to wage war, then they should also pay for it and not bequeath the costs to future generations through borrowing. This was not merely just: it would act as a check upon wasteful and destabilizing wars.[151] These of course were normative judgements, the merits of which could be argued either way. More significantly, a number of writers have argued that Britain's ability to see the war through to a successful conclusion (unlike Russia) reflected Gladstone's effective conduct of the national finances. It was Buxton's judgement that

> [g]overnment finance during the Crimean War was most satisfactory and testified to the strength imparted by the 1853 budget. Gladstone made a determined attempt to fund the war through increased taxation rather than adding to the national debt [...] At first this was wholly provided through an increase in income tax, which doubled between March and May 1854. In May taxes on spirits, salt, and malt were also increased.[152]

Morley writes that the financial settlement of 1853, 'by clinching the open questions that enveloped the income-tax, and setting it upon a defensible foundation while it lasted, bore us through the struggle', while Hirst argues that if a 'fresh stimulus had not been given to commerce, and if the credit of the income tax had not been revived, it is hardly possible that our trade and finance could have stood out so stoutly against the strain of the Crimean War'.[153]

Yet this optimistic assessment has received something of a mauling in recent years. In a 1963 article, Olive Anderson argued that 'even Gladstone's war finance was less purely in the classical tradition associated with his name than is often realized, or than he himself cared to admit. In particular, he made greater use of borrowing than is always appreciated.'[154] She contends that it is untrue that Gladstone's 1853 budget had settled the income tax controversy, with many complaining at its unjust failure to differentiate between permanent and precarious incomes, and this meant Gladstone could

---

[151] Morley, *Gladstone*, I. p. 515.
[152] Buxton, *Finance and Politics*, I. p. 155.
[153] Morley, *Life of Gladstone*, I. pp. 474–75; Hirst, *Gladstone as Financier*, p. 152.
[154] O. Anderson, 'Loans versus Taxes: British Financial Policy in the Crimean War', *Economic History Review*, New Series, Vol. 16 (1963), p. 315.

not raise it sufficiently to cover the war's costs.[155] A trenchant critic has been Feuchtwanger:

> The whole tradition of Peelite finance [...] mixed with war as little as oil does with water. Gladstone was forced to abandon his own principles step by step and when the British public, after a winter of disasters in the Crimea, demanded an all-out effort to win the war, Peelite canons of economy were laughed out of court as petty cheese-paring.[156]

Gladstone 'soon came up against the limits of income tax' and he turned to the loans he had previously rejected, using exchequer bonds and bills to make up for short-term deficiencies in the revenue. 'In fact, 46 per cent of the total expenditure on the Crimean War was met by loans, in spite of the fact that it was a relatively short war.'[157]

Shannon echoes Feuchtwanger's strictures. 'What is so noticeable about Gladstone at this time is a certain helpless inflexibility, a lack of resourcefulness and consequently, ultimately, "evasions and sophistries."'[158] His 'obsession with his new vocation [...] led him to invest in this already excessively moralistic financial policy an overwhelming and unbalancing element of his own intense moralism'.[159] His determination to avoid paying for the war through borrowing led him to try to disguise the need for it by issuing redeemable Exchequer Bonds – which were never redeemed and were in fact added to the national debt. By the time he left office in 1855 a budget deficit of £2 million had emerged.[160]

> This fiasco seriously compromised Gladstone's financial reputation [...] It was as well [...] for Gladstone's reputation that the Aberdeen coalition fell at the beginning of 1855, for by then the discrepancy between his doctrine and his policy was of embarrassing proportions. He was contemplating a loan of £12 million and a large increase in indirect taxation.[161]

---

155 Ibid., p. 319.
156 Feuchtwanger, *Gladstone*, p. 89.
157 Ibid., p. 90.
158 Shannon, *Gladstone: Peel's Inheritor*, p. 287.
159 Ibid., p. 288.
160 Anderson, 'Loans versus Taxes: British Financial Policy in the Crimean War', p. 316.
161 Shannon, *Gladstone: Peel's Inheritor*, p. 288. See also Anderson, 'Loans versus Taxes: British Financial Policy in the Crimean War', p. 315.

By the time of his resignation, remarks Hawkins, '[p]olitical pundits and the city came to consider Gladstone "rash, obstinate and injudicious"', while Hoppen concludes 'that by 1857 Gladstone was being widely regarded as something of a financial crank'.[162] In reality, Roland Quinault has recently observed, Gladstone's approach to war finance was less doctrinaire than he often appeared to suggest and there was a significant contrast between theory and practice: 'he justified higher taxation as a moral check on the lust for war, but he also recognised the need for loans to fund major conflicts'.[163]

Were Gladstone's financial policies a political asset or liability?

It is commonly argued that Gladstone's financial policies were a political asset for himself and the governments of which he was a member. With respect to Gladstone's own position, Shannon sees his financial policy as forming the basis of a 'second vocation'. Although his first foray into this field in 1853 ended prematurely, during the mid-1850s he returned to the theme in more systematic fashion, drawing up a programme for financial reform:

> With this programme [...] Gladstone signalled the revitalising of his second vocation. He was picking up the threads of the aborted mission of 1853 and forming them into the sinews of a grand strategy for a financial policy big enough and bold enough to remoralise politics by the sheer weight of its gravitational pull.[164]

Hawkins similarly sees the financial framework established by his 1853 budget as central to Gladstone's negotiation of the personal and public crises afflicting him in the 1850s. While Whig governments under Palmerston diverged from Gladstonian principles by spending more money on defence and covering this through increases in borrowing and indirect taxes, Gladstone, in a series of articles, defended his 1853 settlement, calling for retrenchment so as to make possible the phasing out of income tax.[165] 'The question of the income tax', Hawkins concludes, 'offered the Peelites, and in particular Gladstone, the opportunity to re-establish their authority within Westminster.'[166]

Gladstone's reputation for financial acumen was, says Biagini, all the more important given his lack of social connections or regular party ties. 'Faced

---

[162] Hawkins, 'A Forgotten Crisis', p. 293; Hoppen, *Mid-Victorian Generation*, p. 153.

[163] R. Quinault, 'Gladstone and War', in Quinault et al. (eds), *William Gladstone* (2012), p. 243.

[164] Shannon, *Gladstone: Peel's Inheritor*, p. 319.

[165] Hawkins, 'A Forgotten Crisis', p. 299.

[166] Hawkins, *British Party Politics*, p. 40.

with such odds, Gladstone elaborated a strategy for turning his weakness into strength.' Central to this were 'his rhetorical powers and newly developed links with the press. The aims were to reap the political benefits of his well-advertised financial prowess, and to present his own comparative political isolation as a noble stance adopted in the national interest, to which he appealed above the old cliques.' Gladstone understood how public opinion could be 'worked' through the press, and the latter, grateful to Gladstone for scrapping the paper tax, 'celebrated his budgets as patriotic responses to the needs of the economy and the expectations of the people'.[167]

Matthew emphasizes Gladstone's politicization of the chancellorship. Thus the 1860 trade treaty with France was really a foreign policy move to counter Whig bellicosity. While his attempt to abolish the paper duties in 1860 was rebuffed by the Lords, his martyrdom in the cause of abolishing the taxes on knowledge consolidated his radical credentials.[168] More generally, Matthew argues, Gladstone saw financial policy as securing the political legitimacy of the established order. This he endeavoured to do in three ways: first, by harmonizing the tax system to the electoral system through the so-called Victorian social compact; second, by removing potential popular opposition by reducing the size of the state and purging it of wasteful spending; and third, by engaging in continual fiscal reform to demonstrate that the political system was responsive to the needs of the population. 'For Gladstone, therefore, big bills and big budgets represented a means of regular renewal of the legitimacy of Parliament and the political system.'[169]

It is, further, argued that Gladstone's financial policies were popular with wide sections of the electorate – financiers, businessmen and the working class. This vindicated Gladstone's claim that he was chancellor for the entire nation, thereby facilitating his transition from Peelite executive politician to the 'People's William'. Hirst writes that from the time of the 1853 budget 'the middle classes reposed their confidence in Gladstone'.[170] Given the low-tax laissez-faire thrust of Gladstone's finance, this might not seem particularly surprising. What is surprising is that he was appreciated equally by the working class – a point emphasized by Biagini. Gladstone's fiscal rules of avoiding waste and balancing the budget resonated with ordinary people and seemed to represent an underlying moral vision.[171] He was 'revered as the liberator of the "people's breakfast table" [...] the minister who had removed duties and

---

[167] Biagini, *Gladstone*, pp. 34–35.
[168] Matthew, *Gladstone*, p. 114.
[169] Ibid.
[170] Hirst, *Gladstone as Financier*, p. 223.
[171] Biagini, *Gladstone*, p. 40.

taxes from many items of mass consumption and necessities of life'. With the repeal of the paper duties in 1861, Gladstone's 'popularity among working-class radicals increased by leaps and bounds' – as was demonstrated by his triumphal entry into Northumberland in 1862.[172] Parry elaborates this point, suggesting that Gladstone changed the radicals' relationship to taxation, convincing them that the fight for economy no longer had to be conducted *against* the state. 'Liberal governments could link up with the people in an ongoing crusade for pure administration.'[173]

Lastly, it is contended that Gladstone's performance as chancellor provided political plausibility to governments otherwise struggling for relevant policies. Thus, Hawkins believes that his 1853 budget ended the probationary period of the Aberdeen coalition.[174] Similarly, Buxton observes that during the years of Palmerston's dominance, 'domestic legislation [...] was of the most meagre description', and in 'financial matters alone was there any real activity; and the reforms, the relaxations and remissions of taxation of the time redeemed the period from absolute nonentity'.[175] For Parry, Gladstone's 'financial administration remained one of the principal unifying factors in Liberalism'.[176]

Yet, these arguments for the political effectiveness of Gladstone's finance have been contested. Hawkins questions the idea that Gladstone's financial policies commanded widespread respect. His free-trade doctrines were already the consensus among politicians, while his views on tax policy were challenged by the likes of Cornewall Lewis, who argued that indirect taxes should be spread over a wider base of products, and many Tories as well as Whigs preferred Lewis's views to those of Gladstone, who was increasingly regarded as a doctrinaire crank.[177] Neither were Gladstone's policies popular with all the electorate. His failure to differentiate income tax disappointed radicals, while landowners disliked his property taxes. Gladstone's insistence upon cutting spending proved steadily less attractive during the 1860s: with taxation low and the economy expanding, his preoccupation with reducing expenditure appeared pedantic and anachronistic. His calls for further retrenchment met, says Biagini, with growing resistance among educated elites, who favoured increased defence spending.[178] This represented the unravelling of his fiscal

---

[172] Ibid.
[173] Parry, *Democracy and Religion*, p. 186.
[174] Hawkins, 'A Forgotten Crisis', p. 291.
[175] Buxton, *Finance and Politics*, II. pp. 4–6.
[176] Parry, *Democracy and Religion*, p. 269.
[177] Hoppen, *Mid-Victorian Generation*, p. 215.
[178] Biagini, *Gladstone*, p. 42.

social compact. As initially conceived, fiscal policy was designed to stabilize the political system, but by the later 1860s Gladstone was looking to political reform to stabilize the fiscal system, hoping that working-class voters would apply the pressure to cut spending that the middle class were no longer willing to do. Yet even after the 1867 Reform Act, his pledge to abolish income tax in 1874 fell flat with the electorate.

Third, it is countered that Gladstone's finance, far from strengthening governments, destabilized them. His battles with Palmerston over expenditure, remarks Hawkins, threatened the government's unity – which was only preserved by Gladstone's willingness to back down.[179] Indeed, his own 1868 government was brought down by Gladstone's obsession with cutting spending. Believing his chancellor, Robert Lowe, too weak with the spending departments, Gladstone dismissed him and made himself chancellor in order to push for a further £1m in defence cuts as a prelude to abolishing income tax. When ministers resisted, Gladstone called an election – which he lost. 'The whole affair', says Parry, 'alarmed Whigs, not least because they did not want income tax abolition and believed that Gladstone could only make up the shortfall by taxing property, such as death duties.'[180]

More generally the Whigs were, says Parry, uncomfortable with Gladstone's doctrinaire financial policy, contrasting it unfavourably with the more flexible approach of Wood (1846–52) and Lewis (1855–58), neither of whom shared the Peelite drive for tariff reductions. They believed

> that the promotion of trade was only a marginal concern of the Treasury, whose job should be to raise revenue as fairly and uncontentiously as possible. They held that the most successful fiscal policy was a flexible one which reacted quickly and pragmatically to the shifting burdens borne by different social groups. It was not a suitable arena for the application of long-term theories and stratagems which were bound to be falsified by unpredictable events.[181]

For these reasons they favoured retaining income tax, which they thought reduced class animosity by demonstrating a commitment to taxing property.[182]

---

[179] Hawkins, *British Party Politics*, p. 92.
[180] Parry, *Democracy and Religion*, pp. 269–70.
[181] J. Parry, *The Rise and Fall of Liberal Government in Victorian Britain* (1993), p. 184.
[182] Ibid., p. 185.

Gladstone's overall record as chancellor

According to Morley, Gladstone was 'recognised through Europe as the most successful financier of his age', while the American Methodist and educational reformer Frank Gunsaulus stated that Gladstone 'gave England the consciousness that she possessed the greatest Finance Minister in the world'.[183] Advocates of Gladstone's success point to several achievements. First, he realized his goal of making Britain a free trade nation. By 1866, writes Hirst, Gladstone had

> removed nearly all the Customs and Exercise duties on the necessaries of life and raw materials of industry, as well as the protective taxes on manufactured articles. Yet by keeping the indirect taxes on a few articles well suited for fiscal purposes, such as beer, wines, spirits, tobacco and tea, he had maintained a large revenue from Customs and Excise. Trade flourished.[184]

With government spending being held in check, income tax was steadily reduced until in 1865, says Buxton, it came within sight of being abolished entirely.[185]

> It was this increase of trade, this improvement of revenue, and this diminution of expenditure, that made the period of Mr. Gladstone's second term of office at the Exchequer on the whole the most satisfactory and the most prosperous in English financial history.[186]

Barnett Smith believed that the 'prosperity of the country was largely aided by Mr. Gladstone's financial legislation, and [...] those extensive remissions of taxation which distinguished his occupancy of the Chancellorship of the Exchequer'.[187] While Morley noted that Gladstone did not attribute the prosperity of the 1860s to his financial policies alone, 'the special cause of what was most peculiar to England in the experience of this period he considered to be the wise legislation of parliament, in seeking every opportunity for

---

[183] Morley, *Life of Gladstone*, II. p. 371; F. Gunsaulus, *William Ewart Gladstone* (1898), p. 179.
[184] Hirst, *Gladstone as Financier*, pp. 228–29.
[185] Buxton, *Finance and Politics*, I. p. 346.
[186] Ibid., p. 353.
[187] Smith, *William Ewart Gladstone*, p. 507.

abolishing restrictions upon the application of capital and the exercise of industry and skill'.[188]

Second, it is argued that Gladstone profoundly affected public opinion. 'He was', said Russell, 'the first Chancellor of the Exchequer who ever made the Budget romantic', raising, commented Morley, 'finance to the high place that belongs to it in the interest, curiosity, and imperious concern of every sound self-governing community'.[189] More importantly, adds Morley, 'Gladstone had the signal distinction of creating the public opinion by which he worked, and warming the climate in which his projects throve.'[190] Matthew concurs: 'through his oratory the creed of the Cobdenites became the orthodoxy of the electorate'.[191] Gladstone, Dick Leonard has recently written, effectively created the modern post of chancellor of the exchequer, and 'none of his successors has rivalled the impact which he made'.[192]

Third, it is contended that Gladstone significantly enhanced the political position of the chancellor. Ramm emphasizes this point. His chief aim upon assuming the chancellorship in 1859, she writes, was to strengthen Treasury control over the departments and turn the chancellor of the exchequer into a powerful finance minister. This was achieved. Treasury control was secured by having the spending estimates of the departments submitted to him by December, allowing him to assess them before presenting his proposals to the Cabinet.[193] He sought to consolidate his achievements by increasing the accountability of the government's financial administration. In 1861 the House of Commons Public Accounts Committee was set up to examine the accounts of expenditure, while the 1866 Exchequer and Audit Act provided for the auditing of all public expenditure by an audit board.[194] This Exchequer and Audit Act was, agrees Morley, a 'monument of his zeal and power [...] It converted the nominal control by parliament into a real control.'[195]

But some historians question this optimistic assessment. Gladstone had not, after all, cut government spending – only slowed its rise. What disguised this fact, says Hoppen, was the buoyancy of the economy, which allowed Gladstone to cut income tax rates from 10d to 4d in the pound. Even so, 'such

---

[188] Morley, *Life of Gladstone*, II. p. 68.
[189] Russell, *William Ewart Gladstone*, p. 279; Morley, *Life of Gladstone*, II. p. 54.
[190] Ibid.
[191] Matthew, *Gladstone*, p. 135
[192] D. Leonard, *The Great Rivalry: Gladstone and Disraeli* (2013).
[193] Ramm, *William Ewart Gladstone*, p. 40.
[194] Ibid., p. 42.
[195] Morley, *Life of Gladstone* II. 61–62.

reductions were no more than pale shadows of his earlier plans to abolish income tax completely'.[196] Indeed income tax was by 1874 a confirmed part of the revenue system. Ian St John questions how much the mid-Victorian prosperity owed to Gladstone: the progress of transport communications and the growth in the global gold supply all promoted growth, and nations 'from the United States and Prussia to South Africa and Canada, shared in this expansion, even without the benefits of Gladstonian finance'.[197] Biagini admits that free trade yielded many improvements, but from the 1870s it was recognized that poverty was far from disappearing and the economy was still undergoing periodic slumps. For these problems there yet existed no credible strategy.[198] By this time free trade was in global retreat while government spending was rising steadily under the combined pressure of armament spending and the increasing complexity of social problems. Neither was the Commons Public Accounts Committee of much use. It lacked, argues Shannon, 'technical expertise or political authority, so that disputed military spending had to be settled in the Cabinet. Further, Gladstone was unwilling to allow the Committee to discuss fiscal policy in advance – it could only consider tax decisions already taken. Gladstone had no willingness to concede executive authority to such a body.'[199] Hoppen agrees that the Public Accounts Committee and the appointment of a comptroller and auditor-general in 1866 'proved less successful in containing expenditure than he had hoped'.[200]

Conclusion

Gladstone's great achievement as Chancellor was to embody a systematic approach to finance that he had evolved in opposition and then applied in government. Programmatic politics of this kind was, as Matthew, Shannon and Ramm have emphasized, unique in the nineteenth century. As a result Gladstone commanded confidence, and as Morley and Matthew argue, his principles became the consensus. And he brought to the dry data of accounting a strong moral ethos which chimed with the self-righteousness and evangelical perspective of the mid-Victorians. As chancellor, Gladstone reflected back to the Victorians the image of themselves of which they were most proud.

---

[196] Hoppen, *Mid-Victorian Generation*, pp. 14–15.
[197] I. St John, *Gladstone and the Logic of Victorian Politics* (2010), p. 103.
[198] Biagini, *Gladstone*, p. 42.
[199] Shannon, *Gladstone: Peel's Inheritor*, p. 446.
[200] Hoppen, *Mid-Victorian Generation*, p. 119.

Yet Gladstone's tenure as chancellor was not, as Feuchtwanger points out, an unblemished success – his 1853 budget, for example, naively resting upon assumptions about the future that never materialized. More fundamentally, many of his goals remained unrealized: income tax became an accepted piece of the fiscal furniture, government spending did not fall in absolute terms, and the national debt was hardly reduced. Above all, what seemed like permanent principles of finance were already appearing, by the 1880s, to be only mid-Victorian expedients. In seeking to perfect a Platonic minimal state, Gladstone failed to recognize the historical dimension to all social institutions and practices. Just as he had found himself the last man on a sinking Church–State ship, so he was later to compare his commitment to disciplined finance as a piece of driftwood on the shore. He had struggled to defend an approach to finance that would not survive even his own lifetime. And this he, at least, would have regarded as a failure.

2.3   How Effective an Opposition Leader Was Disraeli?

Disraeli was opposition leader for longer than anyone else in British history. But was he any good at his job? The Conservatives failed to command a majority between 1846 and 1874, and historians have questioned how far this reflected Disraeli's deficiencies as an opposition leader – or was it due to circumstances over which he had minimal influence? Below we evaluate the historiography of four arguments advanced by historians who have sought to vindicate Disraeli's opposition strategy.

Disraeli provided strong leadership to the Conservatives

It is commonly said that Disraeli pioneered the concept of the modern opposition leader. He was, says Robert Blake, 'perhaps the first statesman systematically to uphold the doctrine that it is the first duty of the Opposition to oppose'.[201] In this guise he was a 'superb parliamentarian, one of the half-dozen greatest in our history'.[202] He was certainly, writes Machin, one of the most energetic: 'He wanted to galvanise his colleagues into constant activity, making the most of every chance to challenge government policy and obtain a majority [...] The actual merits of government policies were of minor importance when compared with the overriding desire to give perennially

---

[201] Blake, *Disraeli*, p. 355.
[202] Ibid., 764.

active opposition.'[203] In the wake of the 1846 schism over the Corn Laws, writes Paul Smith, upholding an actively critical stance was necessary for sustaining the Conservatives 'as a fighting force in the dispiriting circumstances of apparently permanent minority'.[204] His work to do this constituted his claim to be 'the outstanding opposition leader of the century'.[205] By this aggressive stance Disraeli not only rallied the Conservative party around his leadership but also restored it as a credible candidate for office. Thomas Kebbel, a Tory journalist and friend of Disraeli's, wrote in 1908 how it was apparent by 1852 that

> [o]ut of the broken and dispirited remnants which accepted his leadership in 1848 he had built up a powerful Opposition [...] and had shown the world that there was again a Conservative Party qualified both by numbers and ability to take the reins of government whenever the Liberals should drop them.[206]

This was Disraeli's personal achievement, for, as the Liberal critic Bagehot recognized, Disraeli '*did* lead the Tory Opposition through long and melancholy years, when one did not know who else *could* have or who *would* have'.[207] The Conservatives, writes Machin, 'could not do without his talent, initiative, and vigour'.[208] He was, agrees Jenkins, 'an invaluable asset to his party', the only Conservative capable of competing with government speakers like Palmerston, Russell, Gladstone and Graham.[209] Brandes found much wisdom in the policies he advocated: he abandoned protection; criticized Palmerston's meddling foreign policy; denounced the wretched administration of the Crimea campaign; perceived the underlying causes of the Indian Mutiny; and exhibited self-control and patience. Above all, says Brandes, 'he possessed the gift of never wounding anybody's vanity; as leader of the opposition, he did not thrust any aspiring colleague into the shade'.[210] The sheer professionalism of Disraeli's long commitment to the 'business of the front bench was', concludes Bruce Coleman, 'to be [...] a major factor in

---

[203] Machin, *Disraeli*, pp. 82–83.
[204] Smith, *Disraeli*, p. 117.
[205] Ibid., p. 212.
[206] T. E. Kebbel, *Lord Beaconsfield and other Tory Memories* (1907), p. 3.
[207] W. Bagehot, 'Mr. Disraeli as a Member of the House of Commons', in N. St John-Stevas (ed.), *Collected Works of Walter Bagehot* III. p. 502. Italics in the original.
[208] Machin, *Disraeli*, pp. 86–87.
[209] Jenkins, *Disraeli and Victorian Conservatism*, p. 61.
[210] Brandes, *Lord Beaconsfield*, p. 210.

his eventual success'.[211] William Monypenny and George Buckle suggest that it gradually earned for Disraeli the respect of the British people, such that by the 1870s there was 'an awakening to the fact that his patience, his courage, his genius, his experience, and his patriotism constituted a character round which popular feeling, disappointed in its idol [Gladstone], might safely rally'.[212]

But several writers question whether Disraeli was a galvanizing force for the Conservative Party. While acknowledging that 'Disraeli was the greatest leader of the opposition modern Britain has known', John Vincent adds that '[g]enius is a strange word to use of a man who, as party leader, lost six general elections and won only one'.[213] Hawkins is similarly frank in his assessment:

> Disraeli's solid achievements as Conservative leader were relatively few [...] The only election Disraeli won for his party was in 1874. Only on two occasions, in 1867 and 1877, did he convincingly achieve his political aim of breaking the Liberal party down into its constituent parts.[214]

In opposition the 'countless alliances and tactical manoeuvrings his fertile mind envisaged largely failed to materialise'.[215] Far from providing a figure around which the Conservatives could unite, Disraeli never inspired trust or respect and remained unpopular with his own party. This, remarks Vincent, was Disraeli's chief deficiency: he failed to put down roots in his own party.

> Before 1868 he was tolerated because he was expected to retire with Derby; after 1868 he was tolerated [...] because he was not expected to last long anyway [...] From 1849 to 1881 Disraeli held his position only on sufferance; it was only posthumously that he became the inspiration of his party.[216]

The idea that Disraeli was a relentless critic of government has also been qualified. While indefatigable in his attempts to bring down the Whig and Peelite governments of the 1850s, by the early 1860s he appeared to have run out of steam. He faced in Palmerston a prime minister whom many Tories

---

[211] B. Coleman, *Conservatism and the Conservative Party in Nineteenth Century Britain* (1988), p. 96.
[212] Monypenny and Buckle, *Life of Benjamin Disraeli*, II. p. 522.
[213] Vincent, *Disraeli*, p. 6.
[214] Hawkins, *British Party Politics*, p. 216.
[215] Ibid.
[216] Vincent, *Disraeli*, p. 56.

preferred to himself, and this meant, says Jenkins, that when he did try to put pressure on Palmerston 'he was unable to command the unanimous support of his own backbenchers'. 'The extraordinary fact is that, even after some fifteen years as Conservative leader in the House of Commons, it was still doubtful whether Disraeli would be acceptable to the party as its overall chief.'[217] With the prospects of power seeming remote, Disraeli's zest for politics declined: in the 1863 session he voted in just 8 of 188 divisions; in 1864, 17 out of 156; and in 1865, 9 out of 104.[218] 'Between 1863 and 1865', concurs Hawkins, 'despondency rendered Disraeli an apathetic and fading political presence.'[219] Indeed, Bagehot's 1867 description of Disraeli's performance as opposition leader contradicts the 'opposition for opposition sake' model expounded by Blake: 'For years he has sat almost silent, – never raising petty discussions and confusing old people who thought a Leader of [the] Opposition ought to be always opposing.'[220] Defeat by Gladstone in 1868 prompted, observes Jenkins, a further lapse into 'apathetic opposition leadership [...] During 1870 rumours were rife [...] as to Disraeli's imminent retirement.' January 1872 was the nadir of Disraeli's standing as party leader, and influential Tories plotted his removal. 'It appeared he could not win elections, inspire confidence, or effectively challenge Gladstone.'[221]

Disraeli rebuilt and modernized the Conservative Party

Disraeli, it is argued, sustained the Conservatives as the second great party in Westminster. This was not, Matthew reminds us, inevitable.

> With the departure of the Peelites the Tories became [...] merely an interest group, the 'landed interest', not a party. It was not foreordained that the Conservatives should re-emerge as a national party; they might have remained an interest group for a very considerable period [...] It was of course Disraeli's triumph that they did not.[222]

A party representing the country squirearchy in a Britain becoming ever more urban and commercial surely faced political marginalization. It was

---

[217] Jenkins, *Disraeli and Victorian Conservatism*, p.59.

[218] Ibid., p. 60.

[219] Hawkins, *British Party Politics*, p. 179.

[220] Bagehot, 'Why Mr. Disraeli has Succeeded', in St John-Stevas, *Collected Works of Walter Bagehot* III. p. 492.

[221] Hawkins, *British Party Politics*, p. 181.

[222] Matthew, 'Disraeli, Gladstone, and the Politics of Mid-Victorian Budgets', p. 619.

this prospect, Monypenny and Buckle contend, that Disraeli averted, as he maintained the claim of the Conservatives to be a truly national party. 'Throughout the period he was building up his party so as to fit them for office, and keeping constantly before them a national rather than a sectarian or territorial ideal.'[223] He did this in three ways.

First, he modernized the party's policies in the hope, says Machin, of commanding middle-class support by rivalling the Liberals 'in pursuing progressive, reforming policies'. In so doing he echoed many of Peel's initiatives, such as abandoning protection and confirming the Maynooth grant, while also pursuing parliamentary and social reform. It was, according to several historians, Disraeli's decision to distance the Conservatives from the Corn Laws that was most important. 'National finance', claims Matthew, 'was the issue Disraeli used to educate his party.'[224] Hence, in 1852 he formulated a budget that appealed to the nation as a whole, not just the landed interest, with a reduction in tea duties and differentiated income tax, while rejecting restoration of the Corn Laws. Disraeli thus 'came to support the mid-century Peel-Gladstone fiscal settlement'.[225] For Hoppen, Disraeli's achievement was to persuade the Tory party that they should look not for a return of the Corn Laws but for some alternative compensation such as reduced local taxation.[226]

Disraeli's second contribution to the survival of the Conservatives was his overhaul of party organization. This had disintegrated with the Peelite secession in 1846, and Feuchtwanger notes several of the steps Disraeli took in the 1850s to strengthen the Tories' position, working with a new chief whip, Sir William Jolliffe, and with his own solicitors, Rose and Spofforth, in the sphere of elections.[227] Harold Hanham, in his *Elections and Party Management* (1959), relates how 'Disraeli himself took a great deal of interest in questions of organisation', though he admits that 'he preferred to leave the detailed work of supervision to someone else'.[228] It was from 1868 that Conservative organization really made significant strides. 'During these years of reserve in opposition', observe Monypenny and Buckle, 'when he appeared to colleagues and followers to be apathetic, he had been quietly working at Conservative reorganisation, and creating

---

[223] Monypenny and Buckle, *Life of Benjamin Disraeli*, II. p. 113.
[224] Matthew, 'Disraeli, Gladstone, and the Politics of Mid-Victorian Budgets', p. 619.
[225] Ibid., pp. 621, 640.
[226] Hoppen, *Mid-Victorian Generation*, 136–37. See also Jenkins, *Disraeli and Victorian Conservatism*, p. 42.
[227] Feuchtwanger, *Disraeli*, p. 97.
[228] H. J. Hanham, *Elections and Party Management: Politics in the Time of Disraeli and Gladstone* (1959), pp. 357–58.

a machine which was to lead to the victory of 1874.'[229] The 1868 election showed that in an age of household suffrage a more comprehensive electoral organization was required, and Disraeli instructed John Gorst to provide one. Though Disraeli left Gorst 'a free hand, he paid nevertheless constant personal attention to all that was being done'. 'Disraeli was thus', conclude Monypenny and Buckle, 'responsible for starting the first great party machine, and he reaped the harvest in the victory of 1874.'[230] Harold Hanham similarly relates how Gorst set up a rejuvenated Central Office, while in 1870 he took over the National Union of Conservative Associations which had been formed in 1867 to mobilize Tory support among the working class.[231] By the 1870s, says Paul Smith, 'the Conservatives were the best organised party in Britain'.[232] William Jennings believes that Disraeli's 'most important contribution to the practice of party politics was [...] the party organization, which he first developed [...] Disraeli began the modern organization of party conflict.'[233]

Third, he evolved, according to Parry, a 'more or less coherent Conservative creed' based on moderate domestic reform, fiscal discipline, electoral reform and calls for restraint in foreign policy.[234] Thus he assiduously pursued reductions in income tax and criticized increased defence spending; advocated a conciliatory foreign policy to avoid 'war scares' and build improved relations with France; argued for reform in the government of India, establishing direct British control of India in the wake of the Mutiny; and repeatedly returned to the issue of electoral change, being determined that the Conservatives not be typecast as unthinking opponents of reform.[235] Ian Machin agrees that Disraeli sought to break the Conservative image of reaction by making parliamentary reform 'his most continuous domestic concern'.[236] Richard Davis similarly writes that 'Disraeli's most bold attempt to find an issue with which to breathe life into the Tory party and steal a march on the Liberals, was to advocate the Conservatives taking up electoral reform. He proposed this to an indifferent Derby in 1857 and in 1859 actually brought forward a reform bill.'[237]

---

[229] Monypenny and Buckle, *Life of Benjamin Disraeli*, II. p. 524.
[230] Ibid., pp. 525–26.
[231] Hanham, *Elections and Party Management*, p. 366.
[232] Smith, *Disraeli*, p. 117.
[233] W. I. Jennings, 'Disraeli and the Constitution', *Journal of Comparative Legislation and International Law*, Third Series, Vol. 13 (1931), p. 197.
[234] Parry, *Benjamin Disraeli*, p. 56.
[235] Ibid., pp. 56–61.
[236] Machin, *Disraeli*, p. 81.
[237] Davis, *Disraeli*, p. 140.

In 1872 Disraeli's ideology took a less Liberal turn as he deployed a discourse of Empire, social reform and respect for established institutions. Through his Manchester and Crystal Palace speeches, contends Hawkins, he provided

> Conservatives with a potent language about themselves that enabled them to be a national anti-Liberal party. The diverse and disruptive expectations excited by Liberal fervour, he asserted, were best calmed by reverence for ancient institutions, pride in Empire and a quiet good faith in the good sense of the English people. Disraeli therefore rescued the Conservatives from both narrow sectionalism and atavistic bigotry. His rhetoric gave the Conservative party a future.[238]

Indeed, Bentley judges 1872 to be Disraeli's 'only good year as opposition leader'. His 'highly effective speeches at Manchester and the Crystal Palace helped him establish in the public mind the rhetoric of a Conservatism dedicated to the empire and the advancement of social reform at home'.[239]

However the idea that Disraeli inherited an anachronistic Tory party and supplied it with a progressive ideology and a party machine to carry that message to the people has been rejected by a number of historians, who counter that the culture of the Conservatives changed little under his leadership, that his impact upon party organization has been exaggerated and that he failed to develop a distinct Conservative ideology.

Consider, first, Matthew's argument that Disraeli astutely jettisoned agricultural protection and, by developing broadly Liberal policies, prevented the party retreating into a rural redoubt. Two objections have been made to this perspective. Davis questions the 'propriety of his trying so speedily to disembarrass himself' and his party of protectionism. While protection was 'a millstone round his neck', he himself helped to put it there. Protectionist sentiment remained strong in the counties, and Disraeli's actions 'did little to stabilise his own party, and much to further poison the political atmosphere'.[240] Blake agrees that Disraeli's haste to discard the Corn Laws was an error: 'Protection was indeed dead and damned. But MPs could not easily stomach such words from Disraeli. There was an ornate effrontery about him, which provoked intense dislike among his opponents and much mistrust among his supporters.'[241] It has, further, been questioned how far Disraeli truly broke the Conservative Party's association with the rural interest. For Vincent, Disraeli's

---

[238] Hawkins, *British Party Politics*, p. 216.
[239] Bentley, *Politics Without Democracy*, p. 219.
[240] Davis, *Disraeli*, pp. 98–99.
[241] Blake, *Disraeli*, p. 757.

leadership was striking for its 'traditionalism'. He left the party untransformed, preserving its stable rural identity. 'Far more important than social reform in his rhetoric was his idea of the innate solidarity of the English people behind their natural leaders.'[242] Disraeli exhibited disdain toward the middle classes, and Paul Smith comments upon the lack of progress the party had made by the mid-1860s in attracting the votes of the commercial class. The party's situation was 'critical. It had failed to come to terms with urban and industrial Britain and its expanding social forces. It remained overwhelmingly the party of the landed and agricultural interest.'[243]

The idea that Disraeli actively promoted an efficient party machine extending its reach into working-class constituencies has suffered at the hands of recent research, it being argued that the image owed much to later Conservative mythologizing – beginning with the self-promoting reflections of Gorst himself. While, says Feuchtwanger, some Conservatives were seeking to counter Liberal strength in the boroughs with Conservative working men's clubs, linking them together in 1867 with the National Union of Conservative and Constitutional Associations, Disraeli 'was almost dismissive. He [...] did not want a separate working-class movement, perhaps with its own agenda, to grow up within the party.'[244] Machin likewise observes that Disraeli did not want the National Union to 'become too much of a rival to traditional aristocratic paternalism [...] He never had the common touch' and did not pay 'continuous attention to a popular organisation'.[245] Hence Hoppen's remark that Disraeli was 'ambivalent, even suspicious' of Gorst's work with the National Union and Shannon's judgement that the Union came 'into being in spite of the leadership'.[246] After all, comments Vincent, Disraeli's metier was not mass politics but 'parliamentary manoeuvre'.[247]

Vincent questions Disraeli's success in developing a coherent Conservative programme. His opposition leadership 'lacked a theme'. At best,

[m]id-Victorian Toryism became a pale echo of dominant Liberalism [...] 'Conservative progress' became a Tory cry – but Tory progress curiously resembled Liberal progress [...] Disraelian Conservatism before 1874 was open to the charges of latitudinarianism that Disraeli had made against

---

[242] Vincent, *Disraeli*, p. 15.

[243] Smith, *Disraelian Conservatism*, p. 25.

[244] Feuchtwanger, *Disraeli*, p. 147.

[245] Machin, *Disraeli*, p. 60.

[246] Hoppen, *Mid-Victorian Generation*, pp. 136–37; R. Shannon, *The Age of Disraeli, 1868–1881: The Rise of Tory Democracy* (1992), p. 21.

[247] Vincent, *Disraeli*, p. 8.

Peel. The neo-feudalism of Young England had virtually vanished: the clock was not to be put back.[248]

Davis notes that in 1850 Disraeli spoke of preparing some 'great [...] scheme of policy', but 'the policy never emerged'.[249] Instead, he followed 'any policy that offered a prospect of success'. His attitude to foreign policy was 'equally opportunistic'. Thus, Disraeli initially supported the Crimean War and wanted Derby to lead a War Ministry, 'but once this effort failed, he took up instead the cause of peace'.[250] Insofar as Disraeli did pursue any coherent agenda in the 1850s and 1860s, it was Peelite. Having taken a leading role in Peel's downfall, reflects Blake, Disraeli realized that only a Peelite strategy promised the Tories a return to power. 'He never abandoned or denied his own "philosophy" but it had little effect on his actions [...] Disraeli's actual policy was essentially Peelite'.[251] Disraeli's opposition strategy, echoes Maurice Cowling, was to emulate the example of Peel, Palmerston and the Whigs and accommodate the Conservatives to 'every shade of centrally-held, securely based opinion'. Wishing to replace the Whigs at the centre of the political scene, he championed free trade, tax reductions, a restrained foreign policy and measures to appease Irish Catholics.[252]

Advocates of Disraeli's qualities as a leader point to his 1872 speeches in favour of Empire and social reform. Yet the distinctiveness of this programme has been questioned by, for example, Hawkins, who writes that 'Disraeli's message in 1872 was not a new departure in his thinking. Rather it represented a reworking of established themes.'[253] Empire and national prestige, says Vincent, 'looked back to Palmerston more than forward to late Victorian imperial expansion', and they had limited appeal to voters except in moments of excitement. It was small-scale issues that mattered most and here Disraeli was weaker – for example, in his handling of Nonconformist sensibilities.[254] Jenkins agrees that 'there was very little new in Disraeli's speeches of 1872'. A message of support for established institutions, the empire and a spirited foreign policy had made little headway against Palmerston: what changed in 1872 was not Disraeli's political stance but the disruptive impact of Gladstone's government.[255]

---

[248] Ibid., pp. 6–7.
[249] Davis, *Disraeli*, p. 96.
[250] Ibid., p. 126.
[251] Blake *Disraeli*, pp. 758–59.
[252] M. Cowling, *1867: Disraeli, Gladstone and Revolution* (1967), p. 65.
[253] Hawkins, *British Party Politics*, p. 182.
[254] Vincent, *Disraeli*, p. 51.
[255] Jenkins, *Disraeli and Victorian Conservatism*, pp. 67–68.

That Disraeli imaginatively targeted key electoral groups

Disraeli's Conservatives faced a Liberal-led coalition of factions, which together commanded a majority in parliament. His task was to break the hold of this Liberal coalition and replace it with a Conservative one. There were two steps to this strategy: first, to increase the Conservatives' electoral support, and second, to encourage various political interests to shift their allegiance to the Tories.

Several points have been made regarding Disraeli's effectiveness in winning over public opinion. As noted, he broke the association between the Tories and the Corn Laws, which was essential if they were to appeal to the urban electorate. Second, he cultivated support from members of the Church of England, an institution feeling itself beleaguered with the steady advance of Nonconformism and questions regarding its viability as the Established Church. Disraeli, writes Machin, seized the opportunity 'to appear in the guise of Established Church champion [...] This posture [...] helped him to build up distinctive Conservative morale against the seemingly impregnable Palmerston.'[256] Davis agrees that the defence of the Church was the main issue upon which Disraeli was active in the 1860s.[257] Jenkins elaborates:

Jenkins describes how, among the issues Disraeli raised in the 1860s, was the importance of the Tory party posing as friends of the Church of England against the attacks of nonconformists as represented by the Liberation Society. He helped to rally Commons opinion in favour of retaining Church Rates, and motions to abolish them were defeated in the Commons in 1861–63.[258] In a rare moment of praise, Davis describes this as 'a great parliamentary triumph'.[259]

Somewhat incongruously, Disraeli, hoping to win more seats in Ireland, also stepped forward as the defender of the Catholic Church. Hoppen elucidated upon Disraeli's thinking in a 1970 article on the role of the Catholic vote in the 1859 election.[260] Although the Tories were associated with Protestantism, the Whigs had also offended Catholics – notably with Russell's anti-popery response to the creation of a Catholic hierarchy in Britain – and the way

---

[256] Machin, *Disraeli*, p. 95.
[257] Davis, *Disraeli*, p. 143.
[258] Jenkins, *Disraeli and Victorian Conservatism*, pp. 68–70.
[259] Ibid.
[260] K. T. Hoppen, 'Tories, Catholics, and the General Election of 1859', *Historical Journal*, Vol. 13 (1970), p. 48.

appeared to be open for the Tories to make a bid for Irish support. To this end Disraeli, while in office in 1859, recognized Catholic chaplains in the army, introduced payment for Catholic prison chaplains and defended the Pope's retention of temporal powers in Italy, then being threatened by Italian unification. He also made 'vague promises about a charter for the Catholic University, and even more nebulously expressed nothings regarding tenant-right' for Irish farmers. It was not much, says Hoppen, but 'it was to prove almost enough'.[261] The 1859 election was the only one between 1852 and 1868 when the Tories secured a majority of Irish seats. Thus,

> [t]he Tories were presented with, and at Disraeli's insistence took advantage of, a uniquely favourable opportunity for winning the Catholic vote. They had established a bridge-head in what had previously been enemy territory. Had Disraeli received more support from his colleagues in the ensuing Parliament [...] the Tory party might, at least for a time, become the natural repository of a substantial number of Catholic votes.[262]

Lastly, it is pointed out that Disraeli, recognizing the importance of journalism in forming public opinion, sought to redress the Liberal newspaper advantage by, writes Smith, the bold expedient of founding his own paper, *The Press*.[263] Disraeli raised money for the project and contributed to its early content, pushing a Liberal–Conservative agenda as part of his project of appealing to middle-class opinion.

Did these attempts to enhance the electoral presence of the Conservatives yield dividends? Vincent acknowledges several achievements: governments fell more often than ever before in the 1850s; the Derbyites gained control of the House of Lords; there were improved relations with the Court; Party organization was rebuilt. 'Disraeli's efforts nearly worked.' In 1859 the party was eight votes short of a majority that would have made them – not the Liberals – the beneficiaries of the boom of the 1860s. 'Had they achieved office with a majority while Disraeli was in his prime [...] there was no reason why the Derbyites should not have come to look as impressively inevitable as the Gladstonian Liberals.'[264]

Unfortunately, most historians discount Disraeli's achievements in winning votes for the Conservatives. Jenkins believes that positioning the

---

[261] Ibid., p. 53.
[262] Ibid., p. 67. See also Feuchtwanger, *Disraeli*, p. 117.
[263] Smith, *Disraeli*, p. 117.
[264] Vincent, *Disraeli*, p. 8.

Conservatives as defenders of the Established Church carried little salience with an electorate which did not feel that the Church was in danger.[265] Only later did Disraeli reap benefits from his 'Church in Danger' cry – but this, comments Hawkins, owed more to measures pursued by Gladstone's government, notably the disestablishment of the Church in Ireland.[266] Davis believes that Disraeli's whole approach to the Church of England reveals his opportunism, noting that when prime minister in 1868 he 'was tamely to submit to a motion of Gladstone's making Church Rates entirely voluntary [...] By then he had other fish to fry.'[267] Equally, his attempt to win Catholic support for the Conservatives was never likely to yield significant results. Disraeli himself had opposed Peel's proposal to increase funding to the Maynooth Catholic seminary, while in 1851, as Davis points out, he took a strong Protestant line in opposing the Pope's reintroduction of a Catholic episcopal hierarchy to Britain.[268] Besides, as St John reflects,

> [a]nti-Catholic feeling within the Conservative party was simply too strong to allow Disraeli to pursue seriously measures to 'pacify Ireland'. The Conservatives were the party of the Church of England and Ireland and there was similar resistance (in a party of the landed interest) to the idea of interfering with property rights in Ireland in the interests of the tenant. Derby was opposed to both land reform and the suggestion of a pro-Papal policy [...] For most of the period, the Irish remained part of the Liberal's majority coalition.[269]

Given the importance of winning over public opinion, it was a weakness that Disraeli had no great penchant for campaigning. 'He spoke frequently outside parliament', writes Vincent, 'but built up no great oratorical reputation.'[270] Even the appreciative Monypenny and Buckle acknowledge that Disraeli 'never laid himself out' for 'the goodwill of the democracy'. 'No British statesman of recent years was ever less of a demagogue. With few, if striking, exceptions, it was only in Parliament and in Bucks that he opened his lips.'[271] M. S. Miller and M. G. Wiebe have drawn attention to Disraeli's success in

[265] Jenkins, *Disraeli and Victorian Conservatism*, pp. 70–71.
[266] Hawkins, *British Party Politics*, p. 182.
[267] Davis, *Disraeli*, p. 144.
[268] Ibid., p. 115.
[269] St John, *Disraeli and the Art of Victorian Politics*, p. 47.
[270] J. Vincent, 'Was Disraeli a Failure?', *History Today*, Vol. 31 (October, 1981).
[271] Monypenny and Buckle, *Life of Benjamin Disraeli*, II. p. 521.

securing press coverage for his actions in the 1840s, when 'he used the press much as a politician would use the media now', but historians believe that his attempt to woo a wider electorate by establishing his own paper, *The Press*, did him no favours.[272] While the paper, argues Ann Pottinger Saab, gave Disraeli a useful yet nominally anonymous outlet for his ideas, attacking, for example, the Aberdeen coalition's handling of the Crimean War, it was, says St John, 'never a success, political or financial, and by itself made little difference to the public debate. Its circulation struggled to exceed 2,000.' Journalism 'was not yet a wholly respectable trade and his half-concealed association became another count against him within the Conservative party'.[273] Saab admits that 'the reality of its accomplishments certainly fell short of the opportunity Disraeli and Stanley had thought they were grasping', and Feuchtwanger believes that Disraeli 'probably lost more than he gained by contributing to it'.[274]

Yet electoral campaigning was not the mainstay of Disraeli's opposition activity: this was his attempt to assemble vote-winning coalitions within parliament. Mid-Victorian politics was characterized by a fluidity of party alignment and no one party commanded a majority. Hence, observes Machin, Disraeli's main opposition strategy consisted of 'weakening the Liberal party' by 'exploiting its divisions'.[275] As Bentley reflects, any hope the Tories might have 'must lie in driving wedges between the slices of that potential majority by espousing causes and issues which most divided the enemy'.[276]

Disraeli's efforts to this end have been praised. St John remarks that he 'harried governments with flexibility and tactical skill, occupying rival political positions, exploiting party divisions and continually looking to build alliances with alienated groups'.[277] A key objective was to secure the return of the Peelites and hence, says Machin, Disraeli pressed Derby to accept the abandonment of agricultural protection. By 1852 this had been achieved and the majority of Peelites returned.[278] Disraeli also pursued, writes Jenkins, a Conservative fusion with aristocratic Whigs who disliked Russell's predilection

---

[272] M. S. Millar and M. G. Wiebe, '"This Power so Vast…& so Generally Misunderstood": Disraeli and the Press in the 1840s', *Victorian Periodicals Review*, Vol. 25 (1992), p. 80.

[273] A. Saab, 'Foreign Affairs and New Tories: Disraeli, "The Press", and the Crimean War', *International History Review*, Vol. 19 (1997), pp. 291, 302–4; St John, *Disraeli and the Art of Victorian Politics*, p. 62.

[274] Saab, 'Foreign Affairs and the New Tories', p. 308; Feuchtwanger, *Disraeli*, p. 97. See also Blake, *Disraeli*, p. 355.

[275] Parry, *Benjamin Disraeli*, p. 55; Machin, *Disraeli*, p. 61.

[276] Bentley, *Politics without Democracy*, pp. 163–64.

[277] St John, *Disraeli and the Art of Victorian Politics*, p. 58.

[278] Machin, *Disraeli*, p. 72.

for parliamentary reform. The central figure here was Palmerston, and when Derby sought, in 1852, to form an administration Disraeli offered relinquish the Commons leadership to Palmerston. Unfortunately 'Palmerston was too cautious to be willing to commit himself to the Conservatives'.[279] Rather inconsistently, Disraeli also sought to win the support of Radicals who, though generally supporting Liberal administrations, chafed under the leadership of the aristocratic Whigs and were impatient for greater reforms. Thus, notes Davis, in 1850 Disraeli suddenly announced his support for the long-running Radical demand for an end to paper duties, while St John refers to his efforts to secure Radical backing for his 1852 budget by reducing tax rates on income from employment and business as opposed to income from investments.[280] The idea that Disraeli was meditating on working with the Radicals is supported by the Conservative MP William Fraser, who recalled that in 1853 Disraeli asked him, 'What would you think of an alliance with Cobden and Bright?' Fraser replied that the Conservatives would not accept it, but 'I formed a decided opinion that there was no organic change that Disraeli was not capable of favouring' to secure a majority.[281] However incongruous such a step might have appeared, writes Smith, Disraeli had little choice if the Conservatives were to challenge the government or capture urban constituencies.[282]

Nonetheless, most historians question how much Disraeli's manoeuvring achieved. 'He spent much of his life scheming', Vincent observes, 'but hardly one of his schemes materialised. He searched restlessly for allies outside his own party, but never secured them.'[283] E. T. Raymond concurs: 'If he had sometimes contrived to bring Radicals and Tories into the same lobby, he had formed no permanent combination.'[284] Indeed, Disraeli's overt flexibility alienated people, encouraging a sense that he could not be trusted. Thus Bagehot could write in 1876 that '[o]n all minor parliamentary questions Mr. Disraeli has simply no conscience at all. He regards them as a game [...] to be played so as to show your skill, and so as to win, but without any regard to the consequences.'[285] Davis agrees that he 'twisted and turned in a fashion which it is extremely difficult to describe in any way other than unconscionable'.[286]

---

[279] Jenkins, *Disraeli and Victorian Conservatism*, p. 41.
[280] Davis, *Disraeli*, p. 99; St John, *Disraeli and the Art of Victorian Politics*, p. 42.
[281] Fraser, *Disraeli and His Day*, p. 192.
[282] Smith, *Disraeli*, p. 212.
[283] Vincent, *Disraeli*, p. 50.
[284] Raymond, *Disraeli: The Alien Patriot*, p. 229.
[285] Bagehot, 'Mr. Disraeli as a Member of the House of Commons', in St John Stevas, *Collected Works of Walter Bagehot*, III. p. 502.
[286] Davis, *Disraeli*, p. 119.

Such conduct demoralized his own supporters, and Hawkins emphasizes that during the 1850s Disraeli's 'tactical promiscuity' rendered him 'unpopular with many Conservatives and insecure in his position as Conservative leader in the Commons'.[287] Parry elaborates:

> A good part of the unrest was due to Disraeli's insatiable enthusiasm for planning parliamentary sorties against the governments of Aberdeen and Palmerston in the company of other amenable factions, whether Irishmen, radicals, or opposition Liberals [...] Disraeli bewildered his more unimaginatively stolid back-benchers by his sudden parliamentary attacks, which gave further ammunition to his party critics, for whom he remained 'the Jew'. He appeared to them to be consorting with dangerous radical opinion, at a time of widespread fear in propertied circles of the growing power of 'middle-class' 'Manchester' sentiment.[288]

Jenkins agrees that Disraeli's courting of the Radicals 'horrified many Conservatives [...] and he succeeded merely in reaffirming his reputation as an unscrupulous and unprincipled adventurer'.[289] Smith, however, believes it was attempts to win the Catholic Irish that were 'most disturbing' to backbench Tories.[290] Jenkins sums up Disraeli's weaknesses as opposition leader:

> Disraeli [...] was still the object of deep distrust on the part of many Conservative MPs, who regarded him as an unprincipled adventurer of dubious social origins. Furthermore, he aggravated an already difficult set of circumstances by his personal aloofness, and unwillingness to consult with his colleagues and back-bench followers.[291]

Unfortunately the quest for allies that so antagonized Disraeli's own side was, according to several historians, doomed to failure. He was, writes Blake, 'the object of deep distrust among the elements which he and Derby had to win over if they were ever to hold office'.[292] The 'endless manoeuvring and angling for partners', observes Feuchtwanger, 'was keeping distrust and distaste running high'.[293] Bruce Coleman believes that Disraeli's partisan

---

[287] A. B. Hawkins, *Parliament, Party and the Art of Politics in Britain, 1855–59* (1987), pp. 47, 180.

[288] Parry, *Benjamin Disraeli*, p. 55.

[289] Jenkins, *Disraeli and Victorian Conservatism*, pp. 47–48.

[290] Smith, *Disraeli*, p. 117.

[291] Jenkins, *Parliament, Party and Politics in Victorian Britain* (1996), p. 68.

[292] Blake, *Disraeli*, p. 758.

[293] Feuchtwanger, *Disraeli*, p. 101.

Conservatism meant he could never build a moderate Tory–Whig centrist coalition: 'His tendency to polarise issues, an effect at odds with his underlying desire for a consensus style of aristocratic conservatism, held back the disintegration of the Liberal right after Palmerston's death and helped to delay a major reconstruction of parties.' Thus in 1866 Derby and Disraeli rejected the chance to form a Tory–Adullamite coalition in the wake of the failed 1866 Reform Bill, postponing a Liberal schism for 20 years.[294] A more systemic problem was Disraeli's inability to secure the return of leading Peelites to the Conservative party despite having jettisoned agricultural protection. What impeded reunion, argues Davis, 'was not so much differences of principle as distrust and uncertainty about what the principles and policies of a party in which Disraeli took a leading part would be'.[295] David Murray, in an otherwise sympathetic 1925 biography of Disraeli, admits that animosity toward Disraeli prevented the Peelites returning to the Tories.

> Derby said bluntly that the sole explanation was hatred of Disraeli. He was right; Disraeli's enemies hated him, not only as a man, but as a symbol. A symbol of what? It was hard to say, and it was precisely this elusiveness that made him exasperating. He seemed capable of anything. His Toryism would not fuse with the English party tradition.[296]

More recent studies endorse this perspective. For Parry, Disraeli's 'reputation never recovered from [...] interpretations of his political behaviour between 1846 and 1852', when he denounced Peel before abandoning Protectionism without a moment's regret. By this alone the chances of attracting senior Peelites to the Tory fold had been lost.[297] Jenkins agrees that a chief barrier to any return of the Peelites was Disraeli himself, whose 'attacks on Peel in 1846 had not been forgotten'.[298] Certainly, writes Smith, there 'was no prospect of the leading Peelites agreeing to serve [...] under the man who had helped to assassinate their hero'. The fact was that no significant political figure or group was prepared to associate with Disraeli, and this 'failure to make friends doomed the Conservatives to near continuous opposition for twenty years after the disruption of 1846'.[299]

---

[294] Coleman, *Conservatism and the Conservative Party*, p. 96.
[295] Davis, *Disraeli*, p. 118.
[296] Murray, *Disraeli*, p. 166.
[297] Parry, *Benjamin Disraeli*, p. 55.
[298] Jenkins, *Disraeli and Victorian Conservatism*, p. 39
[299] Smith, *Disraeli*, p. 115.

Disraeli's effectiveness in opposition was constrained by factors beyond his control

If Disraeli's achievements as opposition leader were few, it is often suggested that this was largely due to the adverse circumstances he confronted. One such problem was the underlying weakness of the Conservatives as a country party in an increasingly urban and commercial Britain. The 1846 split, observes Smith, threw the Tories back on their rural haunches at precisely the moment when the nation was shifting to a mainly urban society.[300] 'The Tories', says Vincent, 'were the defenders of rural interests in an ever more predominantly urban society', and Disraeli's attempts to enlist support from Catholics or Anglicans were ephemeral compared to adverse demographic changes and the spread of radical political consciousness into lower social strata. '"Practical politics" was not the answer: the solution was to change the political culture.'[301] But constructing a counterculture to the Liberal monopoly of wisdom was, concludes Vincent, hugely difficult and could only be achieved 'in the very long term'. Ideas such as laissez-faire, religious toleration, meritocracy, utilitarian ethics and the desirability of progress had moved from the political margins to the centre and this coincided, as Froude recognized, with an unparalleled economic prosperity that seemed to vindicate the free-trade optimism of Richard Cobden and Peel. It was Disraeli's 'fate to steer the vessel in the stream when it was running with the impetuosity of self-confidence'.[302] He could do little else but pursue a Liberal agenda.

A second frequently noted problem was the presence on the Liberal benches of the former Tory, Lord Palmerston. Monypenny and Buckle regarded Palmerston as the chief difficulty confronting Disraeli. Having failed to secure Palmerston for a Tory administration, Disraeli faced 'the dreary prospect of an uphill fight in opposition against a nominally Liberal Prime Minister whom many of the Tory rank and file considered a better Conservative than himself'.[303] The 1859 government was just what the middle class wished to see: 'Palmerston as Prime Minister to sustain and guard the national honour and interests, with Gladstone at the Exchequer to promote the national prosperity'.[304] In the Palmerstonian 'Age of Equipoise', asks Coleman, why have a Conservative party at all?

---

[300] Ibid., p. 117.
[301] Vincent, *Disraeli*, pp. 47–48.
[302] Froude, *Lord Beaconsfield*, p. 152.
[303] Monypenny and Buckle, *Life of Benjamin Disraeli*, I. p. 1, 416.
[304] Ibid., II. p. 149.

How far were the Conservatives the party of order any more than the Whigs? […] With Palmerston in charge even the patriotism which had once served the Tories so well was no longer theirs to command […] To many Conservatives Palmerston looked like the best prime minister they had.[305]

For Feuchtwanger, Derby's understanding with Palmerston, under which the Tories would support him against Radicals within the Liberal ranks, made the task of leading the opposition extraordinarily difficult. More than ever Disraeli 'became a lightning conductor for the dissatisfaction which this indeterminate situation was bound to generate'.[306] To this the research of Paul Gurowich suggests a further problem: British politics, he argues, in the later 1850s and early 1860s were far less fluid than has often been contended and 'party continued unobtrusively to furnish the real basis of parliamentary politics'.[307] In which case, the Conservatives' minority position was a handicap Disraeli had little prospect of overcoming.

Lastly, those appreciative of Disraeli's qualities attribute his limited achievements to the deadening hand of the party leader, Lord Derby, who is portrayed as an unimaginative and fatalistic politician who not only frustrated Disraeli's more daring initiatives but also whose lapidary approach to opposition politics contrasted with Disraeli's eagerness to oppose. The irony was that Disraeli needed Lord Derby, who had the political and social weight to hold the protectionist Tory rump together. As Vincent states it, 'Disraeli, at best, was Lord Derby's House of Commons manager. Disraeli proposed; Derby decided.'[308] Monypenny and Buckle admit Disraeli needed Derby, but add that he hindered Disraeli's ardour for a 'bold and decided course', citing, as an example, Derby's unwillingness in 1857 to take up Disraeli's suggestion for a Tory initiative on electoral reform.[309] They refer, too, to Derby's preference for supporting Palmerston after 1859, which 'obliged Disraeli to spend some of the best years of his life leading an Opposition which did not seriously oppose'.[310] Indeed, the two men, it is argued, differed fundamentally in their conception of opposition tactics: where Disraeli was keen to strike at the government whenever possible, Derby, observes Blake, preferred to wait for

[305] Coleman, *Conservatism and the Conservative Party*, pp. 85–87.
[306] Feuchtwanger, *Disraeli*, p. 120.
[307] P. M. Gurowich, 'The Continuation of War by Other Means: Party and Politics, 1855–1865', *Historical Journal*, Vol. 27 (1984), p. 606.
[308] Vincent, *Disraeli*, p. 5.
[309] Monypenny and Buckle, *Life of Benjamin Disraeli*, I. p. 1, 481.
[310] Ibid.

the governing forces to fracture. This clash compromised the Conservatives, and Blake notes that for significant parts of the 1850s the two men failed to work together.[311] In 1855, remarks Machin, Disraeli was furious with Derby for turning down the chance to form a ministry during the Crimean War.[312] Hence Feuchtwanger's judgement that 'Disraeli was sorely handicapped by the fact that he was not in untrammelled command'.[313]

A number of historians take issue with this characterization of Disraeli as a victim of circumstances. First, it is pointed out that Disraeli was in large measure the author of his own fate. Peel's Conservatism, combining respect for institutions and social order with an acceptance of the need for reform, looked set to dominate mid-Victorian politics – until Disraeli sabotaged it by opposing the increased Maynooth grant and Corn Law repeal. 'Disraeli', says Vincent, 'destroyed the only chance of Tory supremacy in the Victorian period when he destroyed Peel.'[314] The Tory party's difficulties, writes Davis, 'were in large part of Disraeli's own making'.[315] The principles that united the Tories were 'agricultural protection and religious intolerance. No one else wanted protection, and few wanted religious intolerance.' Disraeli realized this, but it was he who had led the Tory pack against Maynooth and Corn Law repeal.[316]

Second, Derby's biographer, Angus Hawkins, vehemently rejects the 'Beaconsfield myth' that Disraeli was a 'frustrated genius [...] hampered by the dead weight of Derby's social prominence'. Quite the opposite: Derby was a great asset to the Conservatives and without him Disraeli's prospects would have been zero. In the mid-1850s Disraeli, he writes, was 'deeply mistrusted by many of the Conservative rank and file, and only Derby's endorsement preserved his Commons leadership'.[317] Derby's restrained approach to opposition did not reflect 'apathy or inertia', but an 'astute recognition of the persistent irritant that Disraeli's strategic ingenuity proved to Conservative sensibility'. Disraeli was a 'restless presence spurred on to constant activity by his own insecurity', repelling supporters and potential allies alike.[318] Against this Derby sensibly advocated a policy of watchful inaction in the hope that the differences between Peelites, Whigs, Liberals and Radicals would

---

[311] Blake, *Disraeli*, p. 355.
[312] Machin, *Disraeli*, p. 85.
[313] Feuchtwanger, *Disraeli*, p. 97.
[314] Vincent, *Disraeli*, p. 49.
[315] Davis, *Disraeli*, p. 96.
[316] Ibid., p. 98.
[317] A. Hawkins, *The Forgotten Prime Minister: The 14th Earl of Derby*, II. (2008), p. 114.
[318] Hawkins, *Parliament, Party, and the Art of Politics in Britain*, pp. 275–76.

gradually widen until the governing coalition broke apart.[319] Contradicting the likes of Monypenny and Buckle and Matthew, Hawkins further argues that it was Derby, not Disraeli, who 'educated' the Conservative Party during the 1850s and 1860s. It was Derby, the former Whig, who advocated that the Conservatives stand for 'moderate progress and responsible centrism; a party fit for government responding to the need for genuine reform as opposed to reckless innovation'.[320] Thus, it was Derby who pushed forward the question of reform during 1858–89, against the wishes of Disraeli, and did so again in 1866.[321] Jenkins endorses Hawkins analysis, adding that

> Disraeli was only tolerated by the Conservatives in the House of Commons because he was clearly subordinated to Derby [...] Derby's patrician presence was reassuring to the country gentlemen on the backbenches, making it easier for them to accept the unavoidable necessity of Disraeli's leadership in the absence of any viable alternative candidate.[322]

Conclusion

Disraeli represents the ideal type of an opposition leader, deploying almost every possible tactic in the search for power: targeting the centre ground, overhauling party organization, working on public relations, engaging in parliamentary manoeuvres, seeking to build coalitions, appealing to diverse electoral interest groups. Yet even sympathizers such as Parry concede that his exertions left him, by 1865, 'not much nearer power [...] He was over sixty, still widely distrusted personally, and a leading member of a party that could neither win elections on its own nor attract parliamentary support from other potentially sympathetic factions.'[323] Thus, the question is: did Disraeli make the best of a bad hand or did he contribute to the weakness of the Tory position?

Some historians, led by Monypenny and Buckle, see him as making a positive contribution: without him, the Tories would have been uninspired and possibly moribund, and in no position to benefit from the death of Palmerston and Gladstone's mistakes as prime minister. Most, however, portray him as having a neutral or even negative impact on Conservative fortunes.

---

[319] Ibid., p. 16. See also Jenkins, *Disraeli and Victorian Conservatism*, p. 48.
[320] Hawkins, *British Party Politics*, p. 47.
[321] Hawkins, *Parliament, Party and the Art of Politics in Britain*, pp. 275–76.
[322] Jenkins, *Disraeli and Victorian Conservatism*, p. 45.
[323] Parry, *Benjamin Disraeli*, pp. 70–71.

His vicious and opportunistic attacks on Peel helped create the debilitating split of 1846. Disraeli understood this, for once Peel was out of the way he took up his liberal reformist strategy. But by then he had discredited his reputation as a moderate reformer and rendered himself an insurmountable obstacle to Peelite-Conservative reunion, while his relentless scheming, argue such historians as Hawkins, Machin and Jenkins, further compromised his standing. If Disraeli found himself in a cul-de-sac, it was largely of his own making. The only solution, Vincent argues, was to construct an ideology to challenge the Liberal hegemony. But surprisingly, given his earlier fertility in counter-Liberal thinking, this is what he failed to do, following an essentially Peelite agenda which, contends Hawkins, Derby wished to pursue anyway. Only in the 1870s did he assemble a set of ideas to capitalize on Liberal failings. But there was little here that was truly new or properly worked out. Disraeli remained an essentially reactive figure: he reacted against Peel in the 1840s, found it hard to react against Palmerston in the 1850s and 1860s, and only found a foil against which to deploy his abilities in Gladstone's restlessly reformist government. And then it was quite possible that Derby could have capitalized just as effectively. It was Disraeli's misfortune that circumstances were against him, but it was his weakness as an opposition leader that having helped to make those circumstances he was unable to surmount them.

Chapter 3

WHY DID DISRAELI OVERSEE THE PASSAGE OF SUCH A RADICAL REFORM ACT IN 1867?

Outline of Events

The death of Lord Palmerston in 1865 revitalized British politics. For ten years his charismatic personality had dominated Westminster, and with his demise a host of personalities and issues asserted their claims to attention. First among these was Lord John Russell. Despite having played a prominent part in passing the 1832 Reform Act, and serving as prime minister in the late 1840s, Russell had found his career blocked by Palmerston's popularity, and his hopes of revisiting the subject of reform had been frustrated. Now again the leader of a Liberal government, he moved quickly to bring forward a Reform Bill, the passage of which through the Commons was delegated to William Gladstone. This 1866 Reform Bill was a moderate one, lowering the voting qualification in boroughs from the occupancy of a house commanding a rent of £10 per annum to one liable to an annual rent of £7. It was intended, thereby, to enfranchise the skilled working class, who were not only associated with an estimable sobriety but also had the additional virtue of being expected to vote Liberal. Unfortunately, Russell and Gladstone had not anticipated the emergence of a group of about 40 Liberal MPs vehemently opposed to extending the vote to the uneducated working class. Led by Robert Lowe, these Adullamites were able to defeat the measure by allying with the Conservatives. The government resigned and a Tory administration was formed, with Lord Derby as prime minister and Benjamin Disraeli as leader of the House of Commons. What should this government do about Reform? Disraeli preferred to do nothing. But the emergence of a popular protest movement, triggered by the failure of the Liberal Bill, persuaded Derby that it would benefit the Conservatives to bring forward their own Bill, rather than allow the Liberals to take up reform at the earliest opportunity. The result was a proposal to extend the vote in the Boroughs to all men who personally paid rates (household suffrage). To counterbalance the radicalism of this measure, additional votes were to be given to members of the propertied class (the Fancy Franchises). However, the Bill became ever more radical as Disraeli, who piloted it through the Commons, accepted a series of Liberal amendments that removed the Fancy Franchises and took the number of working-class electors enfranchised above one million. By the time the 1867 Reform Act had passed, Britain had taken a long stride toward a mass urban electorate – though in the counties the working class were still excluded from the vote, and, with astute handling by the Tories, the redistribution of constituencies was limited, with the large urban centres still under-represented compared with the small towns of the south and rural districts, where the Conservatives were stronger.

3.1   Why Did Disraeli Oversee the Passage of Such a Radical Reform Act in 1867?

Among the most contested questions of nineteenth-century history is why Disraeli, having helped block a moderate Liberal Reform Bill in 1866, proceeded within a year to guide through parliament a Reform Act enfranchising twice as many new voters. Five lines of argument can be discerned. First, that Disraeli wished to extend the vote to the working class as part of a commitment to a democratic Toryism. Second, that his actions reflected a strategic assessment that reform could benefit the Tories at the expense of the Liberals. Third, that the Conservative leadership was pushed into reform by a popular agitation. Fourth, that Disraeli was driven to pass a radical Bill by the necessities of the parliamentary situation. Finally, some historians reject the premise of the question, arguing either that the Bill was not Disraeli's work but Derby's, or that it was not a radical Bill but a conservative one.

Tory democracy

Barely had the ink dried upon the Reform Act than Disraeli claimed, in an Edinburgh speech, that it was the product of his long-nurtured ambition to connect the Tory party with a wider electorate. The working class, he argued, instinctively supported the nation's ancient institutions, and it had been his duty to 'educate' his party into recognizing this fact.[1] Georg Brandes wrote in 1878 that the Reform Act was 'the realization of Disraeli's old programme:

---

[1] For Disraeli's Edinburgh speech, see Blake, *Disraeli*, pp. 481–82.

the maintenance of the people's rights by Tory leadership', while the idea that Disraeli's Toryism was inclusive of all social classes was articulated in a *Times* editorial on the second anniversary of his death.

> What distinguished Lord Beaconsfield from the ordinary Tory leaders was his readiness to trust the English people [...] In the inarticulate mass of the English populace which they held at arm's length he discerned the Conservative working man, as the sculptor perceives the angel prisoned in a block of marble. He understood that the common Englishman, even when he has personally nothing to guard beyond a narrow income and a frugal home, has yet Conservative instincts as strong as those of the wealthiest peer.[2]

This theme was taken up by politicians like Lord Randolph Churchill, who sought to exploit Disraeli's legacy to push the Tories in a more popular direction, speaking of 'the great Tory Democracy, which Lord Beaconsfield partly constructed'.[3] Also keen to associate Disraeli with the idea of reaching out to the working class was Harold Gorst, the son of Disraeli's party organizer Sir John Gorst, who said of Disraeli in 1900 that

> [w]hen he entered Parliament the Tories were a party of privilege. He saw the democratic tendencies of the age, and grasped the fact that the people would not remain satisfied with the Reform Act of 1832. The Tories [...] were a party doomed to failure. He took them in hand and educated them. He formed out of them a great national and popular party, and taught the people of this country that the Conservative was their true friend.[4]

The idea that Disraeli's actions in 1867 were shaped by an ideology of popular Toryism has always found advocates. The legal philosopher, A. V. Dicey, saw Disraeli as a key instigator of that shift from individualism to collectivism that he considered the central change in public opinion during the nineteenth century:

> The lesson which Disraeli taught his party was the possibility [...] of an alliance between the Tories and English wage-earners; and the true basis of this alliance was their common dissent from individualistic liberalism

---

[2] Brandes, *Lord Beaconsfield*, p. 213; *Times*, 18 April 1883.
[3] Quoted in Smith, *Disraeli*, p. 214.
[4] Quoted in Shannon, *Age of Disraeli*, p. 3.

[...] the changes in the constitution of the House of Commons, begun by the Act of 1867 [...] were strictly the result of [...] the belief on the part of the Tories [...] that constitutional changes would in practice produce no revolutionary effect, but would diminish the influence of liberalism.[5]

William Monypenny and George Buckle, while admitting that Disraeli's attitude toward reform fluctuated with tactical considerations, add that he 'kept ever before his eyes the establishment of the Conservative party on a national and popular basis'.[6] Interwar biographies of the Conservative leader repeated this theme. Thus Andre Maurois wrote in the 1920s that

> [i]n his heart of hearts he had always been friendly to the idea of a suffrage extended to the more responsible section of the working-classes. That union of the aristocracy and the people which he had preached in *Sybil* would thus find its expression, and the boldest step would perhaps be also the wisest.[7]

Harold Beeley in 1936 attributed Disraeli's tactical agility on reform to the fact that there 'was no man on either front bench with fewer misgivings on the subject of the working-class elector than Disraeli. He still believed in the natural affinity between the aristocratic party and the masses [...] His determination to pass some kind of reform [...] was aided by a genuine sympathy with Radical amendments.'[8] John Marriott, historian and Conservative MP for Oxford, believed that

> Disraeli had always held that if the question [of reform] were tackled at all it must be tackled boldly: that if the settlement of 1832 were upset there was no resting-place, in the boroughs, short of the acceptance of "the principle of rated household suffrage" [...] The Act of 1867 gave precise expression to Disraeli's life-long convictions.[9]

But it was not only Conservatives who articulated this perspective: the liberal historian George Macaulay Trevelyan wrote in his popular *British History in*

---

[5] A. V. Dicey, *Lectures on the Relation between Law and Public Opinion in England during the Nineteenth Century* (1905), p. 253.
[6] Monypenny and Buckle, *Life of Benjamin Disraeli*, II. p. 297.
[7] A. Maurois, *Disraeli: A Picture of the Victorian Age* (1927), p. 214.
[8] Beeley, *Disraeli*, p. 96.
[9] J. A. R. Marriott, *England Since Waterloo* (1913), p. 355.

the Nineteenth Century that with the resignation of Russell's government 'a situation had suddenly arisen in which a Conservative leader who believed in the working classes could become the man of the hour'.[10]

Two more recent historians championing the role of ideology in Disraeli's conduct have been Asa Briggs and Gertrude Himmelfarb. Briggs sees 'a remarkable continuity' in Disraeli's ideas on reform. During the 1830s he had argued that the Tory party was the truly democratic party as it represented the will of the entire nation, and that an extension of the electorate would strengthen the aristocratic settlement of the country. Although he departed from this line when attacking Gladstone's 1866 Reform Bill, by '1867 he had returned to his instinctive position, and seven years later he reflected that his zeal for Tory democracy had served as the consistent element in all his work'.[11] Disraeli 'trusted the electorate', believing that a larger working-class element would strengthen the popular institutions of the country.[12] Himmelfarb is equally emphatic that Disraeli's One Nation Tory ideology played an important part in his approach to the Bill. Disraeli believed that society was governed by traditions of leadership and deference and that no reform bill could not affect this. Secure in his faith in a 'natural social order', he 'took amendment after amendment since there was, for him, no principled place to stop before a household suffrage'. This move to democracy was encouraged by 'the belief that the lower classes were not only naturally conservative in temperament but also naturally Conservative in politics. Thus the party had a practical interest as well as a philosophical disposition towards democracy.'[13] Whereas Liberals like John Bright regarded poorer members of the working class as too dependent or ignorant to be trusted with the vote, the Conservatives assumed that the masses identified themselves with their betters.[14] Disraeli's 'leap in the dark was made in the confidence that he would land securely on his feet'.[15]

A weaker version of the Tory Democracy thesis holds that Disraeli enfranchised the mass of working-class borough electors not because he wanted to incorporate them within the political system but because he

---

[10] G. M. Trevelyan, *British History in the Nineteenth Century* (1922), p. 345.

[11] A. Briggs, *Victorian People: A Reassessment of Persons and Themes 1851–1867* (1954), pp. 286–87.

[12] Ibid., p. 303.

[13] G. Himmelfarb, 'The Politics of Democracy: the English Reform Act of 1867', *Journal of British Studies*, Vol. 6 (1966), pp. 112–13.

[14] Ibid., p. 131.

[15] Ibid., p. 132. For a critique of Himmelfarb's interpretation, see F. B. Smith, 'The "Dependence of License upon Faith": Miss Gertrude Himmelfarb on the Second Reform Act', *Journal of British Studies*, Vol. 9 (1969), pp. 96–99.

believed they would vote Conservative – unlike the skilled working men who would vote Liberal. This was the complaint made by Liberals like Walter Bagehot. 'Mr. Disraeli', he wrote in 1867, 'all along wished to go down very low, to beat the Whigs – if possible, the Radicals too – by basing the support of the Conservative party upon a lower class than those which they could influence.'[16] His aim was to deprive the Liberals of the '"praetorian guard" of select artisans'.[17] Lord Cranborne, a Tory critic of reform, also made this allegation. The Reform Bill, he wrote in 1869, gained some acceptance on Tory benches from the idea that the 'poorer men are the more easily they are influenced by the rich' and that 'the ruder class of minds would be more sensitive to traditional emotions', and this 'went to make up the clear conviction of the mass of the Conservative party, that in a Reform Bill more Radical than that of the Whigs they had discovered the secret of a sure and signal triumph'.[18]

That Disraeli was influenced by the electoral possibilities of an extended franchise has been suggested by more recent historians. He realized, comments Lewis Seaman, 'that the Liberals did best in constituencies with a small working class and the Conservatives did best in boroughs with a large working class vote. Creating a large workingclass electorate therefore did not alarm him.'[19] F. B. Smith lends weight to this interpretation:

> Disraeli shared the widely held view that below a Radical, often Nonconformist labour aristocracy[...]there was a layer of Conservative working men. He hoped that his party would benefit from the enfranchisement of this lower layer not only through their own votes, but by frightening the middle classes into the Tory fold.[20]

Richard Shannon supports this understanding of Disraeli's thinking, arguing that he believed that 'the only chance of loosening the Liberal grip on the boroughs would be by an enfranchisement larger than that proposed by the Liberal government in 1866 [...] somewhere beneath the social stratum of reliably Liberal support there might be hitherto untapped resources of popular Toryism'.[21]

---

[16] W. Bagehot, 'Why Mr. Disraeli Has Succeeded', in N. St John-Stevas (ed.), *Collected Works of Walter Bagehot*, III. p. 491.

[17] W. Bagehot, 'Mr. Disraeli's Administration', in St John-Stevas, *Collected Works of Walter Bagehot*, III. p. 497.

[18] Quoted in Smith, *Disraelian Conservatism*, p. 95.

[19] L. C. B. Seaman, *Victorian England* (1973), p. 162.

[20] F. B. Smith, *Making of the Second Reform Bill* (1966), p. 230.

[21] Shannon, *Age of Disraeli*, p. 13.

Overall, however, historians have queued up to knock down the Tory Democracy interpretation of the 1867 Reform Act. It is argued, first, that Disraeli never called himself a 'Tory Democrat' and that the concept was a construct of later politicians wishing to evoke the shade of the Tory leader to vindicate their own populist Tory politics. Thus Douglas Hurd and Edward Young observe that so 'far as we can tell', Disraeli 'never used the phrase', while for Seaman '"Tory Democracy" was little more than a colourful theory about Disraeli's Conservatism invented by Lord Randolph Churchill in the 1880s for the purpose [...] of embarrassing Lord Salisbury'.[22] Edgar Feuchtwanger elaborates how the term 'Tory Democracy' was developed by Randolph Churchill and John Gorst in their attempt to develop a Fourth Party critical of the traditional Tory leadership, evoking Disraeli as a man who discerned the possibility of a populist Toryism.[23] In his 1886 *History of Toryism*, T. E. Kebbel described Disraeli as being throughout his career interested in the welfare of the poor, and whose 1867 Reform Bill and subsequent social reforms were 'but the natural development of views which he had previously enunciated'.[24] The idea of Disraeli as Tory Democrat met a need for the Conservative Party as it sought to retain relevance in the face of advancing democracy.[25]

Second, many historians deny that Disraeli was a democrat. He did not, wrote D. L. Murray, 'think the masses fit to govern'. His One Nation Toryism meant only that he thought the lower classes 'ought to be governed for their own benefit and not for that of any class or oligarchy'.[26] Jonathan Parry has more recently contended that, although Disraeli talked of the Tories as the 'national and popular party', this was to contrast them to Whig exclusivity. He inhabited an essentially predemocratic mindset, deploying language that used patriotic and monarchical themes to appeal to the British public.[27] Disraeli, concurs Feuchtwanger, 'believed in the aristocratic settlement and could in no way be described as a democrat'.[28] Monypenny and Buckle agree that 'Disraeli was not a democrat': the suffrage was not a right but 'a privilege to be gained by virtue, by intelligence, by industry, by integrity, and to be exercised for the common good'.[29] As late as 1866, they note, he opposed lowering the borough franchise as it would 'introduce many others who are

---

[22] Hurd and Young, *Disraeli*, p. 171; Seaman, *Victorian England*, p. 206.
[23] Feuchtwanger, *Disraeli*, pp. 212–13.
[24] Quoted ibid., p. 214.
[25] Ibid., p. 215.
[26] Murray, *Disraeli*, pp. 225–26.
[27] Parry, *Benjamin Disraeli*, pp. 125–26.
[28] Feuchtwanger, *Disraeli*, pp. 115–16.
[29] Quoted in Monypenny and Buckle, *Life of Benjamin Disraeli*, II. p. 144.

unworthy of the franchise', urging the House to 'sanction no step that has a tendency to democracy, but that it will maintain the ordered state of free England in which we live'.[30] As Maurice Cowling remarks, Disraeli gave 'no sign in late 1866 or early 1867 of extensive sympathy for working-class political rights'.[31]

It is thirdly argued that Disraeli did *not* expect the lower classes to vote Tory. The idea that he did, claims Feuchtwanger, was pushed by Liberal opponents – who portrayed Disraeli as engaging in a rather 'sinister' ploy to reach beyond the enlightened upper-working class to the residuum in search of Tory votes.[32] Robert Blake denies this was ever Disraeli's intention:

[He] was never a Tory democrat, and, whatever he and Derby may have said in the first euphoria of victory, it is certainly not true that either of them had been planning to enfranchise the artisan householder as a safe Conservative. If they had, Disraeli would surely not have devoted so much care to neutralising the effect of household suffrage by redrawing the county and borough boundaries [...] They had the wide franchise of 1867 forced on them as the price of staying in power [...] Disraeli saw the electorate in traditional terms of rural voters being Conservative, urban voters Liberal.[33]

Contradicting Seaman's assertion that Disraeli believed the Conservatives did best in large boroughs, Blake cites a remark of Disraeli's to the effect that, while the working class in small boroughs were under the control of the upper classes and would vote Conservative, in the large boroughs the workers, organized in unions, would not vote Tory.[34] F. B. Smith likewise points out that, if Disraeli had assumed the 400,000 extra working-class electors he planned to enfranchise would vote Tory, he would hardly have needed to propose to give 350,000 extra votes to members of the propertied classes.[35] Concurring with Blake, Smith believes that Disraeli anticipated that, in the large boroughs, Liberalism would remain ascendant and gave only four extra MPs to the great cities of the midlands and north. 'This fact in itself proves the limited faith Disraeli had in the reality of the Conservative working man.'

---

[30] Ibid., 143–45.
[31] Cowling, *1867: Disraeli, Gladstone and Revolution*, p. 334.
[32] Feuchtwanger, *Disraeli*, p. 166.
[33] Blake, *Disraeli*, p. 476.
[34] Ibid., p. 460.
[35] Smith, *Disraeli*, pp. 146–47.

Lastly, it is pointed out that Disraeli only spoke of the Reform Act as the completion of his wish to broaden the electoral basis of Conservatism *after* the measure had passed. It was never his intention to enfranchise large numbers of the urban working class. After all, writes Paul Smith, Disraeli first advocated a rate-payer franchise since it would exclude the compounders and prevent 'a working class predominance that no one desired'. It was only later that he spoke of 'the interests of the labouring classes as essentially the most conservative in the country'.[36] Disraeli's course, contends Feuchtwanger, was 'dictated by the exigencies of parliamentary tactics and it was only after the event that he justified it as the logical consequence of views he had always held'.[37] It was subsequently, observes F. B. Smith, that Disraeli propagated 'the myth that the Bill had been conceived in its entirety at the outset, and that the successive alterations in it had been the result of a deliberate plan by Derby and himself'.[38] This made sense, adds Cowling, once it was clear that the next election would be fought with a working-class majority in the boroughs.[39] For T. A. Jenkins too Disraeli's narrative of events at Edinburgh was more myth than reality:

> Herein lay the origins of what was later to be called 'Tory Democracy' – the doctrine which held that the Conservatives' enactment of Parliamentary Reform in 1867 was incontrovertible proof of their confidence in the loyalty and good sense of the masses. This belief may have borne little relation to the truth [...] but it generated a mythology of great potency which survived for almost a century.[40]

However against these denigrations of the role of Tory Democratic ideology in Disraeli's conduct, Paul Smith has countered that while Tory Democracy was not the motivation behind the Bill, his belief in the trustworthiness of the working class made such a radical Bill possible since he 'was certainly operating with a conception of Toryism which made it easy and in a sense obligatory to trust the political reliability of the people to any extent necessary to pass a Conservative reform bill'.[41] Thus while Disraeli was guided by the dictates of parliamentary advantage, his ideology afforded him flexibility by assuring him that any extension in the right to vote would

---

[36] Ibid., p. 149.
[37] Feuchtwanger, *Disraeli*, p. 130.
[38] Smith, *Making of the Second Reform Bill*, p. 242.
[39] Cowling, *1867: Disraeli, Gladstone and Revolution*, p. 334.
[40] Jenkins, *Disraeli and Victorian Conservatism*, p. 80.
[41] Smith, *Disraeli*, p. 145.

be compatible with a stable, hierarchical society. Seaman similarly observes that the 'continuous concessions he made during 1867 to the Radicals suggest that […] he was not frightened of the artisan class'.[42] Hurd and Young agree: 'It did not really matter whether Disraeli was a deep convert to democracy. The point is that he was not afraid. He was confident he could handle a change in the electorate.'[43] Disraeli's principle during these events, according to F. B. Smith, was to preserve the predominance of the landed interest, but on the matter of the enfranchisement of the artisans he was 'indifferent': when his party was against it, he was, but when pressed to give them the vote, he did so with no qualms.[44] If not a causal factor, Tory Democracy was a permissive one.

Strategic Conservative interests

It is often argued that Disraeli pursued reform in 1867 for strategic reasons. Ever since the 1850s he had been endeavouring to associate the Conservatives with moderate institutional change, and there was no better way to do this than by taking up electoral reform. Having brought forward a limited Reform Bill in 1859, Disraeli and Derby now returned with a more thorough measure which would consolidate the reforming credentials of the Tories while allowing them, not the Liberals, to shape the details of the measure. Parry agrees that a reform bill promised several advantages for the Conservatives: it would deprive the Liberals of a monopoly of the reform issue; by going for household suffrage it would settle the reform question while avoiding manhood suffrage; it would give the Conservatives the chance to manipulate constituency redistribution in their interests. Thus, by bringing forward a reform initiative the Tories were 'attempting to keep alive not only their own careers but also the Conservative Party'.[45] Bruce Coleman broadly endorses this analysis: 'Conservative leaders were keen to re-capture the political centre-ground from the Whigs and preserve the aristocratic constitution through moderate reform. This would associate the Tories with the cause of moderate reform and allow them to recover the traditions of Lord Liverpool and Peel.'[46] For Angus Hawkins, too, the evidence suggests that 'no deeply-held vision of Tory Democracy was driving ministers forward. What did exist was the intention to prove Conservative government responsive, enlightened,

---

[42] Seaman, *Victorian England*, p. 163.
[43] Hurd and Young, *Disraeli*, pp. 171–72.
[44] Smith, *Making of the Second Reform Bill*, p. 72.
[45] Parry, *Benjamin Disraeli*, p. 72.
[46] Coleman, *Conservatism and the Conservative Party*, p. 132.

and capable of reform'.[47] Kebbel recalled that Disraeli spoke to him in 1859 of his determination that reform should not be a Whig monopoly from which the Tories were shut out – destined to wither away.[48]

Rendering this reasoning especially compelling was that further electoral reform was seen as highly likely. 'All agreed', wrote James Anthony Froude, 'that reform was inevitable; if conducted by the Conservatives with a drag upon the wheel, it might be harmless, and might add to their strength.'[49] The goal of Disraeli and Derby was to settle the franchise question while shaping it in a Conservative direction. 'It was only by dealing with Reform themselves', adds Paul Smith, 'that the Conservative leaders could hope to turn the situation to profit.'[50] Household suffrage recommended itself as offering a 'permanent resting point' and because 'it was widely (and perhaps correctly) thought that it would be more beneficial to the Conservatives than a £5 or £6 franchise'. However, they did not intend a democratic measure, 'deliberately smothering it with checks and counterpoises', such as the personal payment of rates.[51] Robert Saunders agrees that what most attracted the Tories to reform was the chance to shape its terms: 'taking charge of a bill would enable the Conservatives to set the terms of the redistribution and the county franchise, and to control the qualifying details by which the franchise was surrounded'.[52]

Several historians see the strategic advantage of the Bill to the Tories, not so much in its particular provisions but in the fact that by passing a major piece of legislation at all the Conservatives could show they were again a governing party able to settle major issues.[53] According to Derek Beales,

> Derby and Disraeli [...] cared more that their party should pass some great measure [...] than they cared about its precise terms [...] The Conservatives had never held a Parliamentary majority since 1846. They could hardly be worse off under a new electoral dispensation. If they were in charge of carrying a Reform Bill, they might hope to make it more advantageous to their party than a Liberal measure would be.[54]

---

[47] Hawkins, *British Party Politics*, p. 121.
[48] Kebbel, *Lord Beaconsfield and Other Tory Memories*, pp. 16–17.
[49] Froude *Lord Beaconsfield*, p. 194.
[50] Smith, *Disraelian Conservatism*, pp. 89–90.
[51] Ibid., pp. 90–91.
[52] R. Saunders, 'The Politics of Reform and the Making of the Second Reform Act', *Historical Journal*, Vol. 50 (2007), p. 587.
[53] Feuchtwanger, *Gladstone*, p. 134.
[54] D. E. D. Beales, *From Castlereagh to Gladstone 1815–1885* (1969), p. 204.

In this connection Hawkins sees the Conservatives' poor showing in the 1865 election as a 'tipping point': having been comprehensively beaten, the idea of overhauling the electoral system was more attractive. Derby, says Hawkins, was determined to hold on to power as long as possible and stake a claim to the Tories being 'a credible and moderate party of government'.[55] And of course, as Paul Smith points out, if their Reform Bill was rejected they could take it to the electorate as 'a useful election cry'.[56] Cowling agrees that the fact that the Conservatives had never done especially well out of the existing electoral system predisposed them to reform. But he adds another strategic consideration: while lowering the electoral threshold in the boroughs might not help the Tories, it would definitely hurt the Whigs, who would come under pressure from the forces of urban radicalism, so pushing the Liberal party to the left, 'with the result that the Conservative party would establish total control of the respectable middle-classes'.[57]

A response to popular protest

The above interpretations all assume that the Conservatives in 1867 were following their own agenda. However a widely held alternative explanation holds that they were forced into bringing forward reform by the strength of public opinion. The defeat of the 1866 Reform Bill, occurring against the backdrop of economic recession and rising unemployment, awoke a desire for reform among the working class and there occurred a series of pro-reform demonstrations across the country – most famously a riot in Hyde Park when a proposed meeting was blocked by the authorities. Several well-placed observers believed that fear of unrest prompted the government to pursue reform as a means of diffusing social tension. Thus John Morley wrote that

> [t]he secret of the strange reversal in 1867 of all that had been said, attempted, and done in 1866, would seem to be that the tide of public opinion had suddenly swelled into a flood. The same timidity that made the ruling classes dread reform, had the compensation that very little in the way of popular demonstration was quite enough to frighten them into accepting it. Here the demonstration was not little. Riots in Hyde Park, street processions measured by the mile in the great cities from London up to Glasgow, open-air meetings attended by a hundred, two hundred, two hundred and fifty thousand people at Birmingham, Manchester,

---

[55] Hawkins, *British Party Politics*, p. 122.
[56] Smith, *Disraeli*, p. 136.
[57] Cowling, *1867: Disraeli, Gladstone and Revolution*, p. 65.

Leeds, showed that even though the workmen might not be anxious to demand the franchise, yet they would not stand its refusal.[58]

Writing in 1880, Justin McCarthy argued that '[n]othing can well be more certain than the fact that the Hyde Park riot [...] convinced her Majesty's Ministers of the necessity of an immediate adoption of the reform principle'.[59]

Interwar biographies of Disraeli repeated this narrative. For E. T. Raymond, the clamour of popular pressure was 'too loud and too insistent to be resisted', while Murray spoke of reform becoming an 'inevitability' once the Court and Parliament had been 'frightened by the tumultuous meetings of reformers in the provinces and by the Hyde Park riots'.[60] G. M. Trevelyan, although accepting the reality of Disraeli's Tory Democracy, added that 'even Disraeli would not have ventured to [...] take the famous "leap in the dark" of working class enfranchisement, but for the agitation in the country over which Bright presided in the autumn of 1866'.[61] E. L. Woodward, in his volume for the *Oxford History of England*, argued that the Hyde Park disturbance 'convinced conservative opinion that electoral reform could not be delayed'.[62] Postwar historians have revisited this theme. Paul Smith, in his *Disraelian Conservatism*, drew attention to 'the powerful working class agitation for Reform which appeared in mid-1866 [...] Downright resistance to this pressure offered serious risk of an explosion.'[63] In his later *Disraeli: A Brief Life*, Smith acknowledges that 'if popular pressure did not force the Conservatives into reform, the need to quieten "agitation" became an additional argument in favour of taking action'.[64] F. B. Smith lists among the factors inducing MPs to pass a Bill they disliked, the 'mass agitation which had sprung up after the defeat of the Liberal Bill'.[65] Beales also credits pro-reform meetings from the autumn of 1866 with an important role since politicians 'felt themselves compelled to pass some measure [...] with a view to placating respectable reformers and detaching them from the extremists'. Without this pressure, 'Disraeli would not have retained control of his party as he allowed the Bill to become radical'.[66]

---

[58] Morley, *Life of Gladstone*, II. p. 227.

[59] J. McCarthy, *A History of Our Own Times*, IV. (1880), p. 83.

[60] Raymond, *Disraeli: The Alien Patriot*, p. 241; Murray, *Disraeli*, p. 194.

[61] Trevelyan, *British History in the Nineteenth Century*, p. 345.

[62] Woodward, *The Age of Reform*, p. 178.

[63] Smith, *Disraelian Conservatism*, pp. 89–90.

[64] Smith, *Disraeli*, p. 139.

[65] Ibid., p. 229.

[66] Beales, *From Castlereagh to Gladstone*, p. 208.

Freda Harcourt attaches particular importance to the role of popular unrest in the passing of the Reform Act. She notes that 1866 saw a serious economic recession coinciding with rising food prices. 'For the very poor and the casually employed the crisis was catastrophic.' Ruling elites were acutely aware of 'the threat to the social order, not from the respectable working classes but from the submerged and dangerous masses'.[67] When the Tories were confronted in 1866 by a huge Hyde Park demonstration which the police were unable to stop, the government was 'accused of failing in its primary task of keeping order' and 'could not ignore the popular movement for electoral reform'. Later another great demonstration in Hyde Park (6 May 1867) was followed by the decision to extend the vote to compounders. While it is true, she argues, that the Bill evolved out of a complex of parliamentary considerations, 'this interpretation also certainly underestimates the forces "out of doors" [...] The safest way to diffuse the danger was to hurry on with an acceptable Bill and so legitimize the agitation, stop the demonstrations and avoid the chances of a violent eruption from the mob.'[68]

But were senior Tories really influenced by popular pressure? Historians generally argue that they were not. For Monypenny and Buckle the idea that the pro-reform demonstrations over the summer of 1866 convinced Disraeli 'that the demand for Reform [...] must be treated comprehensively without further delay [...] is an erroneous assumption'. During August 1866 Disraeli 'thought it most prudent to postpone further action' on reform. If he had fears over the popular protests, they were not significant.[69] The six-month delay between the Hyde Park riots of July 1866 and the introduction of the Reform Bill has often been noted by historians, such as Seaman.[70] After all, he points out, the chief reason given by parliamentarians for conceding the vote to the working class was their respectability. 'Popular clamour', says Hawkins, 'merely stimulated Conservative instincts for order.'[71] Derby 'regarded the disorder with patrician calm'.[72] F. B. Smith notes that 'Disraeli remained outwardly unperturbed by the Riots and they did not impel him towards introducing a Reform Bill,'[73] and T. A. Jenkins concurs:

---

[67] F. Harcourt, 'Disraeli's Imperialism, 1866–68: A Question of Timing', *Historical Journal*, Vol. 23 (1980), pp. 89–90.

[68] Ibid., pp. 91–92.

[69] Monypenny and Buckle, *Life of Benjamin Disraeli*, II. p. 187.

[70] Seaman, *Victorian England*, pp. 153–54.

[71] Hawkins, *British Party Politics*, p. 121.

[72] Hawkins, *The Forgotten Prime Minister*, II. p. 314.

[73] Smith, *Making of the Second Reform Bill*, p. 132.

[T]he crushing of some iron railings and the trampling of a few flowerbeds during the demonstration in Hyde Park in July, organised by the Reform League, was hardly symptomatic of a revolutionary atmosphere. Nor can it be said that such activities were decisive in determining the subsequent course taken by Lord Derby's Conservative ministry.[74]

The Cabinet, continues Jenkins, showed little sign of urgency, as late as January 1867 planning to proceed by resolutions and a Royal Commission, with legislation to follow in 1868.[75]

Cowling, whose 1967 study of the Reform Act pioneered the detailed analysis of the motives of those who actually passed the measure, discounted the role of events outside Westminster:

The passage of the Reform Act of 1867 was effected in the context of public agitation: it cannot be explained as a simple consequence. Parliament in the sixties was not *afraid* of public agitation: nor was its action *determined* by it. Its members did not believe that public agitation necessarily represented public opinion [...] It is in Parliament, and in the light of Parliament's view of public feeling, that the centre of explanation will be found.[76]

While Queen Victoria was alarmed, Derby's correspondence with Disraeli 'makes it impossible to see the Queen as a major policy-maker'. The agitation may have concerned the Whig–Liberal leaders – it did not alarm Conservative backbenchers, for whom 'resistance to public agitation was likely both to conform to Conservative instinct and to be politically advantageous for the party'. If there was one consistent theme operating throughout the Bill's passage it was that any concessions must be made in deference to 'respectable opinion' within Parliament, and not in response to the terrors of outside agitation evoked by Gladstone.[77] Disraeli accepted Grosvenor Hodgkinson's amendment after the Reform demonstration in Hyde Park, not because he feared unrest but because he would cut the ground from under the Radicals.[78] Cowling's work shaped much subsequent writing on the Reform Act. Michael Bentley sees the masses 'not as players but as spectators in a match between overheated politicians locked in a scrum over Palmerston's

---

[74] Jenkins, *Parliament, Party and Politics in Victorian Britain* (1996), pp. 96–97.
[75] Jenkins, *Disraeli and Victorian Conservatism*, p. 78.
[76] Cowling, *1867: Disraeli, Gladstone and Revolution*, p. 3. Italics in the original.
[77] Ibid., pp. 20–21, 26–27.
[78] Ibid., pp. 42–43.

mantle', while Feuchtwanger writes that 'Derby and his colleagues [...] knew what really mattered in the end was the parliamentary situation and not an agitation in the country which they never mistook for the early symptoms of a revolution'.[79]

Himmelfarb, in a 1966 article, criticized the idea that the Reform Act owed much to the economic crisis of 1866–67 or the Hyde Park disturbances. 'Unemployment and rising prices may have accelerated the movement in its later stages, but even then the economic motif was not nearly so conspicuous as might be thought even in public meetings, still less in the counsels of party and Parliament.'[80] Similarly, the demonstration at Hyde Park 'was more an assertion of the right of assembly [...] than of the right to vote'. 'The violence of this affair has been as grossly exaggerated', involving 'little more than broken railings and trampled flower beds'.[81] While it 'did result in a quickening of the public temper on the subject of reform', the 'particular measure remained as indeterminate as before'.[82] Most recently, Robert Saunders has argued that it was not popular unrest that motivated the Tories to reform but the commitment of the Liberals to do so – in which case 'the Tories must either follow suit or appear hostile to reform on principle, which was neither accurate nor likely to secure them in office'.[83]

However, a number of historians contest the idea that popular protest played no part in the Bill's passage. While not alarmed by the demonstrations, Disraeli and Derby did consider them expressions of popular opinion and saw the political capital that could be made by taking up the issue. Monypenny and Buckle attribute Disraeli's conversion to reform to Bright's reform campaign: the 'evidence was conclusive' that 'the country had determined to obtain Reform'.[84] Briggs believes Disraeli's change of mind on reform 'came when he appreciated the extent of parliamentary and extra-parliamentary support for a new reform bill [...] The more active public opinion became, the more tempted was Disraeli to resort to a policy of parliamentary opportunism.'[85] F. B. Smith sees the same process at work – only he considers that it was Derby who was responsive to 'the growing impressiveness of the mass meetings', urging upon Disraeli the need 'for some gesture towards Reform'.[86] In contrast

---

[79] Bentley, *Politics without Democracy*, p. 182; Feuchtwanger, *Gladstone*, p. 134.
[80] Himmelfarb, 'The Politics of Democracy: the English Reform Act of 1867', p. 101.
[81] Ibid., p. 104.
[82] Ibid., p. 106.
[83] Saunders, 'The Politics of Reform and the Making of the Second Reform Act', p. 587.
[84] Monypenny and Buckle, *Life of Benjamin Disraeli*, II. p. 221.
[85] Briggs, *Victorian People*, pp. 277–78.
[86] Smith, *Making of the Reform Bill*, p. 134.

to Cowling, Smith follows the more traditional line that Queen Victoria's concerns were also important:

> The Queen had a clearer sense than her Ministers of the strength of popular feeling and the necessity to maintain social harmony. Her agency gave the agitations a much greater influence in the counsels of the Tory Government than they would otherwise have possessed.[87]

Finding the Queen and Derby ranged against him, 'Disraeli could hold out no longer' and accepted Derby's scheme of bringing forward reform resolutions.[88]

A final view contends that while the Bill was not a direct response to unrest, it disturbed backbench MPs into passing the measure, not wanting to risk the consequences of another defeated bill. The agitation, wrote Beeley in 1936, filled 'the House of Commons with a new sense of urgency, and predisposed it to accept the proposals of a minority Government'.[89] F. B. Smith is, again, receptive to the idea that popular protest played a part in shaping the Bill. While 'there is no reason to suppose that the Riots led the Government to introduce its resolutions when it did, the mass agitation, the apparent breakdown of authority and the belief that the lower classes were ready to demand Reform did ultimately persuade many members that Reform was an urgent question, while the need for a settlement gave the Ministry a powerful coercive argument in the debates of 1867'.[90] The willingness of MPs to enfranchise the compounders reflected, he believes, 'their fear of social unrest', and it was the demonstrations that 'finally forced the issue by intimidating enough members into accepting the Bill'.[91]

A response to parliamentary politics

Ever since Cowling's study of the passing of the Reform Bill there has been a tendency to regard the measure as a product of a particular parliamentary situation. Disraeli's prime motives in 1867 were to split the Liberals, defeat Gladstone and hang on to power. To achieve these ends he had to pass a Reform Bill, and given the Conservative's minority position, this necessitated appealing beyond Gladstone to his more Radical backbench supporters. By

---

[87] Ibid., p. 135.
[88] Ibid.
[89] Beeley, *Disraeli*, p. 93.
[90] Smith, *Making of the Second Reform Bill*, pp. 133–34.
[91] Ibid., pp. 4, 235.

thus studying the Conservatives' actions in microscopic detail, says Paul
Adelman,

> a whole political mythology has been virtually destroyed. It is now clear
> that Disraeli's attitude during the Reform crisis was purely opportunist.
> He neither sought to 'educate his party', nor displayed either firmness
> or consistency of purpose in his support for 'democracy'. Indeed, during
> these months Disraeli had only one major aim: to destroy Gladstone's
> leadership over a united Liberal Party, and, by seizing the initiative in
> reform himself and promoting a Reform Bill, to consolidate his own
> leadership over the Conservative Party.[92]

The 'demythologizing' of 1867 had already begun with Blake's 1966 biography.
Blake believes it 'absurd' to claim that Disraeli viewed Reform other than in
the light of party expediency. His 'attitude to parliamentary reform was [...]
purely opportunist'.[93] He opposed the Liberals' 1866 Bill because he hoped
to bring the government down, while in the conduct of his own measure he
was equally inconsistent. Thus, he initially expected household suffrage to
exclude compounders, but later admitted them. The Bill that emerged 'bore
little resemblance' to the one initially introduced. What began as a limited
addition to the Borough franchise, hedged with careful safeguards, ended
as simple household suffrage This transformation 'is explicable only by the
determination of Derby and Disraeli to [...] stay in office and pass a Bill of
some sort'.[94]

The centenary of the 1867 Reform Act saw the publication of two major
studies of its passage. Both agreed that Disraeli's conduct reflected not some
Tory Democracy ideology but the parliamentary situation. Thus F. B. Smith
wrote of 'Disraeli's resolve to carry the Reform Bill, *a* Reform Bill, to
consolidate his leadership and to humiliate Gladstone'.[95] Disraeli had to fight
on two fronts.

> On one side he had to outbid Gladstone and persuade his men of his
> fighting qualities and of the opportunities for parliamentary success
> inherent in the Bill; and on the other, he had to [...] re-assure the House
> that it would make a conservative settlement. He could win as long as
> he could keep these ends confused and the opposing forces divided.

---

[92] Adelman, *Gladstone, Disraeli and Later Victorian Politics* (1970), p. 12.
[93] Blake, *Disraeli*, 396–97; 438.
[94] Ibid., p. 463. Italics in the original.
[95] Smith, *Making of the Second Reform Bill*, p. 229.

The genius of his achievement in 1867 was that he managed to do all these things and [...] give the appearance of logical consistency and high purpose to the ignoble scramble to settle the question.[96]

Lacking a majority, Disraeli could not impose his will on the House and 'could only play on the Liberals' distrust of Gladstone, their dread of further agitation and on their fears of a dissolution'.[97]

Cowling agrees with Smith that the parliamentary situation determined the form the Bill took, but differs in seeing Disraeli as using reform as part of a wider strategy to secure a political advantage over the Liberals in general and 'destroy Gladstone's control of the Liberal party' in particular.[98] He was continuing the policy he had adopted since the early 1850s – namely of seeking allies from a range of potential sources. In 1865 he tried to prize away dissident Whigs; in 1866 it was the Adullamites; in 1867, abandoned by the Adullamites and Cranborne, he turned to the Radicals.

Disraeli's was a policy of consistent opportunism – an attempt to be prepared for any chance that might arise to occupy as much of the central ground as he could, to hold out expectations to such Liberal or Irish groups as might be detached and to smooth down the rough edges of reactionary Toryism.[99]

Far from being a Tory Radical, he was seeking to pursue a central line that would make his government appear 'a credible instrument of sane, sensible and safe government'.[100] From the perspective of the Conservatives it would have been desirable to combine with moderate Whigs and Liberals to form a broad centrist coalition. But for Disraeli this would end his chances of becoming leader and hence he resisted fusion with the Adullamites in 1866. Yet he was also to lose the support of Cranborne and the Tory anti-reformers. Thus, while Disraeli did shatter the political coalition that sustained the Liberals, he failed to construct an alternative Conservative–Liberal alliance and was forced to appeal to Radical support and make concessions greater than otherwise intended.[101]

The notion that the Reform Bill reflected the contingencies of Westminster politics has become commonplace. Thus, in 1967 Paul Smith acknowledged that

---

[96] Ibid., p. 170.
[97] Ibid., p. 230.
[98] Cowling, *1867: Disraeli, Gladstone and Revolution*, p. 303.
[99] Ibid., pp. 302–3.
[100] Ibid., p. 307.
[101] Ibid., p. 310.

neither Derby nor Disraeli 'had bargained for a measure as large as that which they actually passed', arguing that 'it was a product neither of their principles nor of their stratagems, but of their necessities'.[102] Disraeli was determined to 'bring off a great coup' and 'preferred almost any concession to defeat'. Yet Smith also admitted that wider considerations, including working-class protest, actuated the Conservative leadership: 'Derby and Disraeli and their followers [...] did what they had to do, to satisfy the popular agitation, reconcile the upper strata of the working classes to the established political system, and "dish the Whigs."'[103] While not aiming at 'Tory Democracy', Disraeli was, said Smith, ready to go far to align his party with the popular and progressive trend. However, revisiting the topic 30 years later Smith couched his explanation far more in terms of the contingencies of the parliamentary moment. Once the Bill was in the Commons, he writes, 'passing it became a matter of disrupting Gladstone's hold on the Liberal majority'.[104] 'It needs', says Smith, 'no more than the inspiration of party conflict and the ambition at all costs to succeed and stay in office to explain Disraeli's conduct of the 1867 reform bill.'[105] The Reform Act was 'a brilliant opposition manoeuvre, executed in office'.[106]

Many historians agree. Thus R. W. Davis attributed the fact that the Bill became ever more radical to Disraeli's willingness to 'take the Bill as far as the House chose to take it'.[107] He 'had no convictions about democracy [...] He pursued parliamentary reform solely for its political advantage to himself and his party.'[108] For T. A. Jenkins the Reform Act 'can properly be understood only as an improvised measure, the details of which were largely dependent on the tactical situation facing Disraeli in the House of Commons'.[109] 'Disraeli's governing tactic', he adds, 'was to defeat any amendment from Gladstone, even if it meant accepting a more extreme one from another source.'[110] Bentley, too, attaches most importance to the need of the Conservatives to do down Gladstone. The Conservatives 'anxieties arose neither from the mob nor General Peel: the worry was Gladstone and the likelihood of his return for another long spell of government by sabotage and hypocrisy'.[111] Recognizing this, Disraeli set about 'throttling every amendment to which [Gladstone] lent

---

[102] Smith, *Disraelian Conservatism*, p. 93.

[103] Ibid., p. 97.

[104] Smith, *Disraeli*, p. 142.

[105] Ibid., p. 143.

[106] Ibid., p. 212.

[107] Davis, *Disraeli*, p. 154.

[108] Ibid., p. 171.

[109] Jenkins, *Disraeli and Victorian Conservatism*, p. 75.

[110] Ibid., p. 271. Cf. Hurd and Young, *Disraeli*, p. 165.

[111] Ibid., p. 192.

prominent support'. While haste marked the later stages of the Bill's passage, this reflected not Conservative alarm at the continuing protest movement but Disraeli's recognition that if he were to 'extract permanent advantage from Gladstone's current failure as a politician, he had to charge on to the crucial party question of redistribution. For he who controlled the reallocation of seats and the mapping of constituency boundaries could redesign nothing less than the electoral geography of Britain.'[112] Coleman, asking how the Tory party came to pass such a radical Bill, answers, 'One factor was the firm determination of Derby, Disraeli and most of their colleagues to retain office for as long as possible and to use the opportunity it offered of reversing Tory fortunes.' For Disraeli and the Tory backbenchers 'undermining Gladstone's authority and influence was the main sport'.[113] What they dreaded was a Liberal government with Gladstone at the helm, for a 'new Liberal bill would hardly be tender to Tory interests'.[114]

This interpretation of Disraeli's conduct was far from new. It was the initial gloss on events provided by his Liberal opponents, who claimed that credit for the Reform Act actually lay with the Liberals. Homersham Cox, a Liberal writing in 1868, thought the Bill chiefly reflected the influence of Gladstone. Of the 20 leading clauses of the Bill, 16 were the same as the Liberal Bill of 1866, and of Gladstone's 10 main objections to the original Bill, 9 were incorporated. 'The allegation that the Reform Act of 1867 is mainly or substantially the work of the Conservative Government is one of the most impudent falsifications of history that was ever attempted.'[115] Another Liberal, T. Hayes, saw only cynical ambition in Disraeli's conduct, the passing of the Bill being 'accomplished by his complete reversal of every Tory maxim, the tricking of his opponents, and the betrayal of his own party'.[116]

The bill was a conservative bill

Two final arguments question the assumption that Disraeli passed a radical bill. First, it is contended that the Bill was seen as basically conservative by most Tories. Household suffrage was designed not to initiate democracy but avoid it, for it meant not one man, one vote, but the vote for the head of a propertied household. The bulk of the urban working class would not get the vote, and neither would the working class in the counties. It was thus

---

[112] Bentley, *Politics without Democracy*, p. 193.
[113] Coleman, *Conservatism and the Conservative Party*, p. 132.
[114] Ibid.
[115] Quoted in Himmelfarb, 'The Politics of Democracy', p. 108.
[116] Hayes, *Lord Beaconsfield*, p. 20.

a moderate measure designed to remove pressure for more thorough reform. There is little doubt that this was the Conservatives' initial intention. As F. B. Smith remarks, what eventually emboldened Derby and Disraeli to press for household suffrage was a meeting of Tory MPs in February 1867, at which it was agreed that household suffrage was the surest way to hold the line against the 'democracy'.[117] Shannon agrees that household suffrage was attractive to Tory backbenchers, especially as it offered a sense of finality in matters of franchise reform.[118] Further diluting the apparent radicalism of this proposal was the intention to grant around 300,000 additional votes to members of the propertied classes through various forms of plural voting. By this means, says Davis, household suffrage would be so hedged around with restrictions as to 'render its democratic implications nugatory'.[119] Parry sees the Reform Bill as motivated by a desire to 'defuse agitation for Reform permanently by *ostensibly* adopting the principle for which urban radicals had long lobbied, male household suffrage'.[120] Cowling, too, believes that 'rated residential suffrage with safeguards was regarded as a socially conservative measure' that had the advantage of 'enabling the party to take a step which would not be a capitulation to Gladstone'.[121] And of course, as originally proposed, it would not be a household suffrage – for the many occupiers who had not resided at the same address for two years or who did not personally pay rates would be excluded. With these restrictions a household rating suffrage would settle the borough franchise 'for a generation' in a way that would be 'very conservative'.[122]

Yet it was just this line the government was unable to sustain for, as Parry reflects, 'Disraeli had hoped to preserve propertied rule in the counties by giving the appearance (but not the reality) of household suffrage in the boroughs. The Liberals had no choice but to force him to concede the reality instead.'[123] Thus the fancy franchises were rejected, the residency requirement reduced to one year, and the abolition of compounding meant the enfranchisement of double the number originally intended. It might thus be concluded that the Bill as passed was a thoroughgoing piece of reform. However, a number of historians contest this. Adelman points out that, while the Act added

---

[117] Smith, *Making of the Second Reform Bill*, p. 160
[118] Shannon, *Gladstone: Heroic Minister*, p. 33.
[119] Davis, *Disraeli*, p. 150.
[120] Parry, *Rise and Fall of Liberal Government in Victorian Britain*, p. 215. Italics in the original.
[121] Cowling, *1867: Disraeli, Gladstone and Revolution*, p. 162.
[122] Ibid., p. 167.
[123] Parry, *Rise and Fall of Liberal Government in Victorian Britain*, p. 280.

134 percent to the urban franchise, the county electorate increased by just 40 percent. With boundary changes moving the suburbs into the boroughs, in the counties 'the old order continued almost undisturbed, and they remained the chief stronghold of the Conservative Party'.[124] The conservative nature of the Bill was even more evident in the matter of redistribution. Only 45 seats were redistributed, and of these, 25 went to the counties. Manchester, Liverpool, Leeds and Birmingham gained only one seat each. 'This lack of a fundamental redistribution of seats meant that [...] Liberal votes piled up and wasted in the great centres of population.' The Reform Act, Adelman concludes, 'did not mark a fundamental break in English political life'.[125] Theodore Hoppen believes that Disraeli was fatalistic about the details of the Bill because his objectives were limited and realistic. He and Derby's object was to maintain sufficient non-democratic features in the new situation as to give the Tories a chance. This they did by heaping up working-class votes in the boroughs (which Disraeli had written off as potential sources of Tory support), by keeping many smaller boroughs and by ensuring that still only about one in three men above 21 had the vote in England and Wales. 'For Derby and Disraeli it was such things, not visions of urban Toryism, which gave immediate and partisan justification to what they had done.'[126] Indeed, historians point out that the Conservatives were able to offset concessions on the franchise by their astute handling of redistribution. As Parry describes, the Boundary Commission was instructed to transfer urban areas from counties to boroughs to prevent urban Liberals weakening the Tory position in countryside, this measure alone gaining the Conservatives 25 seats. 'Overall, the structure of parliament was hardly different in 1868 from 1865.'[127]

The Reform Bill was the work of Derby

Lastly, for some historians, the Reform Act was primarily the work not of Disraeli but of Derby. It was Derby who pressed upon a reluctant Disraeli the advantages of a Tory reform measure and who first raised the idea of household suffrage. As Sir William Fraser reflected in the 1890s, 'Upon the late Lord Derby's shoulders must rest most of the responsibility. Without him Disraeli was utterly powerless: we are indebted for the Reform Bill of 1867, to Lord Derby.'[128] Surprisingly, given their overall objective of vindicating Disraeli's

---

[124] Adelman, *Gladstone, Disraeli and Later Victorian Politics*, p. 13.
[125] Ibid., p. 14.
[126] Hoppen, *Mid-Victorian Generation*, p. 253.
[127] Parry, *Rise and Fall of Liberal Government in Victorian Britain*, p. 217.
[128] Fraser, *Disraeli and His Day*, p. 363.

status as an imaginative and commanding statesman, Monypenny and Buckle admit that it was Derby who pushed for a 'moderate and Conservative' reform measure in the autumn of 1866, and although he gradually persuaded Disraeli of the merits of the case, Disraeli was still wary that the Conservatives faced defeat on the issue and urged that a Royal Commission be established to bury the whole matter.[129] It is, they write, 'quite clear that, throughout the autumn and early winter, Disraeli, far from being stimulated into drastic action by the Reform demonstrations throughout the country, was anxious to postpone legislation as long as possible to secure a moderate measure'.[130] Similarly, it was Derby who first floated the radical notion of 'household suffrage' as a basis for reform – something Disraeli had always opposed.[131] 'Disraeli was reluctant to admit the weight of the accumulating evidence. His attitude in the autumn of 1866 makes indeed a serious deduction from his reputation for foresight.' Disraeli was, they conclude, 'an opportunist on Reform'.[132] Saunders has recently stated categorically that a 'rated household suffrage was not Disraeli's idea'.[133] Blake agrees that the Reform Act 'was largely Derby's responsibility', and John Vincent makes the point rather more acerbically:

> Disraeli's part in this [electoral reform] was limited. If he had sublime insights, he kept them to himself. He made three proposals about reform. The first was to settle the matter without delay; the second was to do nothing; the third was to play for time by setting up a commission. All were brushed aside. Disraeli was left to execute other men's plans.[134]

Unsurprisingly, Derby's biographers champion his role in the 1867 Reform Act. Wilbur Jones, in his *Lord Derby and Victorian Conservatism*, points out that it was Derby who pressed the point that the Tory party would have to deal with reform, finding Disraeli at first 'opposed to bringing up the subject', just as it was Derby who became 'convinced that household suffrage, balanced by plurality of voting was the only way out of their dilemma'.[135] Hawkins, Derby's most recent biographer, presents the case for Derby in powerful terms, situating the Reform Act within the wider context of Derby's programme to locate the Tory party within the moderate centre ground of British politics.

---

[129] Monypenny and Buckle, *Life of Benjamin Disraeli*, II. p. 188.
[130] Ibid., p. 196.
[131] Ibid., p. 219.
[132] Ibid., pp. 295, 197.
[133] Saunders, 'The Politics of Reform and the Making of the Second Reform Act', p. 587.
[134] Vincent, *Disraeli*, p. 9.
[135] W. D. Jones, *Lord Derby and Victorian Conservatism* (1956), p. 301.

Disraeli was to claim that in 1867 he 'educated' the Conservative party. In truth, this was Derby's achievement. It was Derby who transformed the protectionist rump of the 1840s into a moderate party, prepared to support far-reaching reform as a lasting settlement. In 1866, as in 1858, it was Derby who forced Conservative attention on parliamentary reform [...] Derby believed there existed a genuine demand for reform [...] If the destructive slide to manhood suffrage and radical fomenting of extreme aspirations was to be prevented, a clear defensible line demarcating a responsible electorate had to be drawn. By December 1866 Derby believed that [...] household suffrage provided such a principle. Disraeli's conversion followed.[136]

However, the argument for Derby's primacy has not gone unchallenged. While Monypenny and Buckle acknowledge Disraeli's uncertain role during the origination of the Bill, once having accepted the need for reform he carried the measure in the Commons and by determining which amendments to accept 'was almost solely responsible' for the Bill's final shape.[137] 'The carrying of the Reform Bill through Committee in the House of Commons was the work of Disraeli, and Disraeli alone.'[138] Davis, too, reflects that, once having accepted the case for household suffrage, Disraeli followed it 'with an agility, boldness, and success which some in the history of parliamentary management may have equalled, but few have surpassed'.[139] Even Hawkins admits that once the Bill entered the Commons 'it became Disraeli's measure'.[140] With Derby ill and distanced from events in the House of Lords, it was Disraeli's audacity and tactical virtuosity that was the leading fact. 'By May 1867 Disraeli had clearly become the directing mind of the ministry. With surgical precision he dissected the Liberal opposition.'[141] Jones similarly admits that 'Derby had little control over the bill in the Commons during April and May [...] Probably he would have preferred to exclude the compound householders, and to keep the two years' residency qualification.'[142] Raymond even suggests that Disraeli's initial coolness on reform was a ruse: he recognized that a moderate measure would not suffice,

---

[136] Hawkins, *British Party Politics*, p. 129.
[137] Monypenny and Buckle, *Life of Benjamin Disraeli*, II. p. 296.
[138] Ibid., p. 282.
[139] Davis, *Disraeli*, p. 149.
[140] Hawkins, *The Forgotten Prime Minister*, II. p. 315; Hawkins, *British Party Politics*, p. 129.
[141] Ibid., p. 126.
[142] Jones, *Lord Derby and Victorian Conservatism*, p. 315.

yet realized that distrust of him within the Tory party meant he could not advance a radical measure and 'therefore allowed the idea of Reform to simmer in Derby's mind, well knowing that it would presently come to a boil in the heat of outside agitation'.[143] But of course, such an interpretation involves reading Disraeli's motives back from the events of 1867, relying more upon an assumption of consistency on Disraeli's part than any actual evidence.

Conclusion

Amid the myriad of interpretations that have clustered around the 1867 Reform Act, it is possible to delineate a 'best fit' with regard to the current thinking upon the subject. Nearly all historians agree that the idea that the Conservatives should proceed with a Reform Bill chiefly lay with Derby. Disraeli was not averse to a Reform Bill, and he advocated one in June 1866, but he was insufficiently confident about the parliamentary arithmetic to press the case and inclined toward inactivity. Impressed by the strength of public opinion, Derby advocated household suffrage in the boroughs – a proposal which was sufficiently radical to snuff out Liberal and popular pressure but which would, when combined with checks and balances like plural voting and the exclusion of compounders, rule out a mass working-class franchise. At this point, as even Derby's biographer Hawkins admits, Disraeli took centre stage since it was his responsibility to direct the Bill through parliament. What determined Disraeli's conduct was his minority position: to pass the Bill he had to take Liberal amendments which pushed him in an ever more radical direction. He was willing to accept this because he had no objection to widening the franchise. It is here, if at all, that Tory Democracy entered the fray: Disraeli did not fear the working-class vote because he thought working men were like any other – products of British society and not a revolutionary menace to the status quo. But he did not assume, as Blake emphasizes, that they would vote Tory. Rather, they would probably vote Liberal, and Disraeli countered this by limiting redistribution and protecting county boundaries, so whatever extra votes the Liberals received would not translate into many extra seats. Disraeli was thereby free to use the parliamentary stage to advance *his* agenda – to demonstrate that he could lead the Tories and outmanoeuvre Gladstone. Disraeli had nothing to lose provided he did not lose – and by a series of astute tactical retreats this is exactly what he avoided. The Reform Act, therefore, had no one author and

---

[143] Raymond, *Disraeli*, p. 243.

no one explanation. Public opinion, Derby's bold response, the Tory wish to see reform dealt with, Liberal pressure in the Commons, and Disraeli's willingness to do whatever was required to keep himself in the driving seat all combined to make the 1867 Reform Act. It was only subsequently that Disraeli claimed an ideological ownership over its terms that was never more than what Blake calls 'retrospective boasting'.[144]

---

[144] Blake, *Disraeli*, p. 465.

Chapter 4

GLADSTONE IN AND OUT OF POWER 1868–1874

Outline of Events

No sooner had Benjamin Disraeli savoured victory over William Gladstone with the passage of the 1867 Reform Act than he was confronted by a resurgent Gladstone formulating plans to heal the wounds of Ireland by disestablishing the Irish Church. Unable to resist a Liberal party reunited behind its leader, Disraeli called a general election – an election which saw Gladstone crush Disraeli's Conservatives and win a hundred-seat majority. The moment was assuredly propitious for the simultaneous apotheosis of those two great forces of the mid-Victorian age: liberal reformism and Gladstone's ethical vocation in the united form of 'Gladstonian Liberalism'. Yet there in fact was the rub. In 1868 these two great rivers of energy converged, but they did not combine and within a few short years their courses were diverging again. At first Gladstone's government did great liberal work – reforming the civil service, the judiciary, the education system, Irish Church and Land, the armed services and local government. Yet each of these reforms, however meritorious, inflicted a series of cuts upon the body of the Liberal Party – cuts which by 1872 had become seriously debilitating. For the Liberal Party was a coalition of interest groups which, if they agreed on some matters, disagreed on still more. The legislation that emerged from this creative tension increasingly failed to satisfy the full range of Liberal interests. It also failed to satisfy Gladstone, who became more and more detached from the policies being implemented in his name. As the government's tribulations mounted, Disraeli, who had responded to defeat by writing a novel, stirred himself during 1872 to deliver a series of speeches lambasting the Liberals for their dysfunctional restlessness and weakness in international affairs, and staking out a new Tory rhetoric of social reform and imperial prestige. With pressure upon the government intensifying and Liberal divisions widening, the prime minister called a snap election in January 1874 on a platform of abolishing income tax. But far from uniting his party, he only heightened its disarray and played into the hands of Disraeli, who assumed the agreeable Palmerstonian pose of promising to restore Britain's reputation as a major power while bringing stability to a nation harassed by Liberal activism. The result was the first Conservative majority since 1841 and Gladstone's withdrawal from the Liberal leadership – for now.

4.1   How Successful Was Gladstone's First Administration?

Gladstone's first government is widely seen as undertaking the work of adapting Britain's institutions to the needs of a modern urban society. Opportunities for the advancement of talent were widened, the basis for a national education system laid, military organization overhauled, government efficiency promoted and the problems of Ireland confronted. Directing this wind of change was Gladstone, defining by his actions what has become known as Gladstonian Liberalism. Thus we find R. C. K. Ensor describing Gladstone's 1868 administration as 'under many aspects the greatest during the long reign of Queen Victoria'.[1] The government's aim was 'to abolish class privileges and unbar to all the doors of political, economic, and cultural opportunity'.[2] F. W. Hirst called it 'the greatest Peace and Reform Government of modern times', while Erich Eyck believed that

> Gladstone's first ministry was epoch-making, as the Ministry of the great administrative reforms. More than any other Ministry of the nineteenth century it may claim the credit for sweeping aside the survivals of the past [...] and making way for a modern conception of the State and its functions.[3]

This view of the reforming work of Gladstone's ministry has persisted. Colin Matthew labels the disestablishment of the Irish Church, the Irish Land Act and the Education Act as 'three of the triumphs of the century', while Hawkins writes that the 'for the first three years of its existence Gladstone's government proved itself, arguably, the greatest reforming ministry of the century'.[4] Yet historians have more recently subjected the claims made on Gladstone's

---

[1] R. C. K. Ensor, *England: 1870–1914* (1936), p. 26.
[2] Ibid., pp. 2–3.
[3] Hirst, *Gladstone as Economist*, p. 255; Eyck, *Gladstone*, pp. 201, 211.
[4] Matthew, *Gladstone*, pp. 207–8; Hawkins, *British Party Politics*, p. 141.

behalf to more searching analysis. The more closely the government's record is examined, the more questionable become the sweeping claims made on its behalf.

Did Gladstone's ministry improve the efficiency of government?

Peter Stansky believes that the aim of Gladstone's ministry was 'to eliminate those various obstacles that prevented individuals from functioning to the best of their ability'. While the traditional class structure was not seriously modified, 'there were fewer restrictions on opportunities, and more of the talented who had not begun at the top were enabled to improve themselves and their country'.[5] Theodore Hoppen agrees that the objective of Gladstone's government was 'to create what mainstream Liberalism regarded as a legitimate order based upon the maximisation of personal opportunities [...] the ideological thrust of Gladstone's thinking at this time was firmly concentrated upon placing all citizens under such conditions as would allow them to make the most of their talents and stations in life.'[6]

Indicative of this approach was reform of the civil service, appointment to which became subject to competitive exams. As a result, so Hirst argued, the 'long reign of patronage and jobbery was ended': candidates could be selected on the basis of ability, while competitive tests motivated universities to improve their teaching to better prepare their students.[7] These reforms, writes John Morley, 'placed the whole educated intellect of the country at the service and disposal of the state [...] stimulated the acquisition of knowledge, and [...] rescued some of the most important duties in the life of the nation from the narrow class to whom they had hitherto been confided'.[8] Hoppen, however, argues that the change in public life has been exaggerated. Not all government was involved: Lord Clarendon successfully resisted the application of competitive exams to the Foreign Office. More important, the introduction of an academically demanding exam meant that the stranglehold on appointments held by the Oxford- and Cambridge-educated elite continued. For all the 'energetic surface disturbance' there remained, below, 'submarine stability'.[9]

---

[5] Stansky, *Gladstone*, p. 117.
[6] Hoppen, *Mid-Victorian Generation*, p. 593.
[7] Hirst, *Gladstone as Economist*, p. 262.
[8] Morley, *Life of Gladstone*, II. p. 315.
[9] Hoppen, *Mid-Victorian Generation*, p. 601.

Also subject to modernizing reform was the army. Ever since the incompetency revealed by the Crimean War there had been calls to clear the way for promotion by merit not wealth or birth, and reform of training and the provision of equipment. Recent victories by the Prussian army over Austria and France reinforced the need for action. Edward Cardwell's army reforms were praised by Morley, who believed that the 'most marked administrative performance of Mr. Gladstone's great government was the reform and reorganization of the army'.[10] Sydney Buxton remarked in 1888 that Cardwell's reforms 'have done much to strengthen the power of England', while Ensor calls Cardwell 'the greatest British army reformer during the nineteenth century'.[11]

> Without them not only would prompt and crucial successes, such as the Egyptian campaign of 1882, have been unobtainable, but the power-prestige, which Lord Salisbury had behind him in his diplomacy, would scarcely have existed in the same way. Not their least exceptional feature was their economy. Cardwell left the estimates lower than he found them.[12]

But again Hoppen is sceptical, considering Cardwell's reforms to be 'at best partial, at worst ineffective [...] No planning department was established and no chief of staff appointed to set out the purpose and strategy of the army as a whole.'[13] Thomas Gallagher points out that there was widespread criticism from among Liberals and also some Conservatives (including the press) at Cardwell's failure to carry out a more thorough reorganization of the army.[14] The abolition of the purchase of commissions had, as Hoppen remarks, no effect on the social composition of the officer corps since 'pay was not increased and expenses were not reduced', so only the well-to-do could afford to become officers, and promotion was based on seniority, not merit.[15] 'The abolition of purchase', summarizes Gallagher, 'involved the spending of very large sums of money, which of course many Radicals opposed in principle. Cardwell's bill made no noticeable change in the army's organization [...] The abolition of purchase brought no promise of an increase in the number of middle-class officers. The whole tone and spirit of the bill [...] sounded unmistakably conservative on the class issue.'[16]

---

[10] Morley, *Life of Gladstone*, II. p. 359.

[11] Buxton, *Finance and Politics*, II. p. 68; Ensor, *England: 1870–1914*, p. 9.

[12] Ibid., pp. 15–16.

[13] Hoppen, *Mid-Victorian Generation*, p. 113.

[14] T. F. Gallagher, '"Cardwellian Mysteries": The Fate of the British Army Regulation Bill, 1871', *Historical Journal*, Vol. 18 (1975), p. 342.

[15] Hoppen, *Mid-Victorian Generation*, p. 604.

[16] Gallagher, 'Cardwellian Mysteries', pp. 345–46.

Further undermining the effectiveness of the reforms was the desire to save money. The introduction of short-service periods was undertaken to save money on pensions, while joint-service manoeuvres were discontinued after 1873 for reasons of cost.[17] Eventually even Cardwell rebelled against demands for further reductions in military spending, and his threat to resign caused Gladstone to call the snap election in January 1874 that led to his downfall.

Financial policy

According to Matthew, financial policy was central to the effectiveness of the administration as Gladstone hoped to put the finishing touches to the minimalist low-tax state he had been perfecting since the 1850s. In some way things ran to plan as, writes Morley, 'sound and substantial results were achieved, testifying to a thrifty and skilful management'.[18]

> In spite of the increased cost of education, of army purchase, of the rise of prices, and all the other causes that swell estimates, the country was still spending no more in 1873 than when Mr. Gladstone took office in 1868. To this story we have to add that nearly thirty millions of debt were paid off in the five years. Well might men point to such a record, as the best proof that the promises of economy made at the hustings had been seriously kept.[19]

But, as Matthew emphasizes, spending was not reduced and given Gladstone's desire to carry through the kind of retrenchment that had been blocked by Lord Palmerston, this was a major disappointment. 'Now Prime Minister […] he should have been in a good position to achieve his ends.'[20] However the record was uneven. Defence spending fell dramatically in 1869 and 1870, but army expansion after the Franco-Prussian War, and the abolition of purchase meant that spending rose again and that from the military departments came steady pressure for increased spending. Gladstone became ever more dissatisfied with his chancellor, Robert Lowe, finding him an 'ineffective ally in his battles with the spending departments'. Discontent with Lowe crystallized over his failed budget of 1871 when, exaggerating

---

[17] Hoppen, *Mid-Victorian Generation*, pp. 113–14.
[18] Morley, *Life of Gladstone*, II. p. 371.
[19] Ibid., p. 375.
[20] Matthew, *Gladstone*, p. 220.

the risk of a budget deficit in the wake of the Franco-Prussian War, he proposed a new tax on matches. Gladstone, admits Matthew, did not object to the match tax 'nor does he seem to have seen soon enough the political dangers involved'.[21] But the tax, relates Morley, 'was greeted with violent disfavour. It was denounced as reactionary, as violating the first principles of fiscal administration, and as the very worst tax that had been proposed in recent memory.'[22] Lowe was forced to abandon the tax and recast his entire budget.

> Competence in fiscal management was the long, strong suit which the Liberals had played throughout the 1860s [...] It was therefore a major blow to the reputation and self-respect of the government when, in 1871, Lowe's budget had to be withdrawn.[23]

In 1873 Gladstone assumed the chancellorship himself, aiming to use financial policy to recover the government's position by abolishing income tax. According to Matthew, Gladstone took up this issue because he feared the extended electorate yielded by the 1867 Reform Act would vote to drive up government spending unless checked by the difficulty of raising revenue. 'Abolition of the tax in the new circumstances thus took on a new urgency for Gladstone as a means of maintaining the minimalist state.' However abolishing income tax meant cutting the military budget by a further £600,000, and when George Goschen and Cardwell declared they could not do this, Gladstone called an election in January 1874. 'The dissolution was therefore essentially a dissolution against the defence departments. Even combining the offices of First Lord and Chancellor of the Exchequer had not allowed Gladstone to prevail against them.'[24] Angus Hawkins's interpretation of Gladstone's motives in turning to income tax abolition in 1873 is more cynical:

> In 1869, religion strained Liberal party connection; in 1870, Irish land reform and elementary education; in 1871, Lowe's finance; in 1872, the *Alabama* question, local taxation, and the ballot; and again religion in 1873. By 1874 financial orthodoxy, the Peelite trump of the 1860s, was the only card Gladstone had left to play.[25]

---

[21] Ibid., p. 219.
[22] Morley, *Life of Gladstone*, II. p. 373.
[23] Matthew, *Gladstone*, p. 219.
[24] Ibid., pp. 224, 227.
[25] Hawkins, *British Party Politics*, p. 171.

Even so, Hawkins believes the decision to play the finance card was ill-judged:

> Ignoring accusations of reckless cuts in defence spending, the premier during 1873 doggedly persisted in a policy of strict economy and retrenchment in government expenditure. Complaints about niggardly cheese-paring increased.[26]

The electorate displayed little appetite for further defence cuts to fund income tax abolition, and the election was lost. Ironically finance, which had appeared to be Gladstone's strongest asset, ended up being a source of weakness.

Education reform

Probably the most important, and certainly the most controversial, reform undertaken by Gladstone's government was the establishment in 1870 of a national system to supply basic schooling to all children. Although William Forster's Bill only fleshed out the existing provision of schooling by the (mainly Church of England) voluntary schools, he provoked considerable criticism, especially from Nonconformists who thought the proposals too accommodating to the established Church. While the measure passed, it was significantly changed through amendments like the Cowper–Temple clause establishing Bible-based religious instruction. Many historians consider the Education Act the government's most impressive achievement. It established the principle of access to education for all children, and while this education was not free or compulsory, school boards could pay the fees of some poor children and gradually school attendance became a legal necessity. The Conservative historian (and educationalist) John Marriott enumerated the Act's beneficial consequences:

> The Act of 1870 was one of the most splendid legislative achievements of the century [...] [Forster] had the supreme satisfaction of knowing that he had laid broad and deep the foundations of a truly national system of elementary education. The citizen rulers of the greatest empire the world has seen were at last to be taught their letters.[27]

---

[26] Ibid., p. 161.
[27] Marriott, *England since Waterloo*, pp. 402–3.

Edgar Feuchtwanger calls the Act 'the single most important achievement of Gladstone's first ministry'. Although Gladstone was not its initiator, the Act 'bore the stamp of much that he believed in: his concern for the work of the Church in education, his preference for voluntary over state action and his distrust of compulsion'.[28] Jonathan Parry concurs that controversy over the Act 'should not detract from the massive significance of the act, nor disguise the satisfaction in the party at its passage'.[29]

But, of course, this is precisely what controversy over the Act *has* done, and most historians dwell chiefly upon its negative political repercussions. For Morley, himself an 1870s Radical, the Bill was half-baked: instead of grasping the nettle and creating an education system 'worthy of the high name of national', it sought to bolt additional schools onto a fundamentally Anglican system, thereby placing religious disputes at the centre of education.[30] Historians emphasize the damage arising from the offence caused to Nonconformists, a key sector of Liberal support. They were antagonized by the increased grants to Church of England schools, and objected to the idea that a school board might (under Clause 25) contribute toward the fees of a poor child attending an Anglican school. Parry elucidates the political context of the Act. In the wake of Irish Church disestablishment, the body of the Liberal party expected the government to turn its attention to English education and attack denominational ascendancy in a similarly thoroughgoing way.

> Liberals did not anticipate that Gladstone's clericalism and Forster's Establishmentarianism would militate against the pursuit of such a policy. In consequence, the nonconformist optimism and enthusiasm of 1868–69 was, before the end of 1870, to be transformed into resentment, and then into mobilisation for fundamental educational and ecclesiastical reform.[31]

Hawkins observes how the education debates exposed Liberal divisions, causing the reform impetus to falter.[32] With backbench support doubtful, ministers, writes Richard Shannon, got their Bill through 'by grace of the Conservative Opposition. Unquestionably this compromised their prestige.'[33]

---

[28] Feuchtwanger, *Gladstone*, p. 158.
[29] Parry, *Rise and Fall of Liberal Government*, p. 237.
[30] Morley, *Life of Gladstone*, II. p. 304.
[31] Parry, *Democracy and Religion*, p. 289.
[32] Hawkins, *British Party Politics*, pp. 155–56.
[33] Shannon, *Gladstone: Heroic Minister*, p. 82.

'The passing of the Act', continues Morley, 'did not heal the wound.' The Nonconformist revolt was organized through Joseph Chamberlain's National Education League, which targeted the issue of Clause 25 – and indeed, says Morley, the 'twenty-fifth section was a real error, and it made no bad flag for an assault upon a scheme of error'.[34] When the election came, the party remained disunited, and of 425 Liberal candidates in England, Scotland and Wales, 300 were pledged to repeal Clause 25.[35] According to Morley, these controversies expressed a fundamental cleavage in an entire way of life:

> At bottom the battle of the schools was not educational, it was social [...] quarrels about education and catechism and conscience masked the standing jealousy between church and chapel [...] From the point of view of party strategy, the policy of this great statute was fatal. The Church of England was quickened into active antagonism by Irish disestablishment, by the extinction of sectarian tests at Oxford and Cambridge, and by the treatment of endowed schools. This might have been balanced by the zeal of nonconformists. Instead of zeal, the Education Act produced refrigeration and estrangement.[36]

Ensor believes Radical and Nonconformist disappointment made 1870 a 'watershed in the administration's fortunes. Before that date it had been popular as well as strenuous, backed by a majority in the country no less than in the house. But from about then a change set in. The majority at Westminster remained [...] but that in the constituencies continuously trickled away'.[37] Yet for Parry it was not the loss of Nonconformist support that was important, but of moderate Anglican opinion, alienated by the apparent threat posed by Liberal policies to the established position of the Church. The Liberal defeat of 1874, he writes 'can be blamed mostly on the defection or abstention of substantial numbers of influential property-owners because of the threat to the church'.[38]

Much of the responsibility for this disputatious atmosphere surrounding the Act has been attributed to Gladstone, who, writes Morley, felt no zeal on the matter of public education, and as a result 'rather acquiesced than led'. 'What Mr. Gladstone cared for was the integrity of religious instruction', by which he meant children receiving religious instruction from Anglican clergymen.[39] If

---

[34] Morley, *Life of Gladstone*, II. pp. 308–9.
[35] Ibid., p. 311.
[36] Ibid., p. 307.
[37] Ensor, England 1870–1914, p. 19.
[38] Parry, *Democracy and Religion*, p. 263.
[39] Morley, *Life of Gladstone*, II. pp. 298–99.

this was impossible – which it was, given the prevalence of Nonconformism – then he wanted schools to teach only secular subjects. But this, too, was a non-starter, given that most MPs wanted to educate the poor precisely to inculcate the Christian message among them. In response Gladstone lost interest in the Bill, and his reluctant acceptance of the Cowper–Temple amendment allowing the board schools to teach Bible-based religion was, argues Matthew, 'a major personal blow [...] it was a personal concession that rankled more than any of the many concessions Gladstone made to hold his ministry together'.[40] The one element of the Bill reflecting Gladstone's imprint, the doubling of government grants to Church schools, only fuelled, says Morley, Nonconformist opposition.[41] Thus Hoppen lays responsibility for the problems of the 1870 Education Act squarely at Gladstone's door. By blocking Forster's initial proposal that only non-denominational religious instruction be allowed in board schools he opened the way for the Cowper–Temple clause, the terms of which were loosely drawn and which, by apparently allowing board schools to promote creeds associated with the Anglican worship, stirred the discontent among Nonconformists.[42] The fundamental division of opinion between Gladstone and the Nonconformists, adds Parry, meant that the government was unable to construct compromise solutions to educational dilemmas, allowing extremist movements like the National Education League to exploit the situation with proposals that alienated mainstream voters.[43]

Foreign and colonial policy

Having consistently objected to Palmerston's meddling in European affairs, Gladstone looked forward to a period of calm in foreign policy, permitting him to focus on reducing military spending. In colonial policy, too, Gladstone wished to save money by making the settler colonies responsible for their own defence. There was, says Matthew, none of the interest he had shown in colonial development in the 1840s. 'Undoubtedly this was a mistake from the point of view of domestic politics: failure to present the positive side of the emotional "kin beyond the sea" view of colonial relationships [...] made it all the easier for the opposition to link patriotism with Conservatism and claim', as Disraeli did at the Crystal Palace, that the Liberals were bent on destroying the Empire.[44]

---

[40] Matthew, *Gladstone*, p. 205.
[41] Morley, *Life of Gladstone*, II. p. 304.
[42] Hoppen, *Mid-Victorian Generation*, p. 599.
[43] Parry, *Democracy and Religion*, p. 332.
[44] Matthew, *Gladstone*, pp. 191–92.

Unfortunately for Gladstone, two issues rendered foreign policy another controversial area. The first was the Franco-Prussian war of 1870 and the use Russia made of this to renounce the Black Sea clauses of the Crimean settlement.[45] Gladstone kept Britain neutral in this conflict and arranged for a diplomatic validation of Russia's actions. This stance has been broadly endorsed by historians such as Feuchtwanger, who believes Gladstone's approach to these events was well judged. The problem was that the 'public felt that Britain had stood by helpless while great decisions were being made and the feeling was widespread that Gladstone was unable to handle foreign affairs. Disraeli was waiting in the wings to come out with more assertive statements about England's imperial mission and her power and these proved to be more in harmony with the mood of the moment.'[46]

The second issue challenging the government was the settlement of the Alabama compensation claim, where Gladstone accepted the ruling of an international committee set up to adjudicate a dispute over compensation between Britain and the American government arising out of damage inflicted upon Federal shipping by a British-made ship during the American Civil War (1861–65). Despite the size of the award against Britain (£3.25 million), Gladstone met its terms. This action has been applauded by many historians. Thus for Morley,

> [t]he Treaty of Washington and the Geneva arbitration stand out as the most notable victory in the nineteenth century of the noble art of preventive diplomacy [...] For the moment the result did something to impair the popularity of Mr. Gladstone's government, but his association with this high act of national policy is one of the things that give its brightest lustre to his fame.[47]

Roy Jenkins likewise describes the settlement as 'the greatest nineteenth century triumph of rational internationalism over short-sighted jingoism'.[48] Feuchtwanger admits that, while the compensation payment 'contributed even more than the other foreign policy problems to the unpopularity of the government', the 'verdict of history has gone most unequivocally in favour of the course taken by Gladstone and his government. Even from the standpoint of *Realpolitik* it was right that every effort should be made to remove the irritants from the Anglo-American relationship.'[49] Biagini agrees that the

---

[45] The Black Sea clauses formed part of the Treaty of Paris that settled the Crimean War in 1856. Under the clauses, Russian was forbidden from stationing warships in the Black Sea.

[46] Feuchtwanger, *Gladstone*, p. 162.

[47] Morley, *Life of Gladstone*, II. p. 413.

[48] Jenkins, *Gladstone*, p. 356.

[49] Feuchtwanger, *Gladstone*, p. 162.

settlement was a 'great success for the British Empire', preventing a damaging tension between the United States and Britain.[50]

Yet others emphasize the damage done to the government's reputation by its conciliatoriness. 'Gladstone's putative weakness in dealing with the *Alabama* affair', writes Hawkins, 'was seen as confirmation of his alleged shortcomings in handling foreign affairs.'[51] Parry, too, comments upon the damage done to the Liberal party by the 'government's apparent submissiveness in its negotiations with the United States', which 'inspired much whig–liberal criticism'.[52]

Legislative activism

According to Hoppen, what distinguished Gladstone's 1868 government from its predecessors was his belief that legislation was the main function of government.[53] The government legislated across a wide range of areas, be it the licensing of public houses or the organization of the judiciary or the overhaul of local government or the legal status of trade unions. Although this legislative dynamism has earned plaudits for the administration, historians have increasingly seen Gladstone's government as trying to achieve too much, confusing energy with effectiveness. Parry talks of the government's 'overstuffed legislative programme'. In 1871 Goschen's ambitious local government and finance reform, Henry Bruce's badly drawn Licensing Bill, and other legislation from Royal Parks to Scottish Education had to be withdrawn after parliamentary criticism.[54] 'The government's reforming zeal', agrees Hawkins, 'brought on legislative congestion in parliament [...] the very wide number of issues on which different sections of the Liberal party expected government action demanded legislative initiative [...] Yet to attempt too much, with consequent failure, was seen to be inefficient.'[55] It was not just government business that brought on arrears – it was the increasing number of private members bills brought forward by restless backbenchers. In what Shannon calls 'a kind of saturnalia of indiscipline', Liberal members put forward ever more private bills – 82 in 1869 and 98 in 1871.[56] 'The greatest failure' of the government, says Agatha Ramm, 'was political.'

---

[50] Biagini, *Gladstone*, p. 82.
[51] Hawkins, *British Party Politics*, p. 164.
[52] Parry, *Democracy and Religion*, p. 352.
[53] Hoppen, *Mid-Victorian Generation*, p. 99.
[54] Parry, *Rise and Fall of Liberal Government*, p. 271.
[55] Hawkins, *British Party Politics*, p. 161
[56] Shannon, *Gladstone: Heroic Minister*, pp. 94–95.

Legislative congestion was the trouble. The large number of government bills, the arrears when a proportion of these failed and had to be reintroduced, the large number of private members' bills, the increase in bills coming under general acts as provisional orders or schemes, all these things threw the parliamentary timetable into chaos. This in turn produced more discouragement and more abandonment of bills, more late-night sittings, count-outs and ultimately government defeats.[57]

Gladstone's personal performance

Gladstone is conventionally depicted as the driving force of his administration, defining Gladstonian Liberalism through his reform agenda. Frank Gunsaulus exemplifies the kind of eulogy his first administration inspired among sympathizers:

> Never did an administration astonish a country with such a succession of nobly conceived and eloquently advocated measures as was now about to be introduced. Gladstone infused his own party with his supreme conviction that these measures were the logical outgrowth of all that the centuries of constitutional monarchical government in England had brought forth, and the Liberal party [...] caught and reflected the luminous quality of his mind and the magnetic influence which his spirit exercised.[58]

More sober historical studies echo this refrain. Thus Feuchtwanger writing in 1975,

> In terms of legislative achievement the government which Gladstone had now formed was to become one of the greatest of the nineteenth century [...] If one wishes to define the substance of Gladstonian liberalism the actions of this government are much the best point of reference [...] The extent of this achievement would have been impossible without his gargantuan powers of work and his prodigious parliamentary ability.[59]

More recently, Euginio Biagini emphasizes how Gladstone not only oversaw his own legislative priorities such as the 1870 Irish Land Act but also

---

[57] Ramm, *William Ewart Gladstone*, p. 69.

[58] Gunsaulus, *William Ewart Gladstone*, p. 250.

[59] Feuchtwanger, *Gladstone*, pp. 149; 170–71.

'presided over the drawing of other important Bills, and loyally supported his ministers in Parliament and the country. In contrast to the view that he focused his mind and attention on only one issue at the time, he was in fact able to divide his energy across most of the many Bills, projects and proposals which the government and leading backbenchers produced between 1868 and 1874.'[60]

For others, Gladstone's leadership was more equivocal. Both Gladstone's most important recent biographers, Matthew and Shannon, see his government less as the fulfilment of political liberalism and more as the perfection of Peelite reformism. Gladstone, writes Shannon, regarded himself 'as the restorer and fulfiller of' the golden age of heroic Peelite reform of the years between 1832 and 1854, which had been superseded by the epoch of 'political bad faith' represented by Palmerston and Disraeli. It was thus a form of statesmanship 'curiously mingling old-fashioned references to the days of Peel with the most modern exigencies of the instant'.[61] Matthew agrees that Gladstone's goals were limited, consisting of perfecting the minimalist state he had helped build from the 1840s.

> Looking at the architecture of the State in the late 1860s, Gladstone saw the grand design as largely fulfilled. The odd cornice remained to be completed, but the foundations and superstructure were built. Gladstone saw his first government not as the new dawn of thoroughgoing liberalism emancipated by democracy, but as the setting of the sun at the end of the day of the building of the mid-century edifice [...] Unlike 1859, Gladstone came into office in 1868 with no overall legislative programme.[62]

Indeed, Matthew believes that Gladstone remained wedded to Peelite fiscal liberalization and was 'sceptical about the value of political liberalism'.[63]

Unfortunately many of his supporters were not sceptical about political liberalism and saw the election victory of 1868 as the prelude to great legislative changes. It was this misapprehension between Gladstone and his backbench followers that lay at the heart of the government's difficulties. For as Matthew observes, Nonconformists, intellectuals, Radicals and Temperance reformers all anticipated that the government would drive forward with the reforms they wished to see – only to find Gladstone viewing

---

[60] Biagini, *Gladstone*, p. 50.
[61] Shannon, *Gladstone: Heroic Minister*, p. 62.
[62] Matthew, *Gladstone*, pp. 172–73.
[63] Ibid., p. 174.

most such reforms 'with caution, and some with hostility'.[64] Parry likewise notes how the reforms introduced by the government in areas like education, local government and pub licensing arose from within 'the Whig-Liberal tradition [...] hardly any of it' was Gladstone's. As a Peelite, Gladstone's preoccupation was with 'finance, religion and the immorality of coercive or careless government; everything else in politics was to him just mundane administration'.[65] Gladstone accordingly viewed with increasing irritation and indifference the measures that defined his administration. As a result, says Stansky, 'even this great ministry ran downhill'. As politics became more tiresome, Gladstone's 'interest in religion grew even greater, and he found himself more concerned with eternal questions rather than immediate ones before the House of Commons'.[66] Although he put through modernizing reforms like the Secret Ballot and the Judicature Act, 'these were not steps with which he was particularly concerned'. Indeed the Secret Ballot Bill 'was not much more welcome to Gladstone than had been the Elementary Education and the University Test Bills [...] he had retained [from the 1830s] a certain resistance towards the idea that those who deserved the vote also needed the protection of being able to exercise it secretly'.[67] By 1871, reflects Hawkins, Liberal dissensions and difficulties were seriously mounting. As Gladstone's Cabinet wilted under the strain, Gladstone took on more of the business of government himself, becoming increasingly irritable, and some 'speculated on his going mad before the next general election'.[68] As we have seen, Gladstone became increasingly preoccupied with defence cuts as a prelude to abolishing income tax, and this brought him into conflict with his own Cabinet. Paradoxically, therefore, if the 1868 government was the exemplification of Gladstonian Liberalism, it owed very little to Gladstone.

Party division

In 1868, Gladstone, by raising the issue of Irish Church reform, had united around his leadership a formidable Liberal majority. Unfortunately, remarks Morley, as 'time went on, the essentially composite character of a majority that was only held together by Mr. Gladstone's personality, his authority in the House, and his enormous strength outside, revealed itself in awkward fissures'.[69]

---

[64] Ibid., p. 175.
[65] Parry, *Rise and Fall of Liberal Government*, p. 247.
[66] Stansky, *Gladstone*, p. 118.
[67] Jenkins, *Gladstone*, pp. 354–55.
[68] Hawkins, *British Party Politics*, pp. 161, 163.
[69] Morley, *Life of Gladstone*, II. p. 388.

Morley identified three Liberal fault lines: first, the Whigs, who never forgot that Gladstone had been a Tory and felt no attachment to him; second, the middle-class liberals, who revered Gladstone's capacity for finance and high moral ideals; and third, the left wing, who thought Gladstone too fond of the Church, too deferential to aristocracy and not sufficiently a reformer. By 1872, he concludes, the 'wide popularity of the government' had undergone 'a marked decline'. To recover party unity Gladstone turned to reform, but, as Hawkins remarks, reforms only exposed Liberal divisions. On Ireland, while Church disestablishment united Liberals, land reform caused disquiet, and prolonged Cabinet discussion 'milked Gladstone's own proposals of their bite'.[70] At the Home Office, Bruce's legislation rarely struck the right note. While, writes Hawkins, his 1871 Act gave trade unions legal recognition of their funds, his formalization of the law relating to peaceful picketing allowed the courts to declare against picketing as such. Union leaders complained of 'Liberal indifference', and in 1874, the Labour Representation League put forward 16 of its own candidates at the general election.[71] Similarly, his 1872 licensing legislation 'offended [...] the publicans and the brewing interest, without securing the support of the temperance movement' since it did not go far enough to regulate the drinks trade.[72] Parry emphasizes the disillusionment with Gladstone's leadership among Whig-Liberals, who believed that he was failing to resist radical pressure from Nonconformists on issues like calls for reform of the Education Act and the rise in republican sentiment. They objected to Bruce's Licensing Bill and Goschen's Local Government Bill and also to the drift of events in Ireland.[73]

Gladstone then, argues Hawkins, made the mistake of trying to reunite his party around the Irish Universities Bill, for which there was little enthusiasm. The government was defeated by three votes and Gladstone resigned. Despite his seeking to force Disraeli to become prime minister and form a government, Disraeli refused and 'Gladstone limped back into office [...] The remainder of the 1873 session proved largely barren.'[74] The Liberals lost ten by-elections between May and January 1874. 'This haemorrhaging of electoral support drained the life-blood of the ministry. Fear of Liberal extremism seemed the main cause of by-election losses.'[75] Thus, concludes Matthew, 'Gladstone's

---

[70] Hawkins, *British Party Politics*, p. 153.

[71] Ibid., p. 158.

[72] Ibid. See also Ensor, *England: 1870–1914*, p. 19.

[73] Parry, *Democracy and Religion*, p. 324.

[74] Hawkins, *British Party Politics*, pp. 165–69.

[75] Ibid., p. 170.

first government petered out, never recovering from the abortive resignation of March 1873.'[76]

Conclusion

Assessments of Gladstone's first government depend primarily upon the perspective from which it is viewed. When judged from the viewpoint of the liberal meritocratic state, Gladstone's government stands out as an episode of outstanding progress. So it was depicted by the contemporary biographer, Barnett Smith:

> That period [1869–1871] which [...] witnessed the passing of the Irish Church Act, the Endowed Schools Bill, the Bankruptcy Bill, the Habitual Criminals Bill, the Irish Land Act, the Elementary Education Act, the Abolition of Purchase in the Army, the negotiation of the Washington Treaty, the passing of the University Tests Bill and of the Trades Union Bill, and the repeal of the Ecclesiastical Titles Act, may well be entitled to the appellation of the 'golden age of Liberalism.' There have been few periods in the history of this country [...] when measures of equal magnitude have been passed within this limited space of time.[77]

A century later Ramm remarked of Gladstone's government that the mark it left on 'almost all British institutions, was outstanding [...] Administrative reform had gone on within departments and parliamentary procedure had begun to be scrutinized. Externally, British relations with the continent and the United States were all better in 1874 than they had been in 1867.'[78]

Historians casting a more critical gaze make two points. First, that Gladstone's reforms counted for much more on paper than they did in reality, the eulogies of the likes of Ramm, Feuchtwanger, Barnett Smith and Gunsaulus resting upon the symbolism of the measures passed rather than a detailed inquiry into the actual changes they yielded – which were often limited or equivocal. Hoppen has been the leading advocate of this view, arguing that many of the reforms 'promised more than they were able to deliver'.[79] Second, it is contended that, whatever the government's policy successes, *politically* it was an abysmal failure. Within two years of its victory, the Liberal Party was

---

[76] Matthew, *Gladstone*, p. 232.
[77] Smith, *William Ewart Gladstone*, p. 424.
[78] Ramm, *William Ewart Gladstone*, pp. 70–1.
[79] Hoppen, *Mid-Victorian Generation*, p. 113.

fracturing into futility, the measures the administration proposed only adding to its woes by offending some interest group or other, while its leader proved increasingly disengaged from the 'Gladstonian Liberalism' his ministry was meant to be defining. The case against Gladstone's government from this perspective is made by Hoppen:

> Gradually, however, so much went awry that the frequently hailed triumphs of Gladstone's first administration produced comparatively few political benefits for their author. When legislation united his party (as over Irish disestablishment) it yielded little or no party advantage after the event. When it divided the party (as over education) bitter Liberal malcontents long continued to roam the landscape seeking revenge. When it sought to remedy a 'great wrong', it could prove notably ineffective and – as happened in the case of the first Irish Land Act – anger rather than pacify its supposed beneficiaries (the tenants). When it seemed to promise dramatic action – as with Civil Service and university reforms and the abolition of purchase in the army – the practical results were generally modest [...] Nor did controversial laws concerning the secret ballot, trade unions, and the drinks trade fare any better. Their supporters soon forgot the kindness. Their opponents neither forgot nor forgave.[80]

4.2   Why Did Gladstone Lose the 1874 Election?

Gladstone's election victory of over 100 seats in 1868 was replaced, in 1874, by a winning margin for Disraeli's Conservatives of more than 50. Historians have sought for an explanation for this electoral turnaround in two different directions: for a majority, the election was lost by Gladstone – reflecting the actions taken during his 1868 government, but for others, it was won by Disraeli, serving to vindicate his Conservative leadership and opposition strategy. For some the outcome was not the responsibility of either man, but a result of more fundamental social and ideological forces.

1874 as a defeat for liberalism

Bruce Coleman contends that in 1874 'Liberal disintegration was more in evidence than Tory resurgence and in many constituencies it was the fall or division of the Liberal vote since 1868 [...] that led to seats changing

---

[80] Ibid., p. 592. See also St John, *Gladstone and the Logic of Victorian Politics*, pp. 210–11 for a negative assessment.

hands [...]'.[81] Why might such a loss of Liberal support have occurred? Two themes are identifiable.

Long-term Liberal problems

One school of thought traces the seeds of defeat back so far as 1870, though the factors identified as relevant differ radically.

Alienation of nonconformist opinion

A well-established explanation attributes Gladstone's defeat to the disaffection of Nonconformists. After raising their hopes with his move against the Anglican Church in Ireland, he failed to follow this up with a reduction in the power of the Established Church in England. In particular, the 1870 Education Act represented a humiliation for Nonconformists with its increased grants to Anglican schools and the infamous Clause 25. From this point the Nonconformist conscience, which had provided the local impetus behind the Liberals' 1868 victory, was at odds with Gladstone. This idea was advanced by the Liberal journalist Peter Clayden in 1880, who observed that the Nonconformists remained cool toward the government, the Education Act remaining a great grievance. The 'breach between the Government and this large, active, and most important section of its supporters was never healed'.[82] Eyck agrees that 'the greater proportion of the Nonconformists, who could not overlook the fact that the Church was unduly favoured by the Education Act, now joined in the chorus of the discontented', while Davis believes that 'the main factor' behind the Liberal defeat was the 1870 Education Act, which led Dissenters either to abstain or support anti-Act candidates.[83] This was important for, as Feuchtwanger observes, Nonconformists had been 'the activists in many constituencies [...] Now they had been disappointed by the Gladstone government and were apathetic.'[84]

Although venerable, this explanation of Liberal failure has been subject to significant qualification. Parry argues that the small number of cases in which the intervention of alternative Liberal candidates helped the Conservatives take seats was exaggerated by Radicals like Chamberlain to give them more influence in the party.[85] In fact, Liberals 'performed better, in terms of seats

---

[81] Coleman, *Conservatism and the Conservative Party*, p. 144.
[82] P. W. Clayden, *England under Lord Beaconsfield* (1880), pp. 27–28.
[83] Eyck, *Gladstone*, p. 233; Davis, *Disraeli*, p. 166.
[84] Feuchtwanger, *Gladstone*, pp. 176–77.
[85] Parry, *Democracy and Religion*, p. 396.

retained, where nonconformity was stronger'. Nonconformist grievances were not sufficient to shake their personal attachment to Gladstone, 'an attachment founded on emotion and reverence rather than on considerations of policy'.[86] In addition, in areas like the north, education had ceased to be a major issue since Nonconformists dominated the School Boards and were not implementing Clause 25, while in the large northern boroughs most Liberal candidates were Radicals who already supported disestablishment, so there was no reason to oppose them. The Education League was 'out of touch with local nonconformist sentiment' and its campaign 'failed to rouse local enthusiasm'.[87] Thus, concludes Parry, 'abstentions on the "left" of the party therefore probably bear relatively little responsibility for the election defeat – which must rest squarely on those from the "right" who retracted their support'.[88] It seems 'fairly certain', concurs Paul Adelman, that 'the importance of the League generally as an influence in the Liberal *debacle* has been exaggerated'. Nonconformist voters were concentrated in the under-represented cities of the north and midlands, and though there were 34 unauthorized Liberal candidates, the Liberal chief whip thought only 13 seats lost as a result.[89]

Alienation of the brewing interest

An equally august interpretation traces Liberal defeat to the Licensing Act, which restricted pub opening hours and controlled the granting of pub licenses – thereby antagonizing brewers, barley growers, publicans and thirsty members of the working class. Gladstone himself famously lamented that 'we have been borne down in a torrent of gin and beer'.[90] Clayden took up the theme in 1880, suggesting that it yielded an unlikely combination:

> The public house found itself allied to the rectory or the vicarage; the tap-room and the school-room were engaged in similar political propaganda [...] This alliance was the main feature in the election contest. Everything else was dwarfed by it.[91]

The historian most associated with the role of drink in the government's defeat is Ensor. Bruce's attempts to legislate to control drinking 'raised a

---

[86] Ibid., p. 398.
[87] Ibid., pp. 381–82.
[88] Ibid., p. 401.
[89] Adelman, *Gladstone, Disraeli and Later Victorian Politics*, 10–11. Italics in the original.
[90] Quoted in St John, *Gladstone and the Logic of Victorian Politics*, p. 205.
[91] Clayden, *England under Lord Beaconsfield*, pp. 28–29.

storm of opposition from the publicans and the liquor trade generally', and the implications of this were far-reaching:

> From midsummer 1871 till the dissolution of 1874 nearly every public house in the United Kingdom was an active committee room for the conservative party. The consequences of this upon actual voting, well attested by contemporary evidence, probably outweighed all the other factors in the government's unpopularity. But the current of it ran deeper; for here [...] was one of the source-points in the history of parties. Down to then the liquor industry, like other industrial interests, was apt to be liberal.[92]

But this all changed as the drinks interest shifted its allegiance to the Tories:

> Money, workers, and support of every kind flowed to it inexhaustibly from the liquor trade [...] Nor was money all. Few people are so well placed to influence voters as publicans; and there practically ceased to be any liberal publicans. These facts [...] provide no small part of the explanation why conservatism was so much more successful in the forty years after 1871 than in the forty years before that date.[93]

Yet like all monocausal explanations of complex events, the idea that the 1874 election result owed most to the Licensing Act has been much refuted, notably by Harold Hanham, who points out that the view the election was lost due to the drinks issue came from Liberal papers and the UK Alliance, while it suited Gladstone, defeated in Greenwich by a Conservative brewer, to attribute this calamity to the drinks trade. But the pages of the *Licensed Victuallers' Guardian* and the *Morning Advertiser* contained no systematic attack on the Liberals. In few constituencies did Liberal publicans change their allegiance, and neither did Liberal brewers like the Basses, Buxtons and Whitbreads. Where an anti-Liberal shift was visible was in constituencies where the temperance movement was strong. Here 'there really was a rush to the Conservatives'. In other words, it was not Gladstone's licensing reform, but the agitation of disappointed temperance reformers that exerted a damaging effect.[94] But Ensor's claim that brewing money was central to later Tory success 'must be entirely rejected. The main support of the Conservative party was and remained the landed interest.' In 1874 the 'issues before the electors were

---

[92] Ensor, *England: 1870–1914*, p. 21.
[93] Ibid., pp. 21–22.
[94] Hanham, *Elections and Party Management*, p. 225.

so clear and the swing against the government was so strong, that no amount of free beer was likely to have a decisive effect on the result'.[95] Paul Smith, while broadly endorsing this analysis, acknowledges that the Conservatives were more favourable to the drink interest than the Liberals, and differs from Hanham in believing that the *Morning Advertiser* was openly Conservative. 'How much the support of the licensed trade contributed to the Conservative victory is a matter of controversy', concludes Smith, 'but bearing in mind the smallness of many of the Conservative majorities, it seems possible that without it the party would have been deprived of several valuable seats.'[96]

Alienation of trade unions and the Irish

Another key constituent of the Liberal majority held to have been antagonized by Gladstone's government was the working class, who were offended by the Criminal Law Amendment Act, which rendered it difficult for them to use picketing in the prosecution of disputes, as well as the government's general failure to advance working-class interests through social reform. The administration's surplus revenues, writes Francis Birrell, 'merely went to reduce income tax', which 'failed to stimulate enthusiasm in a class of voter which would not pay income tax anyhow'.[97] 'Even more important', says Adelman, 'was working-class opposition to the Criminal Law Amendment Act.'[98] Although, writes Matthew, the government recognized the need to revise the Act, it failed to do so and the 'election manifesto promised much to the middle classes, but nothing specific to the unions [...] Not surprisingly some unions and unionists worked for the Tories at the general election, or ran their own candidates.'[99] Smith, too, believes working-class exasperation diminished 'the Liberals' electoral strength, even if it showed itself only on a limited scale in increased support for the Conservatives'. The Trade Union Congress pressed for the repeal of the Criminal Law Amendment Act, the nine-hour day and compensation for accidents, and Conservatives standing in the larger boroughs endorsed these demands.[100] Also deserting the Liberals were the Irish. Notwithstanding Gladstone's determination to pacify Ireland, the Irish, notes Hawkins, feeling that parliament had not done enough to

---

[95] Ibid., pp. 225–26.
[96] Smith, *Disraelian Conservatism*, p. 190.
[97] Birrell, *Gladstone*, p. 85.
[98] Adelman, *Gladstone, Disraeli and Victorian Politics*, pp. 10–11.
[99] Matthew, *Gladstone*, p. 217.
[100] Smith, *Disraelian Conservatism*, p. 188.

secure their interests, abandoned the Liberals for Home Rule parties.[101] In 1868 Liberals won 65 Irish seats; in 1874 only 17.

Alienation of moderate Anglican opinion

While Nonconformists might have been repelled by a government too indulgent to the Established Church, several historians point out that Anglicans were repelled for the opposite reason. Disestablishment of the Irish Church, the 1870 Education Act and the removal of religious tests at Oxford and Cambridge led many to conclude that the Liberals were too beholden to Nonconformists and could not be depended upon to uphold the status of the established Church. Parry is the most articulate advocate of this view, arguing that the defeat of 1874 was a product of 'propertied Anglican disaffection [...] Too many electors believed that vociferous Dissenters, "Little Englanders" and Irish Catholics had excessive power over the party, and that Gladstone had not done enough to keep these provincial pressures in check.'[102] This sentiment encompassed the Whig-Liberal right of the party, and it was the withdrawal of their support that led to the 'extremely powerful swing of opinion against the government'.[103] If the Education League contributed to the Liberal defeat, it was primarily by 'further antagonising Whiggish voters'.[104] 'The cry of the "Church in Danger", therefore almost certainly inflicted immense damage on the Liberals in 1874.'[105]

Excessive reformism

A more general explanation attributes Liberal defeat to the sheer extent of its reforming ambitions. By legislating so extensively, Gladstone's government irritated the electorate, trampling on too many vested interests and evoking a desire for peace and stability. 'The Liberal statesmen', wrote the Irish Liberal MP Justin McCarthy in 1897, 'had tried too much, had done too much, had spent their force in too many splendid efforts, and the time came at last when the spirit of Conservative reaction prevailed over them.'[106] Another writer sympathetic to Liberalism, Eyck, believes the Liberal ministry fell because it had 'taken its reform programme so seriously that many of the voters deserted

---

[101] Hawkins, *British Party Politics*, p. 173.
[102] Parry, *Rise and Fall of Liberal Government*, p. 272.
[103] Parry, *Democracy and Religion*, p. 382.
[104] Ibid., p. 383.
[105] Ibid., pp. 407, 431.
[106] McCarthy, *Story of Gladstone's Life*, pp. 278–79.

it. After so many exciting years they wanted peace.'[107] This viewpoint is not confined to Liberal authors. The Conservative J. A. R. Marriot writes that 'the tide had begun to turn against the Liberal Government. Their appetite for legislation had been prodigious, and the digestion of the country proved to be less robust than their own.'[108] James Anthony Froude spoke in 1890 of a wider rejection of Liberalism:

> The exhausted volcanoes continued on the Treasury bench; but England had grown tired of them [...] The Premier [...] had irritated powerful interests on all sides, from the army to the licensed victuallers; while of work achieved he had nothing to show but revolutionary measures in Ireland, which had hitherto been unattended with success [...] England [...] had recovered from her revolutionary fever-fit, and desired to be left in quiet after half-a-century of political dissipation.[109]

The idea that 1874 represented a reaction against legislative activism has been much advocated. Despite the government's achievements, says Birrell, it was by 1872 'one of the most unpopular administrations that England has experienced. Everybody was offended, nobody satisfied, and the party was at sixes and sevens.'[110] Coleman sees the rise in Tory fortunes after 1871 as reflecting the actions of the government, whose measures 'far from settling questions, had tended to provoke antagonisms and to inspire unrealistic expectations, leaving supporters dissatisfied and divided and generating resentment among interests that had suffered'.[111] Hawkins concurs:

> Gladstone's defeat in 1874 was [...] principally the result of the defection of moderate support [...] In a well-orchestrated campaign Conservatives exploited moderate Liberal foreboding. Gladstone's administration was portrayed as restless, unpredictable, and a prey to popular agitation.[112]

'Disraeli's greatest asset', remarks John Vincent, 'was Gladstone. The radical wind of the late 1860s could not last forever. While it blew, Disraeli lay low. In 1871 the tide began to turn. The main issue between then and the 1874 election was an over-active, overbearing Gladstone.'[113]

---

[107] Eyck, *Gladstone*, p. 245.
[108] Marriott, *England since Waterloo*, p. 416.
[109] Froude, *Lord Beaconsfield*, pp. 232–33, 235.
[110] Birrell, *Gladstone*, p. 84.
[111] Coleman, *Conservatism and the Conservative Party*, p. 141.
[112] Hawkins, *British Party Politics*, p. 174.
[113] Vincent, *Disraeli*, p. 10.

Campaign mistakes

The idea that Liberal defeat was prefigured as early as 1870 has been challenged, it being argued that Liberal failure owed more to specific mistakes made by Gladstone in the last year of his ministry.

Income tax abolition

The decision to base his election campaign on the proposal to abolish income tax has been portrayed as at best irrelevant, at worst as opportunistic. Large parts of the electorate did not pay income tax and would incur the increased indirect taxes required to fund its abolition: 'Gladstone's dream of a taxpaying franchise', reflects Michael Winstanley, 'had been shattered by 1867 and with it the overwhelming appeal this issue had.'[114] The propertied classes on the other hand did not favour renewed financial austerity at the price of reduced spending on national defence – while they too resented the likely prospect of increased taxes on property. Thus, according to Feuchtwanger,

> In selecting the abolition of the income tax and economy as the core of his appeal Gladstone revealed himself as still a Peelite. What had been the focus of political debate and the basis of his own reputation in 1860 could, however, serve that purpose no longer in 1874. The electors were no longer so interested in details of public money saved; the working class were beginning to look to the public purse as a provider. Gladstone was beginning in some respects to look like a man of the past.[115]

It is from historians sympathetic to Gladstone that the most stringent criticisms of the income tax plan have come. Stansky, for instance, writes that by 1874 'Gladstone was temporarily exhausted of inspiring ideas [...] The cheeseparing side of Gladstone [...] was not part of his grand appeal, which rested on the use of politics for moral ends.'[116] Matthew, although seeing political merit in the proposal, admits that it contained important weaknesses. First, it was too narrowly directed at the middle and propertied classes; second, abolishing income tax would have put tight constraints on government revenue and it would probably have soon been restored.[117] Roy Jenkins is especially unimpressed. It was not, he writes, a truly Gladstonian

[114] M. J. Winstanley, *Gladstone and the Liberal Party* (1990), p. 52.

[115] Feuchtwanger, *Gladstone*, p. 176.

[116] Stansky, *Gladstone*, p. 119.

[117] Matthew, *Gladstone*, p. 225.

manoeuvre – his 'natural appeal was moralizing rather than materialistic'.[118] And if he believed the proposal would unite the Liberals 'he was profoundly mistaken'. Joseph Chamberlain and Walter Bagehot of the *Economist* both condemned the proposal as narrow and selfish. It also brought him into conflict with the military departments of the Cabinet. Jenkins concludes that 'Gladstone's 1874 fiscal programme was [...] manifestly the last shot of an old war rather than the harbinger of the future'.[119]

But was income tax abolition really such an ill-considered piece of opportunism? Clayden writes that the proposal had been 'diligently prepared for' and represented 'the crown and finish of an unequalled series of legislative reforms'. Gladstone's mistake was not to present his income tax plan to parliament in a budget and then call an election.

> Mr. Gladstone's Address was a budget speech incompletely developed and untimely born. It was a sign that he is either ignorant of the arts of the political tactician or indifferent to them. He mis-reckoned his position and misunderstood his countrymen. He should not have taken them into his counsels; he should have acted first and consulted them afterwards.[120]

In practice income tax failed as a cry 'probably because the prosperity of the country was so great, that the mass of the people were indifferent to questions of taxation'.[121]

Matthew contends that Gladstone's motives were not opportunistic but strategic: by abolishing income tax he hoped to entrench the minimalist state in an age of an ever-wider franchise. The policy had the further advantage that it would give the Liberal party a policy to unite around in the wake of the Irish University Bill. Gladstone believed that 'only the budget could restore the party to something like a coherent and companionable body'.[122] Biagini goes further, arguing that Gladstone's tax proposals represented an 'elaborate and sophisticated attempt to update the "social contract"'.[123] Gladstone saw that rising incomes meant that more lower-middle-class people were being brought into the £100 per annum tax bracket – and these same people were being hit by rises in rates to pay for expanded local government activity. Abolishing income

---

[118] Jenkins, *Gladstone*, p. 375.

[119] Ibid., p. 377.

[120] Clayden, *England under Lord Beaconsfield*, pp. 17–18.

[121] Ibid., p. 23.

[122] Matthew, *Gladstone*, pp. 224, 226.

[123] Biagini, *Gladstone*, p. 54.

tax would bring this electorally significant (and largely Liberal) group much relief. Further, 'the chief aim behind the 1874 proposal was that of discouraging imperialism and what Gladstone saw as military overspending […] Without the income tax […] military estimates would inevitably become rigid.'

> Thus the 1874 proposed repeal of the income tax served a variety of purposes and would affect the conduct of both home and foreign affairs […] It was […] aimed at relieving the lower and professional middle classes – which had been overtaxed in comparison with other social groups – by redistributing the fiscal burden on land and real property through local taxation […] It was one of the most ambitious proposals Gladstone had ever conceived.[124]

The snap election

Facing Cabinet resistance to further defence cuts, Gladstone suddenly called a general election. This decision has been much criticized, with Clayden calling it 'the most needless, most untimely, and unfortunate dissolution in English history'. 'Everybody', he continues, 'was angry with Mr. Gladstone for springing the dissolution so suddenly on the country.'[125] There was no chance to mobilize the Liberal forces, and sections of the party believed Gladstone had sprung the election on them so as to set the agenda and eclipse their interests in matters like education reform. Goldwin Smith recalled that 'all Liberals saw at once that it was ruin. It seems that the leader himself contemplated, and almost counted on, defeat.'[126] Gladstone, says Sarah Bradford, 'had hoped that his lightening move would take his opponents by surprise, but in the event it was the Liberals themselves who were found unprepared'.[127] All that Gladstone succeeded in doing, continues Hawkins, was to highlight 'the fact that Liberal organisation in the country was far less advanced than the Conservative structure […] In 1868 Liberals had won an overwhelming victory based upon the "virtuous passion" excited by a single moral issue. In 1874 there was no single transcendent cry and no party organization to fall back upon. Popular Liberal support collapsed.'[128] Hoppen agrees: 'Among

---

[124] Ibid., pp. 53–54.

[125] Clayden, *England under Lord Beaconsfield*, pp. 14, 25.

[126] G. Smith, 'Mr. Morley's Life of Gladstone. II', *North American Review*, Vol. 178 (1904), p. 51.

[127] Bradford, *Disraeli*, p. 303.

[128] Hawkins, *British Party Politics*, p. 172.

Liberals there was confusion and discord [...] Indeed, the whole affair involved Liberal disintegration more than anything very positive on the other side.'[129] It was now, says Hanham, that the Liberals 'suffered for the foolishness of their government in alienating its supporters in the Liberal associations [...] The most energetic party workers of 1868 were either indifferent or had gone over to the anti-government pressure groups, the National Education League, the United Kingdom Alliance and the Home Rule League, and to make matters worse there was scarcely any central direction of the election campaign.'[130]

A failure to persuade

Having called an election upon so controversial a pretext, Gladstone gave himself only two weeks to rally support and failed to utilize the resources at this command. He had little opportunity, concedes Biagini, 'to deploy one of his chief assets – electoral rhetoric. Virtually no national debate took place [...] and the comparatively low turnout helped the Conservatives.'[131] Despite, says Matthew, developing the 'prototype of a new style of popular executive politician' in the 1860s, he had set public speaking aside during his government, addressing only three popular audiences between 1868 and 1873. During the campaign itself 'only three election speeches were made' – as such he 'forfeited one of his major assets'.[132] 'There was', summarizes Jenkins, 'no nationwide campaign, and the government went down to a heavy defeat without deployment of its greatest battering-ram.'[133]

1874 as a Conservative victory

Yet other writers depict the election of 1874 not as an indictment of Gladstone's Liberalism but as a vindication of Disraeli's Tory leadership. Again this can be seen as a reflection of long- or short-term Tory actions.

Long-term Tory strengths

Disraeli's modernized Toryism

In the early 1870s, it is alleged, Disraeli finally brought into focus a conception of Toryism that met the needs of late-Victorian Britain. To traditional Tory

---

[129] Hoppen, *Mid-Victorian Generation*, p. 611.
[130] Hanham, *Elections and arty Management*, p. 222.
[131] Biagini, *Gladstone*, p. 54.
[132] Matthew, *Gladstone*, p. 230.
[133] Jenkins, *Gladstone*, p. 377.

support for established institutions he added a glorification of Empire and a call for social reforms to improve working-class living conditions. Each of these points struck a Gladstonian nerve: Gladstone's government was seen as undermining institutions like the House of Lords and monarchy; lacking in patriotism; being tepid in its support for Empire; and eschewing social provision for the poor, looking to self-help and trickle down to improve the condition of the masses. Thus Disraeli's Tory vision brilliantly exploited Liberal weaknesses. Hence, while Marriott believes that Disraeli's 'success in 1874 was due, primarily perhaps, to the blunders, unpopularity, and internal dissensions of his opponents', it was due also 'to a gradual inclination of the mind and instinct of the electorate towards the objects for which modern Conservatism was to stand. These objects had been in the last few years clearly re-stated and defined by the leader who was now [...] to reap the tardy reward of patience and sagacity.'[134] In his 1872 speeches at Manchester and Crystal Palace, Disraeli, remarks Morley, displayed genius in his ability to 'read aright the signs and characteristics of the time', saw the mood of damaged national pride engendered by Gladstone's pacifistic foreign policy and 'found for it the oracle of a party cry in phrases about Empire and Social Reform'.[135] Disraeli, declare Monypenny and Buckle, gave 'utterance [...] to the ideas that were beginning to stir the nation's heart'.[136]

What, asks Terence Jenkins, was innovative in these speeches? While sharpening his attack on the government's Empire and constitutional policies, what was new was the reference to social reform: although 'he had had much to say in his Young England days about the need to elevate the condition of the people', he had since shown little interest in social issues.[137] Prompting Disraeli's words on social reform were the discussions between leading Conservatives and workers' leaders in 1871 that were known as the 'new social alliance'. This pointed to the possibility of using social reform to appeal to the newly enfranchised working class. Hoppen concurs that while Disraeli's 1872 speeches 'said little that was new', it was the close combination of social reform and Empire 'which created both contemporary and subsequent resonances', yielding a conception of Toryism uniting social improvement with the nation's greatness.[138]

Most historians have, however, been sceptical of the part played by Disraeli's Tory vision in the electoral victory. The Liberal journalist Clayden

---

[134] Marriott, *England since Waterloo*, p. 434.
[135] Morley, *Life of Gladstone*, II. p. 392.
[136] Monypenny and Buckle, *Life of Disraeli*, II. p. 617.
[137] Jenkins, *Disraeli and Victorian Conservatism*, pp. 91–92.
[138] Hoppen, *Mid-Victorian Generation*, pp. 610–11.

complained that at Manchester and Crystal Palace he had largely confined himself to criticisms of the Liberal ministry. 'The Conservative Leader [...] had no policy to state [...] The indefiniteness of the Opposition Leader's views disappointed his audiences, and for a time disheartened his friends.'[139] His election address, too, 'contained no statement of political principles, and no outline of legislative measures'.[140] These words find some support from Terence Jenkins, who writes that Disraeli's electoral address was 'entirely negative'. The ideas of Tory Democracy were conspicuously absent: 'Disraeli offered nothing specifically designed to attract the working men, not even a vague commitment to "social" reform, the emphasis being placed instead entirely on the need for a period of stability and repose.'[141] 'Disraeli's lofty expressions in his speeches of 1872', agrees Ian Machin, 'had not been translated into any definite, detailed intentions.'[142]

Coleman believes this was no accident, arguing that Disraeli did little to reshape Conservatism in either thought or policy. Crown, Empire and social reform had been useful slogans for a leadership nervous of the enfranchised working man, but they were opportunistic responses, and even before 1874 the emphases had changed to criticism of Gladstone's harassing legislation.[143] The party, Disraeli now believed, 'had only to assert its conservative credentials, criticize the government for weakness abroad and for reckless hyper-activity at home and wait to reap the benefits of Liberal difficulties'. Disraeli offered 'conservatism in Conservative clothing'.[144] Smith similarly writes that Disraeli presented an 'essentially negative and quietest front, adapted to appeal to those elements of the middle classes which were seeking a refuge from Radicalism and "democracy"'. The party could not show zeal for the interests of the working class – 'whose force its new bourgeois adherents were relying on it to contain. The theme of social reform, so boldly proclaimed in 1872, was now muted, though not entirely abandoned.'[145] Stanley Stembridge likewise believes that 'Imperialism apparently played no important role in the Tory victory of 1874'.[146] Tory charges of Liberal separatism 'did not really stick, for the Liberals immediately struck a pose as good colonial reformers' and Disraeli hardly referred to it during the campaign.

---

[139] Clayden, *England under Lord Beaconsfield*, pp. 5–7.
[140] Ibid., p. 21.
[141] Jenkins, *Disraeli and Victorian Conservatism*, pp. 95–96, 100.
[142] Machin, *Disraeli*, p. 125.
[143] Coleman, *Conservatism and the Conservative Party*, p. 157.
[144] Ibid., p. 158.
[145] Smith, *Disraelian Conservatism*, p. 185.
[146] S. R. Stembridge, 'Disraeli and the Millstones', *Journal of British Studies*, Vol. 5 (1965), pp. 133–34.

Conservative Party organization

It has alternatively been argued that what delivered Conservative success in 1874 was improved party organization. Disraeli had long sought to improve this, and with the appointment of John Gorst as chief organizer in 1870 the Conservatives began to build up a powerful electoral organization, linking the party with the National Union and targeting the larger borough constituencies of the midlands and north. Gorst himself promoted this version of events, writing in the *Times* in 1874 that Disraeli's victory was the culmination of a deliberate strategy:

> The principles of Tory Democracy were proclaimed in speech and pamphlet, and working men's Conservative Associations were established all over the country to propagate them […] The Conservative working men gave him the majority of 1874, the only Tory majority there has been since the days of Peel.[147]

Gorst's interpretation has received some support from historians. Adelman notes how by the end of 1873, 33 of the 49 largest boroughs had Conservative Associations and there was a candidate for every reasonable constituency, concluding that 'Gorst's efforts seemed to be rewarded by the Conservative victory at the polls'.[148] Jenkins acknowledges that 'by 1874 the party was much better prepared for a fight in the critically important large English boroughs'.[149] Paul Smith agrees that the Conservatives broadened their appeal among working men and in the larger boroughs 'there were significant advances'. In towns of over 50,000 inhabitants, the Conservatives secured 44 of the 144 seats, compared to 25 in 1868.[150] J. L. Hammond and M. R. D. Foot, reflecting upon the reasons for Gladstone's defeat, attach most importance to improved Conservative organization:

> Above all, Disraeli had not wasted his five years in opposition. He had set up the first efficient centralised English party organisation […] It had won him seats steadily at by-elections in the previous autumn, and it had candidates ready in every constituency which he could conceivably hope to win. The general election of 1874 was the first triumph of the Conservative Central Office.[151]

---

[147] J. Gorst, *Times*, 6 February 1907.
[148] Adelman, *Gladstone, Disraeli, and Later Victorian Politics*, p. 27.
[149] Jenkins, *Disraeli and Victorian Conservatism*, p. 97.
[150] Smith, *Disraelian Conservatism*, p. 192.
[151] Hammond and Foot, *Gladstone and Liberalism*, pp. 124–25.

Blake refers to the 'great improvement which under Disraeli's auspices had been made to the Conservative party's organization' such that for 'the moment the Conservative organisation was better than that of the Liberals'.[152] While Hawkins admits that Gorst was building on the work of predecessors and exaggerated his contribution, it was 'the Conservatives under Gorst at Central Office who first moved towards a centralised party bureaucracy harnessing the popular enthusiasm of the constituencies'.[153] Hence, says Hoppen, we find the Conservatives, unlike the Liberals, fighting 'a smooth and well-concerted campaign. And their addresses [...] followed more or less coherent lines: defence of the Church of England, an end to Gladstone's domestic hyperactivity, more religious teaching in schools, opposition to Home Rule, relief for local tax payers, and the vaguest of vaguenesses on foreign affairs.'[154] As Hanham summarizes, in 1874 the Conservatives benefited from the zeal of borough Conservative associations, the vigour of landed magnates in the Counties, the improved central organization of the party 'and the activity of the Conservative publicans who became, for the first time, active politicians'.[155]

Yet a number of historians are sceptical of the role of party organization in the Conservative victory. Shannon labels the idea that Tory success reflected a 'triumph of improved organisation' a myth.[156] It is pointed out, for instance by Jenkins, that Gorst constructed a narrative of his own importance to serve his political agenda within the Tory party. While the Conservatives did do well in the bigger boroughs, it does not follow that his efforts caused the success.[157] This is the point made by Coleman. 'If the Tories were better organised, financed and co-ordinated in the boroughs in 1874 than in 1868 [...] it owed something to Gorst's willing labours but more to an independent shift in the balance of certain kinds of opinion the Tory way, to the alarm and urgency felt within the party in reaction against Liberal measures and to the simultaneous disorganisation of the Liberals.'[158] After all, as both Coleman and Feuchtwanger point out, the Conservatives enjoyed a triumph in the counties 'where the new kinds of organisation were scarcely in evidence'.[159] All Gorst did, argues Hawkins, was 'assist in a movement already under way'.[160]

---

[152] Blake, *Disraeli*, pp. 536–37.
[153] Hawkins, *British Party Politics*, p. 186.
[154] Hoppen, *Mid-Victorian Generation*, pp. 611–12.
[155] Hanham, *Elections and Party Management*, p. 222.
[156] Shannon, *Age of Disraeli*, p. 179.
[157] Jenkins, *Disraeli and Victorian Conservatism*, p. 98.
[158] Coleman, *Conservatism and the Conservative Party*, p. 145.
[159] Feuchtwanger, *Disraeli*, p. 166.
[160] Hawkins, *British Party Politics*, p. 185.

Disraeli's tactical astuteness

A wide range of historians have located Disraeli's real contribution to the 1874 victory to the tactical agility he exhibited in the months leading up to the election. Disraeli saw how the nation was being antagonized by Gladstone's restless reformism and positioned the Conservatives as a moderate party that would sustain ancient institutions and be tender of vested interests. It was this strategy, write Monypenny and Buckle, that was in evidence from his speeches at Manchester and Crystal Palace onwards, as Disraeli made a series of attacks on Gladstone's policies, accusing him of harassing every institution, vexing every trade, despoiling churches and leaving no man certain of his property.[161]

> To an Opposition which, little more than a year before, was discredited, discontented, factious, and hopeless, Disraeli had given organisation, policy, popular respect, the assurance of high and unselfish leadership, and the expectation of early and definitive success.[162]

While Disraeli's election address was negative, he 'was well advised in basing his main appeal on the desire of the electorate for rest, and on their sense of wounded pride at the disrepute of their country abroad'.[163] Robert Blake agrees that the 'rather negative line' of Disraeli's election address 'probably accorded better with the public mood than a more strenuous declaration of policy. Often after a period of strenuous reform a moment arrives quite suddenly when the British people tires of being improved. The winter of 1873–74 was just such an occasion.' By pursuing a policy of shrewd patience, Disraeli became 'a rallying point for the forces of property disturbed at excessive innovation though ready to accept the need for cautious piece-meal reform'.[164]

    The strategic advantages of pursuing a cautious line and downplaying talk of social reform have been recognized by historians. According to Coleman, the Tories benefited from a move of centrist opinion away from a government that had 'lost the image of Palmerstonian success and assurance'.[165] Disraeli, of course, was more than ready to annex the Palmerston tradition of moderate reform at home and a patriotic policy abroad. 'Little was said of empire or social reform.'[166] Parry praises the 'remarkably well orchestrated' Conservative

---

[161] Monypenny and Buckle, *Life of Disraeli*, II, p. 546.
[162] Ibid., p. 560.
[163] Ibid., p. 616.
[164] Blake, *Disraeli*, p. 535.
[165] Coleman, *Conservatism and the Conservative Party*, p. 142.
[166] Ibid., p. 143.

campaign as candidates criticized the government's harassing legislation and warned of its vulnerability to radical pressure. 'The Conservatives' specific electoral pledges were thus designed to furnish a contrast with Liberal unpredictability. By far the most common [...] was their defence of the Church Establishment, and its corollary, the retention of religious education in school-hours, against the threat posed to both by radical Liberals.'[167] The adroitness with which Disraeli deployed Palmerstonian rhetoric is emphasized by Hawkins:

> Conservative victory was also a measure of the effectiveness of the rhetoric with which Disraeli clothed the Conservative party after 1872. He donned Palmerston's mantle and captured new constituencies of electoral support [...] The general election of February 1874 delivered the suburban vote *en masse* [...] it was this achievement which transformed Disraeli from a dispensable liability into an inspiring leader.[168]

The election as the expression of underlying trends

Each of the above interpretations traces the election result to the actions of individuals. An alternative perspective holds that the Conservative victory was a reflection of deeper social changes. Feuchtwanger, for example, sees the election as signalling a shift in the ideological climate away from laissez-faire individualism toward a more collectivist ideology in which there was a role for the state to improve social welfare. This rendered Gladstone's state minimalism out of date and pointed toward Disraeli's social reform agenda. 'The whole ethos of Gladstonian liberalism', he writes, 'self-fulfilment, self-help, individual and social morality, for the moment no longer satisfied the nation as a collectivity as much as it had done.'[169] The problem with this analysis is that it reads too much back from a supposed shift to 'collectivist' thinking in the later nineteenth century as identified by Dicey. In reality, the Tories had not abandoned laissez-faire and made little of any social reforming ambitions.

A phenomenon more commonly pointed to was the growth of a prosperous suburban middle class. As the middle class gained in wealth and prestige they moved to villas in the suburbs, exchanging the Liberalism of their youth for the propertied Conservatism of middle age. It was this demographic change – not Gorst's Tory machine – that yielded Conservative success in

---

167 Parry, *Democracy and Religion*, p. 390.
168 Hawkins, *British Party Politics*, pp. 178, 184.
169 Feuchtwanger, *Gladstone*, p. 168.

the boroughs. Thus for Jenkins the key to Conservative victory was 'the drift towards Conservatism on the part of the middle classes'. Unease at the rise of trade union militancy, Fenianism in Ireland, Gladstone's restless reformism and the growth of suburbia, all contributed to the middle-class shift toward the Tories.[170] Feuchtwanger, again, points to the 'continued drift of the middle and propertied classes towards Conservatism', which was not only due to 'policies of the Gladstone government' but also events like the Paris Commune.[171] Disraeli's moderate message, says Hoppen, meant that the Conservatives 'were increasingly able to profit from the slow anti-Liberal shifts that were taking place in leafiest suburbia'.[172] Hanham attaches the utmost importance to this process, remarking that the 'most important and permanent result of the 1874 election [...] was the marked swing to the Conservatives in middle-class constituencies [...] the City itself, suburban Surrey, Kent and Essex all changed their allegiance [...] By 1880 the Liberals had lost control of suburbia altogether.'[173]

Conclusion

Electoral behaviour is not a science, and the lack of data for the nineteenth century means that we can rarely draw any fine conclusions. At best we can narrow down the range of probable determinants. References to underlying social change seem unpersuasive: in 1868 the Liberals swept to victory – it is hard to believe that suburban expansion or a shift to collectivist ideology could yield a Liberal collapse within six years. The alienation of Radicals and Nonconformists seems unconvincing also: they were too regionally concentrated and they had nowhere else to go. Parry is more suggestive in highlighting the movement of moderate Church opinion away from the Liberals – Gladstone had challenged too many respected interests and would surely do so still more if returned to power. It was now that Disraeli's studied moderation was so important. It was probably enough for Disraeli to pose as the heir to Palmerston, upholding British prestige abroad while overseeing moderate government at home. As Paul Smith concludes, 'Most observers agreed that the verdict of the polls was a negative one [...] what the people wanted was what Palmerston had given them – quiet. The government had been returned on a platform of immobility.'[174] Disraeli did not need a new

---

[170] Jenkins, *Disraeli and Victorian Conservatism*, p. 98.
[171] Feuchtwanger, *Gladstone*, p. 177.
[172] Hoppen, *Mid-Victorian Generation*, p. 612.
[173] Hanham, *Elections and Party Management*, p. 226.
[174] Smith, *Disraelian Conservatism*, p. 198.

Tory vision or enhanced party machine to win in 1874. He needed only for Gladstone to discard the mantle of Palmerston and to allow it to fall upon his shoulders. Gladstone always hated Palmerston's politics and was eager to break with all Palmerston stood for. In 1874 the ghost of the former Liberal leader exacted his revenge.

Chapter 5

GLADSTONE VERSUS DISRAELI
1874–1880

Outline of Events

'Power', Benjamin Disraeli lamented, 'it has come to me too late.'[1] He was fortunate that, at the age of 70, it came to him at all. Ironically, it was William Gladstone who made it possible as he disintegrated the Liberal coalition that had dominated politics since 1846. But Disraeli had played some part in his downfall, for with his 1872 speeches at the Crystal Palace and Manchester he had belatedly constructed a serviceable Conservative ideology for the politics of the wider electorate he had brought into being in 1867. The revived One Nation vision had two components: first, an association of the Conservatives with the idea of social reform, in contrast with the Liberal obsession with institutional tinkering, and second, a celebration of the British Empire, as opposed to Gladstone's embarrassed reserve upon colonial issues. These two themes ought to have provided matter enough for a Conservative government. Unfortunately, they were always more rhetorical than practical conceptions, and Disraeli entered office with no programme for either. This fact has fuelled two of the most controversial debates concerning his politics. Was Disraeli a social reformer, and was he ever really an imperialist? The answer to both questions is an equivocal one. Yes, Disraeli was content to see his government associated with social reform and imperial gestures, but this still this leaves the issue of how far Disraeli personally encouraged these developments as elements in a definite strategy of governance. In either case the matter is debatable, and it is hard to avoid the conclusion that the coherence of Tory policy in

---

[1] Quoted in St John, *Disraeli and the Art of Victorian Politics*, p. 143.

both these areas has owed more to the subsequent writings of friends and critics than to the thinking of Disraeli himself. In any case, the narrative of Disraeli's government was shaped more by external events. In 1876 the Eastern Question was reignited by the heavy-handed methods deployed by the Turks to suppress Balkan nationalism. While Disraeli sought to apply the Eastern policy he had learned from Lord Palmerston, the massacre of civilians in Bulgaria provoked a popular outcry that summoned Gladstone from retirement, thereby initiating an exercise in popular campaigning that was to set a new style in politics and, after four years of invective against Disraeli and all his works, carried Gladstone back to power in 1880 and returned Disraeli to the opposition benches (though this time, as Lord Beaconsfield, in the House of Lords). Adding traction to Gladstone's campaign was the series of mishaps in South Africa and Afghanistan that turned Empire from an asset to a liability for Disraeli. Within a year Disraeli was dead: yet Gladstone, it turned out, was more than capable of generating enough trouble by himself.

5.1   Was Disraeli a Serious Social Reformer?

In a Conservative publication of 1977 extolling the party's contribution to welfare reform, Margaret Thatcher wrote that '[p]ractically every measure of social amelioration passed through Parliament in the nineteenth century was passed by the Conservatives [...] And while its rivals concentrated solely on the propagation of unlimited economic competition – the so-called policy of *laissez-faire* – whatever the human cost to workers and their dependents, it was the Tories who, throughout the century, sought to mitigate the rigours and consequences of the Industrial Revolution.'[2] It is to Disraeli's 1874 administration that Conservatives most naturally point to substantiate her claim. Indeed, the publication's author, Charles Bellairs, argues that Disraeli made it one of the great objects of the Conservative party to 'elevate the condition of the People', that a leading feature of his Government was 'the attention given to practical social legislation', and that by its end 'enormous progress' had been achieved.[3] Is this view correct? Here we consider three questions: did Disraeli demonstrate a consistent interest in social reform; how significant were the reforms of 1874–80; and how important was Disraeli's contribution to the reform process?

---

[2] M. Thatcher, Foreword to C. E. Billairs, *Conservative Social and Industrial Reform* (1977), p. 7.
[3] Ibid., pp. 16–20.

Was Disraeli a committed social reformer?

Disraeli as a committed social reformer

From the late nineteenth century, authors extolling Disraeli's contribution to the Conservative tradition highlighted his social-reforming credentials and characterized them as part of a wider project to unite the working class behind aristocratic leadership in the guise of Tory Democracy.[4] Thus Walter Sichel, writing in 1904, claimed that Disraeli's 'sympathy with the labouring classes proved unceasing, and indeed was destined to carry many alleviating measures in the teeth of the Radical champions of capital some 30 years later.'[5]

> If one had to point to the definite measures of which he was proudest, it would [...] be to the unshowy and many-sided social, sanitary, and industrial reforms that ever engaged his heart [...] Disraeli waited long and patiently for the ripe moment [...] He was still true to the cause of 'Young England'.[6]

William Monypenny and George Earle Buckle affirmed the importance of social concern in Disraeli's Conservatism, describing 'the consolidation of the commonwealth at home by promoting the moral and physical improvement of the people and by welding all classes into an harmonious whole' as one of the ideas by which Disraeli's reputation will live.[7] The merit of this analysis is that it situated the social reforms of the 1874 Government within a narrative of Disraeli's career as a whole. Although, writes R. C. K. Ensor, Disraeli always 'cared sincerely for social reform', he was unable to advance its cause during the 1850s and 1860s since 'few, if any, of his followers in parliament supported him for its sake'.[8] It was only when he became prime minister that he was able to realize the agenda of his youth. 'Now was the moment', declares André Maurois, 'to put into action the ideas of *Coningsby* and *Sybil*. Law after law was passed: equality of obligations between employers and employed; enlargement of the rights of Trade Unions; reduction of the hours of work to fifty-six in the week; half-holidays on Saturday; and numerous sanitary laws.'[9] Although this interpretation of Disraeli's motivation has been widely

---

[4] Adelman, *Gladstone, Disraeli and Later Victorian Politics*, p. 16.
[5] Sichel, *Beaconsfield*, p. 49.
[6] Ibid., p. 167.
[7] Monypenny and Buckle, *Life of Disraeli*, II. p. 1,518.
[8] Ensor, *England: 1870–1914*, p. 31.
[9] Maurois, *Disraeli*, p. 261.

questioned, historians continue to speak of social reform as a defining feature of Disraelian Conservatism. Thus the generally sceptical R. W. Davis writes that

> Disraeli, with a consistency which is especially remarkable in him, had been not only one of the earliest proponents, but also one of the staunchest supporters of a policy of social reform throughout his career. It is the one area of politics in which his self-interested opportunism never seriously subordinated the warm and generous elements in his nature.[10]

Paul Smith too, while developing in 1967 an essentially qualified account of Disraeli's connection to social reform, acknowledges that he 'did more than anyone' to establish the 'tradition of Conservative social reform'.[11] He admits, also, that Disraeli in the 1840s had been 'deeply impressed with the dangers inherent in the abandonment of the working classes to the vicissitudes of an industrial society', and against the doctrines of political economists and Utilitarians he pitted the concept of an organic society 'ready to employ the force of government to promote the well-being of the masses'.[12] Through his 1872 speeches at Manchester and Crystal Palace he consecrated 'social reform as one of the abiding objects of the party'. In his later *Disraeli: A Brief Life*, Smith perceives an imperialist dimension in Disraeli's thinking. If Britain was to remain a great power, it could not do so with a population declining in number and bodily stature. 'An imperial destiny required an imperial breed, and the breeder must to some extent be the state.' As such, social reform complemented his vision of an 'organic' British society made up of mutually interdependent orders, all of which had a vested interest in the 'healthy functioning of the organism'.[13]

For historians emphasizing Disraeli's reformist credentials it is the measures of the 1874 Government that command attention. The year 1875 was, says Ensor,

> quite an *annus mirabilis* for useful domestic legislation. Ministers worked from half a dozen sides to redeem Disraeli's promises of social reform. His home secretary, Cross, sponsored a group of important measures – a Trade Union Act amending the Gladstonian Act of 1871 in a sense

---

[10] Davis, *Disraeli*, p. 173.
[11] Smith, *Disraelian Conservatism*, p. 4.
[12] Ibid., pp. 15–16.
[13] Smith, *Disraeli*, pp. 162, 166.

decidedly more favourable to the trade unions; an Artisans' Dwellings Act, which is one of the milestones in English legislation on the housing problem; and a Sale of Food and Drugs Act, which was the first really comprehensive measure on its subject [...] Even more epoch-making was the great Public Health Act of 1875 [...] *Sanitas sanitatum, omnia sanitas* had been the motto propounded by Disraeli in 1872. These admirable statutes proved [...] his own good faith [...] Certainly this first full session [...] drove a remarkable number of nails into *laisser-faire's* coffin.[14]

Questioning Disraeli's social reform credentials

This view of Disraeli's career has been robustly contested, notably by Smith, who, in his *Disraelian Conservatism and Social Reform*, argued that his interest in social reform was shallow and largely opportunistic. As Paul Adelman reflects, what 'Dr Smith has shown [...] is how little of real substance there is in the popular view of Disraeli as an apostle of social reform'. In practice all Disraeli provided for his party 'were the verbal trappings of reform'.[15] Parry calls the idea that Disraeli was a social reformer a 'myth': he referred to social reform at Manchester to appease Conservative MPs sitting for northern boroughs; he took small interest in the details of such measures; and he made no reference to the social reforms in his 1880 election manifesto.[16] What gave the myth wings was the Conservatives later needed to attract the lower classes by promoting the idea that Disraeli was 'a man of the people, who had the insight to appreciate the merits of a policy of imperial consolidation and social reform'.[17] In reality, observes John Vincent, Disraeli was less actively concerned with social policy than many of his colleagues: 'It is difficult to find a Conservative who was not more active than Disraeli in some form of voluntary social work.'[18] While Ian Machin believes that he did have a humanitarian 'appreciation of the need for reforms', this was always subordinated to 'political expediency'. Hence his support for social measures was 'sporadic and inconsistent'.[19]

According to this sceptical reading, Disraeli took up social issues in the 1840s chiefly as a means to taunt Sir Robert Peel. Smith talks of 'Disraeli's

---

[14] Ensor, *England: 1870–1914*, p. 36.
[15] Adelman, *Gladstone, Disraeli and Later Victorian Politics*, p. 17.
[16] Parry, *Benjamin Disraeli*, p. 91.
[17] Ibid., p. 121.
[18] Vincent, *Disraeli*, p. 53.
[19] Machin, *Disraeli*, p. 7.

popular Toryism' as being 'an idea, an attitude, not a policy', and even this was dropped after 1846 when with Peel's defeat it became a liability.[20] His attachment to his own ideas was 'shallow enough': he opposed the 1848 Public Health Act because of its centralizing tendencies, and voted against an 1850 plan for government inspection of coal mines out of his friendship with Lord Londonderry. 'If Disraeli's professions of social concern were heartfelt, he should have supported this measure, vital to the welfare of the miners.'[21] David Roberts is still more critical. During Peel's ministry, when he might have been pushing social reforms, he 'was busier writing of these ideals in his novels [...] He showed little practical interest in the construction of a benevolent state.'[22]

> The voting record of the author of *Sybil* was hardly distinguished by a compassion for the working class. He voted against the Education Order of 1839, against cheap bread in 1846, against the Public Health Act of 1848, against the Mining Act of 1850, and against the General Board of Health Act in 1854 [...] His single speech for the ten hour factory bill was the only time he spoke for any reform designed to better the condition of the working classes.[23]

Disraeli was basically the spokesman for the landed squires and extolled the virtues of a traditional social hierarchy led by the aristocracy, placing a premium upon social provision by an elite conscious of its obligations to the poor. Hence, while prepared to highlight the sufferings of the working class, his 'fear of a strong central bureaucracy and his alliance with [...] a propertied aristocracy persuaded him to express his paternalism in appeals for rejuvenation of national character and not in mining inspectors and boards of health'.[24]

The tenuous nature of Disraeli's reforming commitment was revealed during the 1850s and 1860s when, observes Smith, 'very little effort was made to use social questions as a means to cultivate working class support'.[25] The economy was prospering, social tensions easing and the Tory party leadership was reviving Peel's strategy of cultivating 'urban

[20] Smith, *Disraelian Conservatism*, pp. 17–18.
[21] Ibid. See also Machin, *Disraeli*, p. 7.
[22] D. Roberts, 'Tory Paternalism and Social Reform in Early Victorian England', *American Historical Review*, Vol. 63 (1958), p. 331.
[23] Ibid., p. 332.
[24] Ibid., p. 336.
[25] Smith, *Disraelian Conservatism*, p. 18.

middle-class support'. By the 1860s the Tories 'had no shadow of a social policy' and accepted the free trade orthodoxy of political economy.[26] Disraeli's reversion to social reform discourse in the early 1870s was, says Smith, a response to the 1867 Reform Act. Even then he was slow to react because the electoral logic was running more strongly the other way as middle-class voters, alarmed at the prospect of radical reforms, turned to the Tories as a safe haven, thereby placing 'severe constraints on the party's approach to the working man'.[27] Only in 1872 did Disraeli manage to square social reform with the need to reassure propertied supporters by arguing that the Tory party was the party of all classes, and that the working class were loyal to the established institutions. 'The progressive Conservatism of Peel fused at last with the romantic Toryism of Young England – such was the formula that was to enable the party to reconcile the assimilation of the apprehensive middle class with the cultivation of the urban working man.'[28]

But the degree to which this message represented a genuine shift toward a reformist policy has been questioned. As Edgar Feuchtwanger notes, for Disraeli 'rhetoric and image making' were at least as important as practical proposals and he offered no specifics.[29] Even rhetorically there were limitations. Ian St John observes that references to social reform accounted for only four percent of the Manchester speech, while Smith believes that the imperialism he proclaimed at the same time was a more potent influence.[30] Thus, summarizes Smith, the 'record of 1872–3 shows how poorly the Conservative party responded to the call to patronise social reform which Disraeli had issued at Manchester and the Crystal Palace [...] No concerted attempt was made to appeal to the working-class electorate on a social reform platform.'[31] As ever, electoral considerations were uppermost. With the middle class increasingly alienated by Gladstone's restless reformism and fearing radicals like Joseph Chamberlain, 'the main concern of Conservatives was to avoid anything which might check the swing towards them. This was not the time for challenging policies of social improvement.'[32]

---

[26] Ibid., pp. 30, 33.

[27] Ibid., pp. 98, 100.

[28] Ibid., p. 102.

[29] Feuchtwanger, *Disraeli*, pp. 158, 161.

[30] St John, *Disraeli and the Art of Victorian Politics*, p. 133; Smith, *Disraelian Conservatism*, p. 322.

[31] Ibid., p. 181.

[32] Ibid., p. 183.

How significant were the government's social reforms?

The reforms as an epoch in legislation

Conservative apologists believed that through measures like the Artisans Dwellings Act and Public Health Act, Disraeli redeemed the promises of his 1872 speeches and made a real difference to the life of the working class. John Gorst, Disraeli's party organizer, expounded this view as part of his attempt to validate the existence of a Tory Democratic tradition of which he was the heir. The 'Parliament of 1874', he wrote, 'was rich in measures for promoting the good of the working class.'[33] Monypenny and Buckle lent authority to this interpretation. 'Social reform [...] honourably distinguished all the domestic legislation of the Government.'[34] Disraeli's great ministry

> took the practical pressing needs of the working population one by one, and found a remedy for them, without inflicting hardship on any other class, or affecting our historical institutions in any way, save to strengthen their hold on popular affections [...] The aspirations of *Sybil* and 'Young England', the doctrines in which Disraeli had 'educated' his party for thirty years, the principles laid down in the great speeches of 1872, were translated into legislative form; it was Tory Democracy in action.[35]

Writing in 1913, under a Liberal government similarly associated with social reform measures, the Conservative J. A. R. Marriott was keen to establish Disraeli's reforming credentials.

> The legislative and administrative achievements of the first three years of the Disraeli Government generously fulfilled [...] the general spirit of the programme laid before the electorate by the Tory leader [...] It is impossible to deny that with the author of *Sybil* social reform was a matter of long-standing conviction and genuine enthusiasm.[36]

Harold Beeley, in 1936, similarly drew a link between Young England and the reforms of the 1870s. 'The dreams of Young England, however, were not entirely faded, and he chose as his Home Secretary an ardent social reformer,

---

[33] Gorst, *Times*, 6 February 1907.
[34] Monypenny and Buckle, *Life of Disraeli*, II. p. 651.
[35] Ibid., pp. 708–9.
[36] Marriott, *England Since Waterloo*, pp. 444–45, 447.

R. A. Cross. His work […] forms the most distinctive landmark in that transition from *laissez-faire* to paternalism which was beginning to affect the legislation of both parties.'[37]

While historians, especially since Smith, have tended to reject the idea that the reforms represented a distinctly Disraelian approach to social policy, they still acknowledge that striking results were achieved. Smith himself talks of the 1875 session as witnessing a 'galaxy' of social reforms. 'It was perhaps the first time in British history that Parliament had been called upon to devote the great bulk of its energies to questions concerning the condition of the people, and it was an impressive earnest of the will of Disraeli's government to show that Conservatism could satisfy the needs of the working population.'[38] It was a 'corpus of legislation unparalleled until the ministries of 1905 and 1945'.[39]

Questioning the significance of the reforms

However the status of the 1874 Government as a social-reforming administration has been questioned on a number of levels. First, the very notion that social reform was a conspicuous aspect of the Government's work has been doubted. At the time, argues Richard Shannon, social reform was merely seen to be 'a kind of political bromide, a salutary contrast to Gladstone's alarms and excursions'. It was only when the Tory party needed a social-reforming narrative for populist reasons that publications like the 1891 *Conservative Legislation for the Working Classes* lauded the legislation passed by Disraeli's Government.[40] Only in retrospect, says Vincent, do 'the social reforms of 1875 stand out. They did not stand out at the time. They were seen more as an absence of conventional politics than as a policy that defined a party.'[41] Few contemporaries would have demurred from Peter Clayden's characterization of the 1875 session as 'one of the dullest on record'. It was 'a year of little schemes. It showed conclusively that the Government could not do anything great.'[42]

Second, it is argued that the reforms were unexceptional and owed more to wider social and political forces than any distinctly Conservative agenda. Lewis Apjohn, a popular historian of Liberal sympathies writing in the 1880s, spoke of a 'half-hearted spirit of reform' and a 'virtual mockery of claims

---

[37] Beeley, *Gladstone*, pp. 105–6.
[38] Smith, *Disraelian Conservatism*, p. 218.
[39] Smith, *Disraeli*, pp. 179–80; Smith, *Disraelian Conservatism*, p. 261.
[40] Shannon, *Age of Disraeli*, pp. 211–12.
[41] Vincent, *Disraeli*, p. 11.
[42] Clayden, *England under Lord Beaconsfield*, pp. 124, 138.

nominally conceded'.[43] In his *A History of Our Own Times*, the Irish MP Justin McCarthy talked of the Government's 'not usually very comprehensive or drastic schemes' which were more in the nature of tinkering. He considered them fatally compromised by their permissive nature: '[i]t seemed to be a clever stroke of management to introduce a measure professedly for the removal of some inequality or other grievance, and then make it permissive and allow the parties concerned to contract themselves out of it.'[44] These deficiencies he attributed to the fact that Disraeli 'was not supposed to have any warm personal interest in prosaic measures of domestic legislation'.[45] This scepticism finds an echo among later historians. According to Theodore Hoppen, 'behind the much-trumpeted social reforms of the Conservative government of 1874–80 lay a series of distinctly modest and permissive acts of a type neither very substantial nor very new'.[46] Little of the legislation passed, writes Vincent, 'made any practical difference. Some [...] was simply a matter of consolidating existing laws, as with the Public Health Act. Most of it was permissive, leaving it to local authorities to choose whether to take any action. Very little of it involved the spending of Exchequer funds. The legislation of the 1870s was not a move towards a collectivist state.'[47]

The fact that many of the reforms were already under consideration, or built upon previous legislation, is widely noted. Clayden describes the Artisans Dwelling Bill as 'a Liberal legacy', resuscitating Torrens measure of 1866.[48] The Friendly Societies Bill 'was a mild and timid result of the long inquiry which the previous Government had carried on', and only compelled societies to publish more information about themselves. 'The Public Health Bill, which contained not a single new clause [...] was a mere consolidation of existing Acts.'[49] Paul Smith observes that the Rivers Pollution Act emerged out of investigations by a Royal Commission, and although making the pollution of rivers an offence, no prosecutions of factories or mines were to be undertaken without the approval of the Local Government Board. 'The limited scope and vigour of the measures of 1875–6 reflected the unwillingness of ministers to push central intervention and control too far, or to deal too stringently with vested interests.'[50] It 'has to be appreciated', writes T. A. Jenkins, 'that

---

[43] L. Apjohn, *The Earl of Beaconsfield* (1884), p. 246.
[44] McCarthy, *History of Our Own Times*, IV. p. 424.
[45] Ibid., p. 430.
[46] Hoppen, *Mid-Victorian Generation*, p. 99.
[47] Vincent, *Disraeli*, p. 54.
[48] Clayden, *England under Lord Beaconsfield*, p. 125.
[49] Ibid., p. 137.
[50] Smith, *Disraelian Conservatism*, p. 226.

most of their Bills were really the product of the administrative machine and might just have easily have been implemented by another government.'[51]

Unsurprisingly, therefore, most historians have rejected the idea propagated by the likes of A. V. Dicey that the reforms expressed a Conservative anti-laissez-faire ideology. Rather, they were pragmatic and bore no imprint of a coherent programme. Robert Blake dwelt upon this point in his 1966 biography. While the Government's social measures constituted 'the biggest instalment of social reform passed by any one government in the nineteenth century', it is 'an exaggeration to regard them as the product of a fundamentally different political philosophy from that of the Liberals, or to see in them the fulfilment of some concept of paternalistic Tory democracy which had been adumbrated by Disraeli in opposition to Peel during the 1840s'. There was no shift from laissez-faire to state intervention, and 'one is struck by the cautious attitude behind the Conservative social reforms'.[52] It was Smith's study, published the following year, that developed this interpretation most thoroughly.

> Their work cannot […] be viewed as the embodiment of any Conservative social 'policy'. It was empirical, piecemeal reform, dealing with problems as and when they were pushed into prominence by their inherent size and urgency, by agitation and the pressure of public opinion, by investigation and discussion, and by the exigencies of party politics […] Most of what Disraeli's ministers did […] had been long in preparation in the corridors of other minds, and most of it would probably have found its way on to the statute book under any government.[53]

Thus, the Artisans Dwellings Act emerged out of a report by the Charity Organization Society calling upon municipal councils to improve housing by compulsorily purchasing slum properties, and while the Act asserted the state's right to intervene to improve social conditions, it was, with its stress on removing the obstacles to enterprise, in many ways a liberal measure. 'There is', writes Smith, 'no better illustration of the confused and nervous empiricism which lay at the heart of Disraelian social reform.'[54]

Smith's analysis shaped the consensus among historians regarding the significance of Disraeli's reforms. For Bruce Coleman, the most remarkable step was the labour legislation of 1875, but this 'reflected […] a desire to forestall a bid for trade-union favour which was gathering support on the

---

[51] Jenkins, *Disraeli and Victorian Conservatism*, p. 115.
[52] Blake, *Disraeli*, pp. 553–54.
[53] Ibid., pp. 257–59.
[54] Ibid., pp. 222–23.

Liberal benches'.[55] Certainly the measures did not represent 'a theoretical, even romantic, rejection of free-market economics of the kind some of the fringe Tory writers had preached earlier in the century'. Soon the Government had exhausted the interest of ministers and supporters. 'In 1880 the Tories were not a social reform party and indeed they had never been one.'[56] Angus Hawkins considers the idea that the social reforms represented the fulfilment of Disraeli's One Nation ideology an unconvincing 'retrospective' reading.

> With the help of hindsight it was easy to give a false coherence and doctrinal impetus to these social reforms. Disraeli's interest in their details had been slight. No strong collectivist commitment saw him requiring a broad package of social reforms from ministers.[57]

Social legislation was seen as sober business attending to matters of practical utility and did not mark a collectivist departure from the principles of political economy.[58] Indeed, as Hoppen observes, 'economic orthodoxies had now come to encase the Tory heart almost as firmly as the Liberal.'[59] T. A. Jenkins agrees:

> Certainly, there was to be no question of the Conservatives embarking on a systematic exercise in paternalistic social reform, inspired by the sort of 'One Nation' principles that Disraeli had laid down in his Young England days. Disraeli may still occasionally have used language reminiscent of his earlier views [...] but in reality his government's response to such matters was influenced by the prevailing doctrines of political economy.[60]

Feuchtwanger is equally frank, suggesting that the Conservative social reform legislation 'could equally well have been passed by Liberal governments, was not the result of an ideology originally proclaimed in the trilogy of novels and owed little to the initiative of the Prime Minister'.[61]

Most historians argue that the class composition of the party precluded any real prospect of pursuing a working-class reform agenda. The Conservatives had traditionally opposed measures that would increase the power of central

---

[55] Coleman, *Conservatism and the Conservative Party*, p. 147.
[56] Ibid., pp. 148, 159.
[57] Hawkins, *British Party Politics*, p. 193.
[58] Ibid., p. 194.
[59] Hoppen, *Mid-Victorian Generation*, p. 614.
[60] Jenkins, *Disraeli and Victorian Conservatism*, p. 112.
[61] Feuchtwanger, *Disraeli*, p. 216.

government, and by the 1870s ratepayers, bemoaning the increases in tax burdens brought by the Liberals' modest reforms, were in no mood to see the Conservatives increase these impositions. The only way to resolve the contradiction was to increase central government grants to local councils, but, remarks Feuchtwanger, 'Disraeli had no wish to disturb the fiscal compact of mid-Victorian society, which had to square the middle-class desire for low direct taxes, the working class pressure for removal of the remaining imposts on consumption and the sensitivity of the landed interest to the rate burden.'[62] Thus while the Conservative chancellor Stafford Northcote's first budget provided for £1.25 million in increased annual subsidies to local councils, he also cut income tax to 2d and abolished the sugar duty. 'Conservative backbenchers', comments Smith, 'continued to look jealously at any proposal tending to increase the rates.'[63] Also, as Vincent observes, Disraeli's timing was unlucky. Taking office at the commencement of the 'Great Depression', with declining revenues, the mood of the times was against doing anything that would increase local taxation. 'This virtually ruled out a social programme.'[64]

Further militating against a Conservative reform programme was the accelerating shift of middle-class voters from the Liberals to the Tories. These new middle-class allies had no wish to see an 'active social reform programme aimed at the working class', and hence there 'could be no question of their exploiting social issues in the spirit of the paternalist and radical Toryism of the 'thirties and 'forties'. Very few Tories had any interest in Tory Democracy, and in 'these circumstances, there was no possibility of the party's going far along the "Disraelian" road of popular appeal and social reform'.[65]

Reform was an uncontroversial programme to distract from lack of political reform

In recent years historians have, under the impact of Peter Ghosh's 1987 article 'Style and Substance in Disraelian Social Reform', increasingly questioned whether the social reforms of the 1870s were in fact radical or ever intended to be such. On the contrary, says Ghosh, Disraeli's motive for bringing forward social reform was to provide a less disturbing alternative to

---

[62] Ibid., p. 168.
[63] Jenkins, *Disraeli and Victorian Conservatism*, p. 112; Smith, *Disraelian Conservatism*, p. 207.
[64] Vincent, *Disraeli*, pp. 10, 52–53.
[65] Smith, *Disraelian Conservatism*, pp. 320–1.

the political reforms advocated by Liberals and Radicals for, quite simply, 'the more energy and attention devoted to the anodyne of social concern, the less there remained for radical, organic innovation in political institutions'.[66] Smith developed this theme in his *Disraeli*, arguing that the Government's social measures were 'relatively uncontroversial', being bipartisan and designed to turn people away from the restless pursuit of institutional change.[67] They had little relationship to the speeches of 1872, and were effectively a 'means for ministers to make themselves useful in the vast spaces of parliamentary time freed by the disappearance of the institutional innovations and Irish preoccupations of the previous ministry'.[68]

The reforming impetus soon expired

Those questioning the significance of the social reforms make much of the fact that they were largely concentrated to 1875. By 1876, says Smith, the Government had largely 'shot its bolt in the sphere of domestic reform'. '*Sanitas sanitatum* was little in evidence in the last years of the Beaconsfield ministry.'[69] Why was this? Smith supplies several competing reasons. At one point he attributes it to Disraeli's lack of interest. 'The Disraelian drive for social reform, never very powerful or coherent [...] had slackened and disintegrated. Its protagonist had lost interest.'[70] Any remaining enthusiasm was soon eclipsed by the Balkans crisis which, after 1878, was replaced by imperial issues. T. A. Jenkins concurs, believing that the Conservatives were diverted from social reform to the more high-profile matters of foreign and imperial policy.[71] However, Smith also identifies a more dialectical mechanism. Social reform, he observes, coincided with an economic slowdown, and there arose a view that the social reforms had brought this about by interfering with the market mechanism and placing tax burdens on property.[72] Adelman, however, sees Disraeli's actions as more strategic, arguing that he turned from social to imperial matters so as to escape from the dilemmas created by the pressure to appeal to the contradictory demands of working and middle-class voters. Disraeli's purchase of the Suez Canal shares, his belligerence toward Russia, and his 'forward' policies in Afghanistan and South Africa in 1879, were 'an attempt to escape from the internal contradictions of Conservative domestic policy [...] by a brilliant display abroad'.[73]

---

[66] P. R. Ghosh, 'Style and Substance in Disraelian Social Reform, c. 1860–80', in P. J. Waller (ed.), *Politics and Social Change in Modern Britain* (1987), p. 60.

[67] Smith, *Disraelian Conservatism*, p. 201; Smith, *Disraeli*, pp. 166–67.

[68] Ibid., p. 213.

[69] Smith, *Disraelian Conservatism*, pp. 266, 289.

[70] Ibid., p. 299.

[71] Jenkins, *Disraeli and Victorian Conservatism*, pp. 116–17.

[72] Smith, *Disraelian Conservatism*, pp. 267, 269.

How important was Disraeli's contribution to the government's reforming agenda?

Conservative accounts depict Disraeli as educating a reluctant Tory party in the need to tackle social problems and ensuring that the Government devoted time to the process. Is this characterization justified? Several writers are sceptical, agreeing with Blake that 'it would be wrong to pitch Disraeli's claims too high as the author of this valuable legislation'.[74] It is argued, first, that Disraeli entered government with no coherent reform programme. Smith makes much of this point:

> The great Conservative champion of social reform and the reconciliation of classes came into office in 1874 without a single concrete proposal in his head [...] Not only was Disraeli without a definite policy in 1874, he was virtually incapable of constructing one.[75]

His decision to remove the President of the Local Government Board from the Cabinet 'suggested that the emphasis Disraeli had laid in 1872 on the importance of public health had been less than heartfelt'.[76] Smith's assessment soon found a secure place within textbooks. Thus Beales in his 1969 history of Victorian England wrote that 'Disraeli was totally lacking in the capacity to devise detailed schemes of legislation', while more recently Machin has contended that, while Disraeli saw that the Conservatives needed reform measures in an increasingly populist age, 'he was not the man to draft and issue blueprints [...] He had no conception of a coherent, progressive programme of reforms, and the social bills of his Governments were introduced empirically to deal with individual problems.'[77]

Second, it is claimed that the reforms enacted were the work of Disraeli's Cabinet colleagues, and in particular his home secretary, Richard Cross. Disraeli's role, says Smith, was to dream dreams, 'not to implement them'. He had conceived the vision of a national Toryism, but it was 'left to his subordinates to produce measures which should demonstrate the worth of his past professions'.[78] Numerous commentators endorse this interpretation. Vincent writes that, except at the level of 'broad strategy and parliamentary

---

[73] Adelman, *Gladstone, Disraeli, and Later Victorian Politics*, p. 19.
[74] Blake, *Disraeli*, p. 555.
[75] Smith, *Disraeli*, p. 199.
[76] Smith, *Disraelian Conservatism*, p. 196.
[77] Beales, *From Castlereagh to Gladstone*, p. 261; Machin, *Disraeli*, p. 132.

helmsmanship', what occurred 'had little directly to do with Disraeli'.[79] Richard Weeks remarks that the 'important social reform measures of his second administration were not specifically called for by Disraeli, though he was happy to agree to the proposals of his cabinet colleagues'.[80] Hoppen largely paraphrases Smith:

> Not that there was anything like a Conservative social programme. Disraeli, not by nature a legislative politician at all, simply left relevant ministers to proceed as the need arose. They in turn produced a series of haphazard bills, the timing and contents of which were dictated more by circumstance than anything else.[81]

On the rare occasions, says Coleman, when Disraeli intervened on questions of domestic legislation, electoral considerations were his concern.[82] This was notably the case over trade union reform, but even then, comments Feuchtwanger, his 'part in it was slight and he sometimes dozed when it was being discussed in cabinet'.[83] Why was this? Partly, says Adelman, it had to do with Disraeli – he was old, tired and 'lacked the interest in, or grasp of, administrative detail so essential for the social reformer'. But the fact was, writes Blake, that 'social reform was not the principal or even a leading secondary preoccupation of Disraeli'.[84] He was far more interested in foreign policy and after 1876, reflects Adelman, he found in empire 'ideas more in harmony with his flamboyant imagination'.[85]

Yet these more jaundiced interpretations have not gone unchallenged. To the point that Disraeli lacked a plan of reform, Jenkins responds that it was not accepted practice by party leaders to set out policy commitments in the run-up to elections. Only a 'totally inexperienced Minister like R. A. Cross […] could have seriously expected his leader's mind to be full of matured policies'.[86] It was not, says Vincent, the job of Conservative leaders to legislate: we should not judge Disraeli by Liberal criteria.[87] Nor, writes Feuchtwanger, should we judge by the light of later years. Cross expressed his disappointment at

[78] Smith, *Disraelian Conservatism*, p. 200.
[79] Vincent, *Disraeli*, pp. 12, 54.
[80] R. G. Weeks, 'Disraeli as Political Egoist: A Literary and Historical Investigation', *Journal of British Studies*, Vol. 28 (1989), p. 409.
[81] Hoppen, *Mid-Victorian Generation*, p. 614.
[82] Coleman, *Conservatism and the Conservative Party*, p. 150.
[83] Feuchtwanger, *Disraeli*, p. 172.
[84] Blake, *Disraeli*, p. 556.
[85] Adelman, *Gladstone, Disraeli and Later Victorian Politics*, p. 17.
[86] Jenkins, *Disraeli and Victorian Conservatism*, pp. 110–11.

Disraeli's lack of reforming ideas 30 years later 'when perspectives had greatly changed. What could broadly be called welfare legislation [...] had by then assumed an importance which they did not have in 1874.'[88] As to Disraeli's lack of personal involvement – this too, argues Hawkins, misunderstands his distinctive contribution:

> Disraeli's great achievement was to provide a rhetorical context for the Acts of 1875–6. Disraeli's genius lay in the use of words. His speeches of 1872–3 established the Conservatives as a national party with a positive anti-Liberal message [...] His language gave wider meaning to the substantive detail of others.[89]

It was, acknowledges Blake, Disraeli who 'had emphasised that social rather than political reform would be the Conservative policy'.[90] The legislation of 1875, admits Smith, 'flowed naturally from the policy guidelines' laid down in 1872: Disraeli's 'role as prime minister was to set the course and leave the departmental ministers to settle details'.[91] And here, what is important, argues Ghosh, is that Disraeli was determined that a 'programme of "necessary and adequate" social measures' be carried out. While the particular measures were the responsibility of departmental ministers, 'the size and direction of the whole programme was in the Premier's hands'.[92] Accordingly, the 1875 session recorded 'one of Disraeli's most untypical triumphs – the execution according to timetable of his pledge to legislate *en masse* on social topics'.[93]

> What made the social legislation of 1875 remarkable was not its detailed origins, which were technical, bipartisan, and conventional, but a series of political factors – advance pledges, the focusing of legislative strategy, the management of Parliament, and the presentation of the whole.[94]

Monypenny and Buckle point out that Disraeli always favoured a system of ministerial devolution, and this was more necessary now his strength was impaired. Even so, he took a close interest in social reform measures: 'the carrying into effect of the programme of social policy outlined in 1872 was not less his work than

---

[87] Vincent, *Disraeli*, p. 54.
[88] Feuchtwanger, *Disraeli*, p. 171.
[89] Hawkins, *British Party Politics*, pp. 194–95.
[90] Blake, *Disraeli*, p. 555.
[91] Smith, *Disraeli*, pp. 179–80.
[92] Ghosh, 'Style and Substance in Disraelian Social Reform', pp. 72–73.
[93] Ibid., p. 73.
[94] Ibid., pp. 76–77.

the programme itself'.[95] Davis agrees that, although Cross 'drew up the measures, they were [...] largely inspired by Disraeli's earlier utterances'. Even when they were not, Disraeli backed Cross to the hilt. 'The credit which he has received for the government's social legislation is not, therefore, really misplaced.'[96] Indeed, Smith describes Cross's elevation to the Home Office as indicative of Disraeli's realization that 'labour questions would become pressing'.[97]

Above all, it is contended that there was nothing inevitable about a Conservative social reform programme. As Davis points out, urban sanitary reform had little relevance to the majority of Conservatives who sat for county or market town seats.[98] If one person deserves credit for pushing the Conservatives into reforms they found uncongenial it is Disraeli. Thus, while Blake was among the first of recent historians to re-evaluate Disraeli's relationship to the reforms of 1874–76, he acknowledges that 'Disraeli was at the head of the administration that brought this about, and he encouraged the policy [...] He deserves his share of the credit.'[99] Similarly Smith believes that Disraeli's 'general approval of the measures which his colleagues devised was vital to the development of the ministry's reforming effort'.[100] It was owing to his reforming impetus, concludes Feuchtwanger, that the Conservative party 'was not tarred with the brush of blind reaction'.[101]

Conclusion

In assessing the significance of the Conservative social reforms it is necessary to set them in their appropriate context. Just as we must avoid the temptation to read back into the reforms the origins of the twentieth-century welfare state, so we must resist seeing them as the culmination of a tradition of Disraelian Conservatism stretching back to Young England in the 1840s. The work of Blake and Smith in the 1960s challenged earlier interpretations associated with the likes of Monypenny and Buckle and Sichel, to the effect that Disraeli had a coherent ideology of the need to subject markets to regulation that bore fruit in the reforms of 1874–76. Disraeli had no such ideology and for most of his career devoted little thought to the social needs of the working class. When he did talk the language of social concern, as he

---

[95] Monypenny and Buckle, *Life of Disraeli*, II. pp. 710–11.
[96] Davis, *Disraeli*, p. 175.
[97] Smith, *Disraelian Conservatism*, p. 195.
[98] Davis, *Disraeli*, p. 178.
[99] Blake, *Disraeli*, p. 556.
[100] Smith, *Disraelian Conservatism*, p. 322.
[101] Feuchtwanger, *Disraeli*, p. 173.

did in the mid-1840s and the early 1870s, it was for political reasons, whether to appeal, as Smith suggests, to the enlarged working-class electorate, or, as Ghosh believes, to provide the House of Commons with uncontentious tasks to substitute for the institutional change he hated. Disraeli's rhetoric did not mean that the Conservatives had abandoned their commitment to a small central government or a free market economy.

Yet it does not follow that the reforms were insignificant. It is generally recognized that they *did* constitute the most sustained attempt to legislate on social matters of the nineteenth century. The reforms also represented, as St John argues, an acceptance of the fact that the market mechanism was ill-suited for dealing with the negative externalities generated by economic growth. The mid-Victorian economy had expanded vigorously since the 1840s, but this only exacerbated the problems of urban living. Laissez-faire was not enough, and Disraeli was the first leading politician to recognize this. His rhetoric of social cohesion and imperial strength reconciled Conservative backbenchers to a type of legislative intervention they were prejudiced against, and he installed the men who would make it happen. Most of the reforms would have happened anyway. But they would not have happened so soon had they not served the political purposes of Disraeli.

5.2   How Far Was Disraeli an Imperialist?

The debate surrounding Disraeli's 'imperialism' mirrors that concerning his social reform credentials. Was Disraeli always an imperialist, or did he become one in the early 1870s? Was Disraeli a convinced imperialist during his second administration, or did he attach more importance to the rhetoric of Empire, leaving any shaping of the imperial agenda to others?

Was Disraeli always an imperialist?

That Disraeli's commitment to Empire has been questioned owes much to remarks by him during the 1850s and 1860s suggesting that he regarded the colonies as burdensome. 'These wretched colonies', he remarked to Lord Derby in 1852, 'will all be independent, too, in a few years, and are a millstone around our neck', while in 1866 he asked, 'What is the use of these colonial deadweights, which *we do not govern*?'[102] A number of writers have accordingly argued that Disraeli shared (with Gladstone) the prevalent mid-nineteenth-century view that the white settler communities would

---

[102] Quoted in C. C. Eldridge, *England's Mission: The Imperial Idea in the Age of Gladstone and Disraeli* (1973), p. 178. Italics in the original.

follow the United States toward independence, and that the Empire rested upon shared values and little more. Thus even Stanley Stembridge, who argues that Disraeli attached consistent importance to the Empire, admits that the Tory government of 1852 did nothing to consolidate the Empire, establishing self-governing institutions in New Zealand and relinquishing British claims to the unused wastelands. He admits, too, that Disraeli shared Gladstone's belief that self-governing colonies should be responsible for their own defence.[103] Monypenny and Buckle endorse this point: Disraeli believed that a 'colony that repudiated any interference from home with her local government should [...] pay for her own local defence'.[104] In 1866 he advocated that British troops be withdrawn from Canada, while in 1865 Disraeli stated that Britain's connection with Canada would remain 'until that mature hour when we shall lose our dependency but gain a permanent ally'.[105] To speak so casually about the ending of Britain's formal connection with Canada adds plausibility to the charge that his later championing of Empire was more tactical manoeuvre than authentic conviction.

Carl Bodelsen developed this interpretation in his 1924 *Studies in Mid-Victorian Imperialism*. 'Disraeli does not seem ever to have been deeply interested in the colonial question. In his political life before the Crystal Palace Speech the colonies had played an insignificant part, and even after 1872 he cannot be said to have done much to promote the unity of the Empire.' Before 1872 Disraeli believed 'that the unity of the Empire could not be maintained. That he also at one time thought that separation was not a matter of regret seems to appear from some of his letters.'[106] While Bodelsen concedes that the 'millstones' remark was a 'petulant outburst', it was 'not the sort of thing an Imperialist statesman could write'.[107] E. T. Raymond concurs that 'Disraeli had little of that enthusiasm for the colonies that was the mark of his successors'.[108] Blake writes that 'Disraeli's imperialism was a later development, and essentially concerned India, which appealed to something in his imagination in a sense that the "colonies" did not'.[109] Ghosh notes that for Disraeli in 'private the colonies were always deadweights'.[110] He attached priority to low government spending and recognized that the 'empire was a

---

[103] Stembridge, 'Disraeli and the Millstones', p. 132.
[104] Monypenny and Buckle, *Life of Disraeli*, II. p. 209.
[105] Quoted ibid., pp. 140–1.
[106] C. A. Bodelsen, *Studies in Mid-Victorian Imperialism* (1924), 121–22, 45–46.
[107] Ibid., p. 122.
[108] Raymond, *Disraeli*, p. 261.
[109] Blake, *Disraeli*, p. 455.
[110] P. R. Ghosh, 'Disraelian Conservatism: A Financial Approach', *English Historical Review*, Vol. 99 (1984), p. 286.

vast obligation and a source of material weakness'. If Disraeli was to realize his fiscal objectives 'an aggressive or forward policy was out of the question'.[111]

Can we surmise that Disraeli was pessimistic or even dismissive regarding the future of the Empire? Stembridge rejects this, arguing that Disraeli supported the Empire throughout his career. He refers to Disraeli's 1833 reference to 'our great Colonial Empire', his 1840 hope that 'the national character may yet save the Empire' from Whig attacks, and his pressing upon Lord Derby the idea of a system of colonial tariff preference and colonial representation in parliament.[112] Besides, Stembridge points out that Disraeli's 'millstone' remarks were both made when he was chancellor of the exchequer and under great pressure to balance the books, and that both related to the North American colonies and not the dependent Empire, and especially India, which evoked so much of Disraeli's imperial sentiment. In this 1866 'deadweight' letter he had, in the first part of the sentence, written that '[p]ower and influence we should exercise in Asia; consequently in Eastern Europe.'[113]

Colin Eldridge endorses Stembridge's view regarding the consistency of Disraeli's interest in the Empire, agreeing that negative references to the colonies were 'nothing more than expressions of extreme annoyance' and that to 'interpret them as signalling a general aversion to empire is a gross misconception'.[114] Disraeli always spoke of the Empire as a prop and symbol of Britain's greatness, and whereas 'Little England' Liberals were willing to whittle the Empire away, the Conservatives should defend the colonial relationship.[115] In 1847 he suggested an Imperial customs union, and in 1851 that colonial MPs be admitted to Parliament. In the early 1850s he called for the Crown to assume responsibility for the government of India, something he helped to bring about in 1858 following the Mutiny, while in 1862, observes T. A. Jenkins, Disraeli attacked Liberal colonial policy in words similar to those of 1872, arguing that the Liberals had allowed self-government by the white settler communities without considering their commercial and military relations with Britain.[116] Unfortunately, says Eldridge, Derby had no interest in imperial consolidation, and Disraeli had to wait until 1872 to 'resurrect his ideas and put a long-considered strategy into operation'.[117] In his 1996

[111] Ibid.

[112] Stembridge, 'Disraeli and the Millstones', pp. 127–28.

[113] Quoted in Monypenny and Buckle, *Life of Disraeli*, II. p. 210.

[114] C. C. Eldridge, *Disraeli and the Rise of the New Imperialism* (1996), p. 25.

[115] Eldridge, *England's Mission*, pp. 16, 181.

[116] Eldridge, *Disraeli and the Rise of the New Imperialism*, p. 17; Jenkins, *Disraeli and Victorian Conservatism*, p. 74.

[117] Eldridge, *England's Mission*, pp. 14–15.

Disraeli and the Rise of the New Imperialism, Eldridge makes a strong case for Disraeli's consistent imperialism:

> For thirty years, Disraeli had shown a personal allegiance to the name of empire. In election addresses, pamphlets, letters and speeches, he talked incessantly of defending 'the glory of this country as a great empire'. Empire was both a cause and symbol of Britain's greatness [...] He wanted to make the consolidation of the empire a great Conservative principle [...] It seems perverse, therefore, that for over fifty years [...] Disraeli has been accused of being a separatist and an anti-imperialist.[118]

However a caveat should here be entered. Eldridge does not believe that Disraeli was interested in the Empire as such; rather, what interested him was the *role* Empire could play in 'Britain's position and prestige as a world power'. Disraeli saw the Empire as an emblem of British power – not as the embodiment of a mission to spread British civilization. As Jenkins sums up, Disraeli exhibited 'a consistent concern with the importance of maintaining the Empire, which he regarded as an essential pillar supporting Britain's status as a great power in the eyes of the world'.[119]

Was the Disraeli of the 1870s a New Imperialist?

A more intense debate concerns the extent to which Disraeli became a 'New Imperialist' in the 1870s and subscribed to the kind of expansionary and populist imperialism seen as characterizing the later nineteenth century. While appreciative accounts portray Disraeli as injecting the theme of empire into Victorian Conservative politics, more sceptical commentators doubt this narrative.

Disraeli the New Imperialist

Supporters of Empire regarded Disraeli as the first major politician to raise the standard of Empire as a central policy commitment. In his 1872 speeches he celebrated Britain's imperial connections and affirmed the Conservatives as the imperial party, and once in power he oversaw a government that was proactive in the sphere of imperial policy. Thus, Monypenny and Buckle argue that it is from Disraeli's Crystal Palace speech that 'the modern conception

---

[118] Eldridge, *Disraeli and the Rise of the New Imperialism*, pp. 23–25.
[119] Jenkins, *Disraeli and Victorian Conservatism*, p. 73.

of the British Empire largely takes its rise. In it Disraeli struck a chord that immediately echoed round the Colonies, India and the Dependencies; and the reverberation has never ceased.' The 'consolidation of our far-flung Empire and the assertion of its due influence on the world at large' was, along with social improvement, one of the two great themes of Disraeli's politics.[120] Raymond agrees that in 'his address to the faithful at the Crystal Palace Disraeli began to preach that gospel of Empire with which his name was to be chiefly connected'.[121] It was now, writes Beeley, that Disraeli 'decisively associated the Conservative party with imperialism'.[122] 'He loved', said the Irish-Liberal McCarthy in 1880, 'to feed his mind on gorgeous imperial fancies. It pleased him to think that England was […] an Asiatic Power, and that he was administering the affairs of a great Oriental Empire.'[123] Among more recent historians, Derek Beales endorses the idea that 1872 marked a turning point in Disraeli's politics. Having previously spoken of the colonies as 'a millstone round our neck', in 1872 he 'seized [for the Conservatives] the imperialist position'.[124] Ivan Kalmar goes so far as to claim that '[n]o one was a more potent imperialist than he, the expansionist prime minister of Britain at the Empire's "greatest" hour.'[125]

Support for the idea that Disraeli consciously embraced imperial politics comes from Freda Harcourt. However, she brings forward the dating of Disraeli's imperial moment to 1867, for it was then that he found in a campaign to release British captives held in Abyssinia that colonial enterprises could unite the nation in patriotic feeling. The context for Disraeli's 'new phase of imperialism' was, according to Harcourt, a kind of general crisis, consisting in a need to stabilize political and social hierarchies in the wake of the Second Reform Act, while overseas a series of events, such as the rise of Prussia and the building of the Suez Canal, were threatening Britain's Great Power status. Imperialism was Disraeli's response to this crisis: first, the patriotic appeal of foreign conquest unified the working class around established elites, and second, it evoked the idea that Britain was a global power. It was no accident, she says, that Disraeli asserted Britain's imperial interests only two weeks after Prussia's defeat of Austria, declaring that there 'is no power that interferes more than England. She interferes in Asia, because she is really more an

---

[120] Monypenny and Buckle, *Life of Disraeli*, II. pp. 535–36, 1, 518.
[121] Raymond, *Disraeli*, p. 287.
[122] Beeley, *Disraeli*, p. 103.
[123] McCarthy, *History of Our Own Times*, IV. p. 432.
[124] Beales, *From Castlereagh to Gladstone*, p. 282.
[125] I. D. Kalmar, 'Benjamin Disraeli, Romantic Orientalist', *Comparative Studies in Society and History*, Vol. 47 (2005), p. 348.

Asiatic power than a European. She interferes in Australia, in Africa, and in New Zealand.' Far from his reference to the North American colonies as 'deadweights' indicating an anti-empire mindset, Disraeli wanted to reduce Britain's exposure in the Americas so that she could concentrate on her Eastern empire, which determined her status in Europe.[126] Thus,

> the idea of enhancing Britain's imperial status was seized upon by Disraeli in 1866 as the obvious [...] way of confirming Britain's position as a great power in a rapidly changing world [...] In 1867 he sensed also that a show of aggression, if free from risk, would be popular, and [...] provide a foundation for national unity more compelling than any other that could be devised at the time. The new phase of imperialism he launched was signalled by the Abyssinian Expedition.[127]

The Abyssinian expedition thereby prepared the way for Disraeli's imperial speeches of 1872: 'Disraeli pre-empted empire in 1866 and empire linked with reform in 1872 as the national cause and the medium of integration of the Conservative party.'[128]

Whatever the precise dating, it is argued by those who see Disraeli as a pioneer of the New Imperialism that his 1874 government pursued an expansionist imperial agenda. To 'maintain and heighten' the government's 'imperial character was the special work at which he laboured as Minister', said Monypenny and Buckle.[129] Indeed, for Ensor 'the dazzle of imperialism' was 'soon outshining the sober glow of social reform'.[130] Eldridge relates how the 'government did seem to be especially active in the imperial sphere. There was the annexation of Fiji, the purchase of the Suez Canal shares, extension into the Gold Coast colony, the Queen being made Empress of India, the threat of war with Russia over the route to India, the occupation of Cyprus, the establishment of dual control over Egyptian finance, the annexation of the Transvaal, and expeditions against the Zulus and in Afghanistan.'[131] 'The first indication he gave to the world of the "new Imperialism",' writes Marriott, 'was the purchase of the Khedive's shares in the Suez Canal.' This was 'no isolated speculation, but a move in a coherent and preconcerted plan'.[132] Monypenny and Buckle concur, regarding his purchase of the Canal shares as

---

[126] Harcourt, 'Disraeli's Imperialism, 1866–68: A Question of Timing', p. 97.
[127] Ibid., pp. 88–89.
[128] Ibid., p. 107.
[129] Monypenny and Buckle, *Life of Disraeli*, II. p. 746.
[130] Ensor, *England: 1870–1914*, p. 31.
[131] Eldridge, *Disraeli and the Rise of the New Imperialism*, p. 41.
[132] Marriott, *England since Waterloo*, pp. 448–49.

the opportunity 'for which he had been waiting, of striking an effective and resounding blow for the security of our imperial communications, and for the strengthening of the British position in the whole Eastern world'.[133] Vincent lends support to this interpretation. 'The thought of founding another India in the Middle East was one of his motives in 1876–8. He cast a covetous eye on Constantinople. He acquired Cyprus. He set up a system of military consuls in Asia Minor. It was not an empire; but it was how empires start.'[134]

By his oratory, says Feuchtwanger, it was now perceived that Disraeli's orientation was 'imperialist' and 'forward'.[135] This, it is argued, was most visible in the case of India. Here Britain was fortunate, write Monypenny and Buckle, to have 'a Prime Minister of Oriental extraction and imagination', and they refer to his purchasing of a Suez Canal interest, his concern with the Russian threat to Afghanistan, his support for the Prince of Wales's tour of India, and the proclamation of the Queen as Empress of India.[136] Stembridge agrees that a new approach to Empire was most evident in India, where Disraeli 'put an end to the policy of "masterly inactivity"', advocating pushing British influence into Afghanistan 'in order to obtain a "scientific frontier"' with the Russian Empire.[137] To this end, says Raymond, he 'sent Lord Lytton to India with instructions to [...] bring Afghanistan within the orbit of British influence'.[138] In 1878, Lytton accordingly sent troops into Afghanistan and ordered them to enter Kabul – against the instructions of a British Cabinet alarmed at the prospect of war with Russia. At first Lytton's bold move appeared to have succeeded, but the mission was then massacred by members of the Afghan army and a further invasion was required to restore British authority. For Liberal critics and a number of historians these events bore the imprint of Disraeli's expansionary vision of empire. 'The Afghan war', writes Raymond, 'was one for which Beaconsfield had partly to thank himself [...] He was annoyed by, and yet he seemed to relish, the persistency of the Viceroy [...] he never contrived a sufficient halter to restrain him.'[139] Bradford echoes these words: 'Disraeli, sympathising with Lytton's view of the importance of maintaining British prestige in Indian eyes, had made little effort to restrain him.' He made 'a warlike speech' at the Lord Mayor's banquet talking of the need for a 'scientific frontier', and 'it was precisely

---

[133] Monypenny and Buckle, *Life of Disraeli*, II. p. 779.
[134] Vincent, *Disraeli*, p. 13.
[135] Feuchtwanger, *Disraeli*, p. 200.
[136] Monypenny and Buckle, *Life of Disraeli*, II. pp. 749, 875.
[137] Stembridge, 'Disraeli and the Millstones', p. 137.
[138] Raymond, *Disraeli*, pp. 344–45.
[139] Ibid.

by encouraging such attitudes that he was preparing the way for disaster'.[140] Feuchtwanger, too, acknowledges that as 'long as the "forward" policy in Afghanistan went well he had no objection'.[141] Eldridge lends his authority to this perspective. Lytton arrived in India with instructions to secure the Afghans' acceptance of a permanent British mission, and when he proceeded with his military mission against orders, Disraeli 'decided to uphold the actions of a rebellious Viceroy'.[142]

By thus celebrating and prioritizing the Empire, Disraeli is held to have done two things. First, according to Bodelsen he associated Empire with the jingoistic school of Imperialism 'which dwells on the spectacular aspect of the possession of colonies, which is prone to consider mere extent of territory an advantage in itself'.[143] Second, he connected that jingoistic imperial attitude with the Conservative party. Disraeli, says Blake, seized the imperial idea from the Liberals – partly for opportunistic reasons, but also because 'his own temperamental instincts pointed that way'.[144] Colin Matthew elaborates this theme: 'Recognizing the power of symbol, Disraeli created for the new electorate the myth of the imperial party with its "patriotic" underpinnings of Queen, Church, and Empire.'[145]

Questioning the Imperial Disraeli

Every strand of the preceding argument has been challenged by historians rejecting the image of Disraeli the empire builder. Thus, Eldridge argues that the 1872 speech did not mark a new departure for he had been advocating similar views since the 1830s. 'Disraeli had often reverted to the problem of colonial tariffs, the need for some sort of system of imperial defence and the idea of a representative council [...]. Even the attempt to equate the Liberals with the separatists was not new [...] In fact the whole Crystal Palace speech had been more or less foreshadowed a decade earlier.'[146] Disraeli had not 'laid out a Conservative programme for the future nor had he once advocated imperial expansion'.[147] Stembridge concurs: his views in 1872 were the same as those of the 1840s – he wanted not to expand the Empire but to bind the colonies closer

---

[140] Bradford, *Disraeli*, p. 357.
[141] Feuchtwanger, *Disraeli*, p. 199.
[142] Eldridge, *England's Mission*, p. 204.
[143] Bodelsen, *Studies in Mid-Victorian Imperialism*, p. 124.
[144] Blake, *Disraeli*, p. 760.
[145] Matthew, *Gladstone*, pp. 267–68.
[146] Eldridge, *England's Mission*, p. 177.
[147] Eldridge, *Disraeli and the Rise of the New Imperialism*, p. 36.

to Britain, and his ideas about how to do this had changed little.[148] According to Blake, Disraeli's remarks at the Crystal Palace 'seem to have been thrown out more or less casually and without any special appreciation of their significance'.[149] Far from proclaiming 'a new era of aggressive Imperialism', argues Hawkins, the Crystal Palace speech was a reworking of an element in Disraeli's thinking traceable back to the 1830s.[150] It was not Disraeli who had changed but the political context: the charge that the Liberals were undermining the Empire carried much more resonance now Gladstone had replaced Palmerston as Liberal leader. Disraeli's imperial speeches were a bid to secure the patriotic mantle of Palmerston.[151] In taking up Empire, writes Smith, Disraeli was 'asserting a tactically advantageous Conservative position in a lively current debate'.[152] The ideas of imperial consolidation and emigration to the colonies were then current and there was 'nothing original' in what Disraeli said. Bodelsen, too, believes Disraeli's decision to raise the issue of Empire 'was due, less to his conviction of the greatness of the cause of Imperialism, than to the realization that here was a new chance of "dishing the Whigs"' and monopolizing for the Conservatives a popular cause. In fact, Feuchtwanger points out that the idea that Disraeli *did* advocate an ardent imperialism originated 'with Liberal critics, who wished to portray Disraeli as an aggressive expansionist, corrupting the masses with the un-English concept of imperial dominion'.[153]

The case for Disraeli as the originator of the New Imperialism is stronger if one follows Harcourt in seeing the 1867 Abyssinian expedition as inaugurating Disraeli's imperial vision. Unfortunately, Nini Rodgers argues, there is little to support her argument. The war was provoked by King Theodore of Abyssinia, and 'there is much evidence to show that the passing of the Second Reform Act and the resort to force against Theodore were coincidental rather than consequential, and that the decision to launch a campaign was the product of departmental government rather than of an initiative from a Disraelian cabinet'.[154] There was no question of annexing the territory, and Disraeli justified the mission in terms of humanitarian motives, not imperial prestige. 'Harcourt's hypothesis', says Eldridge, 'remains unproven.'[155]

---

[148] Stembridge, 'Disraeli and the Millstones', p. 139.

[149] Blake, *Disraeli*, p. 523.

[150] Hawkins, *British Party Politics*, p. 183.

[151] Ibid., p. 195.

[152] Smith, *Disraeli*, p. 162.

[153] Quoted in Feuchtwanger, *Disraeli*, pp. 178–79.

[154] N. Rodgers, 'The Abyssinian Expedition of 1867–1868: Disraeli's Imperialism or James Murray's War?', *Historical Journal*, Vol. 27 (1984), pp. 136–37.

[155] Eldridge, *Disraeli and the Rise of the New Imperialism*, p. 30.

It is also contended that Disraeli knew little about the colonies and had no imperial programme. Even in 1872 he was lamenting what had not been done in the past – not sketching a programme for the future. Thus, for Bodelsen,

> [t]he assertion sometimes made that Disraeli was one of the founders, even the founder, of British Imperialism will [...] hardly stand the test of an examination [...] Disraeli was never really much concerned about colonial questions for their own sake [...] His criticism of the colonial policy of the Liberals was [...] directed against the grant to the colonies of fiscal autonomy and the control of waste lands, and the failure to bind the colonies to take their share in imperial defence [...] this criticism shows a considerable ignorance of colonial conditions. Any attempt to resume Imperial control of these subjects would [...] probably have resulted in declarations of independence on the part of the colonies.[156]

Stembridge agrees that at the Crystal Palace Disraeli was only expressing regret for policies not pursued and 'had no intention of resuming imperial control over tariffs or defence or wastelands'.[157] Indeed, Archibald Thornton points out that the decision to allow colonial governments to allocate their waste lands was taken by the Conservatives in 1852 and that Disraeli's regrets 'were some twenty years too late'.[158] Disraeli's failure to evolve any plausible policies regarding the white settler colonies is attributed by Beeley to the fact that he was not interested in them. It was the Asiatic Empire that concerned him. Raymond agrees: where India had 'always fascinated', the colonies 'wearied him [...] and it was probably the consciousness that Canada and Australia were of more interest to the newly enfranchised electorate that explained his sudden enthusiasm for the white constituents of "the Empire of England"'.[159] Blake similarly writes that Disraeli 'had taken little interest in the colonies' and 'was quite content to leave colonial policy to Carnarvon'.[160]

According to this sceptical perspective, then, Disraeli articulated no new ideology of Empire in 1872, and when he came to power, says Michael Bentley, 'neither Disraeli nor his ministers held any ideology about imperial expansion except insofar as they believed that history showed it to be a bad and dangerous thing'.[161] Hoppen holds that Disraeli 'displayed no greater or more

---

[156] Bodelsen, *Studies in Mid-Victorian Imperialism*, p. 123.
[157] Stembridge, 'Disraeli and the Millstones', p. 138.
[158] A. P. Thornton, *The Imperial Idea and Its Enemies* (1963), p. 10.
[159] Raymond, *Disraeli*, p. 287.
[160] Blake, *Disraeli*, p. 665.
[161] Bentley, *Politics without Democracy*, p. 224.

sustained interest in the colonies' than Gladstone.[162] Bruce Coleman agrees that Disraeli had no expansionist agenda for the Empire. Despite earlier Tory criticism of Gladstone's ministry for weakness in colonial policy, 'the new ministry had designed no "forward policy" for the colonies'.[163] 'In spite of his public image as the champion of imperialism', remarks Feuchtwanger, 'he had in fact no consistent imperial and colonial policy and certainly no general policy of expansion.' Colonial policy was largely left to Lord Carnarvon, Disraeli taking little interest in the details, being 'above all concerned to avoid trouble'.[164] Indeed, argues Eldridge, to look for a new colonial policy in 1874 is misguided, for Disraeli wanted to use the *concept* of imperial power to strengthen the impact of British foreign policy.[165]

Given this lack of an imperial programme, it is little wonder that many writers see Disraeli playing an essentially passive part in the Empire-related initiatives of his government, following the lead of others – whether it be his colonial secretary, Lord Carnarvon; Queen Victoria, in the case of the Royal Titles Bill; or 'Men on the Spot' such as Lord Lytton and Sir Bartle Frere. So we find Stembridge writing that the Disraeli's imperial difficulties arose because 'he failed to oversee his administration closely and left too much to subordinates', and Paul Smith arguing that the 'forward movements of empire were the result, not of Disraeli's imperialism, but of his excessively loose control of the cabinet'.[166] In the absence of a firm hand at the centre, the government was buffeted by a series of imperial crises – the one theme being that Disraeli had little or nothing to do with them. Thus, writes Eldridge, W. D. McIntyre 'exploded once and for all the myth of a series of "forward movements" in 1874 – in West Africa, the South Pacific and the Malay States [...] Inheriting a series of crises in the tropics, the Conservatives did little more than implement the policies initiated by their predecessors [...] a policy of minimum intervention was followed.' Disraeli played little part in these matters.[167] With respect to Carnarvon's annexation of the Fiji Islands, Disraeli was, says Eldridge, 'positively obstructive'.[168] Angered by Carnarvon's opposition to his Public Worship Bill, he refused to call a Cabinet meeting and left the entire matter to Carnarvon. Stembridge goes so far as to say that over Fiji, Disraeli 'was no more eager for annexation than Gladstone

---

[162] Hoppen, *Mid-Victorian Generation*, p. 629.
[163] Coleman, *Conservatism and the Conservative Party*, pp. 152, 160.
[164] Feuchtwanger, *Disraeli*, p. 198.
[165] Eldridge, *England's Mission*, p. 185.
[166] Stembridge, 'Disraeli and the Millstones', p. 137; Smith, *Disraeli*, p. 197.
[167] Eldridge, *Disraeli and the Rise of the New Imperialism*, p. 8.
[168] Eldridge, *England's Mission*, p. 189.

had been'.[169] The idea that the Queen should be declared Empress of India derived from Victoria herself. Coming in 1876 at a time of great pressure in international affairs, Disraeli, observes Shannon, 'would have preferred to wait for a less fraught time, but the queen would not be denied'.[170]

Disraeli took even less interest in South Africa. It was, narrates Eldridge, Carnarvon who pushed the idea of federating the British and Dutch settler communities, and even here C. F. Goodfellow showed in 1966 how Carnarvon was taking advantage of a crisis in the Transvaal to push through a failed confederation scheme of his Liberal predecessor, Lord Kimberley.[171] 'Disraeli, as usual, showed little interest.'[172] 'Far from [...] being intent on initiating an aggressive, expansionist scheme, the prime minister responded in a very casual fashion [...] "Do what you think wisest."'[173] Monypenny and Buckle concede that he 'had his doubts' about Carnarvon's 'very forward policy'. However, his mind in 1876 was preoccupied with the Eastern Question and he deferred to his colleague's expert knowledge. It was Carnarvon too, they say, who selected Bartle Frere to be the high commissioner of South Africa. Disraeli was opposed to precipitate action against the Zulus, and it was Frere who was responsible for the disaster at Isandhlwana.[174] 'The war was', says Blake, 'emphatically Frere's war.'[175] Thus, concludes Eldridge,

Disraeli's name became associated in South Africa with an expansionist policy in the Transvaal to which he had paid little attention and a war against the Zulus which he had opposed. Far from being the product of an aggressive intent, the Zulu war was the product of Disraeli's weakness as prime minister.[176]

It was, Maurice Cowling and Blake contend, the same story in Afghanistan. It was Lytton who initiated the military mission that was blocked at the frontier and who then sent a larger force up the Khyber Pass, contrary to instructions. The humiliating massacre in Kabul, argues Cowling, was the result of a rebellious proconsul who ignored directions from London.

---

[169] Stembridge, 'Disraeli and the Millstones', p. 135. See also Jenkins, *Disraeli and Victorian Conservatism*, p. 117.
[170] Shannon, *Age of Disraeli*, p. 278.
[171] C. F. Goodfellow, *Great Britain and South African Confederation, 1868–1881* (1966).
[172] Eldridge, *England's Mission*, p. 195.
[173] Eldridge, *Disraeli and the Rise of the New Imperialism*, p. 44.
[174] Monypenny and Buckle, *Life of Disraeli*, II. p. 1,288.
[175] Blake, *Disraeli*, p. 669.
[176] Eldridge, *Disraeli and the Rise of the New Imperialism*, p. 45.

Again, it was Disraeli's inability to control his imperial governors that was the problem.[177] Monypenny and Buckle had already portrayed Disraeli as a relatively passive figure in the Afghan crisis, feeling 'unduly hustled by Lytton', though recognizing the need to support him once the decision was taken.[178] Blake did nothing to revise this picture in his 1966 biography. While admitting that Disraeli informed Lytton that 'masterly inactivity' had 'ceased to be the official policy' in Afghanistan, he did not approve of Lytton's decision to send a military mission to Afghanistan, concurring with the general view that a reply to Britain's protest to the Russians be received first. Apart from the initial error of appointing Lytton Viceroy, 'Disraeli cannot be held seriously responsible' for the events in Afghanistan. Lytton and Lord Cranbrook (the secretary of state for India) were the main culprits.[179] J. L. Duthie talks of Lytton's 'wilful precipitancy' in dispatching the military mission without authorization and of pursuing his own goal, which was partition of Afghanistan, considering a 'subordinate Afghanistan as the only assurance of India's security'.[180]

Disraeli never seems to have clearly appreciated the options involved, but he was certainly not a notable war-monger before or after the Chamberlain mission's rebuff. Cranbrook, proxy for Lytton, was the pro-war influence in the cabinet. When the general responsibility for the Second Afghan War is assessed, the cabinet's fault was one of omission, the viceroy's one of commission.[181]

Even in the East, concludes Eldridge, 'Disraeli was not the expansionist he is frequently alleged to have been'.[182]

What of the claim that Disraeli sought to lay a new basis for imperial power in the Middle East? This, too, has been rejected. Monypenny and Buckle denied that Disraeli had any wish to occupy Egypt, knowing such a move would be unacceptable to the French. He accordingly welcomed Anglo-French control of Egyptian finance.[183] Similarly, Disraeli's purpose in securing a stake in the Suez Canal company was, says T. A. Jenkins, to

---

[177] Ibid., p. 9.

[178] Monypenny and Buckle, *Life of Disraeli*, II. p. 1, 287.

[179] Blake, *Disraeli*, pp. 659–63.

[180] J. L. Duthie, 'Pragmatic Diplomacy or Imperial Encroachment?: British Policy Towards Afghanistan, 1874–1879', *International History Review*, Vol. 5 (1983), p. 491.

[181] Ibid., p. 494.

[182] Eldridge, *Disraeli and the Rise of the New Imperialism*, p. 50.

[183] Monypenny and Buckle, *Life of Disraeli*, II. p. 1,318.

counteract French influence in the region, not take steps toward a British annexation of Egypt.[184] According to Blake, all the evidence points to Disraeli's 'determination to adhere to the traditional course' of basing the defence of British interests at Constantinople not Cairo.[185] He believed, writes Eldridge, that Constantinople not Egypt was the key to India, for if Constantinople fell to the Russians, they could easily march south to Egypt.[186] Ironically, Disraeli's lack of ambition in Egypt drew criticism from the Liberal journalist Peter Clayden. The purchase of the Suez shares was, he remarked, welcomed as an indication that Britain might establish a protectorate in Egypt. This would 'have safeguarded British interests and kept us out of the miserable complications further East [...] If our Government had got firm hold of Egypt in 1876, they might have left Turkey to its fate.' Unfortunately the chance to establish a Protectorate was missed since 'Disraeli was dreaming of Cyprus and Asia Minor and the Euphrates Valley, and could not see the full extent of England's interest in Egypt'.[187]

Thus, it is the view of a series of historians that, in the words of Stembridge, 'Disraeli's imperialism in the 1870s has been exaggerated [...] He was no exponent of a "new" imperialism and was no more an advocate of expansion for its own sake than Palmerston had been.'[188] Despite the rhetoric of Crystal Palace, there was, says Eldridge, little difference between the approach to Empire of Gladstone and Disraeli.

> Disraeli's contribution to British imperial history needs to be reassessed. With the so-called 'forward movements' of the early years of his administration he had almost nothing to do. The decisions extending British influence in various parts of the world were not even part of a consistent Conservative philosophy, but merely the outcome of earlier events. For the 'forward movements' of the later years of his administration Disraeli also had little responsibility [...] 'Beaconsfieldism' was substantially a product of Disraeli's weakness as Prime Minister rather than his strength.[189]

---

[184] Jenkins, *Disraeli and Victorian Conservatism*, p. 119. Davis takes a similar line, *Disraeli*, p. 210.

[185] Blake, *Disraeli*, p. 587.

[186] Eldridge, *Disraeli and the Rise of the New Imperialism*, p. 47.

[187] Clayden, *England under Lord Beaconsfield*, p. 192.

[188] Stembridge, 'Disraeli and the Millstones', p. 136.

[189] Eldridge, *England's Mission*, p. 170. 'Beaconsfieldism' was the derogatory term coined by Disraeli's political opponents to characterize what they considered to be his aggressive imperialist tendencies.

Disraeli and the rhetoric of Empire

Given this questioning of Disraeli's imperial credentials, how did Disraeli ever become linked with Empire in the first place? Two observations are relevant. First, nearly all historians recognize that Disraeli saw Empire as a subject for socially unifying rhetoric. It was a form of words that resonated with a cross section of the British class system – not a programme for imperial policy. The concept of empire, writes Paul Smith, was

> one which could perform a vital integrating function in providing for all classes a common symbol of national stature, a common source of national prosperity, and a common object of national pride and endeavour. This was image-making, not policy-making.[190]

For Disraeli, says Smith in words that echo Harcourt's analysis of the Abyssinian invasion, the stimulation of an English sense of imperial destiny 'was the means of trying to infuse a common pride and purpose into a society threatened with disintegration and decay' by modern industrial capitalism.[191] Eldridge agrees. The purpose of Disraeli's Crystal Palace speech was to harness patriotism to the Conservative party and reassure 'middle-class supporters and attract new working class voters'.[192] Feuchtwanger takes this argument one stage further by linking Disraeli's imperialism to social reform, thus rendering him a pioneer of social imperialism. 'If social imperialism means transcending class tensions by imperial patriotism and alleviating them by social reform, then Disraeli was a precursor of later, more explicit social imperialists in the Conservative party.'[193] Disraeli's imperial vision, believes Jenkins, 'consisted of little more than flamboyant gestures, designed to impress public opinion. His presentation of the annexation of Fiji, the purchase of the Suez Canal shares and the Royal Titles Act all testified to Disraeli's awareness of the value of imagination in politics.'[194]

Second, it is argued that Disraeli's imperialism was not about the Empire at all; rather, it was about Britain's prestige as a Great Power. What he wanted to do in the wake of Gladstone's passive foreign policy was reassert Britain's position within the counsels of Europe, and glorying in her Empire was a means to this end. An important source for this reading is Thornton's

---

[190] Smith, *Disraeli*, p. 164.
[191] Ibid., p. 216.
[192] Eldridge, *Disraeli and the Rise of the New Imperialism*, p. 70.
[193] Feuchtwanger, *Disraeli*, p. 211
[194] Jenkins, *Disraeli and Victorian Conservatism*, p. 120.

The Imperial Idea and Its Enemies (1959). What Disraeli did, he argues, was fashion a new dress for the argument that he had consistently propounded: 'that England, if she were to remain a Great Power, must *function* as such'.[195] His evocation of Empire was primarily a matter of asserting British power in Europe, especially in the wake of the rise of Prussia and the marginalization of British diplomacy. 'It was not a question [...] of the Khyber Pass: it was a question that concerned the character and influence of England in Europe.' If Britain was to be diplomatically isolated from Europe, then it should be an 'isolation that came from self-confidence, from extreme energy, from abounding resources, and above all from the inspiration of a great cause [...] Here lay the core of Disraeli's case.'[196] Stembridge largely endorsed Thornton's analysis:

> His imperial idea was a powerful England, strengthened by the resources and peoples of a far-flung empire, playing a decisive role in world affairs. For such a purpose more territory was not needed, but the loss of territory had to be avoided as a symptom of decline.[197]

Eldridge made this idea the foundation of his understanding of Disraeli's imperialism.

> Disraeli comprehended the possibility of utilising British possessions to increase British influence and power. It was not 'colonial' policy that Disraeli was interested in but the effect of the possession of empire on British foreign policy.[198]

'Disraeli did not possess any "theory of empire". It was the use that could be made of empire that interested him.'[199] The part of Empire most central to Britain's global status was India. And then, by a dialectical process, the defence of India and the routes to India became the dominant focus of Disraeli's foreign policy. So where India was meant to underpin British foreign policy, British foreign policy became about the strengthening of India.

> During Disraeli's premiership Indian and imperial interests became synonymous with the British national interest. The purchase of the Suez Canal Company shares, the Royal Titles Act, the sending of Indian

---

[195] Thornton, *The Imperial Idea*, p. 19. Italics in the original.
[196] Ibid., pp. 27–28.
[197] Stembridge, 'Disraeli and the Millstones', p. 138.
[198] Eldridge, *England's Mission*, p. 184. See also p. 179.
[199] Eldridge, *Disraeli and the Rise of the New Imperialism*, p. 66.

troops to Malta and the occupation of Cyprus were all part of a design to defend British naval lifelines and the approaches to India.[200]

This reading of Disraeli's imperialism figures prominently in most recent studies. Thus, for T. A. Jenkins, when Disraeli spoke of upholding the Empire, what he meant was 'maintaining Britain's prestige in the eyes of the world'.[201] Parry likewise affirms that by Empire Disraeli meant 'the historic and symbolic greatness of England, exemplified by its power in Europe and its global prestige', while according to Machin, Disraeli was interested in imperialism 'because of the impression it could make on the world in raising British prestige, and because of the enthusiasm which would be aroused at home for a Government which pursued it successfully'.[202] In their recent biography, Douglas Hurd and Edward Young affirm that, for Disraeli, 'prestige was a solid asset [...] A country which enjoyed high prestige would prevail in any contest where otherwise the scales were balanced.'[203]

Another author seeing Disraeli's imperialism as essentially rhetorical is Ghosh. However, he questions the Thornton–Eldridge understanding of the function of that rhetoric. For Ghosh, Disraeli was never an imperialist. His more bellicose language from 1878 was a response to Gladstone's attacks over the Bulgarian atrocities and then in the Midlothian campaign. Disraeli's only counter to Gladstone was 'a positive and assertive policy', and for this reason he 'extended the patriotic image to cover deeds which were not his own'.[204] The differences between Gladstone and Disraeli were not so much practical as ones of 'presentation and imagination'.[205]

Conclusion

It is apparent from the research of Stembridge and Eldridge that Empire, for Disraeli, was about Britain's standing as a great power. While his imperial references of 1872, and the prominence of Empire adventures in the 1874 government, seem to suggest he was a pioneer of the New Imperialism, most historians question this. Disraeli, it is said by writers as diverse as Bodelsen, Eldridge, Blake and Smith, had no interest in the colonies and did not try to expand them. What he wanted to do was exploit Gladstone's embarrassed

---

[200] Eldridge, *England's Mission*, p. 209.
[201] Jenkins, *Disraeli and Victorian Conservatism*, p. 121.
[202] Machin, *Disraeli*, pp. 138–39.
[203] Hurd and Young, *Disraeli*, p. 202.
[204] Ghosh, 'Disraelian Conservatism', p. 292.
[205] Ibid.

reticence on Empire by celebrating the Empire as a means to social cohesion and as a method by which Britain might retain prestige in an age of rising new powers like Germany and America. The problem was that celebrating Empire could not be a matter of words: if you portray the Empire as a great patriotic fact, it is hard to reject the idea that there ought to be more of it. The people running the Empire drew this connection and they did add to the Empire, precipitating a series of imbroglios that contributed to Disraeli's defeat in 1880. An empire can never be a static thing. If an empire is not growing then it is allowing potential challenges to emerge. Carnarvon, Lytton and Frere, who confronted the reality of administering the Empire, realized this. Disraeli, by delegating the business of imperial government, kept his hands clean. It might be argued that historians like Eldridge and Stembridge, who have described Disraeli's colonial attitudes so well, have also supplied them with a coherence they never really possessed.

5.3   Why Did Gladstone Take Up the Balkan Agitation in 1876?

In September 1876, a supposedly retired Gladstone burst upon the public consciousness with a pamphlet denouncing the Eastern policy of the Conservative government in the light of reports of massacres perpetrated by Turks in the Ottoman province of Bulgaria, initiating, thereby, a campaign against 'Beaconsfieldism' works that was to carry him back to the premiership in 1880. What motivated this dramatic personal intervention? Traditionally, Gladstone has been seen as being driven out of retirement by a moral imperative to speak up for the oppressed Christians of the Ottoman territories. Yet in more recent decades historians have questioned this moralistic interpretation, arguing that Gladstone's behaviour was either the product of a specifically evangelical religious impulse or a more prosaic concern with the mechanics of power.

The conventional account of Gladstone's intervention represents one of the contemporary 'myths' of Gladstone's career mentioned by David Hamer: 'The intensely dramatic events of that episode obviously made a deep impression on the popular imagination – the venerable and retired statesman emerging from his study like an embodiment of the wrath of God to denounce immorality in foreign policy.'[206] Formulated by Liberal commentators of the day, this narrative quickly established itself as the accepted interpretation in the early biographies of Gladstone – such as Frank Gunsaulus's 1898 study:

---

[206] D. A. Hamer, 'Gladstone: The Making of a Political Myth', *Victorian Studies*, Vol. 22 (1978), p. 31.

Sitting in Hawarden Castle [...] the stalwart spirit of Gladstone could not be satisfied or acquiescent. He had heard the cry of beleaguered and outraged humanity, and [...] suddenly made his appearance in the House of Commons [...] a profound faith in justice, triumphantly glowing in his face, and a sublime passion for righteousness beaming from those deep-lit eyes, took possession of the House [...] Every facility which his eloquent tongue and scarcely less eloquent pen might employ was used in the unparalleled crusade [...] He organized and led against the policy which now stood revealed in all its satanic features, as the merciless light of Gladstone's mind and conscience played upon it.[207]

That Gladstone's motives were moral and idealistic had already been affirmed in numerous accounts. Thus, as G. W. E. Russell says,

Mr. Gladstone is a humane man: the Turkish tyranny is founded on cruelty. He is a worshipper of freedom: the Turk is a slaveowner. He is a lover of peace: the Turk is nothing if not a soldier. He is a disciple of progress: the Turkish empire is a synonym for retrogression. But above and beyond all else, Mr. Gladstone is a Christian: and in the Turk he saw the great anti-Christian Power standing where it ought not [...] and stained with the record of odious cruelty [...] on its defenceless subjects who were worshippers of JESUS CHRIST.[208]

Barnett Smith spoke of Gladstone rousing 'in so remarkable a degree the feelings of the English people in favour of the oppressed nationalities of Turkey', while for McCarthy, Gladstone 'came to the front and sounded a tremendous note upon his bugle-horn. He put himself in the front of the agitation [...] and [...] threw his whole soul into the movement against the Ottoman Government in Bulgaria.'[209] Recollecting his youthful contacts with Gladstone, the future Conservative prime minister Arthur Balfour testified to the powerful impression his Balkan campaign made upon his contemporaries:

At the zenith of his physical powers, with all the authority of an 'Elder Statesman', all the independence of a simple citizen, all the gifts of

---

[207] Gunsaulus, *William Ewart Gladstone*, p. 287.
[208] Russell, *William Ewart Gladstone*, pp. 244–45.
[209] Barnett Smith, *William Ewart Gladstone*, p. 513; McCarthy, *Story of Gladstone's Life*, pp. 298–99.

an accomplished agitator, he chose a cause which, as treated by him, had appealed to his particular prejudices. The atrocities on which he dwelt were [...] only too real, the indignation which he expressed was genuine.[210]

This account of Gladstone's actions resonated well into the twentieth century. According to Erich Eyck, Gladstone 'was profoundly agitated by the thought that thousands of Christians [...] had been massacred, and that England [...] was standing indifferent, with folded arms – or even worse, was shielding these Turks whose hands were dripping with blood'.[211] Robert Seton-Watson, in a 1935 study of the Balkan crisis, endorsed the evangelical interpretation of Gladstone's intervention. There was, he says, 'a certain crusading trait in his character, and the spirit which had inspired his exposure of the Neapolitan prisons now kindled in the cause of the downtrodden Christians of the East'. His 'chief motive' was a hatred of cruelty and oppression.[212] J. L. Hammond and M. R. D. Foot wrote in 1952 that the former Liberal leader 'felt himself compelled to rouse the feelings of Englishmen against the atrocities of Ottoman rule', while fittingly, perhaps, Peter Esslemont, in a short guide to Gladstone's career designed to galvanize Britain's patriotic resolve in the face of the Nazi threat, declared that '[n]ever in British history had an awakening of conscience been so much the work of one man'.[213]

In general, it is Gladstone's emotional attachment to the cause of the Bulgarian people that is emphasized. But a more personal motivation is also sometimes acknowledged: namely, a deepening hatred of Disraeli that could border on the anti-Semitic as Gladstone suspected Disraeli's indifference to the suffering of Christians as arising from his Jewish predilection for Ottoman over Christian rule.[214] Thus, McCarthy believes that what finally summoned Achilles to 'rush forth of his tent and lead on the battle' were Disraeli's speeches and actions on the Bulgarian question.[215] Balfour, too, noted that Gladstone 'hated the Prime Minister', and Seton-Watson agrees that Gladstone's long developing animosity toward Disraeli, and his suspicion that Disraeli's 'crypto-Judaism has had to do with his policy', 'helps to explain the mentality of the man who after retiring from public life [...] now emerged

---

[210] Quoted in Eyck, *Gladstone*, p. 278.

[211] Ibid., p. 256.

[212] R. W. Seton-Watson, *Disraeli, Gladstone, and the Eastern Question* (1935), p. 77.

[213] Hammond and Foot, *Gladstone and Liberalism*, p. 129; P. Esslemont, *To the Fifth Generation* (1941), p. 79.

[214] Feuchtwanger, *Gladstone*, p. 181.

[215] McCarthy, *Story of Gladstone's Life*, p. 294.

once more from his lair [...] and proceeded to develop a demagogic activity unequalled in the history of Britain'.[216]

These accounts agree in regarding Gladstone's actions as essentially impulsive. A rather different interpretation is provided by Matthew, who situates Gladstone's intervention within the context of his religious interests. His approach to the atrocities 'reflected the theological preoccupations of the previous eighteen months of retirement: it was High Church in conception, Evangelical in conviction, and Broad Church in presentation'.[217] Gladstone's long-standing belief in the Concert of Europe was endorsed by his High and Broad Church perspective, with its idea of reconciling differences between Great Powers through congresses and negotiations. The Bulgarian atrocities necessitated the intervention of the Concert of Europe because the Turks had failed to uphold the principles of justice within the boundaries of European civilization.[218] Matthew notes that Gladstone had been concerning himself with events in the Ottoman Empire from early 1876, arguing, in a series of Commons speeches, for greater self-government within the Ottoman Empire for the Christian people of the Balkans. 'Even before the popular agitation had really begun, Gladstone had by the end of July 1876 measured out the ground and the arguments which were, in language much more strident, to be the essence of his position in subsequent years.'[219] It was reformist, yet moderate and rational. Why, then, did Gladstone's advocacy of the Bulgarian cause become so vociferous in the late summer of 1876? Where Shannon emphasizes the impact of public opinion, Matthew highlights the role of divine opinion. 'Between July and September 1876, Gladstone experienced a conversion of Evangelical intensity.'

> In a true Evangelical spirit, Gladstone believed himself to have been called 'for a purpose', a call carrying 'the marks of the will of God'. This is a sober analysis of his position [...] on this occasion he came to feel that he was the direct recipient of a specific call.[220]

In the process, says Matthew, Gladstone sought to 'turn the crisis to encourage a national debate on national objectives, attempting to rally the electorate to the support of a wide range of policy positions'.[221]

---

[216] Seton-Watson, *Disraeli, Gladstone, and the Eastern Question*, pp. 78–80.
[217] Matthew, *Gladstone*, pp. 269–71.
[218] Ibid., p. 273.
[219] Ibid., p. 267.
[220] Ibid., pp. 282, 285.
[221] Ibid., p. 268.

Other historians concur in portraying Gladstone's intervention less as an emotional spasm and more as the logical outcome of a reasoned position. Francis Birrell argues that it was Disraeli's refusal to endorse the Berlin Memorandum that was crucial, for it 'offended him on his two deepest sensibilities'. Not only did Disraeli reveal himself to be 'the supporter of the Turk against the Christian' but he also 'broke up "the Concert of Europe," on which Gladstone [...] had always insisted as the basis of any respectable polity'.[222] Ramm similarly sees Gladstone's interest in the Balkans emerging over a period of time, becoming acute when the government ceased to work with the European powers. Initially articulating his concerns in Parliament, it was only when Parliament went into recess in August 1876 that Gladstone became involved in a campaigning manner, believing himself free to lead the assault on the government.[223] To the issues of the treatment of Christians and the Concert of Europe, Feuchtwanger adds that of national self-determination. 'As a problem of international policy Gladstone could see the Eastern Question as a perfect demonstration model for his outlook and attitude.'[224]

However, the idea that Gladstone was driven by a profound sentiment, whether humanitarian or theological, was challenged in 1963 by Shannon in his *Gladstone and the Bulgarian Agitation 1876*. Shannon questions traditional narratives of Gladstone's engagement in two ways. First, he argues that Gladstone did not make or lead the agitation; rather, the agitation had been building without Gladstone since early 1876 and Gladstone was slow to enrol himself under its banner. The first reports of the extent of the massacre in Bulgaria appeared in late June 1876, and a popular protest movement led by High Churchmen against the government's eastern policy was soon underway. But as yet, writes Shannon in a later biography, 'Gladstone remained little attuned to these stirrings. For most of July, while public alarm mounted at what seemed Britain's virtual complicity in horrific transactions, Gladstone dallied in desultory activities. He declined a requisition by a group of Liberal MPs to chair a protest meeting.'[225] Only in September did Gladstone commit himself to the campaign.

> Far from being a decisive agent, Gladstone was practically carried into the agitation by others [...] Far from being an impatient crusader against Disraeli, Gladstone, even after committing himself on 6 September,

---

[222] Birrell, *Gladstone*, p. 92.
[223] Ramm, *William Ewart Gladstone*, p. 73.
[224] Feuchtwanger, *Gladstone*, p. 181.
[225] Shannon, *Gladstone: God and Politics*, p. 274.

wasted a vital and precious month in delays and vacillations. Far from deliberately boosting forward the agitation in September, in effect Gladstone did more than anyone else to put a drag on its impetus.[226]

What eventually drew Gladstone from his Hawarden retreat was not the massacres but the public's response to them.

> Before his mind became excited to a pitch where he could commit himself wholeheartedly in the Eastern question, he had to be convinced that the question promised, for him, the elements of a moral crusade; and the basic element of a moral crusade was a significant manifestation of moral sentiment on a popular level and scale. Essentially, the aspect of the Bulgarian affair that excited Gladstone most profoundly was not the horror of the atrocities themselves but the realisation that they had provoked a great mass movement of popular moral passion. The central function of the atrocities agitation [...] was that it restored the moral rapport between himself and the masses which the defeat of 1874 had snapped.[227]

When he saw a notice for a workmen's protest in Hyde Park in mid-August 1876, he remarked that 'the game is afoot and the question yet alive'.[228] As such Shannon says that Gladstone's initial motivation 'was almost nakedly opportunist [...] The critical and decisive moment in the process of his commitment to the agitation came when he realized that a stirring of truly popular moral passion was in being.'[229] What Gladstone perceived among the 'masses' was what he called a 'virtuous passion': 'it was', summarizes Shannon, 'far less a case of Gladstone exciting popular passion than of popular passion exciting Gladstone'.[230]

Shannon's emphasis upon the role of the pre-existing Balkan agitation in explaining Gladstone's actions has found its way into the work of other historians. Already, in his 1954 *Gladstone*, Philip Magnus had admitted that the 'popular indignation' over the atrocities 'gave Gladstone his opportunity to direct public opinion towards the end which he desired. He wrote calmly to Lord Granville on 7 August: "As a Party question this affords no despicable material, but there are much higher interests involved."'[231] Ramm,

---

[226] Shannon, *Gladstone and the Bulgarian Agitation 1876* (1963), p. 90.

[227] Ibid., p. 92.

[228] Ibid., p. 100.

[229] Ibid., p. 101. See also Shannon, *Gladstone: Heroic Minister*, p. 169.

[230] Ibid., p. 174.

[231] P. Magnus, *Gladstone: A Biography* (1954), p. 241.

too, acknowledges that 'Gladstone had a base on which to build in existing agitation', while Stansky writes that the popular response Gladstone's intervention evoked proved that 'between him and his followers the rapport which he felt he had lost in 1874 was stronger than before. He responded to and helped shape a profound feeling of popular indignation.'[232] Although recognizing the 'depth of Gladstone's emotions' on the Balkans question, Feuchtwanger adds that 'Gladstone's fundamental simplicity and innocence did not exclude a great deal of political cunning'.

> In beckoning Gladstone out of retirement the domestic repercussions of this foreign imbroglio were at least as important as the international implications. As the atrocity agitation began to get under way in August 1876 he could perceive that here was a means by which he might re-forge the bond with the masses that had snapped two years earlier. He could not appeal to the material self-interest of the masses, for he was no democrat or egalitarian; for him the bond could only rest on a moral cause and this now lay ready to hand.[233]

Did Gladstone conceive that the campaign might carry him back into Downing Street? Matthew thinks not. Gladstone, he writes, 'was reluctant to accept what were to be the full public implications of his position'. It 'was in no way clear that the Eastern Question Campaign implied an eventual return to office'.[234] Shannon, not unexpectedly, intimates the reverse, remarking that 'there was more than a hint of Gladstone's seeing the people's "virtuous passion" as the means of embodying all the subordinate conditional clauses with which he had invariably qualified his yearnings for retirement'.[235] Parry is more forthright: 'Gladstone [...] blamed the defeat of 1874 largely on the lack of opportunity of "stirring the country". He spent the years in opposition looking for a "virtuous passion." In 1876 he seemed to find it.'[236] Roy Jenkins is most explicit:

> The genesis of Gladstone's fervour on the issue is difficult to analyse. Was he, perhaps semi-consciously, looking for a cause for which, with a clap of thunder and a whiff of smoke, he could re-emerge as the dominating figure of politics after a fairly boring two and a half years

[232] Ramm, *William Ewart Gladstone*, pp. 73–74; Stansky, *Gladstone*, p. 125.
[233] Feuchtwanger, *Gladstone*, pp. 181–84.
[234] Matthew, *Gladstone*, p. 288.
[235] Shannon, *Gladstone: Heroic Minister*, pp. 171–72.
[236] Parry, *Rise and Fall of Liberal Government*, p. 276.

during which he had been trying to persuade himself that he wished to concentrate on theology?[237]

When he turned from theology to the Balkans in 1876 'he was turning from a task he did indifferently to one which he did spectacularly well'.[238]

Conclusion

Not for the first time, we discover that interpretations of Gladstone's actions tend to be overdetermined. We can explain Gladstone's intervention as either the involuntary impulse of a committed humanitarian and long-standing supporter of Balkan nationalism; as a response to a call from God; or as a manoeuvre designed to restore him to a leading place in Liberal politics. Shannon's research makes a simple emotionalist account inadequate: Gladstone tarried too long before entering the fray for his action to be considered that of a man fired by moral sensibilities alone. As several historians recognize, more strategic considerations played a part – notably as to whether the popular outcry was sufficiently strong to sustain a Gladstonian campaign. Did Gladstone, then, picture the Balkan campaign as offering a fast track back to the premiership? This seems unlikely: there were just too many imponderables rendering this a questionable guide to action. It was the exhilaration of launching a popular agitation on behalf of a wholly moral end that seems to have drawn Gladstone into the political fray once again.

---

[237] Jenkins, *Gladstone*, p. 401.
[238] Ibid., p. 402.

Chapter 6

GLADSTONE ALONE 1880–1885

Outline of Events

The Midlothian election of 1880 signalled Benjamin Disraeli's political destruction as assuredly as the cold winds of 1881 brought his demise, and the way was now clear for William Gladstone, at the head of a large majority, to settle his scores with Beaconsfieldism and perfect his political legacy. Yet it soon became apparent that Gladstone had no idea what to do with this new lease of power beyond undoing the wicked excesses of Disraeli's period in office – especially in the sphere of imperialism. But shifting a nation's foreign policy is no easy business in a world where the Empire created a dynamic of its own, and while in Afghanistan the troops were withdrawn, disentangling Britain's relations with the Transvaal was far more difficult, as the First Boer War of 1881 testified. Yet these foreign policy dilemmas were soon eclipsed by Gladstone's annexation of Egypt in 1882. While the motives for this action are much debated, what is not questionable is that by this dramatic act of imperial expansion Gladstone liquidated the moral basis of his anti-Beaconsfield rhetoric. And Egypt led to the Sudan as Gladstone's imperial story mirrored Disraeli's, from glamorous victories to humiliating disasters – this time as General Charles George Gordon was killed at Khartoum.

In domestic politics Gladstone again found himself drawn into the affairs of Ireland, as the agricultural depression brought that island to the brink of crisis. Preoccupied as he was, and hinting repeatedly of his imminent retirement, the government drifted, being buffeted, almost immediately, by the storm over the atheist MP Charles Bradlaugh's claim that he be exempt from swearing an oath of allegiance to the Queen as a Christian. The Bradlaugh controversy, ruthlessly exploited by Tory dissidents of the 'Fourth Party', revealed the splits between Radicals and Whigs on the government benches, and the manoeuvring between these rivals for the post-Gladstone inheritance became a defining feature of the administration. While plans for local government reform were never realized, in 1884–85 long-promised proposals to bring the County franchise into line with that in the boroughs were carried onto the statute book. But with this measure settled, Liberal differences opened still wider, and in June 1885 the government was defeated in a budget vote and resigned. It seemed that Gladstone might finally retire: in reality he was about to embark upon the most tumultuous months of his political career.

6.1 Why Did Gladstone Intervene in Egypt?

It was the supreme irony of Gladstone's second administration that it was responsible for the greatest act of imperial expansion of the nineteenth century – the conquest of Egypt. In 1881 an Egyptian national movement had begun under the leadership of an army officer, Arabi Pasha. Gladstone's instinct was to support Arabi, declaring in January 1882 that "Egypt for the Egyptians" is the sentiment to which I should wish to give scope'.[1] However, as law and order within Egypt deteriorated and, having failed to secure European support for armed measures to restore it, Gladstone approved British military intervention to overthrow Arabi and return the Khedive to his authority. While the removal of Arabi proved straightforward, this was not true of the restoration of the Khedive's authority, and the temporary occupation of 1882 lasted over 70 years. Why, then, did Gladstone so flagrantly contradict not merely his anti-imperial Midlothian rhetoric but also the specific warnings he had uttered in 1877 regarding the inadvisability of occupying Egypt? Here we consider five interpretations: that he was guided by concern for the security of the Suez Canal; that he was upholding law and order; that he was acting in the interests of finance capital; that he was pushed into Egypt by imperial-minded members of his Cabinet; and that he intervened to prevent Egypt from severing its ties to the Ottoman Empire.

Securing the route to India

Ronald Robinson and John Gallagher, in their 1961 *Africa and the Victorians*, argue that Gladstone's Cabinet was initially resolved to avoid military intervention in Egypt by any power, especially France, though sections of the Cabinet, led by Lord Hartington at the India Office, urged that Britain needed secure the Suez Canal route to India. The story of the months running

---

[1] Quoted in Matthew, *Gladstone*, p. 383.

from the autumn of 1881 up to the decision to invade in July 1882, was one of building a majority within the Cabinet on behalf of the need to defend the Canal, which in turn evolved into the conviction that Suez would only be truly secure when Arabi was removed from power and possible French intervention forestalled. By early July 1882, write Robinson and Gallagher,

> the danger to the Indian route had convinced most of the Cabinet that in the last resort they must sanction the British landing which hitherto they had been intent to avoid. Their disillusionment with Arabi's liberalism, despair of Turkish and international action, suspicion of French loyalty, anxiety for the Canal, and their Irish confusions had driven this non-interventionist ministry to the point of action.[2]

What convinced the Cabinet that Arabi posed a threat to the Canal was his construction of gun batteries at Alexandria. They allowed Admiral Seymour to issue an ultimatum calling on the batteries to be dismantled, and when this was not complied with, Seymour's ships opened fire. This in turn provoked anti-Western riots in Egypt and Arabi's declaration of war on Britain. These events completed 'the conversion of the Liberal Cabinet from naval and diplomatic bluffing to urgent and direct action, with or without the Powers'.[3]

But was this the reason Gladstone allowed such a move to be made? Robinson and Gallagher are sceptical. Gladstone did not believe that the Canal was seriously threatened, and when Seymour proposed to send his ultimatum, Gladstone remarked, 'I do not feel the necessity'. It was only *after* the bombardment that the threat to the Canal became serious, and even then Gladstone, say Robinson and Gallagher, protested impotently at the plans for invasion.[4] Colin Matthew similarly observes that 'Gladstone [...] did not associate himself with the India Office argument about the security of the route to India [...] He very strongly opposed independent British seizure of the Canal [...] as Arabi was unlikely to tamper with it unless provoked.'[5] Indeed, Gladstone had always been loath to see Egypt as wrapped up with the British position in India, reflecting during the Midlothian campaign, 'Suppose the very worst. The Canal is stopped [...] It seems to be forgotten that there is a route to India around the Cape of Good Hope.'[6] J. S. Galbraith

[2] R. Robinson and J. Gallagher, *Africa and the Victorians* (1981 edn.), p. 111.
[3] Ibid., p. 113.
[4] Ibid., pp. 111, 115.
[5] Matthew, *Gladstone*, p. 386.
[6] Quoted in Biagini, *Gladstone*, p. 83.

and A. L. al-Sayyid-Marsot similarly write that 'Gladstone did not believe that the security of the Canal justified military action', and suggest that fears for the security of the Canal were only put forward because they 'provided the most palatable explanation to the Liberal party and the general public'.[7] Antony Hopkins has more recently questioned Robinson and Gallagher's claim that security fears over the Suez Canal were the prime reason for British intervention. The Canal, he says, was never seen as being seriously under threat: the Egyptian crisis centred upon Cairo, the Admiralty expressed no fears and neither did the French, who withdrew from taking action.[8] If anything, it was the bombardment of Alexandria that brought forward a potential threat to the Canal as Arabi looked to make a response. 'Evidence from different sources', writes Hopkins, 'points clearly to the conclusion that the Canal was promoted late in the day to [...] provide a rationale for action by suggesting that free trade and international communications were in peril.'[9]

Upholding the public law in Egypt

Gladstone justified Egyptian intervention as an act of duty on behalf of the Concert of Europe to uphold the rule of law within Egypt, and this became, says Hopkins, the conventional explanation of British invasion. Thus, the imperial administrator Alfred Milner wrote in his 1892 *England in Egypt*,

> We had gone to Egypt professedly with no other object than to 'restore order', nor can there be the smallest doubt of the absolute *bona fides* of that profession [...] No one [...] can doubt for one moment that Mr. Gladstone's Ministry was sincerely anxious to avoid any fresh interference in the affairs of Egypt [...] But the English Government and people were swept along in spite of themselves by the current of events [...] the state of disorder already reached was of the extremist gravity. European property was no longer safe; European blood [...] had already been shed [...] Face to face with this frightful emergency, the English Government looked to the European Concert; it looked to Turkey; it looked in the last resort to combined action with France [...] But the flame of anarchy spread too fast for the slow movements of

---

[7] J. S. Galbraith and A. L. al-Sayyid-Marsot, 'The British Occupation of Egypt: Another View', *International Journal of Middle East Studies*, Vol. 9 (1978), pp. 472–73.

[8] A. G. Hopkins, 'The Victorians and Africa: A Reconsideration of the Occupation of Egypt, 1882', *Journal of African History*, Vol. 27 (1986), p. 373.

[9] Ibid., p. 374.

diplomacy. No one else was ready or willing to strike at once [...] Let it always be remembered that Great Britain did save Egypt from anarchy, and all European nations interested in Egypt from incalculable losses in blood and treasure.[10]

John Morley concurred with this analysis. It was only when appeals to Turkey and France had failed that 'single-handed intervention was inexorably forced upon the one Power that had most consistently striven to avoid it [...] The British cabinet had persuaded themselves that the overthrow of the military party was an indispensable precedent to any return to decently stable order.'[11] Edgar Feuchtwanger believes that Gladstone saw himself as working on behalf of the Concert of Europe, considering it 'a just war'. 'England had not wished to act alone but in the end the extent of Egyptian disorder and the reluctance of others to co-operate forced her hand.'[12] Roy Jenkins, too, contends that Gladstone came to see that measures against Arabi were required if 'order' was to be upheld in Egypt. He preferred to work with the Concert of Europe, but with Germany indifferent and France scared of Germany, 'it was the British on their own or nothing'.[13] Richard Shannon agrees that Gladstone 'acted throughout for Europe, within a European frame of assumptions and intentions [...] Once the Khedive's authority was restored [...] British forces would withdraw, having fulfilled their European vocation.'[14] For the imperial historian Bernard Porter, 'what looks like imperialism was not imperialism at all. Gladstone certainly did not intend it as such. In the case of Egypt he saw Britain as [...] representing the whole European community in defence of international law.'[15]

Travis Crosby, however, suggests that Gladstone's talk of acting on behalf of the Concert of Europe chiefly reflected his need to justify his action in the light of his previous denunciations of imperial aggression by claiming that his 'warlike actions [...] were the means to peace'.[16] This was the line he pushed to the pacifist John Bright, to whom he described himself as 'a labourer in the cause of peace'.[17] The notion that Gladstone's references to acting on behalf of the Concert of Europe represented a salve to his own conscience gains support from the fact that the operation owed nothing whatsoever to any

---

[10] A. Milner, *England in Egypt* (1892), pp. 15–17.
[11] Morley, *Life of Gladstone*, III. p. 80.
[12] Feuchtwanger, *Gladstone*, p. 214.
[13] Jenkins, *Gladstone*, p. 504.
[14] Shannon, *Gladstone: Heroic Minister*, p. 305.
[15] B. Porter, *Britannia's Burden* (1994), p. 87.
[16] T. L. Crosby, *The Two Mr. Gladstones* (1997), p. 175.
[17] Ibid., p. 176.

European Concert. On the contrary, by alienating France, which regarded Egypt as within its sphere of influence, it marked, writes Kenneth Bourne, 'the final collapse of Gladstone's Concert of Europe policy'.[18] Besides, as Matthew reflects, the issue remains as to 'what was it that made "order" in Egypt a question on which Britain was to act singlehandedly' despite Gladstone's misgivings?[19]

Cabinet pressure

'The most obvious reason', says Matthew, as to why Gladstone allowed British military intervention to proceed was that, by the end of June 1882, he 'was simply outnumbered and outflanked in his Cabinet, and was anyway physically and mentally exhausted by his constant work in the Commons on the Irish Crimes and Arrears Bills'.[20] Robinson and Gallagher agree that by the summer of 1882 Gladstone could no longer resist Cabinet pressure arising out of fears for the Suez Canal: 'The old man, already at full stretch with the Irish Arrears Bill, for the moment had lost his grip on Egyptian policy.'[21] Numerous historians have endorsed this analysis. For a nineteenth-century admirer like Frank Gunsaulus, such a deviation from Gladstonian Liberalism in the sphere of Empire policy could only be attributed to the shade of Disraeli:

> There can be no question that Gladstone had been forced into despatching this army, and that, as Prime Minister, he was following up an initiative which his own brain and heart and conscience never would have made [...] The Jingo policy of Beaconsfield had gotten into the blood of the present Government.[22]

Angus Hawkins also sees Gladstone as being forced by his Cabinet into a robust line on Egypt – an issue which united Whigs and sections of Radical opinion like Joseph Chamberlain and Charles Dilke.[23] Shannon notes that Gladstone's preferred option was 'Egypt for the Egyptians', but 'he was no longer up to the job of imposing such an eccentric opinion on his colleagues'.[24]

[18] K. Bourne, *The Foreign Policy of Victorian England 1830–1902* (1970), pp. 139–40.
[19] Matthew, *Gladstone*, p. 384.
[20] Ibid., p. 386.
[21] Robinson and Gallagher, *Africa and the Victorians*, p. 111.
[22] Gunsaulus, *William Ewart Gladstone*, p. 317.
[23] Hawkins, *British Party Politics*, p. 231.
[24] Shannon, *Gladstone: Heroic Minister*, p. 293.

'Harassed by the [Irish] Arrears crisis, Gladstone's grip on the Egyptian crisis loosened.'[25] Feuchtwanger depicts a prime minister out of his depth:

> On Egypt Gladstone was not at his best: the discrepancy between his own ideology on foreign policy and the realities of the situation was too great. He could not give the matter enough attention [...] the Cabinet was divided and Gladstone was not a dictator within it.[26]

Hopkins endorses this picture of Gladstone being preoccupied by Ireland and 'ill-informed about Egyptian affairs.' As such he was exposed to pressure for intervention from Dilke, the under secretary at the Foreign Office, who had an expansionist agenda in Egypt, and Lord Hartington. Strengthening their position were the despatches of Auckland Colvin, the controller-general in Egypt, who depicted Arabi as a military thug bent on overthrowing European influence. 'Thus, all the official information reaching London during 1882 fitted the requirements of the forward party in the cabinet perfectly.'[27] Galbraith and al-Sayyid-Marsot make this argument forcibly. 'Gladstone in 1882 had other preoccupations than Egypt. He was deeply involved in the problems of Ireland; and he depended primarily on Granville to make the decisions on Egyptian policy.' He was ignorant about Egyptian affairs and, although wanting to pursue a pacific course, 'was not in control of cabinet decisions'.[28]

Agatha Ramm also sees Gladstone's hand as being forced on Egypt – though she believes that it was Admiral Seymour who took the lead. Seymour wanted Arabi to dismantle the forts at Alexandria, and requested that the government endorse an ultimatum to this end. It was recognized that a bombardment might well evoke a response from Arabi, but the 'forward party' were ready to accept this as any such threat would provide a pretext for a British invasion. However, Seymour exceeded his orders, demanding that Arabi 'surrender' his forts. In doing this, says Ramm, he 'practically committed his Government to take power out of Arabi's hands into his own'. Galbraith and al-Sayyid-Marsot agree. Seymour, they write, was 'ambitious and eager for action, and the information he supplied the Admiralty became the justification for the bombardment'. He exaggerated the danger from the forts and claimed that Arabi was 'dedicated to a holy war against the West, inspired by the Prophet with whom he communicated nightly'.[29] On 11 July he bombarded

---

[25] Shannon, *Gladstone: God and Politics*, p. 339.
[26] Feuchtwanger, *Gladstone*, p. 214.
[27] Hopkins, 'Victorians and Africa', p. 383.
[28] Galbraith and al-Sayyid-Marsot, 'The British Occupation of Egypt', pp. 478–80.
[29] Ibid., pp. 484–85.

the forts, a fire broke out and the town was pillaged. Seymour telegraphed for two battalions from Cyprus, and on 15 July Alexandria was policed by 800 British soldiers. On 17 July he announced that with the Khedive's permission he alone was responsible for maintaining order. 'He had', writes Ramm, 'fully committed his Government', and three days later the Cabinet agreed to send an expedition force to Cyprus and Malta.[30]

But was Gladstone really such a cipher in the events leading up to the invasion? At no point did Gladstone make a principled objection to intervention – however much he expressed doubts, at each stage in the process he ultimately acquiesced. Robert Harrison rejects the idea that Seymour was primarily responsible for bringing events to a crisis in Egypt, whose action was 'a small part of a much larger strategic operation planned well in advance to secure the Suez Canal.'[31] The idea of using the guns at Alexandria as a pretext for provoking conflict with Arabi came from the First Lord of the Admiralty, Lord Northbrook, and was taken up by Lord Granville, who 'ordered Admiral Seymour to require that Arabi halt work on the fortifications'.[32] Roy Jenkins believes that Gladstone was divided on Egypt between two positions – his anti-militarist conscience pulling him away from intervention, his belief in international order drawing him forward. And while he greatly preferred action by the Concert of Europe, still he was prepared for Britain to proceed alone.[33] Once the decision was taken, Gladstone gave it his full backing: Philip Magnus observes that his secretaries 'had never seen him in such extraordinary spirits [...] He was full of praise for the generals, the admirals, the officers, and the men.'[34] Shannon talks of his 'extraordinary [...] outbursts of eager triumphalism and vainglory'.[35]

Finance

Another explanation of Gladstone's Egyptian intervention emphasizes the role of finance. The Egyptian state was heavily indebted to the West and also owed a regular tribute to Turkey, and an Egyptian national government was considered likely to default on these payments. This was a serious concern for Britain, whose investors held the largest share of

---

[30] Ramm, *William Ewart Gladstone*, p. 91.
[31] R. T. Harrison, *Gladstone's Imperialism in Egypt* (1995), p. 11.
[32] Ibid., p. 15.
[33] Jenkins, *Gladstone*, p. 504.
[34] Magnus, *Gladstone*, p. 291.
[35] Shannon, *Gladstone: Heroic Minister*, p. 306.
[36] Hopkins, 'Victorians and Africa', p. 379.

Egyptian debt.[36] The idea that Gladstone intervened in Egypt for financial reasons was raised by the Tory–Democrat Randolph Churchill, who argued in 1883 that Gladstone's invasion was a criminal act undertaken in the interests of bondholders: 'He came among them with his armies and his fleets; destroyed their towns; devastated their country; slaughtered their thousands; and flung back those struggling wretches into the morass of oppression.'[37] This 'bondholder' thesis, according to which the extent of British holding of Egyptian bonds meant that the government could not risk a nationalist government defaulting on its interest payments, was actively propagated by the friend of Egyptian nationalism, Wilfred Blunt. His associate A. M. Broadly wrote in 1884 that the military intervention in Egypt was necessitated by 'the defence of British pecuniary interests in that country', and Blunt himself developed this theme in his 1907 *Secret History of the British Occupation of Egypt*.[38]

Matthew admits that Gladstone was willing to intervene if financial order was at stake, and this included the reliability of Egypt's financial payments. 'Money was tied in with power and imperial strategy in an unusually direct and explicit form in Egypt.'[39] Adding plausibility to this account is the fact that Gladstone was a large holder of Turkish Government bonds guaranteed by the annual Egyptian tribute. His finances, says Jenkins, were 'quite remarkably concentrated' on Egyptian government debts.[40] When the crisis broke, his stock was worth £40,567 – one-third of his entire investment portfolio. British victory over Arabi yielded Gladstone a capital gain of half a million pounds (in modern money) as the value of Turkish–Egyptian stock soared.[41] Matthew believes it a 'matter of speculation as to what part, if any, the Prime Minister's personal stake in the stability of Egyptian affairs played in his eventual agreement to go along with the change from indirect to armed intervention in Egypt by Britain alone'. On the one hand, Gladstone recognized that the interests of bondholders in Egypt *were* a factor in the decision to intervene. On the other hand, Matthew believes that Gladstone's personal holdings were only a subconscious factor since he was preoccupied with his Irish Arrears Bill. He was not an advocate of intervention and proved no friend of the bondholders: in 1884 he agreed to a reduction in the interest on Egyptian debts. 'It would', concludes Matthew, 'be crude and simplistic to infer

[37] Quoted in Magnus, *Gladstone*, p. 310.
[38] Quoted in Hopkins, 'Victorians and Africa', p. 365.
[39] Matthew, *Gladstone*, p. 387.
[40] Jenkins, *Gladstone*, p. 502.
[41] Ibid., p. 508.

any personal corruption, or even a conscious awareness of an association between personal investments and "order" in Egypt.'[42] In this Matthew is followed by Jenkins, who writes that 'I do not believe for a moment that his primary or even his significantly supporting motivation sprang from financial self-interest'.[43] Shannon concurs:

> As he absolutely could not reproach himself with the slightest twinge of doubt that he had, or would, make any decisions about Egypt with any thought of bondholding, his conscience was perfectly clear and no question of improper interest could possibly arise.[44]

'Even so', admits Matthew, 'his holding of Egyptian Tribute Loan is a fact that, once known, is hard to forget.'[45]

The idea that Britain's intervention in Egypt reflected chiefly economic considerations was reaffirmed by Hopkins in his article 'The Victorians and Africa: A Reconsideration of the Occupation of Egypt, 1882'. Like Matthew, Hopkins observes that law and order involved the protection of Britain's economic interests, and these 'played a part, perhaps even a crucial part, in Britain's decision to invade Egypt'.[46] After pointing to the extent of Britain's investment and trade links with Egypt, Hopkins argues that, while intervention was made acceptable to public opinion by stressing issues like the threat to the Canal and law and order, the real motives were 'specific business and financial concerns' formed through the connections between City of London financial interests and leading politicians. Gladstone was not directly involved in this nexus and his role was a passive one: 'Gladstone was a leader who was led throughout this episode.'[47] Lacking the will or knowledge to withstand the pressure of the Cabinet, he convinced himself that intervention was a Christian act taken to put down a tyrant. But in reality,

> [i]ntervention did not spring from any danger to the Canal, from the spread of anarchy, or from French ambitions, but from the conscious and sustained defence of Britain's expanding economic interests in Egypt.[48]

---

[42] Matthew, *Gladstone*, p. 388.
[43] Jenkins, *Gladstone*, p. 508.
[44] Shannon, *Gladstone: Heroic Minister*, p. 303.
[45] Matthew, *Gladstone*, p. 389.
[46] Hopkins, 'Victorians and Africa', p. 380.
[47] Ibid., p. 387.
[48] Ibid., p. 385.

Although Hopkins's argument is more suggestive than conclusive, Theodore Hoppen lends his support to it, observing that there existed in the Home Counties a charmed circle of the great and the good capable of effecting a 'harmonious union between personal and national interests'.[49]

Upholding the Ottoman Empire

The preceding explanations all portray British intervention as forced upon Gladstone by pressure from within his own government. However, Robert Harrison, in his *Gladstone's Imperialism in Egypt*, argues that it was Gladstone 'who most singularly defined and directed various policy aspects in the Egyptian affair as vital to British interests and to his own political morality [...] the principal decisions that propelled the later strategies and military preparations for Egypt's invasion emanated from the highest level of the Liberal government'.[50] While sympathetic to the Egyptian national movement, Gladstone also believed that the security of the Suez route to India was vital and that Egypt should remain within the Ottoman Empire. What wrecked Gladstone's attempt to sustain these two diverse approaches was his discovery that Arabi's goal was not autonomy *within* the Ottoman Empire, but *independence* from it. Gladstone intervened in Egypt to uphold the Ottoman Empire because it underpinned Britain's trading and communication interests in the region.

> Gladstone and Granville had long determined that Egypt should remain in the Ottoman orbit, since all Suez and Red Sea water rights treaties, numerous reforming and internal improvement schemes, and financial obligations to the Europeans remained viable, without international guarantees, only as long as the Porte maintained legal suzerainty over Khedival Egypt.[51]

Having decided to uphold 'Britain's directly controlled Khedival mechanism and securing the Canal route to India', Gladstone's Liberal government sought to obscure the 'blatantly imperialistic' character of their action by pretending to a 'great reluctance to intervene' and claiming they were doing so 'for the sake of the Egyptian people'.[52] But this was, concludes Harrison, only ever a matter of putting 'a good face on a questionable deed'.

---

[49] Hoppen, *Mid-Victorian Generation*, p. 659.
[50] Harrison, *Gladstone's Imperialism in Egypt*, p. 160.
[51] Ibid., p. 13.
[52] Ibid., pp. 78, 161.

Conclusion

By the end of 1882 Gladstone found himself, in Shannon's words, the 'master of the Nile, the Canal, the crossroads of the world'.[53] This was all the more unexpected since he had, in 1877, warned specifically against a British occupation of Egypt. Why, then, did Gladstone oversee such an imperial advance? In confronting this question it is well to observe, first, that historians, with the exception of Harrison, agree that Gladstone did not initiate the policy of occupying Egypt and that the pressure ran from the Cabinet to Gladstone. So why did the Cabinet want to occupy Egypt and why did Gladstone acquiesce in a policy over which he had profound misgivings? What resolved the majority within the Cabinet upon intervention was the belief that order could only be restored by overthrowing Arabi and reaffirming the Khedive as a puppet ruler on behalf of Western interests. Why was this so important? The most commonly aired justification was the need to guarantee the Suez route to India, and Robinson and Gallagher trace the process by which a majority in the Cabinet came to conclude that Arabi had to be removed for this reason. However, Arabi had not threatened the Canal, and, as Matthew points out, Gladstone never accepted that the defence of India required British control of the Canal. What Gladstone *did* talk about was the need to uphold order in Egypt, and he always claimed that Britain was intervening on behalf of the Concert of Europe. This explanation has been accepted by writers ranging from Lords Cromer and Milner at the time to Shannon more recently. But why was order in Egypt more important than elsewhere in Africa? Hopkins has valiantly endeavoured to revive the claims made by critics of intervention such as Blunt that what drove policy on Egypt were British economic interests in the region. Unfortunately, Hopkins provides little evidence to substantiate his claim, and there is nothing to show that this was Gladstone's motivation – despite his substantial holdings of Turkish–Egyptian stock. A paucity of evidence equally bedevils Harrison's attempt to present Gladstone as pushing for invasion to hold Egypt within the Ottoman Empire. It is the current consensus that Gladstone allowed himself to be pressured into intervening by his Cabinet for want of the energy or interest to evolve an alternative strategy, and that his references to upholding the public law on behalf of the Concert of Europe were really an attempt to cover the contradiction between his words and actions on Egypt. What lay behind the Cabinet pressure for invasion – whether it was

---

[53] Shannon, *Gladstone: Heroic Minister*, p. 305.

the Canal, public order, fear of French intrigue or the interests of London financiers – remains unclear.

6.2   Was Gladstone a Unifying or a Divisive Figure in the Liberal Party?

Gladstone was, after 1880, the most commanding figure in British politics, and following his return to front-line politics in 1876 he could not but be Liberal leader. Yet what kind of leader did he prove to be? Was he, as a strong tradition suggests, the one man who could unite a fractious Liberal party around his charismatic personality? Or was he, as has been increasingly argued, a disruptive presence who left the Liberal party more riven with contention than he found it?

Gladstone as unifier

According to the traditional interpretation, from the late 1870s Gladstone was the one figure able to unite the Liberal party sufficiently to be able to form a stable government. With the party increasingly divided between aristocratic Whigs and the rising forces of middle-class radicalism, Gladstone alone possessed the prestige to hold the party together. With his Midlothian campaign he rallied the party around the denunciation of Beaconsfieldism, carrying it to victory.[54] Francis Birrell encapsulates this interpretation:

> At the beginning of 1876, the Liberal Party was almost non-existent; by the end of 1877, it was united, enthusiastic, and self-confident. 'The old man' had indeed performed a miraculous task, of which the coping-stone was the Midlothian campaign [...] No one knew the proportion of 'Whigs' to 'Radicals' in the new House, and Gladstone was the only person who could keep the party together for a few years more.[55]

Morley, himself a Radical of the 1880s, writes that Gladstone's accession to the premiership in 1880 was inevitable, for it 'was Mr. Gladstone, as everybody knew and said, who had led and inspired the assault'.[56] His Cabinet was a vexatious one, with peers led by Lord Hartington often at odds with Commoners like Chamberlain. Morley notes that Chamberlain himself

---

[54] Morley, *Life of Gladstone*, III, p. 3.
[55] Birrell, *Gladstone*, pp. 95, 102.
[56] Morley, *Life of Gladstone*, II, p. 618.

remarked, 'I don't see how we are to get on, if Mr. Gladstone goes.' Here, says Morley, we have 'the key to many leading incidents [...] during the life of this administration'. Gladstone's son, Herbert Gladstone, refrained this theme in his 1928 recollections:

> Mr. Gladstone, in his constant effort to mould all Liberal forces for the purposes of progress, was the sole connecting link between Whigs and Radicals [...] he was the last barrier between the Whigs and the oncoming flood of Radicalism under Mr. Chamberlain.[57]

Feuchtwanger and Hamer endorse this perspective. According to Feuchtwanger,

> [t]he Liberals were in fact so heterogeneous that perhaps the only way to lead them was Gladstone's way: by detachment and the choice of great causes emotionally presented [...] Gladstone could hardly have towered like a colossus had he really been so much out of line with the mood and requirements of the time.[58]

For David Hamer, too, the Liberal party was a coalition of sectional interests, lacking an integrating ideology. Gladstone's response was to evoke great causes around which the party could coalesce, while avoiding allying himself with any one of the competing interest groups.

> Gladstone always and very calculatedly moved on a plane of his own. One result of his deliberate aloofness from internal party disputes and sectionalism was that he never became completely committed to either radical or conservative positions.[59]

While the Radicals felt they shared enough ground with Gladstone to give them hope of realizing much of their programme, the Whigs saw in Gladstone's influence 'a guarantee against the assumption by the Radicals of complete control over the party'.[60]

Most recently, Matthew has forcibly asserted the idea that Gladstone played a uniquely unifying role within the party. First, he emphasizes the heterodox nature of Liberalism by the 1880s and Gladstone's ability to box the compass of contradictory positions.

---

[57] H. Gladstone, *After Thirty Years* (1928), p. 277.
[58] Feuchtwanger, *Gladstone*, pp. 195, 198.
[59] D. A. Hamer, *Liberal Politics in the Age of Gladstone and Rosebery* (1972), p. 74.
[60] Ibid., pp. 75–77.

The Liberal party aspired to classlessness, but it was riddled with class; it hoped for interdominationalism but it divided between Erastianism, sectarianism, and secularism; it tried to offer justice to the three kingdoms but it satisfied none. Gladstone stood outside the Cabinet and the party; his class was indefinable, his religion exceptional; he was an extreme Radical on some questions, and unreconstructed Conservative on others.[61]

Matthew, in other words, agrees with Feuchtwanger and Hamer that Gladstone

had substantial credit with each of the various sections of the party, though each also had substantial reasons for caution about him. Among the radical nonconformists, his opposition to Beaconsfieldism was an impeccable credential [...] To the Liberal centre, he offered executive competence, a safe pair of financial hands, and a strong urge for legislative achievement. For the Whigs, he represented especially a guarantee against something worse.[62]

Second, Matthew argues that the Whigs no longer possessed the intellectual or political energy to lead the party.

The Whigs were ceasing to be a fertile force in British politics and were becoming predominantly reactive [...] The intellectual daring and political initiative of the Russell era was being replaced by the grey conventionality of Hartington: moderately competent, politically respectable, but sterile. Outside the field of colonial government and foreign affairs [...] it would be hard to find any significant contribution [...] for which the Whigs were responsible after 1880.[63]

Hence, Granville and Hartington were 'probably rather relieved' to be passed over for the premiership in 1880: 'neither had the energy nor the political clout successfully to lead the Liberal party in power. 1880 was the last occasion on which the Whigs were offered a government with a good majority, and their leaders were not strong enough to take it'.[64] Gladstone was also, argues Matthew, central to Liberal organization outside Westminster.

---

[61] Matthew, *Gladstone*, p. 228.
[62] Ibid., p. 364.
[63] Ibid., p. 358.
[64] Ibid., p. 353.

Liberal individualism meant there was much resistance to the idea of regular party organization. As such 'the Gladstonian method of rhetorical integration [...] offered a substitution for or alternative to organization at the national level'. Gladstone was the 'arbitrator, mediator, and key-stone of the Cabinet-Party arch'.[65]

Gladstone as a force for instability

The view that Gladstone was indispensable for Liberal unity has come under mounting attack.

Lack of a policy programme

An early criticism, voiced by R. C. K. Ensor in 1936 and taken up by Hamer, was that Gladstone failed to provide his party with a legislative programme. The 1880 government achieved so little, says Ensor, because it was afflicted by divisions which 'palsied the government's counsels and zigzagged its policy. Gladstone had induced extremes to meet in attacking Beaconsfield, but not in the pursuit of any positive programme.'[66] Hamer makes much of this fact. Although Gladstone seemingly possessed all the attributes to lead the Liberal coalition, his government was weak since it had no programme and drifted from 'one session to another without adequate preparation of plans for the use of parliamentary time'. 'The truce of 1879–80 was soon broken. The sections began clamouring for priority of attention, and the Liberal leaders soon seemed to be spending more time in finding excuses for inaction than in getting things done.'[67]

Roy Jenkins believes that the weakness and divisions of the government reflected 'almost entirely' Gladstone's failure to provide leadership.

> The 1868 government, because it had a legislative programme relevant to the dominant issues, was able to make the political weather. The 1880 government not only lacked a structured programme but it also had little idea in advance of the main issues with which it would have to deal. As a result it was always the creature rather than the creator of the circumstances in which it operated.[68]

Ireland dominated the government, but Gladstone, who had no conception of the relations between economics and politics, failed to see that the agrarian

---

[65] Ibid., pp. 361–62.
[66] Ensor, *England: 1870–1914*, p. 67.
[67] Hamer, *Liberal Politics*, pp. 84, 88.
[68] Jenkins, *Gladstone*, p. 443.

depression was pushing Ireland into crisis and had no policy for Ireland – or indeed for anything else. 'Improvisation was the keynote of the government's performance.'[69]

Intention to retire

Another criticism emphasizes the destabilizing effect of Gladstone's repeated talk of retirement. When assuming the premiership in 1880 he was adamant that he was doing so only until he had cleansed the nation of the evils of Beaconsfieldism. His position as prime minister was, therefore, provisional and several historians, including Shannon, Hawkins, Jonathan Parry and Matthew, have highlighted the disabling effect this had. With everyone expecting Gladstone's departure, manoeuvring for the succession began almost from the government's commencement – as Parry explains:

> Uncertainty for the future greatly increased tension. Both Hartington and Chamberlain were driven onto the defensive, acting as protectors of sectional interests within the party. Yet both were forced to defend Gladstone's continued leadership, for fear that if either took the blame for pushing him out, the succession would favour the other [...] The bizarre result was the simultaneous emasculation of all the leading Liberals of the day, and a style of government far removed from the decisive, purposeful yet reassuring Liberal ideal.[70]

By a paradoxical logic, observes Hawkins,

> the very tensions created by the expectations of Gladstone's departure enabled the Grand Old Man to argue that he must reluctantly continue as leader in order to preserve Liberal unity [...] Gladstone's continuing claim on the Liberal leadership by 1883 depended on a persistent sense of emergency. Yet it was precisely the temporary nature of Gladstone's leadership that did much to foment divisions.[71]

Jenkins concurs. So long as uncertainty about the leadership persisted, Gladstone's heirs were disinclined to allow long-term policy decisions to be settled. 'In consequence, Gladstone was confronted with what seemed to him to be disunity amongst his colleagues, and he responded by assuming the

---

[69] Ibid., pp. 444–45.
[70] Parry, *Rise and Fall of Liberal Government*, p. 290.
[71] Hawkins, *British Party Politics*, p. 234.

role of peacemaker in Cabinet, instead of being the director.'[72] According to Shannon, Gladstone further stirred the pot of discord by floating hypothetically large questions with respect to issues like the government of Ireland while insisting he would not be around to resolve them.[73] Thus, with the party unsettled and Radicals and Whigs uncertain of whether they could command the party in Gladstone's absence, all factions 'preferred his staying on to the likely shape of things were he to go'.[74]

Matthew acknowledges that Gladstone's intention to retire 'created widespread unease […] there was a sense of the transitory about the Cabinet of 1880–5'.[75] However, he lays responsibility for this state of affairs at the door of the Whigs.

> The fact was that the Whigs could not let him go. They would not let him go in 1874; they tried to stop him going in 1875; they could not do without him in 1885. For all the rows over Irish property, the Whigs looked to Gladstone for defence.[76]

Feuchtwanger had earlier remarked that whenever 'his resignation appeared to become an imminent reality, irresistible pressures appeared to make him stay. Very often they came from those who frequently opposed him, Hartington and Chamberlain, for only Gladstone could keep the heterogeneous Liberal coalition together and neither of them was yet ready to succeed him.'[77] Hoppen agrees that 'virtually every other leading man in the party needed Gladstone more than the Prime Minister needed any of his lieutenants'.[78] By 1885, summarizes Shannon, all sections of the party agreed that Gladstone had to be the leader:

> For Chamberlain, Gladstone's leadership was a convenience, a means of transition from the old politics to the new. For Hartington, Gladstone's leadership had become a stark necessity.[79]

Gladstone's distance from the Liberal tradition

The above arguments are contingent in character, pointing to the effects of a lack of a clear policy programme and of Gladstone's retirement plans.

---

[72] T. A. Jenkins, *Gladstone, Whiggery and the Liberal Party 1874–1886* (1988), p. 234.
[73] Ensor, *England: 1870–1914*, p. 67; Shannon, *Gladstone: Heroic Minister*, p. 284.
[74] Shannon, *Gladstone: God and Politics*, p. 341.
[75] Matthew, *Gladstone*, p. 354.
[76] Ibid., p. 357.
[77] Feuchtwanger, *Gladstone*, pp. 214–15.
[78] Hoppen, *Mid-Victorian Generation*, pp. 639–40.
[79] Shannon, *Gladstone: Heroic Minister*, p. 385.

However, two more systemically disruptive aspects of Gladstone's political position have been identified.

First, it is argued by Parry and Shannon that Gladstone was not a unifying figure since he did not embody mainstream Liberal politics. Gladstone was still a Peelite and did not subscribe to core Liberal doctrines, such as institutional reform and parliamentary government. Indeed, Shannon suggests that he was not even a Gladstonian Liberal. Compounding this was a developing mistrust of his methods, which were volatile and conviction based. The party, it appeared to increasing numbers of senior Liberals, could never be stable and united with Gladstone at the helm. Parry expresses these ideas in his *Rise and Fall of Liberal Government in Victorian Britain*. Gladstone, he says, 'remained unsympathetic to organic constitutional reform, to anti-clericalism, and to those who tolerated the drift of parliamentary debate, yet these were the three staples of the Liberal tradition'.

> He inspired Liberals on many occasions and for many reasons but, ultimately, large numbers of them proved no more willing to accept his emotive, authoritarian, evangelical, sentimental, unpredictable leadership style than the Conservatives of 1846 had tolerated Peel's. In 1886, Gladstone broke up his party almost single-handedly as his mentor had done forty years before. The Liberal party did not fall apart because of 'sectionalism' or whig 'inflexibility' but because of Gladstone's distance from the Liberal tradition.[80]

Although Gladstone's strategy of maintaining public morality and efficient government was conservative, 'the religious zeal with which he promoted it distanced him markedly from the integrationist, rational and parliamentary whig temper. The whigs believed in organic institutional reform, and open debate in parliament [...] Gladstone disliked institutional reform, abhorred anti-clericalism and, at times of stress, had little respect for "parliamentary government".'[81] Where he was 'excitable, domineering, and impulsive', the 'whig-Liberal tradition held to key ideals: integration, establishment, reason, consensus, law, parliamentary government. At various times, different Liberals concluded that under Gladstone's leadership these values were, or might be, under serious threat.'[82] During the Midlothian campaign it seemed as if the party might be welded together around an ideology of Gladstonian Liberalism. It is all the more ironic, therefore, that Shannon observes that

---

[80] Parry, *Rise and Fall of Liberal Government*, p. 225.
[81] Ibid., p. 250.
[82] Ibid., p. 260.

by 1882 divergences were increasingly apparent between 'Gladstonian Liberalism' and 'Gladstone's Liberalism'. While Gladstonian Liberals wanted a thorough reform of local government, 'Gladstone offered grandiloquent phrases but avoided effective commitment'.[83]

> With his legislative barrenness in the 1880 Parliament, Gladstone was the wrecker of Gladstonian Liberalism. With his invasion and occupation of Egypt he wrecked Gladstonian Liberalism's international morale. The gap yawned between Gladstone's Liberalism and Gladstonian Liberalism.[84]

Even Matthew concedes truth in this charge. While Gladstone felt that 'the most effective way of maintaining party enthusiasm was for him to lead from the front' with 'big bills', the problem was that many of the big measures Gladstone championed did not run with the grain of Liberalism and 'frustrated the anticipated Liberal programme'.[85]

Gladstone prevents Whig–Radical compromise

T. A. Jenkins and Hawkins reject the entire Gladstone as unifier narrative. According to Jenkins, Whiggism was not, as Matthew suggests, exhausted by the 1870s. Historians, he argues, have underestimated the capacity of the Whigs to supply strong centre-ground Liberal politics, just as they have exaggerated the power of the Radicals, who lacked clear policies or a leader. Chamberlain's attempt to weld together the diffuse forces of Victorian Liberalism failed – partly because Liberals in other towns were unwilling to take their direction from Birmingham. By exaggerating Chamberlain's power and antagonistic relations with the Whigs, historians have obscured 'the crucial point that [...] he generally recognized the need to cooperate' with the Whigs.[86] Indeed, efforts were made in the later 1870s by Whig leaders to accommodate the Radicals, with Hartington signalling in speeches that he was prepared to consider the case for Scottish Church disestablishment, temperance reform, reduction in the county franchise and the reform of county government, and this provided a basis for Radical co-operation.[87] The Whigs, he continues, 'were far less conservative in their attitudes to

---

[83] Shannon, *Gladstone: God and Politics*, pp. 334–35.
[84] Ibid., p. 339.
[85] Matthew, *Gladstone*, pp. 359–60.
[86] Jenkins, *Gladstone, Whiggery and the Liberal Party*, p. 14.
[87] Ibid., p. 83.

reform than is usually supposed', being chiefly concerned to regulate the pace of change and retain control over the party.[88] Hence, the Radicals believed Hartington 'was sufficiently responsive to their views for it to be worth their while to accept his leadership [...] because the Whigs were able to tap vital sources of strength through their hold over moderate Liberal opinion'.[89] 'What was *not* apparent by late 1879', writes Hawkins, 'was a vicious Liberal schism [...] between Whig and radical factions, demanding the presence of Gladstone to restore party unity.'[90] Hartington 'fought a successful campaign during 1879–80', criticizing Disraeli's imperialist foreign policy and fiscal extravagance, and it 'was quite on the cards, during the autumn of 1879, that it would be the Whig leaders, rather than Gladstone, who would be the chief beneficiaries of the Liberal revival'.[91] But all such hopes were dashed by Gladstone's Midlothian campaign, which focused popular support on himself. 'Gladstone's pre-eminence had not been a necessary condition for Liberal unity. These ambiguities permeated the tensions within Gladstone's second cabinet.'[92] While Jenkins admits that rank-and-file Radicals wanted a Gladstone premiership, this was not true of leading Radicals, who mistrusted his erratic style of politics, and most senior Liberals considered Hartington and Granville to be 'men who stood for party unity and sober, responsible leadership'. It was the *scale* of the Liberal victory and the view that this reflected the moral forces unleashed by Gladstone that unnerved the Whigs – when, given the economic depression and dissatisfaction with Disraeli's foreign policy, 'it is conceivable that Gladstone's activities made virtually no difference to the result of the general election'.[93]

Once the Liberal administration was formed, Jenkins agrees with Hawkins and Shannon that Gladstone's overbearing personality encouraged faction fighting within the government, as did his teasing talk of retirement. The Liberals, then, were divided because of Gladstone and 'competition for influence over the destiny of the party in the post-Gladstonian era'.[94] 'Gladstone's position', comments Hawkins, 'rested upon the notion that he performed a unique service as a balancing force between the Whig and Radical sections of the Liberal party.'[95] But this 'played down the ability

---

[88] Ibid., p. 76. See also Hawkins, *British Party Politics*, pp. 219–20.
[89] Jenkins, *Gladstone, Whiggery and the Liberal Party*, p. 95.
[90] Hawkins, *British Party Politics*, p. 220.
[91] Ibid., p. 222; Jenkins, *Gladstone, Whiggery and the Liberal Party*, p. 101.
[92] Hawkins, *British Party Politics*, p. 225.
[93] Jenkins, *Gladstone, Whiggery and the Liberal Party*, pp. 137, 139.
[94] Ibid., p. 146.
[95] Ibid., p. 181.

of some Whigs, such as Hartington [...] to align radical aspirations with executive competence and moderate reform. Gladstone's unique authority was not as indispensable to Liberal unity as he believed.'[96] As a corollary, Jenkins questions 'the inevitability of a Liberal schism, after Gladstone's retirement'.[97]

> Whether, on Gladstone's departure, Hartington and Chamberlain could have established a reasonable working relationship, is one of the great imponderables of late nineteenth-century politics. It is possible to detect certain areas of policy, notably concerning foreign and imperial matters, where there was a great deal of common ground between Hartington and the younger school of Radicals, and this might have provided the basis for an accommodation along 'Liberal Imperialist' lines.[98]

This Jenkins–Hawkins understanding of Gladstone's disruptive role gains support from several other historians. Shannon acknowledges that Gladstone's 'unprecedented' ascendancy in the government and country gave Cabinet colleagues the license to pursue their own agendas, and hence 'the longer Gladstone stayed on and the more, consequently, incoherent were his colleagues, the more he needed to stay on as the sole power of coherence'.[99] Even Feuchtwanger, who regards Gladstone as uniquely placed to integrate the Liberal coalition, admits that by the end of his administration he had 'pushed his "leadership by detachment" to dangerous lengths' and 'his colleagues were manoeuvring for position'. At times the Whig–Radical cleavage 'seemed less important than the gulf between his own Cobdenite economism and the imperialist concerns of so many of his colleagues'.[100]

Parry, too, believes that had Hartington been able to head the Liberal party on his own terms he 'might well have been its greatest leader'.[101] But where Jenkins and Hawkins see Hartington as willing to work with the Radicals, Parry argues that, as a natural Palmerstonian, his aim was to attract the support of the gentry, the rising plutocracy and the propertied middle class so as to 'secure a permanent electoral majority for the party and to marginalise radicals who might threaten the rule of property and law'. Hartington knew

---

[96] Hawkins, *British Party Politics*, p. 265.
[97] Jenkins, *Gladstone, Whiggery and the Liberal Party*, p. 191.
[98] Ibid., pp. 196–97.
[99] Shannon, *Gladstone: Heroic Minister*, pp. 252, 284.
[100] Feuchtwanger, *Gladstone*, pp. 228–29. Richard Cobden had been the leader of the free-trade Anti-Corn Law League and was a strong advocate of laissez-faire economic policies.
[101] Parry, *Rise and Fall of Liberal Government*, p. 260.

how to 'keep the Liberal coalition together' and in the wake of Gladstone's 1874 defeat sought to revive the Whig tradition of reason and steady progress, focusing upon a strong foreign policy, fiscal rectitude, unionism and considered legislation. 'In other words, the answer to Liberal problems seemed to be a reassertion of *parliamentary* government' through debate. The Whiggish logic was impeccable – but things did not work out like that.[102]

Conclusion

As is apparent, the debate concerning Gladstone's affect upon the Liberal party from the late 1870s is highly polarized. Certainly, as Hamer suggests, Gladstone *ought* to have been an integrating personality since he could legitimately appeal to almost every one of the wide array of political connections who made up the Liberal party. And according to the traditional interpretation, traceable to Gladstone himself and since reiterated by Morley, Feuchtwanger and Matthew, Gladstone indeed supplied the integrating leadership the Whigs could no longer provide. To this Jenkins, Hawkins and Parry object, arguing that the Whigs were far from a spent force and that in Gladstone's absence they and the Radicals would have compromised around a programme of moderate reform. Which perspective is correct we can never know, for the experiment was never tried. What we *do* know is that Gladstone's leadership was subject to serious debilitating weaknesses, notably the absence of a strong policy programme and an expressed determination to retire which, as even Matthew acknowledges, meant that an atmosphere of transitoriness clung around the government. The Liberals were more divided in 1885 than in 1879. Whether they would have been more or less so in Gladstone's absence is impossible to resolve – but Gladstone assuredly created an unreal political atmosphere in which the politics of the possible was placed in abeyance.

---

[102] Ibid., pp. 261, 272–73.

Chapter 7

GLADSTONE AND IRELAND

Outline of Events

Ireland exerted a pronounced influence upon William Gladstone's political career. It had been one of his first priorities to uphold the status of the Church of England as the official Church of Ireland. Yet his commitment to Anglican exclusivity in Ireland collapsed in 1845 when confronted by Sir Robert Peel's proposal to enhance the state subsidy to the Catholic seminary at Maynooth. Gladstone allied himself with the Peelite project of pacifying Ireland through policies formulated independently (and often at odds with) the views of his party, and this, essentially, was the story of Gladstone's later engagement with Ireland – a story beginning in 1867, when Gladstone responded to Fenian terrorism in England by claiming that the time had come to remove Ireland's legitimate grievances with British rule. To this end he sought to end the status of the Church of England as the official Church of Ireland; amend landlord–tenant relations in Ireland through his 1870 Land Act; and tried (unsuccessfully) to make the Irish University system more accommodating of Catholics. With these measures Gladstone considered he had done enough to pacify Ireland. This was always wishful thinking, and the agricultural depression of the 1870s and 1880s intruded a new bitterness in landlord–tenant relations as farmers struggled to pay what they considered exorbitant rents. Thus, when becoming prime minister in 1880, Gladstone sought to neutralize the land issue by granting the tenants' demands for the 3F's. It was hoped that by following up this initiative with local government reform, the stabilization of Ireland would be realized. But the devolution of powers to Ireland never came; instead, there were the Phoenix Park murders and a further wave of coercion. Thus by 1885 Gladstone was brought to recognize two facts: first, land reform had not pacified Ireland; second, Irish nationalism, far from being in retreat, had consolidated its grip upon Irish opinion. Gladstone's response was dramatic. Concluding that Ireland would only be a peaceful member of the Empire if it ran its own domestic affairs, he drew up the Irish Home Rule Bill of 1886. Unfortunately, Gladstone's conviction that the concession of a separate parliament for Ireland was a price worth paying for peace was not shared by large parts the Liberal party, let alone parliament or the nation. Just as Peel had shattered the unity of the Conservatives over Maynooth and the Corn Laws in 1845–46, so did his greatest disciple shatter Liberal unity over Ireland 40 years later. Although Gladstone campaigned doggedly for Irish Home Rule for a further eight years, his second Home Rule Bill was crushed by the House of Lords in 1894, and the greatest politician of the Victorian age retired at the age of 85 with his mission to pacify Ireland unrealized.

7.1   Gladstone and Irish Church Disestablishment

Gladstone's decision to take up Irish Church reform in 1867 commenced an engagement with the Irish question that determined the trajectory of the remaining 30 years of his career. Evidently, we need to know why he took this first step. Historians disagree upon this issue: for some it was a principled initiative designed to improve Irish government; for others, it had more to do with the needs of the Liberal party, or Gladstone, than with Ireland; for others still, it was but another scene in the ever-continuing rivalry with Benjamin Disraeli.

A necessary reform whose time had arrived

It has often been argued, beginning with Gladstone in his 1868 *A Chapter of Autobiography*, that he arrived by the mid-1860s at the conviction that the Anglican Church needed to lose its established status in Ireland as a necessary step toward reconciling Irish opinion to government from London. Having initially worked to uphold the established status of the Church in Ireland, Gladstone had, from the late 1840s, developed ever greater reservations about this state of affairs, and thus when in 1865, writes John Morley, he considered the position of the Irish Church, his 'indictment' was 'decisive'. So began 'the first advance upon what was to be an important journey'.[1] In 1865 Gladstone judged that British opinion would not allow the disestablishment of the Church in Ireland, and hence he stated 'that the question was out of all bearing on the practical politics of the day'. But by 1868, says Morley, he believed the time had come to act. Why was this?

---

[1] Morley, *Life of Gladstone*, II. p. 141.

Morley cites Gladstone's own words of 1869 that it was the rise of militant Fenianism and, in particular, the attacks in Manchester and London that were key. Though not changing Gladstone's thinking on Ireland, they prepared public opinion to consider 'the vast importance of the Irish controversy'.[2] While the Tories contemplated concurrent endowment of religious faiths in Ireland, Gladstone countered with disestablishment and an end to all endowments. This decision, contends Morley, was 'one of the heroic acts of his life' and showed that he had 'rightly divined the state of public opinion about Ireland'.[3]

The idea that Gladstone took up Irish Church reform in 1867 because the political situation made it possible to implement a policy he already knew was right, has been endorsed by numerous studies. In 1913, J. A. R. Marriott noted that Gladstone vehemently denied that Fenianism had affected 'in the slightest degree' his own convictions on the subject. Fenianism merely suggested the occasion: the causes of the problem lay deep in the past.[4] E. L. Woodward similarly writes that Gladstone's 'mind was made up' before the Fenian outrages, which only convinced him 'that delay was dangerous'.[5] Erich Eyck likewise believes that the Fenian atrocities created a situation within which the causes of Irish unrest would have to be tackled, as does Francis Birrell, who says that Gladstone recognized that, for the first time, the possibility of building a public opinion in favour of disestablishment existed. 'Out of this unpromising material, Gladstone "formed a public opinion" and gained a majority of 100; for few people had taken much interest in the Irish Establishment till Gladstone had drawn their attention to the subject.'[6] More recently, Francis Lyons has written that Gladstone saw terrorism as 'the symptom of a deeper malaise', and that his conviction that 'Irish violence was the product of Irish grievance' antedated Fenianism by many years.[7] Peter Stansky regards Gladstone's Irish initiative of 1867 as representing the coalescence of principle and practicality – of the slow 'change of his mind as well as the gradual maturing of public opinion'.[8] Roy Jenkins echoes this interpretation. The views Gladstone expressed in his 1867 Southport speech on Irish reform were not 'the result of a sudden lurch, but rather the end of a gradual but predictable curve which had started nearly thirty years before

---

[2] Ibid., pp. 240–2.
[3] Ibid., pp. 246, 250.
[4] Marriott, *England Since Waterloo*, p. 383.
[5] Woodward, *Age of Reform*, p. 346.
[6] Eyck, *Gladstone*, p. 180; Birrell, *Gladstone*, p. 79.
[7] F. S. L. Lyons, *Ireland since the Famine* (1972 edn.), p. 142.
[8] Stansky, *Gladstone*, p. 111.

and taken him through almost 180 degrees'.[9] George Boyce believes that Gladstone was 'not motivated' by the Fenian attacks to take up the issue of the Irish Church, but that 'he saw the opportunity that it offered to make a bold move' in that direction.[10]

This interpretation is endorsed by both Colin Matthew and Richard Shannon. Matthew observes that in 1866 Gladstone still considered the disestablishment of the Irish Church an 'unripe' issue. It was the 'heat of Fenianism' that caused the ripening.[11] Gladstone's approach to the Irish Church question reflected his underlying object of marginalizing Fenianism by removing the causes of Irish unrest. 'Gladstone seems to have believed that if the Irish were shown the Westminster Parliament redressing their grievances by spectacular acts of legislation, then this would encourage their adherence to the existing political structure, both as to institutions and political parties.'[12] Shannon likewise notes that Ireland had become an increasing preoccupation for Gladstone during 1866, and the status of the Irish Church in particular. The problem was that in 1865 he had declared the Irish Church to be an issue that would not be settled for five or ten years and 'there is no doubt that it was Fenian terrorism at the end of 1867 which enabled Gladstone to begin to transmute into immediacy the process since 1865 which had passed from "five to ten years" through to "not far distant"'.[13]

But why did Gladstone *want* to disestablish the Irish Church? Most agree with Matthew that his prime concern was to pacify the Irish by removing the grievance of being subordinated to an alien Church. A particular audience to whom Gladstone wished to appeal, says David Bebbington, was the Roman Catholic hierarchy in Ireland, which he hoped might constitute a bulwark against Fenianism.[14] Euginio Biagini, however, contends that Gladstone's preoccupation remained with the fate of Anglicanism in Ireland. 'Gladstone's aim was that of strengthening the Irish Church, as much as implementing religious equality. From his own peculiar Tractarian-Evangelical standpoint he felt that the Irish Church itself would benefit from autonomy and freedom for state control.'[15] Stansky concurs that 'Gladstone believed that the Church of Ireland would [...] find strength and new life through disestablishment'.[16]

---

[9] Jenkins, *Gladstone*, pp. 283–84.
[10] D. G. Boyce, 'Gladstone and Ireland', in Jagger (ed.), *Gladstone*, pp. 107–8.
[11] Matthew, *Gladstone*, p. 145.
[12] Ibid., p. 194.
[13] Shannon, *Gladstone: Heroic Minister*, p. 46.
[14] D. Bebbington, *William Ewart Gladstone* (1993), pp. 146–47.
[15] Biagini, *Gladstone*, p. 48.
[16] Stansky, *Gladstone*, p. 114.

David Hamer, by contrast, believes that Gladstone's chief motive was to strengthen the Anglican Establishment *in Britain* 'by eliminating the indefensible and peripheral anomalies which rendered it vulnerable to criticism' from Nonconformists.[17]

Ireland as a means to Liberal unity

A second widely canvassed explanation for Gladstone's action refers not to the condition of Ireland but to the condition of the Liberal party. The years 1866–67 had left the party in disarray as his own Reform Bill failed and many MPs supported Disraeli's 1867 Reform Act. Gladstone was looking for an issue that could reassemble party unity around his leadership, and this the Irish Church provided. Ireland provided good ground for such a policy: it was, unlike many Liberal concerns, one where Gladstone had come to share the majority view of the party, and it was one which appealed across the spectrum of Liberal opinion, uniting, says Boyce, 'Whig and Dissenter alike'.[18] Michael Bentley has forcefully expressed this strategic imperative:

> If Gladstone could involve all wings of his party in an effective Irish policy it might prove possible to reconstruct Liberalism and throw out Derby and Disraeli [...] The reform difficulty had shown the importance of approaching politics through a realistic conception of what political parties could achieve [...] Seen from an extra-party standpoint, after all, the problems of Irish society required one operation more than any other: an assault on the iniquities of landownership and the plight of the Irish tenantry. Yet Gladstone saw at once that the subject [...] would divide his party even more drastically than reform had done. His attack must rather be aimed at the point where Whiggery met Dissent, and that intersection occurred in the movement to disestablish the Anglican Church in Ireland. Whatever Gladstone's task in Ireland would eventually come to comprise [...] his mission was to pacify the Liberal party.[19]

Theodore Hoppen joins Bentley in placing political considerations to the fore:

> Failure and departure from office in 1866 prompted Gladstone to move beyond reform and to begin turning a very recent interest in Irish affairs

---

[17] Hamer, *Liberal Politics*, p. 26.
[18] D. G. Boyce, *The Irish Question in British Politics, 1886–1996* (1996), p. 19.
[19] Bentley, *Politics without Democracy*, p. 205.

into a sovereign method for reuniting the fractured forces of Liberalism [...] Certainly the unfolding of his engagement does not match the development of serious unrest in Ireland. Probably he realised that Ireland would allow him to divert attention from more divisive issues [...] The disestablishment of the (Anglican) Church of Ireland was, indeed, the only major issue capable of uniting all sections of the Liberal Party.[20]

T. A. Jenkins, alert always to the more personal calculations underlying Gladstone's protestations of principle, considers his own account of the background to his decision to take up the Irish Church question as characteristic of his 'capacity for self-deception'. It is difficult 'to resist the conclusion that Gladstone's conduct was designed – perhaps unconsciously – to secure the fulfilment of his political ambitions' by consolidating 'the inheritance which seemed likely to be his when Palmerston and Russell departed from the scene'.

> This conclusion is strengthened [...] when we remember that, in 1868, the 'remote question' of Irish Church disestablishment suddenly became 'ripe' for settlement, at a time when Gladstone badly needed a unifying issue with which to draw the Liberal party together, after the chaos caused by the reform crisis.[21]

The problem Gladstone faced, says Jonathan Parry, was that he did not share backbench enthusiasm for policies such as secret voting and education reform. 'Divisions within the Liberal party were less obvious on the Irish Church question, because whigs, anti-Catholic Ulsterman and nonconformists could all appreciate the arguments for disestablishment. This increasingly appeared to be the only policy capable of re-establishing party unity.'[22] Selecting Irish Church disestablishment was, says John Vincent, 'a stroke of electoral genius [...] Ireland did as much for the Liberal Party as the Liberal Party did for Ireland'.[23]

Significantly, most historians believing Gladstone was acting out of principle over disestablishment also acknowledge the policy's political benefits. Thus Matthew agrees with Bentley that Gladstone was thinking of both land and church reform in Ireland, but that land reform was too

---

[20] Hoppen, *Mid-Victorian Generation*, pp. 220, 594.

[21] Jenkins, *Gladstone, Whiggery and the Liberal Party*, p. 23.

[22] Parry, *Democracy and Religion*, p. 265.

[23] J. Vincent, *The Formation of the British Liberal Party 1857–1868* (1972 edn), p. 87.

complicated to be brought forward in opposition. 'Resolutions of principle on the Irish Church, however, both unified the party and were possible within the limitations of opposition.' Indeed, Matthew sees the decision to prioritize the Irish Church as an act of instinctive self-healing by the party, with Lord John Russell paving the way with his pamphlet promoting the concurrent endowment of church organizations in Ireland. 'Gladstone's Irish Church Resolutions of March 1868 should therefore be seen [...] as part of a general move by the Liberal leadership to solve both their party and their policy problems.'[24] Shannon lends support to this notion when he notes that Gladstone discussed the Irish question with Russell who, in January 1867, agreed to raise the issue of the position of the Irish Church.[25] Supported by the party, endorsed by the electorate in 1868, opposed in full only by the Anglican Establishment in Ireland, the Irish Church Bill offered a means of stabilizing the majority and 'preventing the dreadful disintegration which had followed the victory in the 1865 general election'.[26] Shannon similarly admits that from 1866 Gladstone had 'the Irish Church question in reserve' as 'a means of keeping the fissile Liberal party united'. Gladstone 'wanted [...] revenge. He was eager that Liberalism should resume forthwith its command of public affairs and legislation. He had, in the Irish Church question, the means of it.'[27] Eyck observes how, with his declaration in favour of Church disestablishment, Gladstone had 're-established, at a single blow, the unity which of recent years had, to his distress, been destroyed'.[28] It was, says Birrell, 'perhaps Gladstone's most brilliant achievement as a leader. Both the strategy and the tactics are beyond criticism [...] Whig and Radical, Adullamite and Manhood Suffragist, united at last behind a leader and a policy, rushed into the fray.'[29] In like manner Feuchtwanger believes that while Gladstone acted from 'deep conviction', 'he had brought off a brilliant parliamentary coup' for 'it united Radicals, Dissenters, Adullamites and all; it divided the Tories because the High Church party was in outright opposition while those of Low or broad church views were prepared to concede that the position of the Irish Church could not remain entirely intact'.[30] Boyce, in his survey of Gladstone's Irish policies, prioritizes the role of domestic politics: the Irish Church question 'offered him an opportunity to rally the forces of Liberalism

---

24 Matthew, *Gladstone*, p. 146.
25 Shannon, *Gladstone: Heroic Minister*, p. 30.
26 Matthew, *Gladstone*, p. 176.
27 Shannon, *Gladstone: God and Politics*, pp. 201, 211.
28 Eyck, *Gladstone*, p. 181.
29 Birrell, *Gladstone*, p. 77.
30 Feuchtwanger, *Gladstone*, p. 143.

and Nonconformity' while allowing Gladstone to assume a 'high moral tone'.[31]

Gladstone's evolving vocation

According to Shannon, the roots of Gladstone's Irish policy lay in his need for a vehicle adequate to his popularity as it had evinced itself in the early 1860s and which the extension of the franchise in 1867 only promised to enhance. The year 1867 was about Gladstone's need to assert his personal authority – within the Liberal party and the nation. To support this contention, Shannon points to the fact that the failings of the Church of Ireland were 'hardly a new revelation' to Gladstone:

> What was new and important for Gladstone in 1863 was that he needed body and work for his forming vocation. The logic which pressed itself upon him with an irresistible cogency now was that, if what he could make of Lancashire and the Tyne as representing body in terms of numbers and releasable energy was available, what would be the most appropriate work upon which to set those numbers and energies?[32]

His answer was religious equality for Ireland, and Gladstone later cited this as one of the four occasions in his life when his grasp of political timing allowed him to see that the materials existed to form a public opinion and direct it to a great reforming end.

> This ripeness in the time bore for Gladstone much deeper import than the mere 'right-timing' or opportunism or the expediency of gathering the Liberal party back into unity [...] The very air presaging great events to come, the exigencies, duties, and opportunities of the state, enlarged in proportion to the widening of the electoral basis [...] now assumed potent urgency in an articulation between the doings and intentions of the minister [...] and the corresponding conviction wrought by them upon the public mind.[33]

Gladstone thus, claims Shannon, felt himself called to take up religious justice for Ireland as a divine imperative, the hand of God being manifested in the 'pattern of things' which had all the attributes of a 'providential dispensation'.[34]

---

[31] Boyce, 'Gladstone and Ireland', p. 108.
[32] Shannon, *Gladstone: Peel's Inheritor*, p. 487.
[33] Shannon, *Gladstone: Heroic Minister*, p. 50.
[34] Shannon, *Gladstone: Peel's Inheritor*, pp. 487–88.

Rivalry with Disraeli

According to Parry, what caused Gladstone to take up Irish Church reform was Disraeli's assumption of the Conservative leadership, for this raised the possibility that he might bid for Irish nationalist support to bolster the position of his minority government. Derby, a staunch supporter of the Protestant ascendancy in Ireland, had always resisted Disraeli's attempts to appease the Irish, but with his retirement Disraeli was free to explore the possibilities of Irish reform, and Gladstone saw the need to trump Disraeli with more radical proposals of his own. Thus, while Gladstone had become convinced by early 1867 that the established status of the Church of Ireland needed to end, he hesitated to move on the issue since the Whigs still favoured joint endowment, that is, a policy of providing financial support for all the leading Irish churches, including the Catholic Church. Although he raised the Irish question following the Fenian attacks in December 1867, this did not unite the party, and Gladstone delayed making any move. What changed matters was Disraeli's becoming Conservative leader in February 1868 and his announcement that the government was considering a plan to establish a state-funded Catholic university in Ireland. It was this scheme, says Parry, that permitted the reunification of the Liberal party, for the idea of endowing a Catholic university in Ireland was unpopular with Liberals. 'Gladstone immediately capitalised on this feeling', attacking Disraeli's plans as an unprincipled attempt to save the Irish Establishment by bribing Catholics, and announcing that 'he would be introducing resolutions discussing the future of the Irish Establishment'.[35] By this means, agrees Feuchtwanger, any 'danger that Disraeli might "dish the Whigs" on Ireland as he had done on reform, was now removed'.[36] Shannon, too, lends support to Parry's emphasis upon Gladstone's rivalry with Disraeli, writing that the 'autumn session in 1867 had left the Liberals as disunited as ever. There was an urgent need to outbid the government's Catholic university bribe.'[37]

Conclusion

There is some debate as to *why* Gladstone believed the Irish Church should be disestablished. Was his concern to remove an injustice to Ireland, as Morley and Matthew suggest? Or was it, as Biagini contends, to strengthen the mission of the Anglican Church in Ireland? Or is Hamer correct to suggest

---

[35] Parry, *Democracy and Religion*, p. 268.
[36] Feuchtwanger, *Gladstone*, p. 143.
[37] Shannon, *Age of Disraeli*, p. 38.

that by cutting off the rotten branch of the Anglican establishment in Ireland the health of the English trunk would be better preserved? Adjudicating between the 'goods' of these respective outcomes is probably impossible since Gladstone no doubt expected all to flow from disestablishment. What is clear is that Irish Church disestablishment was so radical and potentially controversial a course that it is hard to think that Gladstone would have undertaken it without the expectation that it would yield benefits within Ireland. The real debate centres upon why Gladstone prioritized the Church issue *when* he did – for as Shannon points out, the problems raised by the Anglican Establishment in Ireland were familiar to Gladstone long before the 1860s. The obvious causal factor was Fenian terrorist activity in 1867, and a host of historians, including Morley, Matthew and Shannon, see the Fenian outrages as the catalyst that converted an abstract preference for disestablishment into a practical imperative. But there are problems with this formulation. As Ian St John observes, Gladstone 'was never one to overreact to threats of violence, and in any case the link between the activities of Irish émigré nationalists and the status of the Irish Church was a tenuous one. As an explanatory factor it cannot compete with the far more shattering events of Gladstone's humiliation in the matter of Parliamentary reform during 1866 and 1867.'[38] Hence another influential perspective sees Gladstone seizing upon the Irish Church question as a means to restoring Liberal unity around his leadership. The Irish Church offered profound political benefits to Gladstone, and for several historians, notably Bentley, Hoppen and Parry, this was the pre-eminent consideration in his conduct. Are they right? Again, there is no conclusive way to disentangle the elements within Gladstone's thought process. But we can plausibly contend that, just as Gladstone would not have taken up Irish Church reform if it did not promise benefits within Ireland, so, given the precarious status of his Liberal leadership in 1867, he would have been unlikely to have embarked upon such a course if it did not also offer political advantages within Britain.

7.2   Why Did Gladstone Pursue Irish Home Rule?

Most historians see Gladstone's commitment to Home Rule as arising out of a determination to resolve, finally, the Irish question. But for a significant number Gladstone's chief preoccupation was not Ireland but the state of politics within Britain – and especially his continuing status as Liberal leader.

---

[38] St John, *Gladstone and the Logic of Victorian Politics*, p. 137.

Home Rule as a solution to the Irish Question

Many historians have accepted Gladstone's protestations that he was impelled to take up Home Rule by the imperatives of Ireland. Where historians adopting this position differ is in what, precisely, caused Gladstone to turn to Home Rule in 1885 as the ultimate expression of his long-standing desire to pacify Ireland.

Home Rule as a logical development within Gladstone's Irish policies

Gladstone, it is commonly argued, had been seeking to render Ireland a contented member of the Empire since he took up Irish Church reform. Yet Ireland remained disaffected, and Gladstone concluded during 1885 that only the establishment of an elected parliament in Ireland to administer local Irish affairs would secure his aim. Morley, who as Gladstone's Secretary of State for Ireland was privy to his chief's thinking, articulated this view in his 1903 biography. Gladstone's decision to take up Home Rule, he writes, reflected his quest to bring peace to Ireland, and he was contemplating a large settlement before the 1885 election. 'So little true is it to say that Mr. Gladstone only thought of the possibility of Irish autonomy after the election.'[39] Gladstone's son, Herbert, who was equally acquainted with Gladstone's evolving views, rejected in his memoirs the idea that Gladstone's taking up of Home Rule represented a radical departure. There was 'no "conversion". He was on principle an autonomist, and had been so for forty years.'[40] Another Liberal, J. L. Hammond, in his 1938 *Gladstone and the Irish Nation*, characterized Home Rule as the final chapter in Gladstone's 'great struggle for Ireland's freedom' – a struggle for which he was prepared to sacrifice comfort, popularity and power. After the failure of his Church and land reforms to quell Irish unrest, Gladstone 'wanted the Irish question settled not because he wanted to get rid of party difficulties or because he had some ambition of his own to serve, but because he thought it the most serious of all public problems'.[41] As Tom Dunne more recently remarks, 'the home-rule initiative was the culmination of twenty years of conciliation policies towards Irish nationalism by Gladstone'.[42]

---

[39] Morley, *Life of Gladstone*, III. p. 216.
[40] Gladstone, *After Thirty Years*, p. 263.
[41] J. L. Hammond, *Gladstone and the Irish Nation* (1938), pp. iii, 418.
[42] T. Dunne, 'Responses to Gladstonian Home Rule and Land Reform', *Irish Historical Studies*, Vol. 25 (1987), p. 435.

The idea that Gladstone embraced Home Rule because it alone offered the prospect of peaceful relations between Britain and Ireland finds its way into numerous accounts. Thus, according to Feuchtwanger,

> [t]he conviction grew in him that Home Rule, namely a separate Irish Parliament, was the only way in which the tragic Anglo-Irish tangle could be resolved. This conclusion was of course entirely in line with his general philosophy on Ireland, nationality, morality between nations and elementary justice.[43]

For Paul Adelman, Gladstone's decision to take up Home Rule reflected a conviction, arrived at after 'many years of anguish and reflection', that 'traditional Liberal policy towards Ireland was completely bankrupt' and that 'Home Rule was the only solution for the Irish problem'.[44] J. K. Chapman and C. J. Littlejohn agree, though they add that Gladstone had the capacity to convince himself that what ought to be the case really was: '[t]o him the wish was twin to reality. Home Rule would work because he wanted it to [...] His faith and egotism led him to misapprehend and under-estimate the long-range desires of Irish leaders.'[45] More recently, Stansky has argued that Gladstone was convinced 'that Home Rule was the just and fair solution for Ireland', while Boyce writes that 'there can be no doubt that Home Rule was his real goal, his governing passion; for it was only through the policy of Home Rule that government by consent could be rooted in Ireland'.[46]

The strongest case for the view that Home Rule represented a natural evolution of Gladstone's thinking on Ireland is presented by Matthew, who situates Gladstone's conduct within his reading on Irish history, the disappointing effects of his previous reforms, and the political context of 1885–86. 'The idea of "Home Rule" did not', Matthew writes, 'spring up fully formed in an instant', being, rather, part of an evolution of his thinking upon Ireland since the 1840s in the light of 'experience and the recognition of particular contingencies'.[47] It was 'an assessment of opportunity and "ripeness"'.[48]

> The object of the [Home Rule] bill was 'social order', and it was thus the constitutional culmination of that long series of measures proposed

---

[43] Feuchtwanger, *Gladstone*, p. 230.

[44] Adelman, *Gladstone, Disraeli and Later Victorian Politics*, p. 44.

[45] J. K. Chapman and C. J. Littlejohn, 'Home Rule Revisited: an Essay in Historiography', *Historical Reflections/Réflexions Historiques*, Vol. 3 (1976), p. 36.

[46] Stansky, *Gladstone*, p. 157; Boyce, 'Gladstone and Ireland', p. 117.

[47] Matthew, *Gladstone*, p. 466.

[48] Ibid., p. 464.

by Gladstone since 1868 to solve the Irish question. His mission was still to pacify Ireland, not to liberate it [...] Gladstone's experience had eventually taught him that only through liberation could pacification be achieved.[49]

Matthew enumerates the influences that prepared the way for Gladstone's acceptance of Irish self-government. Among these was the predisposition within mid-nineteenth-century Liberalism toward the devolution of decision-making to local governments. In the context of Empire, the devolution of self-government to Canada and Australia had been associated with imperial stability, and when Gladstone began to consider Home Rule in 1885, it was to the Canadian model he turned. Of course, the difference between Ireland and Canada was that Ireland was a member of the United Kingdom, and granting self-government to Ireland might imperil the integrity of the United Kingdom. The solution to this problem, writes Matthew, was suggested to Gladstone by A. V. Dicey's *Law of the Constitution*, which asserted that sovereign power within the United Kingdom lay in parliament. If so, the British parliament could devolve power to Ireland yet still revoke it if necessary. Far from imperilling the unity of the British state, Home Rule would preserve it since a failure to act would cause Ireland to remain in a condition of endemic disaffection.

Gladstone was prepared, reluctantly, to meet violent disorder in Ireland with coercion, but [...] he sought a long-term political solution which would pacify the Irish, achieve social order, and restore the norms of liberal civil society. Pacification and the absence of the forces which made coercion necessary were the goals Gladstone sought through the 'Trilogy' of social order, a complete land settlement, and Irish autonomy in Irish affairs which made up the proposed Irish settlement of 1886.[50]

Home Rule was taken up, not as 'a crude political bargain, but as a recognition of a just demand fairly stated and as a conservative means of maintaining for its most important purposes the unity of the State'.[51]

Matthew's assessment has been endorsed by a number of historians. Angus Hawkins talks of Gladstone's 'righteous sense of mission' over Ireland.[52] By 1885 the Liberal party had reached stalemate on Irish policy at a moment

---

[49] Ibid., p. 501.
[50] Ibid., p. 471.
[51] Ibid., p. 550.
[52] Hawkins, *British Party Politics*, p. 259.

when the anticipation of increased Parnellite strength in the next parliament emphasized the need for a 'large constructive' initiative on Ireland.

> This crisis, moreover, was seen by Gladstone as precisely one of those great problems in national life which required his continued presence at the forefront of politics [...] By September 1885 Gladstone was privately convinced that Home Rule was both necessary and desirable. His Liberal beliefs reinforced the need for a large constitutional settlement restoring social order in Ireland and removing the cancer of the Irish question from the British body politic.[53]

Hoppen likewise believes that 'Gladstone's journey towards Home Rule was neither abrupt nor simply self-interested'.[54] Rejecting the idea that Gladstone was acting out of instrumental motives, he writes that it 'does now seem clear that Gladstone had begun to move decisively towards an acceptance of Home Rule as an efficient and worthy cause well before the general election of late 1885 and that, in doing so, he was committing no violence towards his record on Ireland over the previous four years'.[55] For Roy Jenkins, Gladstone's commitment to Irish self-government was genuine and 'high-minded'. 'He was prepared [...] to devote another eight years of his ebbing life to trying to achieve Home Rule.'[56] Shannon agrees that Gladstone gradually became convinced that Home Rule was the right policy.

> As far as can be determined that insight came gradually upon Gladstone during the Irish turmoils of 1882, was repressed by the onset of the Egyptian and Sudanese issues, revived with the emergence of the franchise and redistribution measures of 1884, and crystallized at a moment he came to identify early in March 1885.[57]

Quite simply, says Parry, 'the "people" of Ireland had a right to rule themselves'.[58]

However some historians question whether Home Rule was a natural progression upon Gladstone's previous attempts to solve the Irish problem. Bentley sees this as a too uncritical acceptance of Gladstone's own

---

[53] Ibid., p. 258.
[54] Hoppen, *Mid-Victorian Generation*, p. 678.
[55] Ibid., p. 679.
[56] Jenkins, *Gladstone*, pp. 524–25.
[57] Shannon, *Gladstone: Heroic Minister*, p. 375.
[58] Parry, *Democracy and Religion*, p. 445.

autobiographical writings and Morley's partisan biography. 'At no time during the 1880 parliament did Gladstone give any indication that he might move beyond some measure of local government for Ireland. When he did move he had more on his mind than Home Rule.'[59] Shannon, too, points out that Home Rule was not the logical next step in Irish policy: there was a developing consensus within the Liberal party that Ireland should receive 'a big measure of democratic local government reform [...] and a measure to begin the shift on Irish land from landlordism to smallholders'. This was the most obvious next step to take, yet 'the key feature of his ministry from 1880 to 1885 was that Gladstone very deliberately prevented these things from happening'.[60] Home Rule did not occupy a point within a continuum: it was a radical departure.

Home Rule as a response to the extent of nationalist feeling

When explaining why Gladstone chose 1885 to press the case for Home Rule, a number of commentators highlight the impact of the 1885 election, when Catholic Ireland returned a near-unanimous set of Irish nationalist MPs, thereby confirming to Gladstone the intensity of nationalist opinion in Ireland. Two important witnesses attest to the importance of this factor. One is the Irish national MP and historian Justin McCarthy, who writes in his biography of the Liberal leader that he had previously been unsure as to what Ireland's true opinion was as most Irish MPs were not supporters of the national cause. The 1885 elections changed this: 'I had some opportunity of talking to Mr. Gladstone, after the general election which made this change, and he told me frankly that his question was answered so far as the national desire of Ireland was concerned.' Gladstone now accepted that there was such a thing as a distinct Irish nationality: '[h]e had learned something to-day which he did not know yesterday, and he felt bound to act upon the knowledge'.[61] Morley's account is similar. During the 1885 election campaign Gladstone had said that what Ireland 'may deliberately and constitutionally demand [...] will be a demand that we are bound at any rate to treat with careful attention'.[62] Much, therefore, depended upon the voice of Ireland, and here the verdict was clear.

As a supreme electoral demonstration, the Irish elections of 1885 have never been surpassed in any country. They showed that neither remedial

---

[59] Bentley, *Politics without Democracy*, p. 248.
[60] Shannon, *Gladstone: God and Politics*, xix.
[61] McCarthy, *Story of Gladstone's Life*, pp. 327–29.
[62] Morley, *Life of Gladstone*, III. p. 237.

measures nor repressive measures had made even the fleeting shadow of an impression on the tenacious sentiment of Ireland, or on the powerful organisation that embodied and directed it. The Land Act made no impression. The two Coercion Acts had made none. The imperial parliament had done its best for five years [...] and this was the end [...] the vehement protest of one of the three kingdoms against the whole system of its government, and a strenuous demand for its reconstruction on new foundations.[63]

The part played by the election in confirming Gladstone's resolve to press ahead with Home Rule is alluded to by many historians. For Matthew it was one of the short-term factors that settled Gladstone's thinking upon the Irish question. His 'commitment to Home Rule involved the Peelite view that government should, through legislation, redress an established grievance, and he saw the 1885 election as the moment at which that establishment of grievance would be publicly confirmed'.[64] Shannon agrees that, having been converted to the justice of Home Rule, the question remained: was the moment ripe for action? This would be determined largely 'by what results the Irish constituencies would return in the coming elections'.[65] Similarly Feuchtwanger writes that, for Gladstone, 'the election of 1885 had created a situation that made it imperative to deal with Ireland, one way or the other [...] The state of Ireland was dangerous and large expectations had been raised; now was the moment to meet the situation with a fully-fledged scheme.'[66]

Ireland's strong support for nationalist candidates carried two messages for Gladstone. One was the reality of an Irish nationalist identity. 'Gladstone', says Parry, 'became obsessed with the notion that the Irish people formed an organic whole through a shared national identity.'[67] He accordingly romanticized the Irish nationalist leaders, believing they would end social and religious tensions, marginalize extremists and uphold the propertied class in leadership. Boyce agrees that for Gladstone, Ireland possessed 'the elements of nationality'.[68] Adelman likewise believes that over the summer of 1885 Gladstone became convinced 'of the reality of Irish nationality: how then could he oppose what a majority of the Irish people wanted?' What 'clinched his support for Home Rule' was the fact that in the election 'the Irish Party

[63] Ibid., p. 254.
[64] Matthew, *Gladstone*, p. 480.
[65] Shannon, *Gladstone: God and Politics*, p. 359.
[66] Feuchtwanger, *Gladstone*, pp. 232, 235–36.
[67] Parry, *Rise and Fall of Liberal Government*, p. 296.
[68] Boyce, *The Irish Question in British Politics*, p. 33.

won every seat in Ireland south of Ulster'.[69] For Roy Jenkins, too, the triumph of Charles Stewart Parnell's Irish party in the election 'made a profound impression […] the clarity with which the Irish constituencies had spoken was unmistakeable'. Such was the solidity of the nationalist vote that Gladstone feared the Irish MPs might 'withdraw from Westminster and set up their own assembly in Dublin […] The choice […] would then have lain between military re-conquest or the acceptance of an illegal and revolutionary break-up of the United Kingdom.'[70] 'Nothing survived politically in Ireland', concurs Geoffrey Garratt, 'except Parnellism and Ulster […] There was no alternative except a bureaucratic system with coercive powers, or some form of Home Rule.'[71]

But did the 1885 election results really intrude a new element in Gladstone's thinking? Shannon thinks not: in 1883 Gladstone had been warned that the effect of electoral reform in Ireland would be a major loss of Liberal seats since 'the Catholic vote would be given solidly against the Liberals'.[72] Yet he nonetheless pressed ahead with lowering the franchise in Ireland to British levels, thereby helping engineer the very expression of Irish national opinion he was now responding to. Alan O'Day estimates that electoral reform trebled the number of Irish voters, creating a 'vastly enlarged Catholic electorate' that included 'a substratum of cottiers and agricultural labourers'.[73] As Jenkins admits, Gladstone lowered the franchise in Ireland in 1884 even though he realized that 'it would mean more than doubling the size of the Parnellite parliamentary party and also the virtual elimination of Liberal MPs […] from Ireland'.[74]

Home Rule as a necessary step toward solving the Irish land problem

Biagini presents a distinctive interpretation of Gladstone's support for Home Rule, locating it in his belated recognition of the need to solve the Irish land problem by creating a class of independent peasant proprietors. The agricultural depression brought falling prices and evictions, and rural outrages had not ceased with the breaking of the Land League. Gladstone concluded that buying out the landlord class was the only solution to the land question. However he believed this complex financial process could only be administered by local representatives within Ireland, who could

[69] Adelman, *Gladstone, Disraeli and Later Victorian Politics*, pp. 45–46.
[70] Jenkins, *Gladstone*, pp. 535–36.
[71] Garratt, *The Two Mr. Gladstones*, p. 259.
[72] Shannon, *Gladstone: Heroic Minster*, p. 323.
[73] A. O'Day, *Irish Home Rule 1867–1921* (1998), p. 93.
[74] Jenkins, *Gladstone*, p. 488.

collect the loan repayments and mediate tensions between farmers and the British treasury. Home Rule was thus necessary for the implementation of a land purchase policy.[75] Biagini agrees with Matthew that Gladstone's aim in 1885–86 was to pacify Ireland and create a political and social system in which indigenous elites would oversee national progress and make coercion unnecessary.[76] However, where Matthew sees the land purchase scheme of 1886 as a means to Home Rule, Biagini sees Home Rule as a means to the land purchase scheme.

Home Rule as necessary to preserve the Liberal state in Britain

According to this argument, Gladstone sought to implement Home Rule in order to uphold the liberal traditions of England. Ireland's alienation from British rule lay behind the chronic lawlessness that was posing an ever-greater threat to the free political institutions of the United Kingdom – as exemplified by the need for near-continuous coercion laws, terrorist attacks on the mainland, filibustering in the Commons and the blackening of Britain's image abroad. The Irish boil needed to be lanced – if only for the health of the British political tradition. Thus Matthew draws attention to the sense of 'the corruption of the British Liberal state which the constant presence of the Irish question in British politics involved', such as the introduction of the guillotine in parliamentary debates, the establishment of secret service police and the imposition of an armed body guard for the prime minister. All this was additional to the perennial need to suspend civil liberties in Ireland through coercion legislation. Gladstone was keen to 'restore the norms of liberal civil society' by pacifying the Irish.[77] Roy Jenkins follows Matthew's reasoning, arguing that 'Gladstone saw that the maintenance of the liberal state was incompatible with holding within its centralised grip a large disaffected community of settled mind'. His 'overwhelming desire was a quick settlement of the Irish question, which he had come to see [...] as an endemic poison to state and society'.[78]

Home Rule as a domestic political strategy

An alternative reading of Gladstone's decision to embrace Irish Home Rule sees it as a reflection not of Ireland's needs but of his determination to secure his own political and personal ends within Westminster.

---

[75] Biagini, *Gladstone*, p. 94.
[76] *Ibid.*, pp. 101, 104.
[77] Matthew, *Gladstone*, p. 471.
[78] Jenkins, *Gladstone*, p. 537.

Home Rule as a policy to justify Gladstone's
continuing Liberal leadership

It used to be alleged by critics of Gladstone's Home Rule policy that he
seized upon the idea after the 1885 election as a means to hold onto power
in conjunction with the votes of Parnell's Home Rule party. So did Goldwin
Smith argue in 1904, 'it is impossible to forget that Gladstone's position was
that of leader of the Opposition, wishing to reinstate his party in power, and
seeing that this could be done only by the help of the Irish vote'.[79] With
the publication of Gladstone's diary and personal papers, however, this
view is no longer seriously entertained, for it is realized that Gladstone was
contemplating Home Rule before the 1885 election. Those seeing Home
Rule as a political stratagem point now, instead, to the fact that in 1885
Gladstone's continuance as Liberal leader was highly doubtful. Not only had
he spent the last five years talking of his retirement but also most senior
Liberals had come to chaff at his leadership and there was a widespread view
that, with the collapse of his 1880 government, the time had come for him
to quit the scene. But Gladstone wanted to remain at the centre of political
affairs and conclude his parliamentary career in a fittingly grand manner –
and this required a cause that would galvanize the party and which he alone
could oversee. Irish Home rule offered this, allowing Gladstone to turn the
tables on his critics and secure for the foreseeable future his dominance of a
Gladstonian Liberal party. It was a political masterstroke.

Alistair Cooke and John Vincent argue this position in their 1974 book
The Ruling Passion. In January 1885, 'Gladstone was as clearly marked for the
axe as any prime minister can be'. He was 'everyone's enemy'. The Whigs
found him too passive abroad and too radical at home, while for the Radicals
he was 'quite unable to give the new lead which they saw as necessary'. 'The
movement of both wings of the Liberal party against its centre was irresistible.'[80]
Yet within a year Gladstone was 'to conduct the most successful party purge
in British history [...] The problem of how his lieutenants were to displace
Gladstone was solved in 1886 by Gladstone displacing his lieutenants.'[81] The
key to this unexpected turnaround was Home Rule. According to Cooke
and Vincent, Irish policy was essentially about Westminster politics. Irish
circumstances were unimportant because neither politicians nor the public
had any interest in the subject. English opinion about Ireland 'had nothing

---

[79] Smith, 'Mr. Morley's Life of Gladstone. II.', p. 56.
[80] A. B. Cooke and J. Vincent, *The Ruling Passion: Cabinet Government and Party Politics in
Britain 1885–86* (1974), p. 24.
[81] Ibid., p. 15.

to do with Ireland, and everything to do with England'.[82] Cooke and Vincent are non-committal when discussing why Gladstone took up Home Rule. They are sceptical of the idea that Home Rule was the logical point to which Gladstone's Irish policies had been tending and doubt that it was a fixed point in his politics. By June 1885 Gladstone's 'ideas on autonomy were still quite restricted, not going beyond those of Chamberlain and many others', and this suggests that 'he left his policies to be formed by the political situation as it developed'.[83] Yet they reject, too, the view that Gladstone was acting wholly out of opportunist or egotistical motives, and do not think he was trying only to cleanse the party of radicalism. He was, they suggest, prepared to move slowly toward the possibility of a Home Rule initiative during 1886, and what forced his hand was Joseph Chamberlain's attempt to bring the issue to the fore in March 1886. This prompted Gladstone to 'bring home rule forward as a question that could serve to unite his cabinet and increase his command of the party'. From this point the purpose of the Home Rule Bill was not to realize Irish self-government: it was introduced too late in the session to do that and opposition from the Lords was inevitable.

> The bill was however meant to unite the Liberal party by committing it to the principle of home rule and to prepare it for further protracted struggle in which there would only be one possible leader [...] All that in the end can be said about Gladstone's short-term political motives, is that he wished to recapture control of his party, control which he had had to share with powerful colleagues in 1880–85.[84]

This he did, driving out, says Hawkins, 'Chamberlain and his radical brand of creeping municipal socialism' as well as Lord Hartington and the cautious Whigs.[85]

T. A. Jenkins also emphasizes how Home Rule became tied up with Gladstone's political future. He accepts that by 1885 Gladstone was looking to Home Rule as the means to pacify Ireland, but 'there remains the question of why he accepted it when he did, and this can only be explained in terms of his need for a new "speciality" which would enable him to justify retaining the leadership of the Liberal party'.[86] For Gladstone, Ireland demanded that special kind of leadership he had evolved from 1880 to unite a Liberal party

---

[82] Ibid., pp. 17–18.
[83] Ibid., pp. 51–52.
[84] Ibid., pp. 54–55.
[85] Hawkins, *British Party Politics*, p. 256.
[86] Jenkins, *Gladstone, Whiggery and the Liberal Party*, pp. 247–48.

too divided to arrive at a solution of its own. By this means 'the Irish cause came to be identified inseparably with Gladstone's leadership'. The policy itself evolved over time, becoming steadily more radical, until what 'had originally been a question of local government expanded, during [...] 1885, into the heroic proportions of a great imperial question'.[87] Like Cooke and Vincent, Jenkins accepts that Gladstone did not expect Home Rule to pass and 'conceived of his task [...] in terms of laying the foundations for eventual action by a united Liberal party [...] on a policy of home rule for Ireland'.[88]

Although Hoppen believes that Gladstone's Home Rule initiative reflected principled motives, he admits that Gladstone was 'casting about for a good reason for remaining at the centre of events, in which respect Ireland clearly possessed all the potential of a new Bulgaria'.[89] The prominent Irish historian F. S. L. Lyons also accepts that 'the particularities of party warfare in 1885–86 evoked from Gladstone a series of reactions which suggest that it was indeed the saving of the Liberal party, and of his own position within the party, rather than Irish exigencies that made him go the way he did'.[90] Parry, too, believes that Gladstone was 'subconsciously looking' for a reason not to quit politics. He is not explicit as to what lay behind this desire – though he mentions Gladstone's disapproval of Parnell's alliance with the Tories and Chamberlain's increasingly undisciplined policy pronouncements. 'Gladstone convinced himself that one last service was demanded of him before retirement.'[91] He found this in Home Rule. Boyce concurs, noting that Gladstone felt a compulsion to connect his political future with 'great and good acts of government' that only he could do. 'Therefore he must stay at his post.'[92]

Home Rule as a worthy task for a Liberal majority

Shannon argues that Gladstone expected the 1885 election to yield a strong Liberal majority based on the extension of the county franchise, opening up a 'golden prospect' for progressive reform.[93] But would his likely successors, Hartington or Chamberlain, be equal to this opportunity? Gladstone believed

---

[87] Ibid., p. 249.
[88] Ibid., p. 284.
[89] Hoppen, *Mid-Victorian Generation*, p. 677.
[90] F. S. L. Lyons, 'Review of *Gladstone and Ireland* by John Vincent', *Irish Historical Studies*, 22 (1979): p. 500.
[91] Parry, *Rise and Fall of Liberal Government*, p. 295.
[92] Boyce, *The Irish Question and British Politics*, p. 29.
[93] Shannon, *Gladstone: Heroic Minister*, p. 369.

not, and he came to regard it as his destiny to remain in politics to realize the force of this powerful majority. To justify this he needed an object 'worthy and appropriate', and this Home Rule provided. Previously, his room for manoeuvre on Ireland had been limited by the caution of the Whigs. But armed with his expected majority he could press ahead without them, while the surge in support for the Irish Nationalists would persuade Liberals as a whole that the time for bold action had arrived. According to T. A. Jenkins,

> there seems little doubt that the discreet tactics adopted by Gladstone in the autumn of 1885 were founded upon the assumption that the Liberal party would obtain a parliamentary majority sufficiently large to allow him time in which to foster an appropriate moral climate for the reception of a home-rule measure. He appears to have been confident that, once confronted with the strength of Irish Nationalist feeling as demonstrated by the election of 80 or 90 Parnellite MPs, British public opinion, the political parties, and even the House of Lords, would be compelled to recognize the need for this concession.[94]

What exploded this strategy was the fact that the November 1885 election yielded no such great Liberal victory. Forced to switch tack, Gladstone, argues Shannon, justified his sudden urgency by portraying Ireland as being on the verge of a revolution that might only be averted by granting self-government, convincing himself that 'there was a plan by the Irish party of a "withdrawal *en bloc*" from Westminster and setting up an Assembly in Dublin'. In fact, adds Shannon, there 'appears to be no evidence that such a plan was ever envisaged […] What seems […] most likely is that Gladstone, having boxed himself in […] with his stipulation for the "absolute necessity" of a clear Liberal majority, now chose to believe and live for the moment completely in a self-induced conviction which would justify his unboxing himself.'[95] As such, he was proposing palliatives to a crisis that existed largely in his own mind.

Home Rule as a means to a Virtuous Politics

The most strategic reading of Gladstone's conduct is provided by Hamer, who argues that Gladstone took up Home Rule as a means to shape the future character of the Liberal party. With his 1880 administration so beset by Liberal factionalism, and with the development of a programmatic approach

---

[94] Jenkins, *Gladstone, Whiggery and the Liberal Party*, p. 246.
[95] Shannon, *Gladstone: Heroic Minister*, p. 395.

to politics among the Radicals that Gladstone disliked, he saw in Home Rule an ideal means to inculcate his own conception of Liberal government as an engine of great virtuous measures. Hamer does not deny that Gladstone thought that 'Home Rule was the right solution to the Irish problem', but, he adds, 'this does not mean that he was innocent of any thought about the effect on the party [...] The idea of devotion to a great national cause was an integral part of Gladstone's concept of what a party, and especially the Liberal party, ought to be.'[96] He had sought to supply the Liberals with such a cause with income tax abolition in 1874 and his Midlothian speeches, and Irish Home Rule was the most thorough campaign to this end.

> [F]rom Gladstone's point of view what he was to do in 1886 was to help create a different kind of party, to effect a transformation of the Liberal party from 'party in the practical and popular sense' to party that was the 'instrument' of 'lofty purpose'. And in the process he believed he was creating a stronger, more coherent, more unified party.[97]

Like Peel in 1846, Gladstone was prepared to go ahead with his initiative and ask his party to support him, and if only part of it did, that would not be necessarily a bad thing:

> [t]here can be no doubt that Gladstone [...] began to accustom himself to during 1885 to the idea that a split might not only be inevitable but [...] desirable and beneficial [...] a split on a clear issue, a single great question, could, paradoxically [...] have the effect of producing a party more united, more coherent, more capable of effective action.[98]

In particular, by adopting Home Rule, Gladstone marginalized Chamberlain's Radical programme. 'The unity of Radicalism was shattered. And the wrecking factor was Gladstone's great hold over Radical opinion.' As Hamer summarizes,

> Two aspects of Gladstone's political thinking were fused in his conduct in this crisis. On the one hand, there was his belief that great national causes [...] needed the Liberal party for their fulfilment [...] On the other hand, there was his belief that the Liberal party needed great

---

[96] Hamer, *Liberal Politics*, pp. 121–22.
[97] Ibid., p. 65.
[98] Ibid., p. 123.

national causes to devote itself to if it was ever to be able to subdue the divisive forces within itself.[99]

Other historians have seen Gladstone as using Home Rule to shape the Liberal party as an agent of Gladstonian Liberalism. Thus, where Hamer emphasizes its role in breaking the challenge from the Radicals, Birrell writes that, by 1885, Gladstone 'recognised that he had to get rid of the Whigs. Hartington had "dug his toes in" since 1883. Having crushed the Central Board in 1884, he was not likely to alter his mind in 1886. The Whigs had got to go, and this was a good moment for getting rid of them.'[100] Bentley likewise emphasizes Home Rule's purgatory qualities:

> A bold stroke of policy aimed at a great moral cause might overcome the preoccupation with property and egalitarianism to which the radicals had become prone and reconvene the forces of progress. If it drove Chamberlain and his crew out of the party, *tant mieux*. If it sent into retirement the set pieces of Whiggery then that, too, could only prove a gain […] Home Rule, in short, made sense.[101]

While not arguing that Gladstone set out to divide the party, Shannon sees Home Rule as the clearest manifestation of the continuing Peelite character of Gladstone's politics:

> The reality of the eventful year of 1886 in Mr Gladstone's career was his imperious foisting upon his party without consultation of a radical policy it would never of its own initiative undertaken; and of how he ignored those backbench Liberals who desperately tried to get him to listen to advice from the party as to how a scheme for Irish autonomy acceptable to the Irish, the Liberal party and the country at large might be achieved.[102]

Conclusion

The debate concerning Gladstone's motives with respect to Home Rule exemplifies the polarization that characterizes nearly all writing concerning his career. As with all the great initiatives with which he was associated

---

[99] Ibid., pp. 116, 123.
[100] Birrell, *Gladstone*, p. 114.
[101] Bentley, *Politics without Democracy*, p. 248.
[102] Shannon, *Gladstone: God and Politics*, xviii.

(income tax abolition, Bulgarian atrocities campaign, disestablishment of Irish Church, invasion of Egypt etc.), so with Home Rule is it possible to present Gladstone's actions as, on the one hand, a considered product of reflection, guided by God, to arrive at the right action on ground of principle, or, on the other, as a calculated act designed to achieve some personal or party gain. A plausible case has been made by the likes of Hammond and Matthew for the view that Gladstone took up Home Rule as the logical fulfilment of his endeavour to bring peace to Ireland. However surprised contemporaries may have been when Gladstone announced his proposals, few contended that they conflicted with the main thrust of his previous measures or his wider politics. In fact the danger in this interpretation is almost the reverse: once it is known that Gladstone *did* take up Home Rule in 1885, it becomes tempting to view all his prior policies with respect to Ireland as a progression toward this end. The vote to accept Maynooth funding, the disestablishment of the Irish Church, the successive land reforms, the decision to bring Ireland's franchise into line with the rest of the United Kingdom: all can be regarded as successive steps Gladstone took on the path to Home Rule. This, in essence, is the story told by Morley, Matthew, Hammond and, of course, Gladstone himself. The problem with it is that it lifts Gladstone clear of the political context within which he made each of these decisions, such that he appears like a great ship steering his course imperviously through the choppy waters of conventional politics to pacify Ireland. This cannot be right, for Gladstone was always an intensely engaged politician, struggling (like all politicians) to sustain his ascendancy or recapture it after a period of eclipse. If Gladstone was a great statesman guided by the light of Christian virtue, he was also a practical politician guided by the need to assemble votes for a policy or preserve his leadership. Thus historians like Hamer, Jenkins and Cooke and Vincent root Gladstone's conduct in 1885 in the schismatic character of the Liberal party and his own desire to avoid retirement. Both, it seems, must be true. Yes, Gladstone did come, in the mid-1880s, to judge that Home Rule was the only way to achieve his goal of a contented Irish nation. But equally, his decision to prioritize Home Rule above all other objectives in 1885 must have involved some recognition of the political situation, namely, his reluctance to retire and his determination to leave behind a Liberal party that was true to his conception of progressive politics. Of all the potential explanatory factors, it is hard to avoid the contention of Jenkins, Parry and Cooke and Vincent that what was of most immediate importance was Gladstone's wish to extend his political career. Only this can explain why Gladstone determinedly pressed ahead with Home rule when the parliamentary situation was certainly *not* ripe. If Home Rule was indeed a logical necessity, then it would have happened at some stage. The most persuasive explanation of why it had to happen in 1886 was that only then would Gladstone oversee the doing of it.

7.3   Why Did Gladstone's 1886 Home Rule Bill Fail?

In December 1885, Gladstone's Home Rule intentions were made known to the British public. The following six months saw him form his third administration, present his proposals to the Commons, see them rejected by a margin of 30 votes and call a general election – which he comprehensively lost. Why, then, did Gladstone, one of the most commanding and experienced politicians, not merely of the Victorian age but of any age, fail to carry a measure which he was convinced would solve the Irish Question?

Gladstone's strategic mistakes

A common explanation, endorsed by the likes of Matthew and Feuchtwanger, traces Gladstone's failure to miscalculations he made in the preparation and presentation of his Home Rule proposals. Gladstone, it is alleged, formulated his plan for an Irish parliament in seclusion from his party, planning to confront the Liberals with his scheme once the expected Liberal landslide in the 1885 general election had been realized. Overawed by the heroic scale of the measure, there would be little resistance from the Commons, thereby placing pressure upon the House of Lords to give way or risk having its powers questioned in a fresh election. Unfortunately, this strategy was riddled with mistakes. First, the secretive way in which Gladstone developed his ideas, argues Matthew, meant he did nothing to prepare a favourable opinion for them. Liberals complained at having not been consulted, and even once his ministry was formed Gladstone continued to prepare his Irish settlement in 'purdah', hoping 'to trump [...] party unease by the production of a great bill'. Even so,

> [t]he sensational production of the Government of Ireland Bill on 8 April 1886, the greatest of all the Gladstonian 'big bills', was also, self-evidently, the riskiest: the lever was to be pulled in one stroke. Consequently, the education of the party could not begin until the examination was almost at hand and it was necessarily unaccompanied by any Gladstonian extra-parliamentary speechmaking [...] The real drive to win the argument through pamphlet warfare did not come until *after* the defeat of the Government of Ireland Bill.[103]

---

[103] Matthew, *Gladstone*, pp. 488–90.

Eyck similarly writes that Gladstone's 'over-estimation of pure tactics and his under-valuation of psychological and material factors' did 'serious injury to himself and to his cause'.[104] 'It was a serious error to present a policy so novel and so revolutionary to the electors in so abrupt a fashion, after so little preparation.' Gladstone mistakenly believed that the electorate would follow him in placing 'confidence in Parnell and his followers, when for years they had regarded them as the enemies of England, who did not shrink even from crime'. Philip Magnus acknowledges that Gladstone had 'failed to educate his party', while Travis Crosby observes that he had 'neglected to cultivate public opinion'.[105] Rank-and-file Liberals, says Shannon, were 'offended at the way Gladstone had treated the party; bewildered at the hurtling pace he was driving; fearful for damage and possible disaster to the party in the constituencies'.[106] Agatha Ramm attributes the flaws in Gladstone's approach to his simultaneously seeking to develop a policy that would bring peace to Ireland while keeping the Liberals united. To the latter end, Gladstone 'kept silent about his intentions until the very eve of introducing the bill' – with the result that he was unable to call upon support for Home Rule when he needed it.[107] For, as George Russell reflected in 1891, up 'to December, 1885, English politicians who were favourable to Home Rule, or, indeed, had seriously considered it, might be counted on the fingers of one hand'.[108]

Gladstone's assumption that the 1884 Reform Act would yield the Liberals a commanding electoral victory proved equally illusory. Having decided, says Shannon, that 'he had to keep his big idea under cover', Gladstone's electoral campaign was feeble: his 'manifesto was anodyne' and, although he referred to the need to grant Ireland greater self-government, the significance of the remark was lost. 'What came across was the majestic fact of the Grand Old Man imperiously demanding a clear majority in Parliament [...] without needing to tell the country quite why he wanted it.' In the event, the Liberals failed to secure even an absolute majority, let alone a mandate that might put the Lords under pressure to accept Home Rule. Thus, while Gladstone had accurately predicted the nature of the Irish problem that would emerge following nationalist success in the 1885 election, 'he failed to produce the Liberal solution to it'.[109]

---

[104] Eyck, *Gladstone*, p. 404.
[105] Magnus, *Gladstone*, p. 346; Crosby, *The Two Mr Gladstones*, p. 206.
[106] Shannon, *Gladstone: Heroic Minister*, p. 422.
[107] Ramm, *William Ewart Gladstone*, p. 108.
[108] Russell, *William Ewart Gladstone*, pp. 257–58.
[109] Shannon, *Gladstone: God and Politics*, pp. 366–68.

Gladstone's intransigence

For several historians, the failure of Home Rule was political. The 1885 election left Gladstone holding a relatively weak hand, but what made failure certain was the inept manner in which he played it. Instead of managing the situation politically – winning over sceptics, cultivating the press or compromising on details – his conviction that he possessed a God-inspired insight into what was required led him to present MPs with a choice of Home Rule or nothing. True to his Peelite inheritance, Gladstone believed it was the party's job to follow the course set by its leader: it was Peel and the Corn Laws all over again. Thus Birrell is critical of the haste with which Gladstone brought forward his Home Rule measure:

> He was now over self-confident. Having searched always for authority, he did so still, and found the authority in himself. He would simply *make* the English public vote away the Union. Whigs, Radicals, Dissenters, what were they? He could call them to heel. The British public would follow where he hollooed.[110]

For Matthew, there was 'an off-hand, "take-it-or-leave-it" quality' about Gladstone's approach to the Bill, 'which relied largely on public rhetoric for its success. Even press contacts […] were not exploited. The Liberal party, perceived from the start as the weak link, was only reluctantly courted.'[111] Though it was clear that the best that could be hoped for was a bare pass on second reading, Gladstone refused to accept any basic changes to the Bill. Indeed, Feuchtwanger notes that when Gladstone did seem willing to compromise on the presence of Irish MPs at Westminster, prospects for a successful vote on second reading rose – only to fall when Gladstone scotched the idea. A 'lesser man, using the skills of the party manager, might well have got the bill through its second reading'.[112] As it was, remarks Matthew, only 'an astonishingly bold, robust, and self-confident politician could have forced the pace the way that Gladstone did between January and June 1886'.[113] This boldness contributed to defeat since a majority of MPs felt Gladstone was stretching the conventions of political behaviour 'too far and too quickly'.[114] Shannon agrees with Matthew that there 'were many tactical

---

[110] Birrell, *Gladstone*, p. 120. Italics in the original.
[111] Matthew, *Gladstone*, p. 506.
[112] Feuchtwanger, *Gladstone*, pp. 240–41.
[113] Matthew, *Gladstone*, pp. 506–7.
[114] Ibid., p. 509.

manoeuvres available in the course of debate and committee to give him ample play in the parliamentary struggle to come [...] It took someone of Gladstone's overweening confidence and wilfulness to create the conditions of failure.'[115] Thus 'instead of approaching the matter of providing enlarged powers of self-government for Ireland on the basis of [...] what Westminster might reasonably be asked to give [...] Gladstone approached the issue as a passionate partisan [...] A *great deal* or *nothing* was of the essence.'[116] Accordingly, Shannon attributes the Bill's defeat to 'Gladstone's deception, wilful haste and imperial style'. In 'the rapture of his peculiarly God-driven style of vanity, he had misread grossly the "facts" of this political juncture [...] his "appreciation of the general situation and its result" had been manifestly awry'.[117] Bentley concurs: by 1886, Gladstone had become 'obsessive' on Irish policy. 'He blinded himself to the manifest truth that, without massive and sustained preparation, the second chamber would never pass his bill even if the first could be induced to do so.'[118] Cooke and Vincent similarly draw attention to the formidable obstacle that was the House of Lords.

> There are strong reasons for thinking a solution was almost impossible in 1886 [...] Even if the bill had passed the second reading, it would have stood in greater peril in committee, and even if it had emerged from the Commons, it would never have passed the Lords [...] On a purely tactical view of the situation, then, 1886 was [...] a trial run whose genuinely Irish purpose, lay at most in forging a link of expediency between Gladstone and the Parnellites.[119]

This analysis has the merit of explaining Gladstone's apparent willingness to court defeat in 1886: he could afford to be imperious if the point of the Home Rule Bill was the fact of bringing it forward. Shannon has a slightly different take on this eventuality, suggesting that Gladstone savoured the prospect of conflict with the Lords:

> There was a sense also [...] that Gladstone's wilfulness in a way welcomed grimly the recalcitrance of the party and the obstacle of the Lords. He had dealt faithfully with the party before. He had also dealt faithfully with the Lords, from whom he had had little gratitude for his mercy to

---

[115] Shannon, *Gladstone: Heroic Minister*, p. 425.
[116] Shannon, *Gladstone: God and Politics*, p. 378. Italics in the original.
[117] Ibid., pp. 395, 398.
[118] Bentley, *Politics without Democracy*, p. 249.
[119] Cooke and Vincent, *The Governing Passion*, p. 163.

them – as he held – in 1884. There is no reason to think that Gladstone would not have relished a collision in 1886 and an ultimate settling of accounts.[120]

Gladstone's mishandling of Chamberlain

A frequently cited error on Gladstone's part was his inept handling of Chamberlain. Despite having recently proposed a bold move to extend local government within Ireland, Chamberlain was to become one of Gladstone's most dangerous critics, resigning in opposition to the Bill, denouncing it from the backbenches and mobilizing Radical opinion against it. With more judicious handling Gladstone could have kept Chamberlain on-side, but his dislike and jealousy of the rising star of radical Liberalism led him to do nothing to secure his support – treating him as disdainfully as Peel did Disraeli, and, says Shannon, what 'Disraeli was to Peel, Chamberlain in due course would be to Gladstone'.[121]

Among the historians considering Chamberlain's alienation to be the most important reason why Home Rule failed are Ensor and Feuchtwanger. Ensor believes 'it was Chamberlain who destroyed his scheme'. It was not merely that he made the most powerful speeches against it. While the hostility of the Conservatives and Whigs could be discounted, 'that of the radical leader could not be. His following all over the country was exceedingly large; and his attitude threw against the bill, when it came to polling, hundreds of thousands of the very voters who would otherwise have felt bound by Gladstone's lead.'[122] Feuchtwanger places similar emphasis upon the loss of Chamberlain. The Radical leader resented the prospect that Irish policy might dominate the government, eclipsing his own reform agenda. And although Gladstone did recruit Chamberlain to his government,

> the slighting treatment which Chamberlain now received at the hands of the Liberal leader was also the greatest single reason for the failure of the enterprise now started [...] [Gladstone] wanted him as a subordinate or not at all. But in this case the mismanagement of personal relations amounted to a major political misjudgement; it was one indication among many that old age was increasing Gladstone's egotism and loss of touch.[123]

---

[120] Shannon, *Gladstone: Heroic Minister*, p. 425.
[121] Ibid., p. 422.
[122] Ensor, *England: 1870–1914*, p. 96.
[123] Feuchtwanger, *Gladstone*, pp. 235–36.

For Roy Jenkins, it was the fact that Chamberlain's defection came on top of that of Hartington that was decisive:

> Gladstone could do without one man but not without both. He would probably have done better to have cultivated Chamberlain and, if necessary, to have let Hartington go before 1886. But he could not bring himself to appreciate Chamberlain [...] there was no instinctive rapport between Gladstone and either of these crucial figures. Nonetheless, given the sulphurous state of their mutual relations throughout the 1880–5 government, it was a remarkable feat of man-mismanagement to drive them into each other's arms by 1886–7.[124]

Gladstone should have neutralized Chamberlain by giving him 'an office from which he would be loath to resign', such as chancellor of the exchequer.[125] Instead he offered the wholly inappropriate Admiralty, and when Chamberlain asked to be secretary of state for the colonies he was rebuffed and given the relatively junior position of President of the Local Government Board. Hammond and Foot describe this as 'one of the gravest errors that Gladstone ever made'. As colonial secretary, Chamberlain would have been distracted from the problem of Ireland and 'the unity of the Liberal party might have been better preserved'.[126]

Even having made this mistake, says Jenkins, Gladstone could have retained Chamberlain if he had allowed him to pursue a series of radical domestic reforms. But instead Gladstone gave him no encouragement and even redeployed the civil servant helping him draw up a local government bill to work on Irish legislation. 'It is difficult to imagine a more wanton gesture. Once he had done it, Chamberlain's departure from the government [...] became a racing certainty.' Eager to find reasons for opposing Home Rule, Chamberlain's 'killer instinct fastened on the point to which there could be no satisfactory answer', namely, the exclusion of Irish members from parliament.

> Once 'battling Joe' was lost to the government, the bill was at his mercy. And the indictment of Gladstone's tactical handling is not what he did or did not do in the run up to fatal second reading in June but that he did not make it worth Chamberlain's while in February-March to stay in the government.[127]

---

124 Jenkins, *Gladstone*, p. 456.
125 Ibid., p. 544.
126 Hammond and Foot, *Gladstone and Liberalism*, p. 178.
127 Jenkins, *Gladstone*, pp. 547, 550–51.

Eyck similarly believes that 'Gladstone was bound to do his very utmost to gain him for the Cabinet', but when Chamberlain made clear his objection to Home Rule and offered his resignation, Gladstone did not exert himself 'to persuade the resigning Minister to remain [...] he quite certainly underestimated the strength which Chamberlain was presently to reveal in battling against him'.[128] The fact was, says Magnus, that Gladstone 'disliked, distrusted, and undervalued' Chamberlain, and it 'never occurred to him that for the sake of Ireland it might be his duty to play Chamberlain like a fish'.[129]

However some historians question Gladstone's culpability with respect to Chamberlain. Adelman argues that Chamberlain disassociated himself from Home Rule because he thought Home Rule was unpopular with the working class, so that if Gladstone called an election on the issue he would go down to a 'terrible defeat', leaving the way clear for Chamberlain to inherit the leadership. What wrecked Chamberlain's plans was that Gladstone did *not* retire after defeat in 1886.[130] Peter Marsh, in his biography of Chamberlain, agrees that Chamberlain believed Home Rule would bring 'electoral death and damnation'.[131] Hamer, too, sees Home Rule as really a battle for control of the Liberal party. Impatient to lead the party in a reforming direction, Chamberlain refused to accept Gladstone's assertion that until Ireland was settled his own radical programme had to be held in abeyance.[132] At the basis of Chamberlain's conduct was a determination not to submit to Gladstone's control over Liberal politics: 'Indeed, one can go so far as to say that Chamberlain's main aim in 1886 was not so much to destroy the Home Rule policy as to destroy Gladstone's influence.'[133]

T. A. Jenkins, by contrast, questions the idea that Gladstone's handling of Chamberlain in early 1886 was misguided. He points out that the party's disappointing performance in the 1885 election had discredited Chamberlain's *Radical Programme*, and it was 'not unreasonable for Gladstone to assume that he would fall into line with his Irish proposals'. Chamberlain in turn 'appreciated the dangers of standing out against Gladstone, and had seemed reconciled [...] to the need for co-operation with the Liberal leader'. It was only when Chamberlain discovered his own 'manifest impotence' to shape

---

128 Eyck, *Gladstone*, pp. 392, 395–96.
129 Magnus, *Gladstone*, p. 359.
130 Adelman, *Gladstone, Disraeli and Later Victorian Politics*, pp. 49–50.
131 P. T. Marsh, *Joseph Chamberlain* (1994), pp. 220, 232.
132 Hamer, *Liberal Politics*, p. 118.
133 Ibid., pp. 120–21.

Irish policy that his 'pride made it impossible for him to swallow any scheme initiated and devised by Gladstone'.[134]

Errors within the proposed legislation

Three weaknesses are said to have compromised the Home Rule Bill's prospects. One was the decision to exclude Irish MPs from Westminster. While for some this was the measure's chief merit, for others it revealed too starkly that Home Rule prefigured Ireland's complete separation from the United Kingdom. This was too much at odds with the developing New Imperialism, and was the aspect of the Bill that Chamberlain most ruthlessly criticized. The fact was, remarks Shannon, that the issue of the Irish MPs raised a dilemma that has confronted all subsequent attempts to devolve power within the United Kingdom: either the Irish remained at Westminster, which would allow them to shape British policy in ways that the British MPs could not shape Irish, or they were removed, which raised the reality of taxation without representation (because Ireland was not to be able to set its own tariffs) and seemed to point toward ultimate independence. Gladstone could not square that circle:

> 'Dualism', or coordinate Parliaments, was logical and intelligible; so was federalism. Imperial authority over self-governing colonies was a pious fiction, theoretically existing to the extent it was patent that it would never be exercised. Gladstone's Home Rule Ireland was a muddled mix of these.[135]

A second problem was the 1886 Land Bill. Intended to smooth the way to Home Rule by buying out the Anglo-Irish landlords and transferring the land to the tenants, thereby removing the grounds for landed opposition to Home Rule, it only produced a new series of potholes – the opposition it generated, says Graham Goodlad, serving to 'reinforce hostility to Gladstonian home rule'.[136] Not only had Gladstone always previously opposed attempts to create a class of small peasant farmers in Ireland, but the sums involved in buying out the landlord class were huge and deeply resented by Radicals who, observes Biagini, 'strongly objected to the burdens it would impose on the British middle and working classes

---

[134] Jenkins, *Gladstone, Whiggery and the Liberal Party*, pp. 278–80.

[135] Shannon, *Gladstone: Heroic Minister*, p. 426.

[136] G. D. Goodlad, 'The Liberal Party and Gladstone's Land Purchase Bill of 1886', *Historical Journal*, Vol. 32 (1989), p. 640.

for the despised Anglo-Irish landlords, who [...] were not entitled to any compensation at all'.[137] Indeed, Shannon writes that the Land Bill failed to please any constituency: the Irish Nationalists denounced it as a 'transparent sham', while its 'intended beneficiaries, the landlords, had but small reserves of gratitude for the author of the Land Acts of 1870 and 1881'. Gladstone 'allowed it to fade quietly out of sight and out of mind. With this fiasco Gladstone's position slumped.'[138] Perhaps the biggest mistake in 1886, says Matthew, was to run the Land and Home Rule Bills independently:

> It may well be that the greatest tactical error of 1886 was not to include both purchase and government in a single bill [...] Certainly the political formula for mutual self-contradiction was there: the landowning classes disliked Home Rule: many Home Rulers in England, Wales, and Scotland, disliked land purchase.[139]

The Bill's third weakness was that it accorded no recognition to the distinctive culture and religion of Ulster. Gladstone, notes Matthew, never attached much significance to Ulster, and 'saw Irish nationality in terms of the Catholic south'.[140] But many MPs felt a greater affinity with the northern Irish and were unhappy with the idea of rendering Protestants a minority within a Catholic-dominated state. 'Perhaps the greatest weakness of the scheme', argues Feuchtwanger, 'was that it made no provision for Ulster [...] Gladstone was hardly aware yet that there was a separate Ulster problem and he certainly was not prepared to accept any Ulster veto on a separate Irish Parliament.'[141] This, says Boyce, was an important omission, for when the Conservatives wished to make the case for the Union, the 'spectacle of a definable, regional, Protestant people, industrious and loyal, placed under the heel of Her Majesty's enemies was a persuasive one'.[142] Unsurprisingly, as the parliamentary debates on Home Rule proceeded, it was, observes O'Day, 'the future position of the loyal Protestant minority' that 'dominated discussions' – though he adds that in 1886 this was a 'minor stumbling block to the passage of his measure'.[143]

---

[137] Biagini, *Gladstone*, p. 106.
[138] Shannon, *Gladstone: Heroic Minister*, p. 428.
[139] Matthew, *Gladstone*, p. 500.
[140] Ibid., p. 486.
[141] Feuchtwanger, *Gladstone*, p. 237.
[142] Boyce, *The Irish Question and British Politics*, p. 35.
[143] O'Day, *Irish Home Rule*, pp. 113, 115.

Home Rule clashed with Liberal values

Parry, in his two studies of nineteenth-century Liberalism, *Democracy and Religion* and *The Rise and Fall of Liberal Government in England*, develops the idea that Home Rule clashed with too many Liberal values to rally sufficient support. One key clash was over method. In objecting to Home Rule, he writes, the Whig-Liberals were objecting 'above all, to Gladstone's manner of conducting government. For them, the essence of government was administration, the preservation of order and balance through the firm but impartial and respected rule of law.' Politicians should be responsible and not push issues ahead of public opinion. Most Liberals recognized that Ireland should be accorded greater self-government. What they resented was Gladstone's subservience to Irish opinion and the erratic and impassioned way he went about prosecuting the case for Home Rule.

> Gladstone was increasingly seen as an unpredictable, irrational leader, prone to mount zealous crusades against misgovernment and extravagance from a self-deceiving notion that he was marshalling a sympathetic public conscience in the cause [...] The manner of Gladstone's commitment to Home Rule suggested that [...] passion had triumphed over reason; separation over assimilation; populist appeals over parliamentary discussion; mob values over manliness; distaste for authority over responsible leadership; sentimentalism over science; 'government by average opinion' over didacticism. The result was the revolt of the Liberal Unionists.[144]

For the Whigs, he had again demonstrated his authoritarian contempt for parliamentary discussion, which they considered the chief method by which different perspectives were considered and compromise arrived at. Far from consulting his party, Gladstone had 'suppressed free debate and exploited "popular idolatry" of himself, in order to impose his policy'.[145]

The second clash Parry identifies was over the content of Gladstone's proposals. While in line with some Liberal ideals, like devolution, Home Rule contravened other, more 'cherished political principles: the rule of law, the defence of property, the superiority of the judgement of the educated, the might of British power, and the probability of the eventual defeat of a superstitious religion by a rational and ethical one'.[146] The Liberal Unionists believed that

---

[144] Parry, *Rise and Fall of Liberal Government*, pp. 305–6.
[145] Ibid., p. 300.
[146] Parry, *Democracy and Religion*, pp. 443–44.

British rule sustained law and order, held the balance between Protestants and Catholics, landlords and tenants and so on. An Irish parliament would quickly fall under the power of nationalists and Catholics and the liberties of the people and the rights of Protestants would soon be suppressed.[147]

Parry's arguments find an echo in the works of other historians. Stansky notes that 'the idea of Home Rule questioned too many firmly held beliefs: in religion, in the nature of Empire, in the menaces of Catholicism, in the weakness of Ulster Protestantism. It also hurt too many vested interests, most particularly those of English landlords of Irish land.'[148] Feuchtwanger, too, points to the array of opinion even within the Liberal party that opposed it. Imperialists objected to the exclusion of Irish MPs from the Commons; many working-class people disliked the Irish as a source of cheap labour and disapproved of Nationalist terrorism; and on the right 'the leading sentiments against Home Rule were national pride and an offended sense of property. Why should the rights of a weak, despised, endemically hostile nation of four million be put above the requirements of a strong nation of thirty million and a powerful Empire?' The Land Bill seemed to represent an attack on property. The moralism on which the case for Home Rule was ultimately based was out of fashion and a 'majority of the intellectuals' lined up against it.[149]

Thus Gladstone failed, says Parry, because his 'commitment to Home Rule was the most convincing demonstration imaginable that his priorities were at odds with those of the mainstream nineteenth-century Liberal tradition'.[150] Once again, Gladstone's distance from the Whig–Liberal tradition stood revealed, as it had been over income tax abolition and the Balkan agitation, and by his 'powerful sense of mission', writes Hawkins, he 'split the Liberal party apart, driving Whigs and Chamberlainite radicals into the arms of Conservative Unionists'.[151] By this means, concludes Parry, Gladstone 'turned the Liberal party from a great party of government into a gaggle of outsiders'.[152]

Conclusion

It is hard to avoid the conclusion that Gladstone made just about every mistake possible in the weeks leading up to the defeat of his Home Rule

---

[147] Parry, *Rise and Fall of Liberal Government*, p. 299.
[148] Stansky, *Gladstone*, p. 165.
[149] Feuchtwanger, *Gladstone*, pp. 239–40.
[150] Parry, *Rise and Fall of Liberal Government*, p. 303.
[151] Hawkins, *British Party Politics*, p. 265.
[152] Parry, *Rise and Fall of Liberal Government*, pp. 305–6.

Bill. 'It is generally agreed', write Chapman and Littlejohn, that Gladstone 'made several political blunders', and they believe that without these errors of judgement 'it is possible, indeed probable, that the Bill would have passed the House of Commons'.[153] To the initial error of failing to prepare either the Liberals or national opinion for the radical departure he had been secretly plotting, was soon added his unwillingness to compromise on essentials, his mismanagement of Chamberlain and the further alienation of opinion through details of the actual legislation, notably the land purchase Bill and the failure to take account of the fact that Ireland contained a Protestant North as well as a Catholic South. If there was one theme uniting these distinct miscalculations it was that highlighted by Parry: namely, that Gladstone's imperious Peelite style of leadership was wholly at odds with the Liberal tradition of free discussion and rational compromise. Gladstone's fixation upon Home Rule as the only solution to the Irish problem, and one that had to be implemented *now*, caused him to overlook the legitimate concerns raised and the discontent within his own party. To this extent Matthew and Shannon are right to portray 1886 as essentially a failure of politics: Gladstone simply could not bring himself to play the Westminster game in the manner required to get his legislation through. The roots of this failure lay in Gladstone's decision to take up Home Rule in the first place. While Gladstone was convinced that Ireland was in crisis and posed *the* greatest challenge to the state, hardly anyone else did. For once, Gladstone's great gift of 'timing' failed him – as Shannon emphasizes. However justified a policy Home Rule was, there was no sign that public opinion was ripe for such a move. The materials for a Home Rule solution to the Irish problem were not at hand, and the one man who might fashion them failed to do so, preferring to bulldoze Home Rule through by means of his evangelical fervour. Why did he proceed with such disruptive haste? The answer must surely be that the closing future of his own political career meant that he simply did not have time to allow a public opinion in favour of Home Rule to ripen. But as Otto von Bismarck once remarked, you cannot ripen a fruit by holding a candle to it.

---

[153] Chapman and Littlejohn, 'Home Rule Revisited: an Essay in Historiography', p. 43.

Chapter 8

GLADSTONE AND DISRAELI: POLITICAL PRINCIPLES

Outline of Events

It is natural to assume that the rivalry between William Gladstone and Benjamin Disraeli reflected not merely a dissonance of personality but also a fundamental divergence in political ideology. To assess this proposition it is first necessary to establish just what, precisely, were the basic political principles of the two men. Predictably, however, there is extensive disagreement as to what Gladstone and Disraeli actually stood for – and indeed, whether either actually stood for anything. The latter possibility is touted much more readily in the case of Disraeli. This, in itself, is somewhat paradoxical, for Disraeli cut his political teeth in the 1840s by championing his Young England brand of true Tory values in contradistinction to Robert Peel's supposedly liberal latitudinarianism, and for most of his life he spoke a recurring language of national unity, patriotism, aristocratic leadership and allegiance to historic institutions. However, contemporary critics and the bulk of subsequent historians have seen Disraeli's rhetoric and practice as two very different things. While Disraeli recognized the importance of ideas, and relished using words and images to convey a political effect, in action he is seen as behaving opportunistically, seizing upon whatever a situation offered to score an advantage. Thus, in each of the major initiatives of his career, from his defence of the Corn Laws in the 1840s to his support for electoral reform in 1867 to his embracing of social reform in the 1870s, Disraeli is portrayed as acting strategically not ideologically. Gladstone, by contrast, is depicted as the conviction politician par excellence, and each of the milestones in his career is regarded as the product of an intense period of internal reflection: if Gladstone advocated a laissez-faire economic policy or the extension of the franchise or Irish Home Rule, he did so because he was convinced that it was the *right* thing to do – so right, indeed, that it was almost certainly God's will.

Where debate has chiefly arisen has been with respect to what principle guided his behaviour. Was Gladstone guided by a profound liberal instinct? Or was he always really a Conservative, and more particularly a Peelite? Or perhaps he is best seen as an Evangelical struggling against the forces of sin? The answer to these questions has implications for the meaning of the rivalry of the two men. If the picture of a principled Gladstone and an opportunistic Disraeli is accepted, then the battle between these great Victorians is reassuringly explicable in ideological terms. But other possibilities exist. If Disraeli was, notwithstanding his attacks upon Peel, really a Peelite, and if Gladstone too was essentially Peel's disciple, then the intensity of their animosity might have arisen from their combat for the same contested ground. Or suppose, as some contend, Gladstone's politics were more pragmatic than principled, then perhaps their rivalry owed more to a clash of ambition and ego than it did to some Victorian morality tale.

8.1   Did Disraeli Possess Any Political Principles?

The degree to which Disraeli's political conduct was shaped by a political philosophy perplexed contemporaries and continues to provoke controversy. For some, Disraeli's career can be understood without reference to ideology at all, being driven by the pursuit of political advantage. For others, Disraeli had ideals, but his practical politics owed little too them. A third group contends that his principles were consistent and relevant to understanding his political actions. A more recent perspective sees Disraeli's ideas not as a source of policy but as a means of justifying his political position and challenging the mid-nineteenth-century liberal consensus.

That Disraeli had no political ideals

From his first entry into politics it was alleged of Disraeli that he had no guiding principles besides a determination to exploit situations for his advancement. Thus the Liberal journalist Walter Bagehot wrote in 1859 that Disraeli 'has never had a political faith, – he probably does not know what it means [...] He has adopted the opinions of parties as he would adopt a national costume. "Tory", "Radical", "Tory-Radical", "Free Trader", "Protectionist", "Conservative", "Reformer", no creed has come amiss to him, and amidst them all he has maintained [...] the same determined will to use them for individual or party ends.'[1] T. Hayes, in a speech before the Leigh

---

[1] Bagehot, 'Mr Disraeli' (1859), in St John-Stevas (ed.), *Collected Works of Walter Bagehot* (1968), III. pp. 486–87.

Liberal Club in 1878, declared that Disraeli's 'guiding star has been his own ambition, and that self has been the only deity he has worshipped'.[2] While old-fashioned Toryism might have been worthy of respect, 'Disraelism, is a mean and contemptible article, founded solely on expediency, and destitute of truth, honour and principle'.[3] In 1907, the Liberal MP J. M. Roberston contended that Disraeli was 'the most notable egoist of his generation'. He 'had no political ideals or convictions, and never cared for any cause as such'.[4] These remarks come from political opponents, but colleagues, too, doubted whether he held any genuine beliefs. Thus, the Conservative MP William Fraser remarked, in 1891, that his 'main object in early life was to make himself conspicuous [...] He looked upon himself [...] as an actor who goes on stage to play a part'. Without 'a drop of British blood in his veins' he could 'watch; study; observe; calculate; do everything but sympathize: he, like Napoleon, used a people to obtain supreme power.'[5] More revealing still is the testimony of his closest political friend, Lord Stanley, who asked in his diary, 'how can I help seeing that glory and power, rather than the public good, have been his objects?'[6]

Early historians shared this perspective on Disraeli's motives. J. A. Froude relates how Disraeli, in the early stages of his career, 'had not concealed that his chief motive was ambition. He had started as a soldier of fortune, and he had taken service with the party among whom, perhaps, he felt that he would have the best chance of rising to eminence.'[7] For the American Frank Gunsaulus, writing in 1898, Disraeli was the 'athletic magician, who was Conservative only by accident', while the Earl of Cromer observed that he 'cared [...] little for principles of any kind, provided the goal of his ambition could be reached'.[8] This tradition of the apolitical Disraeli persists. Indeed, Jonathan Parry suggests that the tendency to view Disraeli as a 'cynical opportunist' is now so strong that historians 'feel obliged to put a sly construction on all his operations, for fear of being branded naive'.[9] Thus, J. H. Plumb believes that 'Disraeli never worked out a coherent political philosophy; at times he stole the programme, if not the principles, of his liberal opponents'.[10] T. A. Jenkins

---

[2] Hayes, *Lord Beaconsfield*, p. 3.

[3] Ibid., p. 20.

[4] Quoted in Smith, *Disraeli*, p. 2.

[5] Fraser, *Disraeli and His Day*, pp. 340–41.

[6] Quoted in Smith, *Disraeli*, p. 3.

[7] Froude, *Earl of Beaconsfield*, p. 236.

[8] Gunsaulus, *William Ewart Gladstone*, p. 231; Earl of Cromer, *Political and Literary Essays* (1913), p. 180.

[9] J. P. Parry, 'Disraeli and England', *Historical Journal*, Vol. 43, (2000), p. 700.

[10] Davis, *Disraeli*, xi.

acknowledges that there is much to be said for the idea that Disraeli was a political adventurer, willing to change his policies in the pursuit of power.[11] Ian Machin presses the point most strongly:

> The most consistent strand in Disraeli's career was his determination to gain and keep political power. There was no similar consistency in the principles or policies he adopted when he was striving to win power or to keep it. He was entirely pragmatic in the way he took up and discarded policies as seemed suitable to his salient quest.[12]

Thus, after initially supporting Peel's commercial reforms, he defended Protection as the prospect of office under Peel receded, only to later abandon it once it became 'politically redundant'. As Machin summarizes,

> Apart from his determination to rise to power and to exploit every opportunity provided by the party and policy to do so, other political considerations in Disraeli's career were of secondary importance. He was completely without any ideological preconceptions which might have made loyal service to ideals a more compelling demand than even rising to a powerful position [...] It is, indeed, difficult to say what ideals he had.[13]

Disraeli's ideology: the aristocratic settlement and one nation

Few historians now accept that Disraeli had no political ideology at all. Quite the opposite: he is widely regarded as having provided an important restatement of Conservative values for the Victorian age. 'Hardly any Victorian politician', writes Parry, 'took more care than Disraeli to work out his ideas.'[14] The question is how far that ideology shaped his practical politics.

According to Robert Blake, Disraeli believed that England's greatness, freedom and happiness depended upon 'the ascendancy of the landed class', and most of his specific attitudes can be traced to a desire to uphold the 'aristocratic settlement'.[15] This 'represented his profoundest conviction and [...] it remained to the end his guiding purpose'. What Disraeli had in mind, explains Blake, was 'the whole ordered hierarchy of rural England' – with

---

[11] Jenkins, *Disraeli and Victorian Conservatism*, pp. 139–40.
[12] Machin, *Disraeli*, p. 5.
[13] Ibid., pp. 164–68.
[14] Parry, 'Disraeli and England', p. 703.
[15] Blake, *Disraeli*, pp. 762–63.

its squires, bishops, dukes, clergy, Lord Lieutenants and so forth. This was the society which Disraeli wished to defend against the Whigs and their 'unholy alliance with' the industrial middle class. Why did Disraeli believe in this territorial aristocracy? Partly because 'he was at heart a romantic', but mainly because 'he had a genuine hatred of centralisation, bureaucracy and every manifestation of the Benthamite state'. He shared Edmund Burke's reverence for independent institutions, which he saw as guarantees of freedom against a levelling state, and believed that the autonomy of the landed classes was the best barrier to centralization.[16] Further, he believed that the urban working class could be won to support a government of the gentry if it legislated on their behalf. These, says Blake, were the defining features of Disraeli's political vision throughout his life. As early as his 1835 *Vindication of the Constitution* 'we have the anti-Whig theory of English history that the Tory party had been the truly democratic party, the party of the majority [...] that the Whigs were the oligarchical anti-national party [...] his contempt for doctrinaires and abstract theories, especially those of the Utilitarians, his deep respect for traditional institutions, and his reverence for landed property and all that goes with it'.[17] Disraeli was articulating the same ideas 40 years later, and his career cannot be understood unless this attachment to the 'aristocratic principle' is remembered.

Blake's emphasis upon Disraeli's attachment to the aristocratic settlement finds support from numerous historians. In 1907 the Tory journalist and friend of Disraeli, Thomas Kebbel, wrote that

> [h]e was an aristocrat of aristocrats. He had no notion of allowing political power to be divorced from the principle of birth and property. He always spoke of the country gentlemen of England as the natural leaders of the rural population. Both in his speeches and in his writings he loved to dwell on the advantages of what he called 'a territorial constitution'.[18]

Paul Adelman acknowledges that many writers have seen a desire to "uphold the aristocratic settlement of the country" as 'the one thread of consistency that runs through all Disraeli's ideas and policies'.[19] One such is Richard Weeks, who accepts that Disraeli's career was governed by the need to uphold

---

[16] Ibid., pp. 278–82.
[17] Ibid., p. 129.
[18] Kebbel, *Lord Beaconsfield*, p. 66.
[19] Adelman, *Gladstone, Disraeli and Later Victorian Politics*, p. 16.

the aristocratic settlement.[20] Another is T. A. Jenkins, who argues that Disraeli believed that the political leadership of the territorial aristocracy 'was both a guarantee of the rights and liberties of the people [...] and the foundation of Britain's greatness among the nations of the world'.[21] Gertrude Himmelfarb, when arguing the case that Disraeli possessed a consistent ideology, finds it in the creed of the Young England novels:

> the belief that the Tories were the national party, that the aristocracy and the working class were natural allies, that the social hierarchy was independent of ephemeral political arrangements, that national character was more important than particular laws, and that politics and society were largely governed by traditions of leadership and deference [...] This creed, so far from being a literary fantasy, was in fact a political ideology of substance and consequence.[22]

Paul Smith has similarly found in Disraeli's writings of the 1830s and 1840s a set of views that resonated through his career and which had, at bottom, a desire to restore an English community out of the 'crowd into which liberal individualism was alleged to have dissolved the nation'. Thus, for Smith, 'there is a case for considering [...] the stance evolved in the 1830s and 1840s [...] *as* his politics, rather than as a colourful but more or less irrelevant prologue to his "real" political career'.[23] This politics he sums up as follows:

> English national rights and liberties were threatened by the centralising state embodied in the Whigs. The only thing that could defend those historic liberties were the national institutions of the Crown, Lords, Church, and the landed interest – which was why the Whigs attacked those institutions in the name of 'liberal' progress. In so doing they deprived the mass of the population of their main bulwarks against industrial and commercial capitalism. The only solution to the social system was to restore the traditional influence of the landed class, which put duty and loyalty before individualism and profit. The political expression of the landed class was the Tory party.[24]

Disraeli, says Smith, said these things through his career, and when speaking at the Crystal Palace in 1872 of the three 'great objects' of the Conservatives

---

[20] Weeks, 'Disraeli as Political Egoist', p. 408.
[21] Jenkins, *Disraeli and Victorian Conservatism*, p. 140.
[22] Himmelfarb, 'The Politics of Democracy: the English Reform Act of 1867', p. 111.
[23] Smith, *Disraeli*, p. 216. Italics in the original.
[24] Smith, *Disraelian Conservatism*, pp. 12–13.

as defence of the institutions of Church and State, upholding the Empire and elevating the condition of the people, he was summing up 'the Tory doctrines he had been preaching for nearly 40 years'.[25] This case for continuity in Disraeli's thinking was made in 1931 by Sir William Ivor Jennings: '[t]he beliefs to which he gave expression in 1832 were not substantially different from those which he maintained as Prime Minister'.[26]

As can be seen from Smith's characterization of Disraeli's politics, much of the purchase of his ideas arose out of a supposed clash with the anti-national tendencies of the Whigs. This point is developed by Angus Hawkins and John Vincent, who emphasize how Disraeli evoked the idea of the Tories as the 'national' party in contrast to the oligarchic cosmopolitanism of the Whig elite. Disraeli's *Vindication* of 1835, writes Vincent, 'foreshadowed his Young England novels of the 1840s, his party leadership, and his premiership [...] Faced with an established Whig supremacy [...] he retorted with an anti-elitist or popular doctrine of national solidarity [...] Since politics is inherently oligarchical, most must suffer from a sense of exclusion. Bring that sense to life, and you have a natural majority.'[27] Hawkins elaborates:

From the beginning of his career [...] Disraeli was [...] consistently anti-Whig [...] The Whigs embraced alien and cosmopolitan ideas. Since 1688 they had burdened England with Venetian politics (an exclusive oligarchy), Dutch finance (a national debt), and French wars. He sought, in contrast, an authentically national party rooted in the ancient institutions of the country. Love of these institutions, Disraeli proclaimed, embraced all classes of society [...] It was the national community, as an organic whole, that was to be brought behind Britain as a great imperial world power; her historic institutions integrating social cohesion with national identity.[28]

Against the rootless theories of the coalition of Whigs, radicals, utilitarians and atheists that constituted the Liberals, adds Parry, Disraeli set the historical continuity of England. 'Hardly any nineteenth century politician was more deeply enthused by the English past; he almost never made a significant speech without evoking it.'[29] Disraeli had an 'intense consciousness of England's

---

[25] Smith, *Disraeli*, p. 165.
[26] Jennings, 'Disraeli and the Constitution', p. 184.
[27] Vincent, *Disraeli*, p. 24.
[28] Hawkins, *British Party Politics*, p. 215.
[29] Parry, *Benjamin Disraeli*, p. 29.

history and character, which drove him to define his political career in terms of a heroic defence of national values, traditions, and power'.[30]

Questioning the practical implications of Disraeli's ideology

But did the ideology of one nation united around a territorial aristocracy shape Disraeli's political conduct? Here we consider four arguments: first, that Disraeli's territorial philosophy, though sincerely held, had minimal impact upon his politics; second, that the territorial constitution was *not* the key to Disraeli's thinking; third, that while Disraeli's ideological goals remained constant, the means he deployed to attain them changed significantly; and fourth, that attempts to discern a link between political ideas and practice are misconceived since Disraeli was deploying ideas for other ends.

That Disraeli's ideas had a minimal impact upon his political practice

A number of commentators contend that Disraeli's political actions were primarily shaped by pragmatic considerations to do with the getting and keeping of power. This was the message of a series of re-evaluations of Disraeli's politics published during the 1960s, including Smith's *Disraelian Conservatism and Social Reform* and Maurice Cowling's *1867: Disraeli, Gladstone and Revolution*, both of which accounted for key episodes in Disraeli's career in terms of the pursuit of political advantage rather than the realization of some ideological vision. Consolidating this more sceptical reading was Blake's 1966 *Disraeli* – the first major biography since William Monypenny and George Buckle's *Life of Benjamin Disraeli* (1910–20). Where the latter argued that Disraeli 'was never without ideas or the courage to follow their guidance', Blake, while acknowledging Disraeli's attachment to the aristocratic settlement, argued that 'he never attempted at all seriously to carry out the sort of programme which he and his friends seem to have envisaged'. 'Indeed, it would have been a vain task in the mid-nineteenth century to have solved the Condition of England question by reviving either the monarchy, the aristocracy or the Church. The extension of the franchise in 1867 and the social reforms of 1875–6 have only a superficial connexion with *Sybil*.'[31] Although 'Disraeli had principles when he led the party [...] they were not the "principles", if that word can be used at all, of Young England'.[32] Disraeli believed that the nation and its liberties would decline with the decline of the landed interest, but this

---

[30] Parry, 'Disraeli and England', p. 700.
[31] Monypenny and Buckle, *Life of Disraeli*, I. p. 303; Blake, *Disraeli*, p. 211.
[32] Ibid., p. 762.

was something few politicians, let alone Conservatives, questioned, and it did little to shape such policies as the Reform Act, social reform or imperialism. To understand these we need to focus upon the particular context within which Disraeli was operating.

Machin elaborates this point. 'Disraeli never [...] pursued a policy which might not aid his political interests.' He had a 'genuine desire to improve social conditions for the working classes, but he did not urge this cause in any consistent or campaigning fashion, maintain it if it went clearly against aristocratic economic interests, or concern himself with its practical details'. For the same reason he raised the need for electoral reform as a means of increasing Conservative support, but he never supported lowering the County franchise or the secret ballot since these reforms were seen as damaging Conservative interests.[33] 'In all aspects of his policy, therefore, the furthering of his party and of his own political fortunes was paramount.'[34] Bruce Coleman agrees. Disraeli kept rhetoric and purpose separate, and subsequent myths have focused too much on his words: 'if one ignores the window dressing, he stuck very close to the mood and requirements of his party [...] his claims to any fundamental creativity and originality are dubious'. Coleman doubts whether there was anything that can be called 'Disraelian Conservatism'.[35] For Douglas Hurd and Edward Young, Disraeli 'had few views on policy which could not be manipulated to suit the situation'.[36] As Vincent summarizes, recent scholars 'all reach essentially the same conclusion – that as a practical politician he was largely uninfluenced by principles or beliefs'. He had an ideology, believing in Britain's greatness and aristocratic rule, but that did not determine his particular policies. 'The opportunist view cannot be wrong, for Disraeli was blatantly opportunist. The question that has been raised recently is whether it is wholly right or only partially so.'[37]

Certainly several historians have presented Disraeli's conduct as something other than purely opportunistic. Parry suggests there is a subtle link between his Young England ideology of the 1840s and his later political strategies, which 'bore some relationship, albeit indirectly, to such ideas'.[38] Disraeli had coherent views on the importance of the land, the church and about the threat posed to society by the decay of 'traditionary influences'. What made this problematic were the rapid changes in Victorian society. He 'could

---

[33] Machin, *Disraeli*, pp. 166–67.
[34] Ibid., p. 169.
[35] Coleman, *Conservatism and the Conservative Party*, p. 159.
[36] Hurd and Young, *Disraeli*, p. 132.
[37] Vincent, *Disraeli*, p. 114.
[38] Parry, *Benjamin Disraeli*, ii–iii.

do nothing about the triumph of free trade, the decline of the old colonial relationships, and the waning of paternalism. For much of his life he had to accept the broad policy assumptions laid down by Liberal politicians.'[39] The challenge of his career was to combine the manoeuvres essential to securing power with his determination to maintain the Conservative party's 'independence and ideals'. Parry believes that he did this, pursuing his conservative objective of frustrating 'radical initiatives which he saw as challenging national institutions and traditions', diffusing conflicts, reducing tension between town and country, capital and labour, striving for 'a unifying synthesis'.[40] In this Parry echoes the earlier words of David Somervell, who writes that Disraeli's mission 'was to preserve the spirit of an ancient order of society, and to create and maintain a political party dedicated to the intelligent, as contrasted with the merely negative and obstructive, pursuit of that end [...] The task of Conservatism was to repair, to defend, and to preserve: strength was to be found in quietness and in confidence.'[41]

Asa Briggs sees as a continuing theme of Disraeli's politics his recognition of the need to 'educate his party' in order to make Toryism popular by adapting to the transforming landscape of Victorian England: 'the first lesson he taught was that [...] Conservatives had to accept the necessity for change and to adapt their tactics accordingly [...] Conservatism could only survive if it considered something more than conservation.'[42] The idea that Disraeli equipped the Conservatives with a set of ideas for the modern age is similarly advocated by J. A. R. Marriott. Where Canning and Peel's attempts to educate the Tories into modern realities ended in failure, 'Disraeli accomplished it' in his 1872 speeches at Manchester and Crystal Palace, which 'defined the principles of the New Toryism [...] "the Constitution, the Empire and Social Reform" represented not merely the battle cry of an opportunist, but the carefully considered and coherent programme of one who aspired [...] to re-found a party'.[43] Hawkins similarly situates the 1870s speeches within Disraeli's politics:

Disraeli's legacy to the party was to provide it, after 1872, with a potent language about itself that defined a Conservative [...] identity [...] In seizing upon the collapse of Gladstonian Liberalism in 1872–4, Disraeli brought the Conservatives forward as a national party [...] They were

---

[39] Ibid., p. 127.
[40] Ibid., pp. 35, 41, 128.
[41] D. C. Somervell, *Disraeli and Gladstone* (1932), pp. 288–89.
[42] Briggs, *Victorian People*, pp. 272–73.
[43] Marriott, *England since Waterloo*, pp. 435–36.

committed to Empire, a robust foreign policy conducted in the light of British interests, associated with support for the monarchy, the defence of property, and protection of the Established Church [...] these were consistent strands in Disraeli's thinking. They provided links between his subversive youth and his role as the pragmatic elder statesman.[44]

Richard Shannon, too, believes Disraeli 'never wavered' from the doctrine he put to Derby in 1848: that the office of the Conservative leader was to "uphold the aristocratic settlement of this country". Compared to this, his 'fleeting adventures with Tory Democracy and wry-faced gestures to the middle-class Conservatism fade into insignificance'.[45] John Walton similarly speaks of the 'enduring principles which underlay Disraeli's political behaviour', notably his belief that 'the rule of the propertied' was 'the best guarantee of traditional liberties as well as of the rights of property'. The Conservative party was his 'vehicle for restoring England to its "natural state" of aristocratic rule, responsible government and social harmony'.[46]

Questioning the aristocratic settlement narrative: Disraeli as Peelite

R. W. Davis takes issue with the emphasis upon the territorial aristocracy as the key to Disraeli's political thinking. Whether 'Disraeli actually had such devotion as Blake suggests to the squirearchy and their interests, much less made them the lodestar of his future career, is highly doubtful'. What Disraeli meant by the landed interest, says Davis, was the rural population more generally, not merely the gentry or aristocrats. The Tory party was dominated by the gentry, and Disraeli was forced to espouse their interests. 'But to see such a course as based on any more than this kind of ultimate opportunism is [...] extremely difficult.' Disraeli 'had a very low opinion of the "gentlemen of England" as represented in the House of Commons' and was not 'on intimate terms with any of the county families'.[47] Ian St John likewise questions 'whether Disraeli himself really believed in the peculiar virtues of the landed aristocracy'. Great territorial magnates were witheringly satirized in the Young England novels, and there 'can be little doubt that this rather cynical attitude towards the existing aristocracy was Disraeli's true opinion. He knew he was superior to them in ability'.[48]

---

[44] Hawkins, *British Party Politics*, pp. 214–15.
[45] Shannon, *Age of Disraeli*, p. 189.
[46] J. Walton, *Disraeli*, pp. 60–61.
[47] Davis, *Disraeli*, pp. 91–92.
[48] St John, *Disraeli and the Art of Victorian Politics*, p. 120.

But if the aristocratic settlement did not drive Disraeli's politics, what did? Despite having launched his career through his conflict with Peel, a number of historians contend that Disraeli was essentially a Peelite. The most prominent advocate of this perspective is Peter Ghosh, who rejects the 'neo-opportunist' interpretation of Disraeli, according to which he possessed principles, but these 'did not determine his actions in any detailed or specific sense'.[49] 'Disraeli, far from being an unprincipled opportunist, can be viewed as a politician whose career displayed a coherent development from the late 1840s.' But it was in finance, not in the sentimentalism of Young England, that Disraeli's ideology can be discerned, as he 'formulated a set of general principles' representing 'an integrated conception covering the related areas of finance, foreign affairs and defence policy'.[50] The basic elements were a pro-French foreign policy and the political importance of low taxation, both of which were combined in the maxim 'expenditure depends on policy'. This basically meant that, since expenditure was determined by foreign policy, low spending and taxation required that Britain maintain good relations with France. Disraeli was, like Gladstone, an advocate of 'economy and retrenchment', and also like Gladstone, he aspired to the 'mantle of Peel'.[51] Yet he failed because Tory defeat in 1859 allowed Gladstone to bring in his 1860–61 budgets and these exhausted 'the issue of financial reform as defined by Peel'. Disraeli's response was to fall back on the defence of the constitution, and for this he looked to social reform 'to divert legislative energy away from assaults in what was vital – the constitutional and institutional framework of the country – and in this way it served a truly Conservative function'.[52] Similarly, Ghosh sees Disraeli's later pro-imperial speeches as a 'deviation' from his traditional foreign policy, provoked by Gladstone's aggressive Bulgarian agitation and existing 'almost solely in the realm of the style and presentation of policy'.

Ghosh is not alone in discerning the lineaments of Peelism beneath the rhetoric of One Nation Toryism. Smith suggests that Disraeli saw from the 1850s that if the Conservative party was to get into power, 'it must resume the Peelite policy which he had wrecked in 1846 and render itself more palatable to urban middle class taste'.[53] Agreeing with Ghosh, Smith sees economical finance as central to Disraeli's politics in the 1850s, attacking

---

[49] P. R. Ghosh, 'Disraelian Conservatism: A Financial Approach', *English Historical Review*, Vol. 99 (1984), p. 268.
[50] Ibid., p. 294.
[51] Ibid., pp. 284, 286.
[52] Ibid., p. 295.
[53] Smith, *Disraelian Conservatism*, pp. 12–13.

Lord Palmerston for the high defence spending necessitated by his turbulent foreign policy. He likewise concurs that it was Disraeli's misfortune that the Conservatives were never in power long enough to wrest 'from the hands of Gladstone [...] the great engine of sound finance and equitable taxation which lay at the heart of mid-Victorian government'.[54] And this was no mere electoral manoeuvre: Disraeli was keen to relieve Toryism of all that was 'obsolete' and 'revive the Peelite tradition of progressive yet moderate reform'. Indeed, he argues that the 1870s, 'the very period which saw the efflorescence of "Disraelian" Conservatism', represented in reality the coming to fruition of 'a line of policy closely comparable to the outlook and approach of Peel', for it was in those years that the Tory party consummated its relations with the urban bourgeoisie. 'The political practice of Disraeli himself seems on close examination to be largely "Peelite" in spirit.'[55]

Machin also believes that Disraeli 'followed the general liberal course' of all British governments from the 1820s, seeking to 'avoid any drift towards revolution and preserve much of the *status quo*' by means of electoral reform, extensions of commercial opportunity and limited social reform.

> In spite of his rift from Peel in the 1840s, he basically agreed with Peel's pragmatic policy of reform [...] even in regard to Gladstone the difference [between the two men] was not fundamental. Both Gladstone and Disraeli accepted a liberal and pragmatic approach to reform which was meant to preserve rather than destroy.[56]

But can Disraeli's politics really be reduced to merely an ersatz version of Peelism? Coleman suggests that Disraeli's politics are better seen as Palmerstonian: he did not pursue a modernization agenda, largely reacting to the mood of the times.[57] Though recognizing a Peelite dimension to Disraeli's conduct, Smith thinks that the 'banal precepts' which Ghosh parades as Disraeli's ideology 'cannot do duty for the fundamentals of Disraeli's political outlook'.[58] Similarly, T. A. Jenkins admits that while, in appealing to middle-class voters, Disraeli was returning the Tories to the Peelite strategy of the 1840s, he made a distinctive contribution through his rhetoric about Britain's ancient institutions, imperial strength and limited social reform. 'Disraeli is

---

[54] Smith, *Disraeli*, pp. 121–23.
[55] Smith, *Disraelian Conservatism*, p. 4.
[56] Machin, *Disraeli*, p. 8.
[57] Coleman, *Conservatism and the Conservative Party*, p. 159.
[58] Smith, 'Disraeli's Politics', p. 67.

therefore reasonably entitled to receive credit for having created his own brand of "Conservatism" by the 1870s.'[59]

Constant ends and changing means: from Tory ideal
to resisting revolution

A historian who has confronted the issue of the significance of Disraeli's political ideas is Clyde Lewis. In his 1961 article 'Theory and Expediency in the Policy of Disraeli', Lewis argues that Disraeli did have a sustained political ideology, but that the policies he deduced from it varied over time, thereby offering a means of reconciling the Aristocratic Settlement and pragmatic/Peelite interpretations of Disraeli's conduct. According to Lewis, Disraeli recognized that with the decline of religious faith there had a risen a spirit of unrest that challenged the traditional hierarchies which underpinned English civilization. The only solution was a 'restoration of faith in those sacred ideals embodied in such traditional English institutions as the old agrarian community, the common law, the Church, and the Monarchy'. Since political change could not be avoided, 'wise statesmanship consisted in the proper evaluation of public opinion, making possible a compromise policy which could preserve the greatest part of the institutional heritage'.[60] 'These principles [...] determined the shifts of policy that characterised his career.' The crucial turning point was the European revolutions of 1848. In his Young England period Disraeli had seen the middle class as the chief threat to ancient institutions, and he sought to resist this by restoring sound Toryism, protecting the rights of labour, abandoning laissez-faire economics and reawakening social responsibility among the ruling class.[61] Yet after 1848 Disraeli, conscious of the destructive potential of such ideas as democracy and socialism, sought to work with the propertied middle class to resist such dangerous innovations. 'The result was a defensive pragmatism which required him to compromise his principles and show more sympathy for the *status quo* than he had shown earlier.'[62] To this end he exhibited 'more sympathy toward liberalism than at any other time during his career', accepting 'free trade, the primacy of the house of Commons, the party system, and even the 1832 Reform Act'. But his purpose remained the same: to

---

[59] Jenkins, *Disraeli and Victorian Conservatism*, p. 100.
[60] C. J. Lewis, 'Theory and Expediency in the Policy of Disraeli', *Victorian Studies*, Vol. 4, No. 3 (1961), pp. 240–41.
[61] Ibid., p. 243.
[62] Ibid., pp. 241, 245

sustain as much as possible of the aristocratic order.[63] Lewis identifies 1867 as a second turning point in Disraeli's policies as he endeavoured to make 'a more direct appeal to the lower classes with what has often been called "Tory Democracy"'. This arose out of Disraeli's growing sense of a European crisis of legitimacy as socialism and secret societies threatened social and political disintegration. In England it was popular unrest over parliamentary reform that opened Disraeli's eyes to the need to appeal 'to the common people through popular slogans, evidently hoping to associate the new democratic movement with respect for traditional institutions'. This seemed like a return to Young England, but there was a difference: in his Young England period he wanted to work with the aristocracy and common people to restore the old order against the middle class, while now he was mobilizing *all* classes against attacks on the social system as such. Thus, through his 1867 Reform Bill he hoped to win the working classes to the support of the aristocratic constitution.[64] Social reforms and imperialism were similarly 'part of a practical policy, designed to satisfy the masses, turn their attention away from constitutional innovations, and enlist their loyalties for the Conservative party'. As Lewis summarizes,

> A review of Disraeli's policy, from beginning to end, reveals a striking consistency. At all times he attempted to further causes which to his way of thinking would foster popular attachment to traditional institutions. At first, when a return to the old aristocratic order appeared possible, he advocated such a course. Then, becoming alarmed by the probability of revolution, he had set aside his absolute ideals in order to wage a defensive fight against immediate dangers. For a while he had sought to establish a new stability in alliance with the middle classes. When this position became untenable, he sought to prevent revolution by appealing to the emotions of the masses.[65]

Lewis's theory fits the facts and Jenkins lends it some support, recognizing that while Disraeli pursued a consistent goal of upholding aristocratic government, he shifted his ground upon becoming Conservative leader in the Commons, accepting both the Whig constitutional settlement of the 1830s and Free Trade 'in the hope of harnessing the middle classes to the support of the nation's institutions'.[66] The problem, as Jenkins admits, is that almost *any*

---

[63] Ibid., pp. 248, 250.
[64] Ibid., pp. 252–54.
[65] Ibid., pp. 256, 258.
[66] Jenkins, *Disraeli and Victorian Conservatism*, pp. 140–41.

action by Disraeli could be interpreted in terms of a desire to uphold England's ancient institutions. Further, Lewis's reference to 1848 as the tipping point in Disraeli's politics has been questioned. Weeks, for instance, believes he places 'too much emphasis' on Disraeli's fear of revolution, and as we have seen, the idea that Disraeli was seriously worried by the Hyde Park events of 1866 is widely discounted.[67] And if 1848 was a turning point in Disraeli's policies, there are other plausible explanations: above all, the simple fact that Peel had been banished and Disraeli had become a senior party leader. E. T. Raymond believes that Disraeli had to sideline his Young England principles once he became a Tory leader. 'To be something politically he must be something very seriously less than his full self [...] Disraeli from now onward must be regarded as a disappointed man.'[68]

Disraeli and the politics of imagery

In recent years historians have taken Disraeli's ideas more seriously *as ideas*. Disraeli's ideas, it is argued, were not a blueprint for action, and the search for a correlation between ideology and policy is misconceived. He used them, rather, to shape perceptions of the Tories, the Liberals – and himself. John Vincent has done most to prompt a re-evaluation of the role of ideas and language in Disraeli's career. Disraeli, he contends, saw the need to fight the battle of ideas with the Liberals, but his room for manoeuvring was limited: economically, free trade ruled supreme and Disraeli 'could not, and probably did not want to, challenge the Victorian economic consensus'. His efforts were accordingly 'deflected to two more productive themes: national identity and religion'.[69] In his Young England novels, Disraeli's solution to the troubled state of English society was the idea of 'class peace, merging into mutual affection'. He did not look to specific policies like Corn Law repeal or emigration: 'His object was to find an attitude rather than a policy' that could unite modern urban society.[70] For Disraeli, political culture mattered.

> Political culture is a question of platitudes, but they must be the right platitudes; and uttering the right platitudes requires genius [...] What public men say, not what they do, is the key to Disraeli's only real social policy: the achievement of an era of good feeling.[71]

---

[67] Weeks, 'Disraeli as Political Egoist', p. 408.
[68] Raymond, *Disraeli*, p. 165.
[69] Vincent, *Disraeli*, pp. 46–47.
[70] Ibid., pp. 82–83.
[71] Ibid., p. 90.

Vincent sees the shifts in Disraeli's politics as reflecting his attempts to strike the right ideological attitude. In the 1830s he made much of national identity; in the 1840s social cohesion; in the 1850s it was defence of the Church. It was 'only in the 1870s that the two themes of social cohesion and national identity were finally integrated' in the advocacy of social reform and imperialism.[72] With ideas such as One Nation, Imperialism and Tory Democracy, Disraeli hoped to challenge the Liberal hegemony and shift the political discourse in ways serving conservative ends. Hence, while Blake might be right in saying that Disraeli's ideas were romantic and unrealistic, it does not follow that they were unimportant in shaping nineteenth-century politics. Vincent's influence is discernible in Smith's 1996 *Disraeli*, where it is suggested that

> Disraeli's art and legacy lay not in the manufacture of measures but in the management of impressions. He was perhaps the first Conservative practitioner to tear at the heart of the prevalent liberal ideologies of his day by denying that politics and government were a primarily ratiocinative activity [...] Image making, for Disraeli, was not charlatanism, but the necessary technique whereby the force of an idea [...] could be brought to bear on the common understanding.[73]

St John, too, suggests that Disraeli, though wanting to promote social unity, recognized that this was impossible given the class system, and that the solution 'had to be psychological. What he wanted to do was not so much change reality as change perceptions of reality.'[74] This theme is strongly advocated by Parry, who contends that Disraeli saw himself as fighting an 'ideological war' to uphold the 'national character'.

> Disraeli identified a set of historical values and traditions that made England unique, and set himself the task of articulating them, promoting them, and, in particular, seeing off attempts to undermine them. This was an ideological war rather than a social one: that is to say, Disraeli did not seek to arrest inevitable changes in underlying social conditions in England [...] His title to fame would be his genius in combating destructive ideas, cosmopolitan ideas that would rot the cohesion and greatness of the country.[75]

---

[72] Ibid., p. 116.
[73] Smith, *Disraeli*, p. 217.
[74] St John, *Disraeli and the Art of Victorian Politics*, p. 123.
[75] Parry, 'Disraeli and England', pp. 704–5.

However, in his earlier work on Disraeli's social reforms, Smith suggested that ideology played a more personal role in Disraeli's politics. His ideas, Smith says, were not rational propositions that might be true or false – they were a set of tools 'loosely related to reality, and designed for inspiration and use'.[76] But tools for what purpose? In his 1987 'Disraeli's Politics', Smith characterizes Disraeli's politics as the 'politics of denization, of settlement, the means by which Disraeli could achieve a sense of home'. Attempting to solve the problem of how a Christianized Jew without social connections could make a public career, ideas offered Disraeli a method by which he could integrate 'his "genius" into English society and history, in terms which should be intellectually coherent, emotionally tolerable, and aesthetically harmonious, as well as operationally viable'.[77] Each of Disraeli's manifestations – radical, Young England feudalist, One Nation imperialist, social reformer – were attempts to construct a vision for England and the Tory party within which he could stake a claim to leadership. They were exercises in 'political self-materialisation'. Thus, it is Smith's argument that Disraeli had coherent ideas, but their primary purpose was to mediate his relations with Victorian Britain. As such, his ideas 'were designed for personal rather than party ends' and it would be a mistake to look for a direct correspondence between Disraeli's ideas and policies.[78] Underlying Disraeli's use of ideas in this way was his Romanticism – his belief that it was possible for an individual to reconfigure reality according to his will. Thus, in the 1840s Disraeli constructed a vision of Toryism that served his needs and excluded the leader of the Tory party, Peel – thereby exemplifying Smith's point that Disraeli's ideas should not be approached from the perspective of truth or consistency, but in terms of what they were intended to do – namely, to serve the 'intellectual and emotional needs, as well as the tactical necessities, of their author'.[79]

Smith's conception of Disraeli using ideas to serve his needs finds support from other historians. Several writers develop this theme in Charles Richmond and Paul Smith's *The Self-Fashioning of Disraeli*, while Hawkins emphasizes the Byronic theme in Disraeli's life. 'It was the heady cultural ferment of Romanticism during the 1820s that shaped Disraeli's imagination and moral sensibilities.' He 'remained throughout his life a Romantic looking to be a hero in the world [...] The inspiration and creativity of language was his medium and the source of his genius'.[80] St John

---

[76] Smith, *Disraelian Conservatism*, pp. 12–13.
[77] Smith, 'Disraeli's Politics', pp. 68, 74.
[78] Smith, *Disraeli*, p. 215.
[79] Ibid., pp. 5–6.
[80] Hawkins, *British Party Politics*, pp. 212–14.

concurs, observing that, as an outsider, Disraeli did not imbibe his political ideology from his social milieu, but had to 'construct his own ideological system', finding it in his 'vision of an organic rural society' which, far from being an 'engine of policy', was 'a psychological device, a literary creation which lived in his imagination and served him well at key moments of his career'.[81] Richard Weeks has similarly suggested that Disraeli 'acted on the political stage out of ambition for personal recognition, and that obtaining power (recognition) was far more important to him than the exercise of power. His political thought consisted largely of grand panaceas impossible of realization.'[82]

Conclusion

Few would now deny that Disraeli had a political ideology. He possessed a set of ideas concerning the role of the rural hierarchy in shaping the nation's character and guaranteeing its freedoms, and he articulated these ideas more explicitly than most of his contemporaries. Blake has, following Disraeli, called this the doctrine of the 'aristocratic settlement' or the 'territorial constitution', and notwithstanding the sceptical noises of Ghosh and Davies, it remains the most widely accepted characterization of Disraeli's political objectives. But what was the *function* of this ideology? Was it the engine of Disraeli's political practice? Early Tory sympathizers like Randolph Churchill, Thomas Kebbel, John Gorst and Monypenny and Buckle, saw Disraeli as seeking to uphold the aristocratic settlement by winning popular support for the nation's traditional institutions and social hierarchy through such measures as electoral reform, social change and imperialism. Clyde Lewis made a determined attempt to reaffirm this One Nation interpretation, and it resonates into our own day.

Unfortunately it received a severe buffeting in the 1960s, as a wave of historians questioned how far Disraeli's initiatives could be ascribed to a One Nation strategy. Paul Smith failed to find an ideological commitment behind the social reforms of the 1870s; Cowling presented Disraeli in 1867 not as an advocate of Tory Democracy but as a reluctant convert to Derby's household suffrage; while Colin Eldridge and Stanley Stembridge rejected the idea that Disraeli initiated a wave of populist New Imperialism. As such, each endorsed Blake's conclusion that Disraeli's conduct was an improvised response to particular circumstances, and this assessment has not been seriously challenged. Yet this has not stopped further debate

---

[81] St John, *Disraeli and the Art of Victorian Politics*, pp. 208–9.
[82] Weeks, 'Disraeli as Political Egoist', p. 388.

concerning the precise place of ideas in Disraeli's politics, and historians such as Vincent, Smith, Jenkins and St John have argued that Disraeli's political ideology existed at one remove from the daily business of politics. In presenting his ideas, Disraeli was seeking to shape a political culture that would at once challenge the liberal hegemony, diffuse class tensions and construct an intellectual world within which his own career would acquire vindication. It was a politics not of pragmatism or policy but of the imagination.[83]

8.2   Was Gladstone's Career Characterized by a Steady Progression toward Liberalism?

It was suggested by Gladstone, and the theme was taken up by a host of near-contemporary biographers, that the key to his career was the gradual abandonment of a Tory ideology in favour of a Liberal one. If the youthful Gladstone was the 'rising hope of those stern unbending Tories', the more mature and wiser Gladstone was the epitome of Victorian Liberalism, advocating free trade, religious toleration, an extended franchise and a minimalist state.[84] But this narrative has been questioned. It has been suggested that Gladstone was never really a Liberal at all, on the grounds that he was always a Conservative or a Peelite, or was out of sympathy with core Liberal values such as individualism. Additionally, the notion that Gladstone broke free from his theocratic approach to politics has been challenged, his later politics being still saturated with the idea that it was the role of public figures to lead the nation to Christian virtue.

Gladstone's Liberal journey

In Gladstone's career, remarked Barnett Smith in 1880, 'may be traced a natural progression [...] With a mind as plastic as the age itself, it was impossible for him to stand still.'[85] And this evolution was in one direction: toward liberalism. As Somervell summarized in 1925,

> He went into Parliament to champion Church monopolies. He became their most conspicuous assailant. He entered Parliament to fight

---

[83] Cf. Jenkins, *Disraeli and Victorian Conservatism*, p. 30

[84] For Gladstone's own account of his evolution through the discovery of freedom into Liberalism, see D. M. Schreuder, 'The Making of Gladstone's Posthumous Career', in Kinzer (ed.), *The Gladstonian Turn of Mind* (1985), pp. 203–4.

[85] Smith, *Life of the Right Honourable William Ewart Gladstone*, p. 576.

Liberalism. He became the leader of the Liberal party. He disestablished the Church in Ireland and tried to disestablish it in Wales. He opened the Universities to live Dissenters and the churchyards to dead ones. He defended the right of an openly blasphemous atheist to a seat in the House of Commons.[86]

This narrative is usually presented in a positive light: having sought in his youth to argue for a medieval union of Church and State, Gladstone lived out his own Whig interpretation of history, discarding successive obscurantist dogmas to enter upon the sunny uplands of reason, tolerance and virtue. G. W. E. Russell was an early advocate of this perspective, writing in 1891 that Gladstone's 'whole life has been spent in unlearning the prejudices in which he was educated. His love of freedom has steadily developed, and he has applied its principles more and more courageously to the problems of government.'[87] Another contemporary Liberal, Justin McCarthy, similarly saw Gladstone's career as a progress from Toryism to Liberalism. One milestone was passed in 1855 when Gladstone agreed to serve under the Whig Lord Palmerston – 'a distinct advance on the way to Liberalism first, and to Radicalism afterwards'. Another was his 1864 'Pale of the Constitution' speech advocating a popular franchise.

Then at last it was plain to everyone that Mr. Gladstone had absolutely broken away from all the traditions of his early Parliamentary career. He had put himself at the head of the free-trade movement. He had put himself at the head of the movement for the repeal of taxes upon knowledge. Now he was putting himself at the head of the movement for the extension of the right of voting so as to admit the working classes and poor generally to the exercise of a vote.[88]

This notion of Gladstone's career as a 'protracted journey from tory to liberal' was monumentalized in John Morley's 1903 *Life of Gladstone*. A friend, colleague and fellow Liberal, Morley portrayed Gladstone's career as, in the words of A. O. J. Cockshut, a glorious achievement in which the guiding theme was the liberation of Gladstone's powers from their initial Conservative constraints.[89] What unshackled Gladstone was his discovery of the precious quality of liberty – both as a personal liberation from inherited dogmas and as

---

[86] Somervell, *Gladstone and Disraeli*, p. 21.

[87] Russell, *William Ewart Gladstone*, pp. 88–89, 275–76.

[88] McCarthy, *Story of Gladstone's Life*, pp. 175, 228.

[89] Quoted in Schreuder, 'The Making of Mr Gladstone's Posthumous Career', p. 199.

the key to social progress. Hence we find Morley reflecting upon Gladstone's first half-century in public life:

> He had learned many lessons. He had changed his party, his horizons were far wider, new social truths had made their way into his impressionable mind, he recognised new social forces. His aims for the church [...] had undergone a revolution. Since 1866 he had come into contact with democracy at close quarters; the Bulgarian campaign and Midlothian lighting up his early faith in liberty, had inflamed him with new feeling for the voice of the people.[90]

Henceforward, as D. M. Schreuder remarks, it became orthodox to view Gladstone's career as pivotal to the history 'of Victorian liberal progress, liberating individual consciences, social and political groups [...] political nationalities and "peoples struggling to be free"'.[91] It is found, for instance, in J. L. Hammond and M. R. D. Foot, who remark of Gladstone's 1851 denunciation of the regime of Naples that it 'marked a definite step in Gladstone's advance towards Liberalism'.[92] Peter Stansky cites Gladstone's resignation over Maynooth followed by his vote in favour of increased funding, as beginning 'his move towards liberalism [...] resigning was the leap into the future necessary for a fresh start'. 'Increasingly he seemed to share the characteristic Liberal belief that all men are potentially capable of trust, of making sensible decisions, of fending for themselves.'[93] A more recent historian empathizing with this evolutionary understanding of Gladstone's politics is Euginio Biagini, who remarks that 'his move towards liberalism did not take the form of a sudden conversion, but of a gradual evolution'.[94]

For those subscribing to the Liberal-evolutionist interpretation of Gladstone's career, the defining feature of his later politics was, in the words of David Bebbington, his 'sublime faith in freedom'.[95] It was not difficult to identify freedom as the key to Gladstone's politics for Gladstone said as much, remarking to Morley in 1891 that 'I was brought up to distrust and dislike liberty, I learned to believe in it. That is the key to all my changes.'[96] Gladstone's concept of freedom, says Bebbington, was a negative one, based

---

[90] Morley, *Life of Gladstone*, III. p. 88.
[91] Ibid., I. p. 631; Schreuder, 'The Making of Mr Gladstone's Posthumous Career', p. 197; Hawkins, *British Party Politics*, p. 261; Shannon, *Gladstone: Peel's Inheritor*, p. 166.
[92] Hammond and Foot, *Gladstone and Liberalism*, p. 62.
[93] Stansky, *Gladstone: A Progress in Politics*, pp. 38–39, 105.
[94] Biagini, *Gladstone*, p. 26.
[95] Bebbington, *Mind of Gladstone*, p. 259.
[96] Quoted in Morley, *Life of Gladstone*, III. pp. 474–75.

on removing obstacles to free expression, freedom of worship, free trade and low taxation. Its clearest expression was in his commitment to what Bebbington labels 'classic individualism'. He believed in a minimal state and rejected the idea that the state could decide what was best for people.[97] As his son Herbert reflected in 1928, 'Individualism is the key to Mr Gladstone's action [...] By training and predilection he was at heart an individualist [...] he remained an individualist to the end.'[98] It was this individualism that drove his championship of laissez-faire economics, with its free trade, minimal state interference, opposition to cartels or sectional interest groups, and low taxation. While Gladstone believed such policies would promote economic growth, their more crucial quality was that they would allow individuals to act morally through their own free decisions. Hence, writes Colin Matthew, a 'powerful sense of moralism buttressed the fiscal case for free trade [...] In Gladstone's view, the Budget was a moral as well as a fiscal engine. It should be regular, balanced and minimal, setting a tone for the nation.'[99]

A second component of his liberalism was a belief in the value of an extensive franchise. As Matthew observes, Gladstone came to regard the mass of ordinary people as possessing an instinct for moral virtue that the established 'classes' with their vested interests lacked and to which he could appeal through his oratory.[100] Gladstone's awakening to the reserves of virtue dwelling among the middle and lower classes became prominent from the mid-1860s, when, argues Bebbington, he recognized the role the 'masses' could play in upholding a just and healthy community. The mass of the public favoured policies that were in the interests of society as a whole, whereas the upper classes sought selfish gains at the expense of the community.[101] The working class in particular had proven more enlightened than the educated classes, and by the end of his career he was looking to them to have a prominent role in government based on a democratic suffrage. Thus, says Biagini, when Gladstone championed the 'masses' against the 'classes' he was not promoting class struggle; rather, his object was to reassert traditional civic virtues against the sectional interest of the privileged elites who had shown a weakness for such things as Disraeli's imperialism.[102] In the process there emerged what Adelman characterizes as Gladstone's 'semi-mystical belief

[97] Bebbington, *Mind of Gladstone*, p. 261.
[98] Quoted in Biagini, *Gladstone*, p. 107.
[99] Matthew, *Gladstone*, p. 340.
[100] Ibid., p. 344.
[101] Bebbington, *Mind of Gladstone*, p. 287.
[102] Biagini, *Gladstone*, pp. 72–73.

that a special *rapport* existed between himself and the people, united together against the unwavering hostility of the Victorian Establishment'.[103]

Questioning Gladstone's liberalism

It has been the effect of scholarship over the last 40 years to challenge most of the assumptions underpinning this happy Liberal-evolutionary narrative, with Gladstone emerging as a more contradictory and ambivalent politician. This has not been an entirely new revelation. That a personality such as Gladstone's could never be defined in terms of conventional liberal formulas alone has long been recognized. Thus Hammond and Foot acknowledged in 1952 that Gladstone did not belong to the Manchester School, had little liking for philosophical radicalism, was hostile to republicanism and was no enthusiast for evolutionary theories. 'Thus of all public men of his time Gladstone occupied the most individual position, finding the origin and vitality of his ideas in sources strange if not alien to most Liberal minds.'[104] As a result he stamped his own character upon Liberalism in the form of 'Gladstonian Liberalism'. But Shannon questions whether Gladstone was even a Gladstonian Liberal:

> If Liberalism is in essence the conclusions arrived at from reasoned lay discussion as to humanity's forward progress, Gladstone remained in essence a being if not quite alien to it, then in most respects other than it [...] The great lesson to be learnt from observing Gladstone's leadership of the Liberal party [...] is that Gladstone's Liberalism was never at home in the Liberal party in Parliament [...] and that Gladstone's Liberalism and [...] parliamentary 'Gladstonian Liberalism' steadily diverged to the point ultimately almost of incompatibility.[105]

Historians have located several sources for this divergence.

Gladstone was always a Conservative

Several historians argue that, while Gladstone's methods changed over time, his objectives were conservative throughout. Having entered politics to uphold the traditional social, institutional and religious structure of Britain, this is exactly what he did throughout his 60-year career. Relevant, here, is

---

[103] Adelman, *Gladstone, Disraeli and Later Victorian Politics*, p. 7.
[104] Hammond and Foot, *Gladstone and Liberalism*, p. 3.
[105] Shannon, *Gladstone: God and Politics*, xiii–xiv

what is held to be his naturally conservative character – pithily captured by Arthur Balfour's 1896 reflection that Gladstone 'is, and always was, in everything except essentials, a tremendous old Tory'.[106] Russell made much of this in 1891, writing that in 'all the petty details of daily life, in his tastes, his habits, his manners, his way of living, his social prejudices, Mr. Gladstone is the stiffest of Conservatives'.[107] His 'natural bias is to respect institutions as they are and nothing short of plain proof that their effect is injurious will induce him to set about reforming them'. For a Whig like Russell, this was a consoling thought:

> [I]t makes some difference to the future of a democratic State whether its leading men are eagerly on the look-out for something to revolutionize, or approach a constitutional change by the gradual processes of conviction and conversion. It is this consideration which makes Mr. Gladstone's life and continued ascendancy in the Liberal party so important to the country [...] he is a restraining and conservative force.[108]

Matthew's depiction of Gladstone as a largely conservative figure undertaking the reforms necessary to sustain the basic structure of British society is not dissimilar:

> Gladstone was a chief agent in the process by which the Anglican university elite adapted itself and public life to the requirements of an industrial age while substantially maintaining traditional institutions and securing, for the most part, its dominant political position.[109]

Shannon is another who argues for the essential continuity of Gladstone's career, which meant that, while he became a leading figure in the Liberal party, what he envisaged was 'not so much an inauguration of new times as a retrieval of old times. He was indeed a very odd and idiosyncratic Liberal.'[110]

Biagini and Bebbington elaborate this point. Biagini contends that Gladstone 'always remained a patrician who believed in the aristocratic principle in government'. He sought not 'an overhaul of aristocratic society' but 'its "moralization", its updating so that it could better face the challenges of democracy'.

---

[106] Quoted in Eyck, *Gladstone*, p. 449.
[107] Russell, *William Ewart Gladstone*, p. 275.
[108] Ibid., pp. 272–73, 275–76.
[109] Matthew, *Gladstone*, p. 639.
[110] Shannon, *Gladstone: Heroic Minister*, xii.

In principle, Gladstone pursued stability, not change. In practice, he realized that stability could be achieved only by establishing a greater degree of justice and equity, and that this required political and economic reform.[111]

However, as Biagini admits, 'the cumulative effect of all such "restorative" measures was to turn Gladstone into a "conservative radical", or even, as he was often perceived, into a radical Liberal'.[112] For Bebbington, too, Gladstone's 'political theory retained a strongly conservative cast. His disposition in all things was to cherish tradition.' What Gladstone stood for was 'ordered freedom', freedom that was balanced 'against principles that can properly be seen as conservative – or at least conserving – attributes of the state'.[113] Hence he championed the landed aristocracy and valued the place of wealth and birth in the governance of the nation, and believed that the wealthy should pass their wealth on within their families 'so that responsibility for social leadership should be transmitted down the generations'.[114] Similarly he was a firm believer in constitutional monarchy and supported the position of the Queen against Liberal critics, while David Nicholls observes that, 'far from being inimical to liberty, a strong state was held by Gladstone to be essential for its preservation'.[115] Indeed, according to E. D. Steele, who emphasizes that Gladstone was 'profoundly conservative' and was attached 'to the idea of leadership and control by rank and inherited wealth', it was the very fact that Gladstone's 'real sympathies lay' with the 'hereditary possessors of power' that he judged them 'more severely than the aspiring bourgeoisie'.[116] Vincent likewise observes that Gladstone's social theory was underpinned by the moral significance he attached to the 'rural social order [...] the hierarchy based on agriculture was the best of all possible hierarchies' for it promoted cooperative relations between the classes.[117]

Gladstone was always a Peelite

Both Shannon and Matthew argue that Gladstone's politics were defined by his encounter with Peel in the 1840s, from which date he endeavoured to perpetuate the goals and techniques of his hero – using executive government

---

[111] Biagini, *Gladstone*, pp. 71

[112] Ibid., p. 72.

[113] Bebbington, *Mind of Gladstone*, pp. 264–65.

[114] Ibid., pp. 265–66.

[115] Nicholls, 'Gladstone on Liberty and Democracy', p. 405.

[116] E. D. Steele, 'Gladstone and Ireland', *Irish Historical Studies*, Vol. 17 (1970), p. 68.

[117] Vincent, *Formation of the British Liberal Party*, p. 244.

to reform institutions so as to render them fit for purpose and to promote economic growth through the liberation of the market mechanism. Thus, Matthew sees Gladstone as a conservative who wished to preserve not so much the heritage of a thousand years but the ideal state that he thought he and Peel had brought into existence between the 1840s and the early 1860s. Here Gladstone's underlying Platonism revealed itself: he believed that something approaching an Ideal Form for the state had been created in the mid-Victorian years, and it was his work to preserve that achievement. Hence, says Matthew, he appeared in 1880 a 'rather conservative figure' defending the 'mid-century liberal state'. 'Gladstone took office in 1880 with explicitly restorative objectives: the removal of the excrescences of "Beaconsfieldism", the restoration of proper financial procedures [...] and a general return to the normality of Whig/Liberal government after the restless adventures of Tory jingoism.' Above all, Gladstone remained dedicated to upholding free trade and the minimalist state in the context of the move to protectionism in Europe following the Great Depression and the first stirrings of social welfare spending.[118]

Peel's legacy, writes Shannon, was equally manifest in Gladstone's approach to governance. 'The lessons Gladstone learned from Peel were those of masterful government and executive prerogative over Parliament. Above all, Gladstone learned from Peel the supreme lesson that the highest exigencies of state might well require heroic sacrifice of the interests of party.'[119]

> It was a doctrine perfectly compatible with being an authoritarian exponent of executive prerogative. That indeed was what Gladstone had always been and ever remained [...] At no point in his leadership of the Liberal party did Gladstone ever consult the party about what it wanted to do. All his great legislative strokes were his exclusive texts.[120]

The difference between Peel and Gladstone is that Gladstone found 'an immense political power outside Parliament by which Parliament, and party, might eventually be brought politically to heel: "the people"'. But even then, for Gladstone the 'people' were a resource he could deploy in his realization of a Peelite agenda. Liberalism offered Gladstone not a new ideology but 'the only plausible prospect of Peelite government. He became a Liberal,

---

[118] Matthew, *Gladstone*, pp. 333–34.
[119] Shannon, *Gladstone: Heroic Minister*, xiii.
[120] Shannon, *Gladstone: God and Politics*, xv.

in short, the better to be a Peelite.'[121] Biagini supports this interpretation, seeing Gladstone's career as being shaped by the Evangelical culture of early nineteenth-century Britain and adjusted in the light of his experience of Peel's 1841–46 government. Gladstone remained a Peelite, and though, after 1876, he assumed the role of a national leader, 'his aim remained that of converting "the masses" to his version of the Peelite gospel'.[122] In this vision of executive leadership for virtuous ends it was not merely political party that was reduced a subordinate supporting role – it was, as Parry explains, parliament too:

> As an institution peopled by sinful men, parliament's tendency would always be apathy and obstruction [...] Gladstone removed the moral centre of Liberalism away from parliament [...] for Gladstone, parliament's main aim was to refine and process a continuous round of corrective, purifying legislation emanating from an executive anxious to satisfy a roused and coherent popular conscience that good was being done.[123]

Gladstone's theocratic approach to government

Another non-Liberal continuity which many have perceived in Gladstone's politics was the dominating role of religion. In his Church and State days Gladstone argued that the state had a duty to promote the Christian good through its policies, and it is contended that he never relinquished this conviction, believing that it was his vocation to promote Christian virtue through public service. Resting upon the assumption that the Christian good was *the* good, and that it was desirable for the state to promote it, this approach to government was far from liberal, being not sceptical and secular, but prescriptive, dogmatic and theocratic. It is often alleged that the agnostic Morley neglected the role of religion in Gladstone's politics, but this is an exaggeration. As he himself wrote,

> Not for two centuries, since the historic strife of anglican and puritan, had our island produced a ruler in whom the religious motive was paramount in the like degree. He was not only a political force but a moral force. He strove to use all the powers of his own genius and the powers of the state for moral purposes and religious.[124]

---

[121] Shannon, *Gladstone: Heroic Minister*, xivx–v.
[122] Biagini, *Gladstone*, p. 115.
[123] Parry, *Rise and Fall of Liberal Government*, p. 252.
[124] Morley, *Life of Gladstone*, I. pp. 2–3.

The centrality of religion in Gladstone's politics has been widely emphasized. Erich Eyck writes that Gladstone remained faithful to the idea that 'the activities of the State must be based upon the comprehensive idea of right and wrong; that the statesman who commits or causes to be committed an unrighteous action involves [...] the State in dishonour, and indeed in sin!'[125] Stansky argues that Gladstone 'never lost his belief that the State was a moral force and that its primary object was to improve those in its care', while Perry Butler notes that, although Gladstone's 'opinions altered on many matters, the overriding sense of God's Providence, the certainty of Judgement, the divine rule and governance of life that was his from childhood, never left him.[126] For Matthew, 'the fixed point for Gladstone was his Christian faith, the preservation of the Church and the triumph of Christian values'.[127] As the title of his 2007 biography Gladstone: God and Politics indicates, Shannon places still more emphasis upon the religious continuities within Gladstone's career:

> It is a story of how a statesman of almost superhuman energy and forcefulness of character strove to realize God's purposes, as he saw them, in the twisting and slippery paths of public service. Striving to realise God's purposes is the theme at the centre of this reading of Gladstone's life and career.[128]

Shannon believes the most important factor shaping Gladstone's career was his 'unswerving conviction, whether as young Evangelical or mature High Churchman, of the manifest providential government of the world, and his growing sense of his own assigned role as an instrument [...] of God Almighty. It was this Christian providentialism which was [...] most significant in explaining the contours and courses of Gladstone's life.'[129] Upon his becoming a Liberal the 'commitment to a concept of spiritual mission [...] underwent no essential diminution'.[130] St John concurs, writing that Gladstone was infused 'with a supreme self-confidence born of the conviction that the logic of his own mind was but the logic of the mind of God'.[131] What changed was his reading of how God's will was to be realized within public life. With the failure of his Church–State doctrine he sought new ways of serving religion

---

[125] Eyck, Gladstone, p. 30.
[126] Stansky, Gladstone, p. 112; Butler, Gladstone, p. 1.
[127] Matthew, Gladstone, p. 1.
[128] Shannon, Gladstone: God and Politics, xi.
[129] Shannon, Gladstone: Heroic Minister, xii.
[130] Shannon, Gladstone: Peel's Inheritor, p. 166.
[131] St John, Gladstone and the Logic of Victorian Politics, p. 404.

through the state and began to see that 'Peel's great ministry of 1841–46 had about it all the cogent marks of providential ordination'. By assisting Peel in his work of fiscal liberation he was 'working to fulfil God's purposes'.[132]

Boyd Hilton sees Gladstone's career as bearing testimony to the sustained influence of an evangelical moral philosophy. Man's life was bounded by sin, righteousness and judgement, and this moral order remained 'an epicentre of Gladstonian Liberalism'.[133] God was not an abstract idea but a Divine Governing power. Every human action brought consequences according to its righteousness, and hence 'if action was the key to the good life, politics [...] now became regarded as an arena for the grandest actions'.[134] In practice this involved Gladstone in a search for passionate causes that would polarize politics and allow him to pit 'his vision of a morally enhanced future against the privileges of a fallen present'. To this end he took up a series of charged issues, including Italy and political reform, until at length 'he hit an electoral jackpot when he hit on Irish Church Disestablishment in 1868'.[135] Underlying this quest for moral conflict was Gladstone's continuing preoccupation with the evangelical idea of redemption – that the world's wickedness had to be combated through perpetual struggle for righteousness and martyrdom for a just cause.

Like Hilton, Parry portrays Gladstone's engagement with public life as a continual struggle to uphold the religious consciousness of the nation against corruption and sin. Realizing that the Church–State connection could not uphold morality in public life, he looked to public opinion to exert this discipline. 'In the 1850s and 1860s, Gladstone awoke to the immense and evolving power of public opinion, and the duty of the politician to adjust to it in order to train its energies to effective ends.' This meant, above all, combating the corrupting effects of power – the search for prestige, self-seeking, domination and sectional interest.[136] It was because the Tory party could not be depended upon to do this that ultimately explained Gladstone's movement into the Liberals in the late 1850s. 'From then on, Gladstone's political task, at its most abstract level, was to draw out the goodness within the human personality, in a crusade against selfishness, materialism and apathy wherever it occurred.'[137] Thus, although his Church–State project collapsed, 'politics and religion remained indissolubly linked in his mind', and his prescription

---

[132] Shannon, *Gladstone: Heroic Minister*, xiii.
[133] Hilton, *Age of Atonement*, pp. 344–45.
[134] Ibid., p. 347.
[135] Ibid., pp. 353–54.
[136] Parry, *Democracy and Religion*, pp. 167–68.
[137] Parry, *Rise and Fall of Liberal Government*, pp. 248–49.

'for the spread of right feeling was simple, but most unwhiggish: religion, not political institutions'.[138] And how was this virtuous public opinion to be aroused? Biagini points out that here, too, Gladstone turned to Evangelical models. Being inspired by the way in which revivalist preachers like Moody and Sankey used charismatic sermons to convey traditional ideas to the masses, Gladstone 'tried to expound the old orthodoxy in a populist style: and [...] was, to a large extent, successful'.[139]

But it was not only in the promotion of Christian virtue that historians discern continuity in Gladstone's career: it is also in the importance he attached to the Anglican Church. While Liberal sympathizers depict Gladstone as embarked on a voyage to religious tolerance, breaking one after another of the privileges the Church of England enjoyed in the state, this, it has been suggested, misconceives Gladstone's true intentions – which were to consolidate the place of the Church in English society. Gladstone, comments Matthew, sought to uphold the privileged status of the Church of England for as long as possible, his tactic being to surrender indefensible positions to preserve the substance.[140] Opposing the Ecclesiastical Titles Bill of 1851 and the 1874 Public Worship Act, disestablishing the Church of Ireland and supporting the atheist Charles Bradlaugh's right to sit as an MP, were all examples of Gladstone's policy of 'giving gold for freedom' – which meant, says Butler, that the Church should make concessions so as to avoid becoming the subject of political action.[141] Butler dates Gladstone's acceptance of this doctrine to the debates over Maynooth in 1845. From this point he recognized that the state could not be guided by Anglican priorities, and that the best that could be achieved was to secure for the Church freedom of action so that it could pursue its work – and this meant conceding freedom to all faiths.[142]

Yet the view that Gladstone's politics continued to be governed by religious imperatives does not command universal support. According to Michael Partridge, 'probably the greatest question still unanswered about Gladstone's life [...] concerns the role of religion'.[143] A. R. Vidler, in his *Orb and Cross*, argues that Gladstone failed integrate his 'faith as a Christian and his faith as a statesman', and that he was too ready to subscribe to the optimistic

---

[138] Parry, *Democracy and Religion*, p. 153; Parry, *Rise and Fall of Liberal Government*, p. 251.

[139] Biagini, *Gladstone*, pp. 115–16.

[140] Matthew, *Gladstone*, p. 339.

[141] Butler, *Gladstone*, pp. 130–31.

[142] Ibid., pp. 124, 134–35.

[143] M. Partridge, Review of *'Reading Gladstone'* by R. Windscheffel, *Victorian Studies*, Vol. 51 (2009), p. 581.

and materialist assumptions of laissez-faire.[144] More recently, Andrew Jones has spoken of a divide between Gladstone's religious self and political self, where in the latter he showed himself to be 'a very normal, if uncommonly clever, political animal'.[145] And there remains, says Jenkins, the suspicion that religion was merely a cloak to hide his ambition and that God's will was really the will of Gladstone.[146]

Was Gladstone an individualist?

The idea that Gladstone subscribed to the liberal tenet that a free and progressive society rests upon the autonomous actions of rational individuals is challenged by Bebbington, who writes that Gladstone was 'far more of a communitarian than a liberal', and that he never departed from the Aristotelian doctrine that the community should take priority over the individual.[147] 'The language of community ran through the whole of Gladstone's discourse as Liberal leader.' While, Bebbington admits, 'typical liberal themes such as self-help, free trade, and the restriction of the state did appear prominently in Gladstone's speeches; and liberty was undoubtedly something he treasured', his subject was rarely the individual in isolation, and he 'was at the furthest possible remove from supposing there was no such thing as society. On the contrary, individuals were always conceived as members of families, churches, cities, and nations [...] There was merit in joining in the life of the local community, which could give individuals their fulfilment.'[148] Bebbington cites Gladstone's support for the national principle, which rested upon an organic conception of the national state as consisting of people bound together by common values, each seeking 'the common good and not just their own sectional interests'.[149] Hence the 'grand aim in politics [...] was the reconciliation of divergent interests', and the chief means to this end was justice – that is, assigning to every class of the community what was its due.[150] Where justice was lacking, as in Ireland, there would be conflict, and it was the job of British statesmen to bring justice about.

---

[144] A. R. Vidler, *The Orb and the Cross* (1945), p. 155.

[145] Jenkins, *Gladstone, Whiggery and the Liberal Party*, p. 20. Cf. A. Jones, 'Where "Governing is the Use of Words"', *Historical Journal* Vol. 19 (1976), p. 256.

[146] Jenkins, *Gladstone, Whiggery and the Liberal Party*, p. 21. Cf. Hilton, 'Gladstone's Theological Politics', in Bentley (ed.), *High and Low Politics in Modern Britain*.

[147] Bebbington, *Mind of Gladstone*, pp. 304, 308–9.

[148] Ibid., pp. 269, 301.

[149] Ibid., p. 275.

[150] Ibid., pp. 294, 284.

Consequently Gladstone's mature political thought appears to have been deeply ambiguous. On the one hand it showed signs of classical liberalism [...] It was individualist, asserting human rights and the value of self-help, while aiming to limit the state through decreasing public expenditure [...] On the other hand it appeared to be imbued with a species of conservatism, endorsing tradition against those who decried it. It was anti-egalitarian, upholding royalty and the peerage [...] His Janus-like views were often the despair of contemporaries [...] But the tension can be understood [...] by an appreciation of the true foundations of his thinking.[151]

St John locates this communitarian dimension of Gladstone's politics in his understanding of liberty. Gladstone was keen to emphasize that liberty did not mean license or chaos, but ordered liberty under the law, and for this it was necessary that there be a community with laws and customs. 'This was Gladstonian Liberalism: freedom of the individual within institutional continuity [...] a willingness to innovate within a context formed by custom and tradition'.[152]

Questioning Gladstone's democratic credentials

The idea that Gladstone was sympathetic to popular democracy has also been challenged. 'Gladstone', says Nicholls, 'never embraced the idea of democracy'.[153] He believed, reflects Bebbington, that voting was a privilege and not a right and that men had different capabilities and responsibilities, and that there could be no question of the average mass of the population taking a leading role in government.[154] Gladstone, says Blake, 'never envisaged a social order in which the landed aristocracy would not be in the governing class'.[155] What has misled people into assuming Gladstone had democratic tendencies was his evocation of the virtue of public opinion – his claim to be on the side of the masses against the 'classes', his passing of the 1884 Reform Act, and the relish with which he cultivated an image as the People's William. But several historians emphasize that Gladstone never valued popular opinion or democratic institutions as such: the people's will was a *tool* to be deployed for ends selected by Gladstone – above all, using the moral purity of the masses to

---

[151] Ibid., p. 268.
[152] St John, *Gladstone and the Logic of Victorian Politics*, pp. 396–97.
[153] Nicholls, 'Gladstone on Liberty and Democracy', p. 405.
[154] Bebbington, *Mind of Gladstone*, p. 265.
[155] R. Blake, 'Gladstone and Disraeli', in Jagger (ed.), *Gladstone*, p. 63.

check the corruption of the ruling elite. The people's role was not to initiate policy but rather, like the chorus in a Greek play, to pass moral judgments on the actors under the directing hand of Gladstone.

Morley himself was keen to refute the accusation that Gladstone was a populist who allowed his policies to be dictated by common opinion. This was 'the exact opposite of the truth'. It was the statesman's role to discern the facts of an era and decide whether the possibility existed to direct public opinion to a given purpose. 'In every one of his achievements of high mark [...] he expressly formed, or endeavoured to form and create, the public opinion upon which he knew that in the last resort he must depend.' Morley cites the 1853 budget, where Gladstone, far from bowing to pressure to abolish income tax, presented a fiscal plan predicated upon its continuance – in the process changing 'a current of public opinion that seemed far too powerful to resist'. Similarly with respect to his Irish Land Act of 1881: 'Here he had no flowing tide, every current was against him. He carried his scheme against the ignorance of the country, against the prejudice of the country, and against the standing prejudices of both branches of the legislature.'[156]

Gladstone, in other words, was in the driving seat, and the role of the public was at best to fuel the engine and at worst to be moulded and carried along to a destination set by Gladstone. As Shannon observes, Gladstone never admitted 'that the virtue and righteousness of the freedom-loving people was translatable into directive popular political prerogative. His position invariably was that virtue and righteousness and love of freedom were the energizing forces in popular materials available to him on occasions defined by him, to be formed, mobilized, and directed for purposes also defined by him.'[157] As Shannon's rather opaque words suggest, the relationship between Gladstone and popular opinion was complex. On the one hand, as Matthew comments, Gladstone was one of the first politicians to realize the potency of the new forum of public debate made possible by the development of the public meeting and the national press.[158] 'His rise in the Liberal party in the 1860s', adds Parry, 'owed almost everything to his ability to suggest that he had a purchase on extra-parliamentary opinion, that he should head the party because he alone spoke the language to which they were willing to listen'. Yet, Parry continues, Gladstone did not regard public opinion as a force to which he or the political system should submit. On the contrary, it was a weapon he could deploy in achieving his goals, developing 'an extraordinary notion of his

---

[156] Morley, *Life of Gladstone*, III. pp. 536–37.
[157] Shannon, *Gladstone: Heroic Minister*, II. pp. 4–5.
[158] Matthew, *Gladstone*, p. 1.

role, nay his duty, as an instrument of God's will [...] Gladstone's definition of the "people's will" [...] bore a remarkable resemblance to the values which he himself wanted to propagate.'[159] And what was the end to which he wished to direct this opinion? It was to uphold the traditional institutional and social structure of Britain which, he believed, was under threat from a new 'plutocratic' moneyed class bent on pursuing its own ends at the expense of the public good. Selfishness and corruption were on the increase, and it was 'only by harnessing the superior morality of the poor that the activity of the British executive could be kept from sinking into the morass of vested-interest legislation'.[160] Gladstone did not want the poor to govern, but he thought 'the pressure for the maintenance of moral government would come from the common man'. The Gladstonian Liberal party, devoid of class bias, would forge links with the mass of the electors who, while unable to make policy decisions, were made moral through their lives of hard toil. Thus, from the 1860s Gladstone saw the role of the Liberal Party as exciting popular enthusiasm behind moral causes, thereby giving legitimacy to a revitalized executive government.

> Gladstone's aims were conservative: to preserve the political balance between the propertied and the masses; to maintain low expenditure and low taxation; to re-establish the authority of central government; to safeguard the doctrinal heritage of the Church of England from attack; to secure stability and the rule of law in Ireland; most importantly, to demonstrate to the enlarged electorate that its proper function was the age-old one of checking corruption and extravagance in government, rather than the disreputable one of using its voting muscle to press for sectional gain.[161]

So while Gladstone was alive to the reality of public opinion, it was to be awoken by Gladstone to basically conservative objectives: 'Economy and propertied rule were to be defended by rousing public opinion to political participation under aristocratic leadership.'[162]

Gladstone as a political opportunist

A theme common to the above interpretations is that Gladstone's conduct was guided by an underlying system of political beliefs. This assumption was

---

[159] Parry, *Rise and Fall of Liberal Government*, p. 251.
[160] Parry, *Democracy and Religion*, p. 170.
[161] Ibid., pp. 171, 173.
[162] Parry, *Rise and Fall of Liberal Government*, p. 253.

challenged in the 1960s and 1970s by historians like Alistair Cooke and John Vincent who argued that Gladstone was best understood as a politician like other politicians, who did things for reasons of personal and party advancement, and that what made him appear different was that he so readily justified his actions in terms of principled language. Historians, it is implied, have given too much attention to the reasons Gladstone gave for his actions, and too little to his more prosaic motivations.

A paradox confronting any vision of Gladstone as a conviction politician is that he changed his mind on just about every political issue of his day. Matthew acknowledges that 'Gladstone was not always consistent in his policies, nor did he seek to be'.[163] He regarded politics as a second-order activity compared to theology, and its principles were not dogmas. Thus, although he portrayed his actions in a language of moral absolutes, his conduct was shaped by a pragmatic recognition of the possibilities of particular situations – and this led him to alter his policies throughout his life.

> Gladstone's political philosophy of learning by experience provided for a reasoned change in his political position on a number of major questions: church and state in the 1830s and 1840s, tariffs in the 1840s and 1850s, political reform in the 1860s, Ireland in the 1870s and 1880s. His consistency was, he contended, one of method of change rather than the maintenance of content.[164]

Gladstone dominated the political agenda for so long precisely because 'he moved with the mind of his age [...] He [...] represented Victorianism more completely than any other person in public life'.[165]

This contrast between the sweeping first principles of Gladstone's rhetoric and his more pragmatic actions was highlighted in an 1864 *Quarterly Review* article, which remarked that Gladstone was not comfortable unless he could base a proposed action 'upon the foundation of some simple, large, grand first principle, which, applied to the existing condition of the world, would turn society upside down'. But in reality his objects were more moderate, and 'he proceeds to cut down his great first principle by limitation after limitation until, for practical purposes, the merest shred of it is left behind'.[166] Shannon similarly notes that several nineteenth-century writers questioned the extent of his commitment to Liberalism. Bagehot famously described Gladstone as

---

163 Matthew, *Gladstone*, p. 640.
164 Ibid.
165 Ibid., p. 644.
166 Quoted in Shannon, *Gladstone: Peel's Inheritor*, p. 510.

a 'man who cannot impose his creed *on* his time, but must learn his creed *of* his time'.[167] Similarly Goldwin Smith believed that Gladstone 'had no clearly thought out political philosophy'. All his ideology really amounted to was a guiding idea of liberty, which he turned to once his early Toryism broke down, according to which 'liberty [...] would of itself be the parent of all good'. Smith's view, says Shannon, was that Gladstone was ambitious and his ideology was simply a justification for his essential desire to serve the nation. Shannon largely endorses this:

> Undoubtedly there is a larger element of validity in this general interpretation of Gladstone's adaptiveness to his times and the consequent elements of fortuitousness and even emptiness of his Liberalism than is to be found in the Liberal pieties of Morley.[168]

T. A. Jenkins argues that Gladstone 'never found an alternative guiding creed to his discredited theory of Church–State relations', and this raises the possibility that his subsequent career was sustained by little more 'than personal ambition and opportunism'. Jenkins believes there was a divergence between Gladstone's secular and religious impulses, but this was obscured because of the way in which he infused 'secular, political questions with an intense religious fervour'. As an example, Jenkins cites the almost religious zeal Gladstone displayed during the 1850s and 1860s in pursuing free trade and retrenchment, presenting laissez-faire as promoting the nation's ethical progress in the way he earlier attributed to the Church.

> In learning to adapt to the reality of conditions in nineteenth-century Britain, then, Gladstone developed an unconscious habit of impregnating political exigencies with his religious enthusiasm in such a way that the political impulse acquired an air of moral righteousness which blinded him to the fact that the original motivation had been political.[169]

Gladstone's conduct was, in other words, fundamentally opportunistic: 'The events of 1868 and 1885–6 [...] suggest that great questions had a habit of becoming "ripe" for settlement very rapidly, when they suited Gladstone's tactical purposes.' In 1868, when Gladstone needed to reunite the Liberal

---

[167] Bagehot, 'Mr. Gladstone' (1860), in St John-Stevas (ed.), *Collected Works of Walter Bagehot*, III. p. 438. Italics in the original.

[168] Ibid., pp. 168–69.

[169] Jenkins, *Gladstone, Whiggery and the Liberal Party*, pp. 20–22.

Party, it was the question of the Irish Church that suddenly became ripe for resolution, while in 1885, when Gladstone's career appeared to be drawing to a close, it was revealed to Gladstone that Home Rule for Ireland was the overwhelming issue of the day.[170] Jenkins calls this Gladstone's 'highly developed faculty for self-deception: that is to say, he had the ability to rationalize his political position, his conduct and his underlying ambitions, in such a way as to create the appearance of having brought them into accordance with the facts of a given situation'.[171]

Conclusion

Gladstone has been treated far more indulgently by historians than Disraeli. Where, in the case of Disraeli, it is assumed that his political behaviour was driven by a desire to advance his career, and that his ideas were, at best, an irrelevance, or at worst a set of attitudes he struck for political advantage, in Gladstone's case the opposite is assumed: namely, that the mainsprings of his actions lay in certain fundamental principles, and that the complexities of his career arose out of the tension between his ideological beliefs and the shifting world within which he sought to apply them. Gladstone was an idealist forced to compromise in the light of realities, while Disraeli was a realist who used ideas only when it suited him. Yet Gladstone's politics were far more fluid than Disraeli's: where Disraeli for most of his adult life was a Conservative who continually reprised his message regarding the importance of historic institutions in preserving the greatness of the nation, Gladstone shifted from High Tory to reforming Peelite to Liberal, in the process revising his avowed stance on just about every major issue he encountered. On electoral reform, the secret ballot, the disestablishment of the Irish Church, the Maynooth grant, the Anglican exclusivity of public office, the admission of Jews to Parliament, the granting of Home Rule to Ireland – in every case Gladstone overturned his previously held position and invariably did so in ways that advanced his career. So why has Gladstone not been portrayed as an opportunist whose politics was driven by an eye on the main chance?

The reason is that Gladstone's career has been interpreted as a progressive evolution from a set of Tory beliefs genuinely held to a set of Liberal–Conservative and ultimately Liberal beliefs equally genuinely held. Thus in the works of Morley, McCarthy, Somervell, Eyck, Magnus and Stansky, among others, the young Gladstone is seen as advocating an anachronistic

---

[170] Ibid., pp. 26–27.
[171] T. A. Jenkins, 'Gladstone, the Whigs and the Leadership of the Liberal Party, 1879–1880', *Historical Journal*, Vol. 27 (1984), p. 343.

Tory philosophy, and that once he came into contact with real-world problems under the guidance of Peel, he was led to bring his thinking into line with the dynamics of the Victorian age by discarding his closed hierarchic Tory vision in favour of an open, free-thinking, tolerant Liberalism. As Magnus summarizes, Gladstone 'started as the foe, became the agent, and ended as the prophet of the Liberal experiment'.[172] More generally, Gladstone's political evolution was part of a wider preparedness to come to terms with modernity. To quote Morley:

> In a new time, marked in an incomparable degree by the progress of science and invention, by vast mechanical, industrial, and commercial development, he accepted it all, he adjusted his statesmanship to it all, nay, he revelled in it all, as tending to ameliorate the lot of the 'mass of men, women, and children who can just ward off hunger, cold, and nakedness.' He did not rail at his age, he strove to help it.[173]

Matthew echoes this characterization:

> Forged by an education essentially pre-industrial, Gladstone mirrored his times in adapting politically, religiously, and socially to new circumstances [...] A radical conservatism, which fused at times with an advanced liberalism, was Gladstone's method.[174]

This progressive interpretation of Gladstone's career has been qualified in more recent years as historians have drawn attention not to what changed in Gladstone's politics but to what stayed the same. For some, such as Biagini, Bebbington and to a degree Matthew, Gladstone remained essentially a conservative who deployed liberal reform to better sustain the class structure of British society; for Shannon, Gladstone, once having fallen under Peel's spell, was always a Peelite whose executive reform-to-preserve arrogance never fitted within the Liberal tradition; while for Hilton and Parry, Gladstone's politics remained saturated with the sinfulness of man and the need for political leaders to assist in ensuring that virtue triumphed over vice by rooting out corruption.

Both liberal and conservative narratives of Gladstone's career are plausible, and it is tempting to combine them to portray Gladstone as a synthesizing politician who worked to secure both reform and stability. Thus, we find Matthew describing Gladstone's 'frame of mind' as 'highly complex and

---

[172] Magnus, *Gladstone*, p. 445.
[173] Morley, *Life of Gladstone*, III. p. 551.
[174] Matthew, *Gladstone*, p. 1.

eclectic, embracing elements both of political Conservatism and of political Liberalism, and certainly offering no simple categorization'.[175] As a result his politics perplexed Conservatives and often disappointed Liberals. For the former, it was almost always too much, too soon, while for the latter, it was sometimes too little, too late.[176] Bebbington likewise observes that 'Conservative characteristics could coexist with obviously liberal views because both found their place within a broader philosophy', while Schreuder describes Gladstonian Liberalism as, 'in the last resort, a force for stability and order in an age of acute destabilizing transition', seeking through timely reform to balance an old order 'in the face of the dynamics of an industrializing Europe'.[177]

For each of these interpretations, Gladstone's conduct was driven by some overarching political philosophy – be it liberalism, theocracy, conservatism or a combination of all three. But suppose the truth about Gladstone were more prosaic? Suppose he was just a politician like Palmerston or Disraeli or Lord Derby whose actions arose out of the getting and keeping of power? While few historians have been prepared to consistently argue this, being still, perhaps, under the spell of Morley or of Gladstone's own narrative of his actions as presented through his monumental diaries, such a reading of Gladstone's behaviour is eminently defensible. For one of the strongest themes to emerge from the historiography of the major controversies of Gladstone's career is that, in every case, whether it be the decision to approve Peel's Maynooth subsidy or to join the Liberals in 1859 or to disestablish the Irish Church or to take up the Bulgarian agitation in 1876 or to champion Irish Home Rule, a case can be made that Gladstone was merely promoting his political prospects. In which case, what may be distinctive about Gladstone is not so much that he acted out of principle, but that he so readily convinced not only others but himself that he did so.

---

[175] Ibid., p. 337.
[176] Ibid., p. 1.
[177] Bebbington, *Mind of Gladstone*, p. 308; Schreuder, 'Making of Mr. Gladstone's Posthumous Career', p. 234. See also Stansky, *Gladstone*, p. 182.

AFTERWORD

If the vigour of the debate generated by a historical subject is testimony to its ability to attract the creative talents of the leading historians of each generation, then the political careers of William Gladstone and Benjamin Disraeli stand out beyond all others of the nineteenth century. Among the most striking features to emerge from the above survey is that controversy regarding the doings and motivations of these two political personalities was present from the very beginning of their careers and shows no sign of abating. Accounts of historiographical debates often deploy the language of traditional and revisionist viewpoints, but in the case of Gladstone and Disraeli this will not do. While both politicians received 'monumental' biographies in the shape of John Morley's *Life of William Ewart Gladstone* (1903) and William Monypenny and George Buckle's *Life of Benjamin Disraeli* (1910–20), each of these books was no mere hagiography – both were sophisticated pieces of historical scholarship and set new standards in the writing of political biographies. Accordingly, both books contained complex assessments that did not fit into any simple heroic account of their subject matter. Morley, for example, showed just how slow and tentative was Gladstone's political journey into Lord Palmerston's Liberal cabinet, while Monypenny and Buckle highlighted Disraeli's reticence with regard to the question of parliamentary reform in 1866. Nevertheless, it is true to say that both large books cast a shadow over subsequent writing on Gladstone and Disraeli through into the post-1945 period. Most writers between the wars tended to take the essential outlines of the careers of Gladstone and Disraeli for granted – whether it was accepting that Disraeli took an active interest in social reform in the 1870s or that Gladstone's engagement with Ireland was motivated by a principled determination to alleviate the sufferings of its people. Even then there were occasional questioning voices – such as Carl Bodelsen's critical 1924 study of Disraeli's commitment to imperialism. But it was only in the 1960s and

1970s that something approaching a revolution in Gladstone and Disraeli scholarship occurred, as a series of books and articles appeared re-evaluating one after another of the assumptions hitherto made about their careers. Robert Blake provided a new narrative of the life of Disraeli which, though significantly influenced by Monypenny and Buckle's, was not merely much more engagingly written but also placed Disraeli the political opportunist centre stage, rejecting the idea that his politics was in any important way an expression of Young England ideals or Tory Democracy populism. Two years later works by Maurice Cowling and F. B. Smith confirmed the picture of a pragmatic Disraeli overseeing the passage of the 1867 Reform Act in the interest of party advantage, while S. R. Stembridge and Colin Eldridge provided new assessments of Disraeli's imperialism, and Paul Smith supplied the first detailed treatment of Disraeli and social reform – highlighting just how little consistent ideological commitment underlay it and how loosely Disraeli was connected with it. At the same time a revolution in Gladstone scholarship was underway, with two writers above all, Colin Matthew and Richard Shannon, exploring in far greater depth than hitherto the complex play of motives that informed Gladstone's political actions. Critical to this more nuanced reading of Gladstone was the proper utilization, for the first time, of the Gladstone diaries – publication of which began in 1968. Outstandingly edited by M. R. D. Foot and then Matthew, these diaries allowed Gladstone's political life to be rooted in the intellectual world of Victorian Britain and the subtle yet insistent imperative of Gladstone's profound religious beliefs. While the new research on Disraeli tended to reveal a more tactical, pragmatic and flexible politician than hitherto assumed (though this would hardly have been news to more critical Victorian contemporaries), more recent writing on Gladstone has emphasized the difficulty of discriminating between tactical and principled motives in his actions. Although the reading of his conduct in the light of the diaries reveals a man who reflected deeply upon political issues and was guided in his responses by a sense of divine calling, there remains the fact that, as the likes of John Vincent, T. A. Jenkins and David Hamer have argued, in so many ways Gladstone functioned like any other politician, exploiting situations for political and personal advantage.

In no sense has closure been achieved in the debates concerning Gladstone and Disraeli, and there remains a steady flow of publications reinterpreting and revaluating aspects of their careers. In recent years Disraeli's romanticism and his Jewish identity have attracted more and more interest, causing historians to cross the boundaries of political, literary and cultural history, while Gladstone's reflections upon diplomacy and the quest for international order, and his iconic significance within Victorian culture, have been explored by writers such as Joseph Miesel, Mark Nixon, Roland Quinault and D. M. Schreuder. Yet whatever the richness of this academic debate, what has done most to ensure that Gladstone and Disraeli have retained a salience today far stronger than that of even the most illustrious of their Victorian contemporaries is that both men, from the very beginning, resonated within the popular consciousness. Time and again journalists and politicians of the left and the right have evoked their names for inspiration and guidance, and all the while a never-ceasing stream of popular biographies has brought them before a modern readership (though here, it must be admitted, Disraeli has proven a more amendable subject for the popular biography than Gladstone). There is no better reflection of this than the current vogue for 'parallel lives' of the great Victorian rivals – a genre pioneered by David Somervell in the 1920s and recently revived by Richard Leonard and, with particular success, Richard Aldous in his *The Lion and the Unicorn*.

It is to be hoped that the foregoing pages have captured not only the vibrancy of the debates concerning the key events in the political lives of the two men but also the imagination and subtlety that has allowed historians to advance new solutions to old problems while opening up innovative avenues for further investigation. There is every reason to expect this interplay of interpretation to continue in the years to come, for neither Gladstone nor Disraeli evinces any sign of having ceased to fascinate historians and their readers alike.

APPENDIX ONE: TIMELINE OF THE CAREERS OF DISRAELI AND GLADSTONE

1804	Birth of Benjamin Disraeli
1809	Birth of William Gladstone
1817	Disraeli converts from Judaism to Christianity
1821	Disraeli commences training as a solicitor. Gladstone goes to Eton
1825	Disraeli's failed share speculations leave him in debt
1826	Disraeli publishes first novel, *Vivian Grey*
1828	Gladstone goes to Christ Church, Oxford
1830–1	Disraeli tours the Middle East
1832	Reform Act. Disraeli unsuccessfully contests High Wycombe as a radical. Gladstone elected MP for Newark
1834	Gladstone appointed Junior Lord of the Treasury by Peel
1835	Gladstone appointed undersecretary for war and the colonies. Disraeli publishes *Vindication of the English Constitution* in defence of House of Lords
1837	Disraeli elected to parliament as a Conservative
1838	Gladstone publishes *The State in its Relations with the Church*
1839	Disraeli marries Mary Anne. Gladstone marries Catherine Glynne
1841	Peel forms Conservative government. No place for Disraeli. Gladstone appointed vice-president of the Board of Trade
1842–45	Disraeli works with Young England colleagues
1843	Gladstone appointed President of the Board of Trade
1844	Disraeli publishes *Coningsby*

1845–46	Corn Law crisis. Disraeli attacks Peel
1845	Disraeli publishes *Sybil*
(January)	Gladstone resigns from Cabinet over Maynooth grant
(December)	Gladstone rejoins Cabinet as colonial secretary
1846	Corn Laws repealed. Fall of Peel. Break-up of Conservative Party
1847–49	Disraeli emerges as deputy Conservative leader to Lord Derby
1847	Disraeli publishes *Tancred*
	Gladstone elected MP for Oxford University
1848	Disraeli takes up residence at Hughenden Manor
1851	Gladstone's *Letters to the Earl of Aberdeen* denouncing government of Naples
1852	Conservative government. Disraeli chancellor of exchequer and leader of Commons. Government resigns on defeat of budget
(December)	Gladstone succeeds Disraeli as chancellor of the exchequer in Aberdeen's government
1853	Gladstone's first budget
1854–56	Crimean War
1855	Gladstone resigns from Palmerston's government
1858–59	Conservative government. Disraeli chancellor of exchequer and Leader of Commons
1858	Gladstone appointed Lord High Commissioner for the Ionian Islands
1859	Government resigns on failure of Reform Bill. Liberals win general election
(June)	Gladstone becomes chancellor of the exchequer in Palmerston government
1860	Gladstone's budget incorporating trade treaty with France
1861	Death of Prince Albert
1864	Disraeli's 'Ape or Angel' speech at Oxford
	Gladstone's 'Pale of the Constitution' speech in the House of Commons
1865 (July)	Gladstone defeated for Oxford University. Elected MP for South Lancashire
(October)	Death of Palmerston. Lord John Russell prime minister
1866 (March)	Liberal Reform Bill brought forward by Russell and Gladstone
(June)	Defeat of Liberal Reform Bill. Government resigns
(July)	Hyde Park pro-reform riots

1866–68	Conservative government
1867	Conservatives pass the Second Reform Act, introducing household suffrage in boroughs
1868 (February)	Retirement of Derby. Disraeli becomes prime minister
(March)	Gladstone moves Commons resolutions for disestablishment of Irish Church
(November)	Gladstone's Liberals win election. Gladstone elected for Greenwich
(December)	Gladstone becomes prime minister
1869	Disestablishment of the Irish Church
1870 (February)	Irish Land Bill
(March)	Elementary Education Bill
(May)	Disraeli publishes *Lothair*
	John Gorst placed in charge of Conservative Central Office
1871	Liberal government abolishes purchase of army officerships
1872 (April)	Disraeli speech at Manchester
(June)	Disraeli speech at Crystal Palace
(September)	*Alabama* compensation claim award
(December)	Death of Disraeli's wife
1873 (February)	Irish Universities Bill
(March)	Gladstone resigns as prime minister. Disraeli declines Victoria's invitation to form a government. Gladstone returns
(August)	Gladstone becomes chancellor of the exchequer
1874 (February)	Conservatives win general election. Disraeli prime minister
(November)	Gladstone's pamphlet denouncing the *Vatican Decrees*
(December)	Gladstone resigns as Liberal leader
1875	The year of Conservative social reform legislation
(July)	Uprising against Turkish rule in Bosnia-Herzegovina
(November)	British government purchases 44 per cent stake in Suez Canal company
1876 (May)	Disraeli refuses to sign the Berlin Memorandum on Turkish reform. Turkish massacre of Bulgarian Christians
(August)	Disraeli becomes Earl Beaconsfield
(September)	Gladstone pamphlet *The Bulgarian Horrors and the Question of the East*
1877 (January)	Victoria declared Empress of India
(April)	Transvaal annexed to British South Africa
	Russia declares war on Turkey

1878 (March)	Russia forces Treaty of San Stefano on defeated Turks Britain begins preparations for war. Derby resigns as foreign secretary
(June–July)	Disraeli attends Congress of Berlin. Returns claiming 'peace with honour'
(November)	British force enters Afghanistan
1879 (January)	British South Africa declares war on Zulus Zulus destroy British force at Isandhlwana
(September)	British mission to Afghanistan massacred
(November)	Gladstone begins Midlothian Campaign
1880 (April)	Liberals win general election. Gladstone prime minister
(November)	Disraeli publishes *Endymion*
(December)	First Boer War begins
1881 (March)	Disraeli's last speech to House of Lords
(April)	Second Irish Land Bill Death of Disraeli
1882 (February)	Charles Bradlaugh affair
(May)	Phoenix Park Murders, Dublin
(August)	Invasion of Egypt
1884 (January)	General Gordon sent to Sudan
(February)	Third Reform Bill introduced
1885 (February)	Death of General Gordon
(May)	Chamberlain's Central Board plan for Ireland rejected by Cabinet
(June)	Liberal government defeated on budget. Resigns
(November)	Election. Liberals largest party but no overall majority
(December)	'Hawarden Kite' suggesting Gladstone's conversion to Irish Home Rule
1886 (January)	Gladstone prime minister
(April)	Home Rule Bill introduced with Third Irish Land Bill
(June)	Home Rule defeated in Commons. Conservatives win general election. Gladstone resigns as prime minister
1890 (November)	O'Shea divorce case. Fall of Parnell
1892 (June)	Liberals win general election
(August)	Gladstone becomes prime minister for the final time
1893 (February)	Gladstone introduces second Irish Home Rule Bill
(September)	Home Rule Bill defeated in the House of Lords
1894 (March)	Gladstone resigns as prime minister
1898 (May)	Death of Gladstone

APPENDIX TWO: HISTORIAN BIOGRAPHIES

Adelman, Paul
Adelman studied at the University of Cambridge and taught history at Kingston Polytechnic, Surrey. He is the author of numerous student guides to British nineteenth- and twentieth-century history, including *Peel and the Conservative Party 1830–1850* (1989) and *The Decline of the Liberal Party 1910–1931* (1982).

Aldous, Richard
Having studied for his PhD at the University of Cambridge, England, Aldous is Currently Eugene Meyer Professor of British History and Literature at Bard College, New York. He previously taught at University College, Dublin.

Anderson, Olive
Professor Anderson was head of the Department of History, Queen Mary and Westfield College, London. She is the author of *Suicide in Victorian and Edwardian England* (1987).

Bagehot, Walter
Born in Somerset, the son of a banker, Bagehot (1826–1877) attended Bristol College and then the University of London, where he studied Classics. While working in the family bank he founded the *National Review* in 1855, and in 1861 became editor of the *Economist*, which had been founded by his father-in-law, James Wilson, in 1843 to advance the case for free trade. Besides his numerous articles on economic, political and literary subjects, Bagehot authored the highly influential *The English Constitution* (1867).

Baring, Evelyn, Earl of Cromer
A member of the Baring banking family, Baring (1841–1917) began his career in the army (he played an important part in developing the plan to implement

Gladstone's policy for abolishing the purchase of commissions in the army), but later entered government service, being appointed British Controller of Egyptian Finance under the Dual Control with France in 1879, and then, in 1883, consul-general of Egypt under the British occupation. He became Baron Cromer in 1892, Earl Cromer 1901, and in 1906 was appointed to the Order of Merit.

Beales, Derek Edward Dawson
Beales (born 1931) was educated at Bishop's Stortford College and Sidney Sussex College, Cambridge, where he has taught since 1955. He was appointed Professor of Modern History at Cambridge in 1980. He has written on a wide array of themes on European, Italian and British history.

Bebbington, David
Having graduated from Jesus College, Cambridge, in 1971, Bebbington (born 1949) completed his doctorate at Fitzwilliam College, Cambridge, before moving, in 1976, to the University of Stirling in Scotland, where he is currently Professor of History. Besides his writings on Gladstone, Bebbington has published extensively on the history of evangelical religion in Britain.

Beeley, (Sir) Harold
Beeley (1909–2001) studied at Queen's College, Oxford, where he wrote his study of Disraeli as a Research Fellow. He was then lecturer in History at the University of Leicester before entering the diplomatic service, assisting in the creation of the United Nations and being appointed British ambassador to Saudi Arabia and the United Arab Republic. In 1969 he became a lecturer in History at Queen Mary College, London.

Bentley, Michael
Having studied for his undergraduate degree at the University of Sheffield and his PhD at Cambridge, Bentley is now Emeritus Professor of History at the University of St Andrews, Scotland. He specializes in the political and intellectual history of Britain in the nineteenth and twentieth centuries, as well as the philosophy of history and historiography.

Biagini, Euginio
Biagini studied at the University of Pisa in Italy before pursuing an academic career in England and America. After holding a research position at Churchill College, Cambridge, Biagini taught at the University of Newcastle, Princeton University and Yale University, before returning to Cambridge in 1996. Since 2008 he has been a Fellow of Sidney Sussex College, Cambridge, where he is Professor of Modern British and European History. He has written widely on liberal thought and politics in nineteenth-century Europe.

Birrell, Francis
Educated at Eton College and King's College, Cambridge, where he was a friend of John Maynard Keynes, Birrell (born 1889) was the son of the prominent Liberal politician Augustine Birrell. During World War I, he served in France for the War Victims Relief Committee of the Society of Friends, 1915–20. He then established a bookshop in London with the writer David Garnett. A member of the Bloomsbury group, he was diagnosed with a brain tumour in 1932, and died in 1935 at the age of 46.

Blake, Robert, Baron Blake
Born in Norfolk, Blake (1916–2003) studied at Norwich School before becoming a student of Magdalene College, Oxford, where he read PPE. He served in the Royal Artillery during World War II, being captured by the Germans at Tobruk in Libya in 1942, before escaping from Italy in 1944. In 1947 he became a Tutor in Politics at Christ Church, and later Provost of The Queen's College, Oxford. Blake was a supporter of the Conservative Party and wrote a popular *History of the Conservative Party from Peel to Churchill* (1970). He was made a peer in 1971.

Bodelsen, Carl
Born in Denmark, where he graduated in English, Bodelsen (1894–1978) studied in Oxford in the 1920s. His *Studies in Mid-Victorian Imperialism* emerged out of his doctoral thesis. He lectured on English Literature at the University of Copenhagen (1926–65). Bodelsen was a member of the Danish resistance movement during World War II.

Bourne, Kenneth
A distinguished historian of British foreign policy, Bourne (1930–1992) was educated at the Universities of Exeter and London, and spent most of his academic career at the London School of Economics, where he became a professor in 1976.

Boyce, D. George
Boyce is a graduate of the Queen's University of Belfast, where he also researched for his PhD. He was an archivist in the Department of Western Manuscripts, Bodleian Library Oxford, 1968–71, and then lectured in the Department of Politics and International relations in Swansea University from 1971 until 2004. He has written books and articles on modern British, Irish, imperial and military history and politics.

Bradford, Sarah Mary Malet Ward
Bradford (born 1938) attended Lady Margaret Hall in Oxford, but left to get married before completing her degree. After first writing a series of books on wine, she has since published a series of popular biographies.

Brandes, Georg
Born to a Jewish family in Copenhagen, Denmark, Brandes (1842–1927) studied at the University of Copenhagen, where he also lectured. He was a proponent of the naturalist movement in Scandinavian literature and wrote extensively on literary and aesthetic themes. A Liberal in politics, he was a friend of John Stuart Mill.

Briggs, Asa, Baron Briggs
Born in Yorkshire, Briggs (1921–2016) was educated at Keighley Grammar School and Sidney Sussex College, Cambridge. During World War II he worked at Bletchley Park. Subsequently a Fellow of Worcester and Nuffield Colleges, Oxford, he was Professor of History at Leeds and Sussex Universities, before becoming vice chancellor of Sussex (1967–76). In 1976 Briggs was appointed Provost of Worcester College, from which position he retired in 1991. Besides his influential books on Victorian history, he wrote extensively on the history of broadcasting.

Buckle, George Earle
Educated at Winchester College and New College, Oxford, Buckle (1854–1935) was a Fellow of All Souls College between 1877 and 1885. Although initially intending to practise law, Buckle joined the staff of the *Times* in 1880, being made its editor in 1889 at the age of 29. During his time as editor the paper was involved in the publication of forged letters connecting the Irish leader Charles Stewart Parnell with the Phoenix Park murders. Buckle was dismissed from the editorship in 1911 by the *Times'* new owner, Lord Northcliffe. Following the death of Monypenny in 1912, Buckle took over the authorship of the official biography of Disraeli, which he finished in 1920. He also edited the letters of Queen Victoria.

Butler, (Sir) Geoffrey Gilbert
Butler (1887–1929) was educated at Clifton College and Trinity College, Cambridge, where he studied History, and was a Fellow of Corpus Christi, Cambridge, where he lectured in History. During World War I, he worked for the Foreign Office, and he headed the British Bureau of Information in New York. He was Conservative MP for the University of Cambridge 1923–9 and served as parliamentary private secretary to Sir Samuel Hoare, the minister of aviation. Butler specialized in diplomatic history and was an expert on the League of Nations.

Butler, Perry
An ordained member of the Church of England, Butler studied at York and Oxford and worked as an assistant to Colin Matthew on the Gladstone diaries. He subsequently taught Church History for the Southwark Ordination Course and served as Rector of St George's in Bloomsbury.

Buxton, Sydney Charles, Earl Buxton

Buxton (1853–1934), the son of a Liberal MP, was educated at Clifton College and Trinity College, Cambridge – though he did not complete his degree due to illness. After serving on the London School Board he became, in 1883, a Liberal MP, remaining in parliament until 1914, serving in the Cabinet as postmaster general (1905–10) and President of the Board of Trade (1910–14), in which post he was responsible for significant social reforms, including the National Insurance Act 1911. In 1914 he was made a viscount and appointed governor-general of South Africa. He was raised to an earldom in 1920 on his return to Britain.

Checkland, Sydney

Checkland (1916–1986) was a Canadian banker who came to Britain in 1938 to study at the University of Birmingham, being elected President of the National Union of Students in 1941. Checkland served in World War II, being wounded in the Normandy landings. In 1945 he contested the general election as a socialist. After teaching at the Universities of Liverpool and Cambridge, he became Professor of Economic History at the University of Glasgow.

Clayden, Peter William

Born in Wallingford, the son of an ironmonger, Clayden (1827–1902) entered business after leaving school. He was a prominent Unitarian minister and founder of the Free Church Union. He then took up journalism, serving as leader-writer and night editor for the *Daily News*, making it a leading organ of nonconformist opinion. In 1893 he was elected President of the Institute of Journalists. He was a strong Liberal, serving on the committee of the National Liberal Federation and standing unsuccessfully for parliament three times. His *England under Lord Beaconsfield* was used by Gladstone in preparing his Midlothian campaign.

Coleman, Bruce

Coleman, a specialist in Victorian political, religious and urban history, studied at the University of Cambridge, and was senior lecturer in Modern History at the University of Exeter.

Cooke, Alistair Basil, Baron Cooke

Cooke (born 1945) was educated Framlingham College, Suffolk, and Peterhouse College, Cambridge, before becoming lecturer in Modern History at the Queen's University, Belfast, in 1971, where he also completed his PhD. In 1977 he joined the Conservative Research Department, and was director of the Conservative Political Centre (1988–97). Since 2009 he has been the official historian of the Conservative Party. In 2010 he became Baron Lexden and sits as a Conservative in the House of Lords.

Cowling, Maurice John

Cowling (1929–2005) was educated at Battersea Grammar School and Jesus College, Cambridge, where he studied History – though his studies were interrupted by war service in India and Egypt. After abandoning a proposed doctorate on British policy in India, Cowling left Cambridge to work briefly for the Foreign Office, before writing leaders for the *Times* and standing as a candidate for the Conservative Party. In 1960 he returned to Cambridge, lecturing first in History at Jesus College and then becoming a Fellow of Peterhouse College, Cambridge, where he remained until 1993. There he made his reputation with a series of books approaching history from a 'high politics' perspective, focusing upon the manoeuvres of leading decision takers, of which *1867: Disraeli, Gladstone and Revolution* (1967) was the first. In 1978 he was a founder of the Salisbury Group of right-wing Conservative thinkers.

Crosby, Travis L.

Crosby is Emeritus Professor of History at Wheaton College, Massachusetts. A specialist in British history in the nineteenth and twentieth centuries, he has focused upon the psychological aspects of the subject. In addition to his work on Gladstone, Crosby has published biographies of Joseph Chamberlain and David Lloyd George, and also a study of *The Impact of Civilian Evacuation in the Second World War* (1986).

Davis, Richard W.

Davis was Professor of History at Washington University, St Louis, where he was a founder (with J. H. Hexter) of the Centre for the History of Freedom. He was the author of *A Political History of the House of Lords, 1811–1846* (2008).

Dicey, Albert Venn

The son of a newspaper proprietor, Dicey (1835–1922) was born in Leicestershire. He attended King's College School, London, and then Balliol College, Oxford. Although winning a Fellowship to Trinity College, Oxford, he also began reading for the Bar, and became a Queen's Counsel in 1890. In 1882 he became Professor of English Law at Oxford, with a Fellowship at All Souls College. An expert on constitutional law, Dicey was the most influential legal thinker of his day. Gladstone used his concept of parliamentary sovereignty when developing his Home Rule for Ireland Bill, though Dicey was a pronounced Liberal-Unionist, and this issue caused him to break with the orthodox Liberalism of his youth.

Dunne, Tom

Educated at University College, Dublin, Dunne is Professor Emeritus of History at University College, Cork. He has published widely on Irish cultural and political history in the early modern and modern periods, and was co-founder and co-editor of the *Irish Review*.

Eldridge, Colin Clifford

Born in 1942 in Walthamstow, Eldridge was an undergraduate at the University of Nottingham, where he also studied for his PhD. He then did postdoctoral research at the University of Edinburgh before becoming a lecturer (and later Professor) of History at St David's University College, Lampeter, Wales. Eldridge has written widely on the history of the British Empire.

Ensor, (Sir) Robert Charles Kirkwood

Born in Somerset, Ensor (1877–1958) was educated at Winchester College and Balliol College, Oxford, where he was President of the Oxford Union in 1900. After an early career as a journalist, writing for publications like the *Manchester Guardian* and *Daily Chronicle*, he returned to Oxford where he was affiliated as a research fellow with several colleges, including Nuffield, Corpus Christi and All Souls. His selection as author of the volume of the *Oxford History of England* for 1870–1914 was a surprise, as he had not written a serious work of history before, but he was well informed about recent events and the book was widely praised. Initially a Liberal, Ensor became a socialist, joining the Independent Labour Party and the Fabian Society and serving on the London County Council (1910–13), though his aversion to German militarism later pushed his politics more toward the Right. Michael Brock writes in the *Dictionary of National Biography* that in 'Oxford as elsewhere he was handicapped by his inability ever to admit that he was wrong'.

Eyck, Erich

A German lawyer who served as a city councillor in Berlin, Eyck (1878–1964) left Germany in 1937, lecturing in history at the Universities of London and Oxford. He produced major studies of Otto von Bismarck.

Feuchtwanger, Edgar Joseph

Feuchtwanger was born in 1924 to a Jewish family in Munich in 1924. His family fled to England following Kristallnacht in 1938. He attended Winchester College, then Magdalene College, Cambridge. Most of his academic career was spent at the University of Southampton.

Fraser, (Sir) William

Educated at Eton and Christ Church, Oxford, Fraser (1826–1898) was Conservative MP for Kidderminster during the 1874–80 Parliament.

Gallagher, John Andrew

Gallagher (1919–1980) was educated at Birkenhead Institute and Trinity College, Cambridge, where his studies were interrupted by service in the

Royal Tank Regiment during the war. After graduating, Gallagher became a Fellow of Trinity and later Beit Professor of Commonwealth History at Oxford (1963–70) and Vere Harmsworth Professor of Imperial History, Cambridge.

Gallagher, Thomas F.
An expert on military history, Gallagher taught at Xavier University, New Orleans.

Garratt, Geoffrey Theodore
Garratt (born 1888) was educated at Rugby School and Hertford College, Oxford, before entering the Indian Civil Service in 1912. He resigned from the Indian Civil Service in 1922, protesting against the wasting of funds on prestige projects in such a poor country. He later worked as a journalist for the *Manchester Guardian*, covering the nationalist movement in India, Mussolini's invasion of Abyssinia, and the Soviet invasion of Finland. He wrote a 1938 Penguin book, *Mussolini's Roman Empire*, and edited *The Legacy of India* (1937). Garratt contested several elections for the Labour party. During World War II he led a company of German volunteers doing war work and died in 1942 from injuries caused by an explosion.

Gaunt, Richard
Gaunt is a specialist in late-eighteenth- and early-nineteenth-century history and the author of *Sir Robert Peel: The Life and Legacy* (2010). He is currently Associate Professor in British History at the University of Nottingham.

Ghosh, Peter R.
Ghosh studied Modern History at Oxford as an undergraduate, and went on to do doctoral research on Victorian finance at Nuffield College, where he was a junior research fellow. In 1981 he was appointed a university lecturer in Modern History at Oxford, and a Fellow and tutor of St Anne's College, the post he continues to hold. Ghosh's recent research has been focused upon historiography, and especially the work of Max Weber.

Gladstone, Herbert John, Viscount Gladstone
Gladstone's last-born child, Herbert Gladstone (1854–1930) was educated at Eton College before entering University College, Oxford, where he studied Classics and History at University College before teaching History at Keble College. He entered parliament as a Liberal MP in 1880, later serving as home secretary (1905–10), playing an important part in passing the Liberal government's social reform programme and dealing with the Suffragette agitation. In 1910 he was appointed governor general of the Union of South Africa and made a viscount.

Goodlad, Graham

Goodlad was educated at Magdalene College, Cambridge, and has since taught at St John's College, Southsea.

Gunsaulus, Frank

Educated at the Ohio Wesleyan University, Delaware, Ohio, Gunsaulus (1856–1921) was a popular and charismatic preacher in the Methodist and Congregational churches, and helped found the Armour Institute of Technology, Illinois.

Hamer, David Allen

Hamer (1938–1999) was educated at the University of Auckland, New Zealand, and the University of Oxford, where he studied for his DPhil. After teaching at the University of Lancaster, he returned to New Zealand, and at the time of his death was Professor of History and chairman of the Department of History at Victoria University, New Zealand.

Hammond, John Lawrence

After attending Bradford Grammar School, Hammond (1872–1949) went to St John's College, Oxford, where he studied Classics. Becoming a journalist, he edited a radical weekly, the *Speaker*, which opposed imperialism and the Boer War. In 1914 he volunteered to serve in the Royal Field Artillery, and from 1916 worked for the Ministry of Reconstruction. After the war Hammond worked for the *Manchester Guardian*, taking a special interest in Irish affairs, and this inspired his major work, *Gladstone and the Irish Nation* (1938). With his wife, Barbara Hammond, he published a series of social histories of the British working class.

Hanham, Harold John

Born in 1928 in New Zealand, Hanham attended the University of Auckland and Selwyn College, Cambridge, where he completed a PhD. He has taught at the University of Manchester, University of Edinburgh, Harvard University and Massachusetts Institute of Technology, and was vice-chancellor of the University of Lancaster (1985–95).

Harcourt, Freda

Until her retirement, Harcourt was Senior Lecturer in History at Queen Mary and Westfield College, University of London.

Harrison, Robert T.

Harrison studied history at the Biola University and the University of Southern California. He is now Professor of History at Southern Oregon University and specializes in Middle Eastern imperial history.

Hawkins, Angus

Angus Hawkins studied at the University of London. He is a Fellow of Keble College, Oxford, and Professor of Modern British History at Oxford University. Hawkins has published extensively on aspects of Victorian political history, including a substantial two-volume study of the career of the 14th Earl of Derby: *The Forgotten Prime Minister: Ascent, 1799–1851* (2007) and *The Forgotten Prime Minister: Achievement, 1852–1869* (2008).

Helmstadter, Richard John

Richard Helmstadter (1934–2012) was Professor of History at the University of Toronto in Canada. An expert on nineteenth-century religion, his publications included *Religion and Irreligion in Victorian Society* (1992).

Hilton, Andrew John Boyd

Hilton (born 1944) studied at Oxford before becoming a Fellow of Trinity College, Cambridge, in 1974. He earlier wrote an influential analysis of Tory party economic policies, *Corn, Cash, Commerce* (1978), and has since contributed a volume to the *New Oxford History of England*, entitled *A Mad, Bad, and Dangerous People? England 1783–1846* (2006).

Himmelfarb, Gertrude

Born in 1922 in the United States to Jewish-Russian parents, Himmelfarb was educated at Brooklyn College and the University of Chicago. She taught at the City University of New York, specializing in the intellectual history of the nineteenth century. She was married to the leading neoconservative thinker Irving Kristol.

Hirst, Francis W.

Educated at Clifton College and Wadham College, Oxford, where he was President of the Oxford Union, Hirst (1873–1953) was strongly committed to Liberal political causes, including free trade and anti-militarism. He opposed the Boer War and contributed (with J. L. Hammond and Gilbert Murray) to *Liberalism and Empire* (1900). Hirst lectured in Political Science at the London School of Economics (1897–1900) and assisted Morley in writing his biography of Gladstone. In 1906 he was appointed editor of the *Economist*, but was forced to resign in 1916 due to his opposition to World War I. In 1931 he led resistance to the National Government's restoration of protective duties, and the publication of his *Gladstone as Financier and Economist* that year was part of his campaign for free trade. A supporter of appeasement, Hirst warned against high government spending during World War II, and after the war was a critic of Keynesian economic policies and the Beveridge Report.

Hopkins, Antony Gerald

Educated at Queen Mary College and the School of Oriental and African Studies, University of London, Hopkins (born 1938) has taught at the Universities of Birmingham, Geneva and Cambridge, where he was Smuts Professor of Commonwealth History and a Fellow of Pembroke College. From 2002 to 2013 Hopkins was Professor of History at the University of Texas, Austin. With P. J. Cain he has written influential studies of the economics of the British Empire since the seventeenth century.

Hoppen, K. Theodore

Hoppen studied at the National University of Ireland and Trinity College, Cambridge. From 1966 he taught history at the University of Hull, where he is now Emeritus Professor of History.

Hurd, Douglas, Baron Hurd of Westwell

Born in 1930 in Wiltshire, the son of a Conservative MP, and educated at Eton College and Trinity College, Cambridge, where he read History and was President of the Cambridge Union, Hurd entered the diplomatic service in 1952. In 1974 he became a Conservative MP, serving as foreign secretary and home secretary. He retired from active politics in 1995.

Jenkins, Roy, Baron Jenkins

Born in Wales, the son of a leading official in the coal miners' union, Jenkins (1920–2003) attended University College, Cardiff, and Balliol College, Oxford, where he read PPE. During the war he worked on code breaking at Bletchley Park, before being elected a Labour MP in 1948. In 1965 he became home secretary in Harold Wilson's government, and oversaw major liberalizing reforms, before becoming chancellor of the exchequer in 1967. In the 1970s Jenkins became a prominent supporter of the European Union (then the European Economic Community [EEC]), and in 1976 became President of the European Commission. Alienated by the Labour Party's move to the Left, Jenkins helped form the Social Democratic Party (SDP) in 1981, leading the party until 1983 and sitting as SDP MP for Glasgow 1983–87. In 1987 he was made a peer and became Chancellor of Oxford University. Jenkins wrote numerous works of history, the last being a biography of *Winston Churchill* (2001).

Jenkins, Terence A.

Jenkins's innovative reassessment of the relationship of Gladstone and the Whigs to the Liberal Party emerged out of his doctoral research at Corpus Christi College, Cambridge. He has since lectured at the University of East Anglia, where he studied for his undergraduate degree.

Jennings, (Sir) William Ivor

Jennings (1903–1965) was educated at Bristol Grammar School and St Catharine's College, Cambridge. A specialist in constitutional law and government, he lectured in law at Leeds University and then the London School of Economics, before helping found the University of Ceylon in 1942 and serving on the Ceylon Constitutional Commission as that state became independent. Jennings was later Master of Trinity Hall, Cambridge.

Jones, Andrew

Jones studied for his PhD at the University of Cambridge, and then lectured in history at the University of Reading.

Jones, Wilbur Devereux

Educated at Youngstown State University and Case Western Reserve, where he earned his PhD in History, Jones (1917–2004) taught at the University of Georgia from 1949 until his retirement in 1983, specializing in Victorian history and Anglo-American relations.

Kebbel, Thomas Edward

Born at Kilby in Leicestershire in 1826, Kebbel was educated at Merchant Taylors' School, London, and Exeter and Lincoln Colleges, Oxford. He intended to read for the Bar, but loose living and declining family finances saw him end up imprisoned for debt in 1853. But in 1855 he joined the staff of Disraeli's newspaper, *The Press*, where he remained until 1858, before writing for a series of papers on conservative politics and country pastimes. In 1872 he joined the staff of the conservative daily paper *The Standard*. Kebbel was a friend of Disraeli from 1858, whose approach to politics he admired. Disraeli appointed Kebbel receiver of fines and penalties at the Treasury in 1877, a post he held until his death in 1917. Kebbel edited Disraeli's speeches in 1882, wrote a short biography of Disraeli in 1888 and contributed the entry on Disraeli to the *Oxford Dictionary of National Biography*. It has been suggested that Disraeli wanted him to write his official biography.

Leonard, Richard (Dick)

Leonard (born 1930) was educated at Ealing Grammar School, the Institute of Education, London, and the University of Essex. After teaching in a school from 1953–5 he became deputy general secretary of the Fabian Society to 1960. During the 1960s he worked as a journalist and broadcaster, before becoming Labour MP for Romford (1970–4). He was subsequently assistant editor of the *Economist* and then a specialist in European affairs for the *Observer* newspaper.

Lewis, Clyde
Lewis completed his Master's degree in History at the University of Cincinnati in 1942, before serving in the United States Air Force during the war. In 1946 he became Assistant Professor of History at Eastern Kentucky State College, receiving his doctorate from Kentucky in 1956 and becoming a professor in 1960.

Lyons, Francis Stewart Leland
Educated at Dover College, Kent, and Trinity College, Dublin, Lyons (born 1923) lectured in History at University College, Hull, from 1947 to 1951 before becoming a Fellow of Trinity College, Dublin (1951–64). In 1964 he was appointed the first Professor of Modern History at the University of Kent. Lyons returned to Trinity College, Dublin, in 1981, and was Professor of History at the time of his death in 1983.

Macaulay, Thomas Babbington, Baron Macaulay
The son of the prominent anti-slavery campaigner and a graduate of Trinity College, Cambridge, Macaulay (1800–1859) sat in Parliament as a Liberal MP on various occasions between 1830 and 1856, during which time he held government office and also served as law officer to the Government of India. The foremost Whig historian and essayist of the nineteenth century, his most notable publication was *The History of England from the Accession of James the Second* (1848).

McCarthy, Justin
Born near Cork, Ireland, McCarthy (1830–1912) was a successful liberal journalist and novelist before, in 1878, publishing his widely read *A History of Our Own Times*. The profits from this book helped fund his political activities, and in 1879 he was elected to Parliament as Home Rule MP for County Longford. He was a member of the Land League and supported Charles Stewart Parnell's leadership of the Home Rule Party until 1890 when, in response to the scandal of the Parnell divorce case, he led the majority breakaway group of Irish MPs and became their chairman until 1896. Struck by blindness in 1898, McCarthy dictated his later books.

Machin, Ian
Professor of British History at the University of Dundee, Scotland, Machin has published extensively on the role of religion in nineteenth- and twentieth-century British history.

Magnus, (Sir) Philip Montefiore
The grandson of a Jewish Conservative MP, Magnus (1906–1988) was educated at Westminster School and Wadham College, Oxford, before entering the civil service and serving in the Royal Artillery and Intelligence Corps in

World War II. He published a series of popular biographies, beginning with a *Life of Edmund Burke* in 1939. Magnus's study of Gladstone was the first extensive treatment of his life since Morley's in 1903.

Marriott, (Sir) John Arthur Ransome

Marriott (1859–1945) was educated at Repton College and New College, Oxford, where he studied Modern History. Upon graduation, he taught History at Worcester College, Oxford, becoming a Fellow of the College in 1914. During this period he took a leading role in the University's extension lectures to non-academic audiences. A prolific author, Marriott was also a committed Conservative and contested several seats until, in 1917, he was elected Conservative MP for the City of Oxford. After defeat in 1922, he returned to parliament for York, retaining his seat until 1929.

Marsh, Peter T.

Having studied for his doctorate at the University of Cambridge, Marsh taught at the University of Saskatchewan (1962–7), before joining the University of Syracuse, where he became Professor of History in 1978.

Matthew, Colin

Colin Matthew (born 1941) graduated from Christ Church, Oxford, in 1963, before taking up a teaching position in East Africa. After returning to Oxford to complete a doctorate on the politics of the Liberal party, Matthew began, in 1970, to edit the Gladstone Diaries with M. R. D. Foot, becoming chief editor in 1972. In 1978 he became Tutor (later Professor) in History at St Hugh's College, Oxford, and in 1992 the director of the new *Oxford Dictionary of National Biography*. He died suddenly in 1999 of a heart attack.

Maurois, André, pseudonym of Herzog, Émile

Born to a Jewish family of textile manufacturers in Normandy, France, Herzog (1885–1967) wrote under the penname of Maurois, which became his official name in 1947. Maurois was the author of many works, including several studies of British culture and history.

Milner, Alfred, Viscount Milner

Born in Germany, Milner (1854–1925) was educated at King's College School, Wimbledon, and Balliol College, Oxford. After working as a journalist under John Morley at the *Pall Mall Gazette*, he entered public life, standing as a Liberal in the 1885 election. In 1889 he entered the government of Egypt, and his *England in Egypt* emerged from this experience. A notable imperialist, Milner later served as high commissioner for South Africa (1897–1901), where he contributed to the outbreak of the Second Boer War in 1899, and served in the War Cabinet during World War I.

Monypenny, William Flavelle

Born in 1866 in Ireland to an Ulster family, Monypenny attended the Royal School Dungannon and Trinity College, Dublin, before entering Balliol College, Oxford, which he left after a year due to ill-health. Taking up journalism, Monypenny worked for the *Spectator* and the *Times*, before travelling to the Transvaal to edit the *Johannesburg Star*. A strong advocate of the British cause against the Boers, he fought in the Second Boer War, being besieged at Ladysmith and then serving in the administration of Lord Milner. Returning to Britain in 1903, he again worked for the *Times*, which commissioned him to write the official biography of Disraeli based on the papers of Disraeli's personal secretary, Montagu Corry. He died of a heart attack in 1912 after completing the first volume.

Morley, John, Viscount Morley of Blackburn

John Morley (1838–1923) studied at Lincoln College, Oxford, but left without completing his degree owing to religious doubts. He became a leading Radical journalist before entering parliament as a Liberal in 1883. Morley was chief secretary for Ireland in 1886 and 1892. He was later secretary of state for India and resigned from the Liberal government in 1914 in opposition to the declaration of war on Germany.

Murray, David Leslie

Educated at Harrow School and Balliol College, Oxford, Murray (born 1888) first pursued an acting career before, in 1920, joining the staff of the *Times Literary Supplement*, which he edited (1937–44). Besides writing numerous novels, Murray wrote a study of the philosophy of *Pragmatism* (1912) and a book of theology, *Reservation: Its Purposes and Methods* (1923). Murray committed suicide in 1962 by taking poison.

Nicholls, David

Educated at the London School of Economics and Kings College, Cambridge, Nicholls (1936–1996) was ordained as a priest in 1963. He lectured in Government at the University of the West Indies, before becoming chaplin of Exeter College, Oxford, and senior member of St Antony's College, Oxford.

O'Day, Alan

Born in 1940 in Detroit, Michigan, O'Day attended the University of Michigan, Roosevelt University, and Northwestern University, before coming to England to study at University College, London, where he completed his doctorate in 1971. From 1976 to 2001 O'Day lectured in History at the University of North London, before becoming a Fellow of Greyfriars Hall, Oxford. Since 2008 he has been a History and Politics Fellow at St. Bede's Hall, Oxford.

Parry, Jonathan
Having been a student of Peterhouse College, Cambridge, Parry is Professor of Modern History at Cambridge and a Fellow of Pembroke College. His studies of nineteenth-century Liberalism have had a major impact upon our understanding of the politics of the period.

Porter, Bernard
A prominent historian of Empire, Porter graduated from the University of Cambridge, becoming first a Fellow of Corpus Christi College, and then lecturing at the Universities of Hull and Newcastle, where he was Professor of History.

Partridge, Michael
Partridge read History at the University of Birmingham and then completed a PhD in History at the London School of Economics. He first lectured at the City of London Polytechnic and joined the Department of History at St Mary's College, Twickenham, in 1985. In 2003 he published *Gladstone 1809–1898*. He died in 2009.

Quinault, Roland
Quinault was an undergraduate at Magdalene College, Oxford, before pursuing postgraduate studies at Nuffield College and Merton College, Oxford. He was Reader in History at London Metropolitan University, and is currently senior research fellow at the Institute of Historical Research, University of London.

Ramm, Agatha
Born in Germany to an English father and German mother, Ramm (1914–2004) taught history at Somerville College, Oxford, from 1952, and specialized in nineteenth-century diplomatic history, editing the Gladstone–Granville correspondence.

Raymond, E. T., pseudonym of Thompson, Edward Roffe
Thompson (1872–1928) was a psychologist and journalist on *John Bull* magazine. He was married to the pioneer film critic Caroline Lejeune and wrote an early self-help book, *The Human Machine: Secrets of Success* (1925). Under the name E. T. Raymond he wrote popular studies of political and historical subjects, including *Mr Balfour: A Biography* (1920) and *Uncensored Celebrities* (1918).

Roberts, Frederick David
Roberts (born 1923) is Emeritus Professor of History at Dartmouth College, New Hampshire, joining the staff in 1957. He has written extensively on the Victorian welfare provision, including *Victorian Origins of the British Welfare State* (1960).

Robinson, Ronald Edward

After attending Battersea Grammar School, Robinson (1920–1999) was a student and then Fellow of St John's College, Cambridge. During World War II he served with the Royal Air Force in Africa and took part in bombing raids over Germany. After serving in the Africa section of the Colonial Office 1947–9, Robinson became a Fellow of St John's College, Cambridge. He was Beit Professor of Commonwealth History at the University of Oxford (1971–81) and a Fellow of Balliol College.

Russell, George William Erskine

Russell (1853–1919) was the grandson of the Sixth Duke of Bedford, and shared the family's Whig traditions – although he was more sympathetic to Radicalism, supporting, for example, the disestablishment of the Church of England. He studied at Harrow School and University College, Oxford. A Liberal MP, he was appointed to the Local Government Board (1883–5) and was undersecretary of state for India (1892–4). Retiring from active politics in 1895, he devoted much time to religious work.

St John, Ian

Educated at Chingford Senior High School, London, St John (born 1965) studied for an undergraduate degree at the University of York before completing a doctorate at Nuffield College, Oxford. Since 2000 he has taught history at Haberdashers' Aske's School, Elstree. He is the author of *Disraeli and the Art of Victorian Politics* (2005) and *The Making of the Raj: India under the East India Company* (2011).

Saunders, Robert

Saunders was educated at Magdalen College, Oxford. He is currently lecturer in Modern History at Queen Mary College, University of London.

Seaman, Lewis Charles Bernard

Seaman (1911–1986) was educated at the Polytechnic Secondary School (The Quintin School), London, and Downing College, Cambridge (1930–3), where he studied History. Seaman then became a schoolteacher, including at Quintin School (1950–8), and was chief examiner in A-level History for the University of London. He was the author of the popular *From Vienna to Versailles* (1964).

Seton-Watson, Robert William

Educated at Winchester College and New College, Oxford, where he read Modern History, Seton-Watson (1879–1951) was a historian and political activist who vigorously advocated the cause of the Slavic people of Eastern Europe and who helped form the state of Yugoslavia after World War I. In

1915 he took a leading role in establishing the School of Slavonic Studies in the University of London, and was a professor there from 1922 to 1945.

Schreuder, Deryck M.
Currently Emeritus Professor of History and Education at the University of Sydney, Schreuder was previously vice-chancellor of the Universities of Western Sydney and the University of Western Australia and President of the Australian Historical Association. His principal research interests have been in modern British and international history, especially in relation to imperial history.

Shannon, Richard
Richard Shannon was born in Fiji. He was educated at the University of Auckland, New Zealand, before studying for his doctorate at Caius College, Cambridge. After lecturing at the Universities of Auckland and East Anglia, he was appointed, in 1979, Professor of History at the University of Swansea, Wales, where he remained until his retirement.

Sichel, Walter Sydney
Educated at Harrow School and Balliol College, Oxford, Sichel (1855–1933) was called to the Bar in 1879. Besides his two books on Disraeli, both published in 1904, Sichel also wrote a study of *Bolingbroke* (1902), as well as patriotic poetry during World War I.

Smith, Francis Barry
Smith (born 1932) was educated at the Universities of Melbourne and Cambridge. He joined the Australian National University in 1966, becoming Professor of History in 1975. Since his early work on reform, Smith has focused on medical history and the history of public health.

Smith, Goldwin
Born in 1823 in Reading, Smith was educated at Eton College and Christ Church and Magdalen Colleges, Oxford, where he was an outstanding classical scholar. He pursued careers in academia (he was a Law Fellow of University College, Oxford, and was later appointed Regius Professor of Modern History by Lord Derby in 1858) and journalism, being a noted liberal in politics and friend of Gladstone. However, he broke with Gladstone over his plans for Irish Home Rule, which he opposed. He settled in Canada in 1871, where he died in 1910.

Smith, G. Barnett
Born near Halifax, Smith (1841–1909) worked as a journalist in London and wrote a series of books on political and literary topics. His biography of Gladstone was one of the first serious and highly detailed treatments of his career.

Smith, Paul
Smith (born 1937) studied for his doctorate at St Antony's College, Oxford, his thesis providing the basis for his highly influential *Disraelian Conservatism and Social Reform* (1967). After lecturing in History at King's College, London, Smith taught at the University of Southampton, where he became Professor of Modern History.

Somervell, David C.
Educated at Harrow School and Magdalen College, Oxford, Somervell (1885–1965) taught at Repton School and, from 1919, at Tonbridge School in Kent. He is best known for his one-volume abridgement of Arnold Toynbee's *A Study of History*.

Stansky, Peter
Stansky (born 1932), who has published prolifically on nineteenth- and twentieth-century British political and cultural history, was from 1968 Professor of History at Stanford, having previously studied as an undergraduate at Yale University and King's College, Cambridge, before completing his doctorate at Harvard University in 1961.

Steele, E. David
Steele did his doctoral research on the Irish land question in British politics. He spent his academic career at the University of Leeds, where he was Senior Lecturer in History. He has published studies of the political careers of Palmerston and Salisbury.

Stembridge, Stanley
Stembridge (1924–1995) studied at Boston and Harvard Universities before teaching at Suffolk, Ohio, and Northeastern Universities.

Thornton, Archibald P.
A notable historian of empire, Archibald Thornton (1921–2004) entered the University of Glasgow after serving in the army in World War II. He then studied and lectured at Trinity College, Oxford, before teaching at the University of Aberdeen and University College West Indies. In 1960 he became Professor of History at the University of Toronto.

Trevelyan, George Macaulay
The son of the Liberal politician and historian, George Otto Trevelyan, Trevelyan (1876–1962) was educated at Harrow School and Trinity College, Cambridge, where he became a Fellow in 1898. In 1903 he resigned his Fellowship and moved to London, where he wrote a series of successful books, including a three-volume study of *Garibaldi*, whom he greatly admired. During World War I, he drove an ambulance in Italy. In 1927 he was appointed Regius Professor of History at Cambridge, and was later Master of Trinity

College (1940–51). A highly influential representative of the Whig school of history, Trevelyan's literary historical style ensured a large audience for his works. Trevelyan was appointed to the Order of Merit in 1930. A passionate walker, he was first President of the Youth Hostel Association.

Vincent, John
Educated at Christ's College, Cambridge, Vincent (born 1937) was a Fellow of Peterhouse College, Cambridge (1962–70), before becoming Professor of History at the University of Bristol. His first book, *The Formation of the Liberal Party*, was published in 1966.

Walker-Smith, Derek, Baron Broxbourne
Walker-Smith (1910–1992) studied History at Christ Church, Oxford, where he published his account of the *Protectionist Case of the 1840s* at the age of only 23. While pursuing a legal career he wrote several books, including a strong defence of Neville Chamberlain's policy of Appeasement. During World War II, he served in the Royal Artillery and on the staff of General Dwight D. Eisenhower. Walker-Smith sat as Conservative MP for Hertford 1945–83. He was minister of health (1957–60) and, although initially a vehement opponent of British entry into the EEC, was a Member of the European Parliament 1973–9. He became Baron Broxbourne in 1983.

Walton, John K.
Walton studied at Merton College, Oxford, and the University of Lancaster, where he was Professor of Social History (1995–8). He has since held research posts at the University of Central Lancaster and Leeds Metropolitan University.

Weeks, Richard G.
Weeks studied History at Macalester College, before continuing his postgraduate studies in Modern European History at the University of Minnesota. He is currently Professor of History and Academic Dean at Defiance College, Ohio. His chief speciality is in the sphere of Russian history.

Winstanley, Michael John
Winstanley was educated at the University of Oxford, where he studied Politics and Economics. In 1972 he moved to Lancaster University to do a Master's in Modern Social History. After a period at the University of Kent, he returned to Lancaster in 1978, and is now Senior Lecturer in History.

Woodward, (Sir) Ernest Llwellyn
Educated at Merchant Taylors' School, Woodward (1890–1971) spent most of his academic career at Oxford – first as a student of Corpus Christie College, and then, following service in World War I, a Fellow of All Souls and New College. In the 1950s he was based at Princeton University. He wrote the official history of *British Foreign Policy in the Second World War* (1962).

BIBLIOGRAPHY

Adelman, P., *Gladstone, Disraeli and Later Victorian Politics* (Longman, London, 1970).

Aldous, R., *The Lion and the Unicorn: Gladstone vs Disraeli* (Pimlico, London, 2006).

Anderson, O., 'Loans versus Taxes: British Financial Policy in the Crimean War', *Economic History Review*, New Series 16 (1963): 314–27.

Apjohn, L., *The Earl of Beaconsfield: His Life and Work* (C. J. Welton, Nottingham, 1884).

Bagehot, W., 'Mr. Gladstone'. 1860. In *Collected Works of Walter Bagehot*, III, edited by St John-Stevas, 415–40.

———. 'Why Has Disraeli Succeeded?' 1867. In *Collected Works of Walter Bagehot*, III, edited by St John-Stevas, 491–94.

———. 'Mr. Disraeli's Administration'. 1868. In *Collected Works of Walter Bagehot*, III, edited by St John-Stevas, 495–99.

Beales, D. E. D., *England and Italy 1859–1860* (Nelson. London, 1961).

———. *From Castlereagh to Gladstone 1815–1885* (Nelson, London, 1969).

Bebbington, D. W., *The Mind of Gladstone: Religion, Homer, and Politics* (Oxford University Press, Oxford, 2004).

———. *William Ewart Gladstone* (Wm. B. Eerdmans Publishing Company, Grand Rapids, 1993).

Beeley, H., *Disraeli* (Duckworth, London, 1936).

Bellairs, C. E., *Conservative Social and Industrial Reform* (Conservative Political Centre, London, 1977).

Bentley, M., *Politics without Democracy 1815–1914* (Fontana, London, 1984).

Biagini, E. F., *Gladstone* (Palgrave Macmillan, London, 2000).

Birrell, F., *Gladstone: Great Lives* (Duckworth, London, 1933).

Blake, R., *Disraeli* (Eyre and Spottiswoode, London, 1966).

———. *Disraeli: Clarendon Biographies* (Oxford University Press, Oxford, 1969).

———. 'Gladstone and Disraeli', in P. Jagger (ed.), *Gladstone*, 51–70.

Bodelsen, C. A., *Studies in Mid-Victorian Imperialism* (Gyldendalske Boghandel, Copenhagen, 1924).

Bourne, K., *The Foreign Policy of Victorian England 1830–1902* (Oxford University Press, Oxford, 1970).

Boyce, D. G., 'Gladstone and Ireland', in P. J. Jagger (ed.), *Gladstone*, 105–22.

———. *The Irish Question and British Politics, 1868–1996* (Palgrave Macmillan, London, 1996).

Bradford, S., *Disraeli* (Weidenfeld and Nicholson, London, 1982).

Brandes, G., *Lord Beaconsfield: A Study of Benjamin Disraeli* (Thomas Crowell Company, New York, 1880).

Briggs, A., *Victorian People: A Reassessment of Persons and Themes 1851–1867* (Penguin Books, London, 1954).

Burdett, O., *W. E. Gladstone* (Constable, London, 1927).

Butler, G. G., *The Tory Tradition* (John Murray, London, 1914).

Butler, P., *Gladstone: Church, State, and Tractarianism* (Oxford University Press, Oxford, 1982).

Buxton, S., *Finance and Politics: An Historical Study 1783–1885* (John Murray, London, 1888).

Chapman, J. K. and Littlejohn, C. J., 'Home Rule Revisited: an Essay in Historiography', *Historical Reflections/Réflexions Historiques* 3 (1976): 27–47.

Checkland, S. G., *The Gladstones: A Family Biography 1764–1851* (Cambridge University Press, Cambridge, 1971).

Clayden, P. W., *England under Lord Beaconsfield* (C. Kegan Paul and Company, London, 1880).

Coleman, B., *Conservatism and the Conservative Party in Nineteenth Century Britain* (Hodder Arnold, London, 1988).

Collieu, E. G., *Gladstone: Clarendon Biographies* (Oxford University Press, Oxford, 1968).

Cooke, A. B. and Vincent, J., *The Governing Passion: Cabinet Government and Party Politics in Britain 1885–86* (Barnes and Noble, New York, 1974).

Cowling, M., *1867: Disraeli, Gladstone and Revolution: The Passing of the Second Reform Bill* (Cambridge University Press, Cambridge, 1967).

——. 'Disraeli, Derby and Fusion, October 1865 to July 1866', *Historical Journal* 8 (1965): 31–71.

Cromer, Earl of, *Modern Egypt* (Macmillan, London, 1911).

——. *Political and Literary Essays 1908–1913* (Macmillan, London, 1913).

Crosby, T. L., *The Two Mr. Gladstones: A Study in Psychology and History* (Yale University Press, New Haven, 1997).

Davis, R. W., *Disraeli* (Hutchinson, London, 1976).

Dicey, A. V., *Lectures on the Relation between Law and Public Opinion in England during the Nineteenth Century* (Macmillan, London, 1905).

Dunne, T., 'Responses to Gladstonian Home Rule and Land Reform', *Irish Historical Studies* 25 (1987): 432–8.

Duthie, J. L., 'Pragmatic Diplomacy or Imperial Encroachment?: British Policy Towards Afghanistan, 1874–1879', *International History Review* 5 (1983): 475–95.

Edinger, G. and Neep, E. J. C., *The Grand Old Man: A Gladstone Spectrum* (Methuen, London, 1936).

Edwards, H. W. J. (ed.), *The Radical Tory: Disraeli's Political Development Illustrated from his Original Writings and Speeches* (Jonathan Cape, London, 1937).

Eldridge, C. C., *Disraeli and the Rise of the New Imperialism* (University of Wales Press, Cardiff, 1996).

——. *England's Mission: The Imperial Idea in the Age of Gladstone and Disraeli 1868–1880* (Macmillan, London, 1973).

Ensor, R. C. K., *England: 1870–1914* (Oxford University Press, Oxford, 1936).

Esslemont, P., *To the Fifth Generation: A Hundred Minutes with Gladstone* (John Avery and Company, Aberdeen, 1941).

Eyck, E., *Gladstone* (George Allen and Unwin, London, 1938).

Faber, R., *Young England* (Faber and Faber, London, 1987).

Feuchtwanger, E., *Disraeli* (Bloomsbury, London, 2000).

———. *Gladstone* (Allen Lane, London, 1975).

Fraser, W., *Disraeli and His Day* (Kegan Paul, Trench, Trubner and Company, London, 1891).

Froude, J. A., *Lord Beaconsfield* (Sampson Low, Marston and Company, London, 1890).

Galbraith, J. S. and al-Sayyid-Marsot, A. L., 'The British Occupation of Egypt: Another View', *International Journal of Middle East Studies* 9 (1978): 471–88.

Gallagher, T. F., '"Cardwellian Mysteries": The Fate of the British Army Regulation Bill, 1871', *Historical Journal* 18 (1975): 327–48.

Garratt, G. T., *The Two Mr. Gladstones* (Macmillan, London, 1936).

Gaunt, R. A., 'Gladstone and Peel's Mantle'. In *William Gladstone: New Studies and Perspectives*, edited by R. Quinault, R. Swift and R. Clayton Windscheffel, 31–50.

Ghosh, P. R., 'Disraelian Conservatism: A Financial Approach', *English Historical Review* 99 (1984): 268–96.

———. 'Style and Substance in Disraelian Social Reform, c. 1860–80'. In *Politics and Social Change in Modern Britain*, edited by P. J. Waller, 59–90.

Gladstone, H., *After Thirty Years* (Macmillan, London, 1928).

Goodlad, G. D., 'The Liberal Party and Gladstone's Land Purchase Bill of 1886', *Historical Journal* 32 (1989): 627–41.

Grant, N., *Benjamin Disraeli: Prime Minister Extraordinary* (Franklin Watts, London, 1969).

Gunsaulus, F. W., *William Ewart Gladstone: A Biographical Study* (American Educational League, Chicago, 1898).

Gurowich, P. M., 'The Continuation of War by Other Means: Party and Politics, 1855–1865', *Historical Journal* 27 (1984): 603–31.

Hamer, D. A., 'Gladstone: The Making of a Political Myth', *Victorian Studies* 22 (1978): 29–50.

———. *Liberal Politics in the Age of Gladstone and Rosebery* (Oxford University Press, Oxford, 1972).

Hammond, J. L., *Gladstone and the Irish Nation* (Longman, London, 1938).

Hammond, J. L. and Foot, M. R. D., *Gladstone and Liberalism* (English Universities Press, London, 1952).

Hanham, H. J., *Elections and Party Management: Politics in the Time of Disraeli and Gladstone* (Longmans, London, 1959).

Harcourt, F., 'Disraeli's Imperialism, 1866–68: A Question of Timing', *Historical Journal* 23 (1980): 87–109.

Hawkins, A. B., *British Party Politics, 1852–1886* (Macmillan, London, 1998).

———. 'A Forgotten Crisis: Gladstone and the Politics of Finance During the 1850s', *Victorian Studies* 26 (1983): 287–320.

———. *The Forgotten Prime Minister: The 14th Earl of Derby. Volume II. Achievement: 1851–1869* (Oxford University Press, Oxford, 2008).

———. *Parliament, Party and the Art of Politics in Britain, 1855–59* (Macmillan, London, 1987).

Hayes, T. T., *Lord Beaconsfield: A Paper Read before the Members of the Leigh Liberal Club* (John Kempster, Hayes, 1878).

Helmstadter, R. J., 'Conscience and Politics: Gladstone's First Book'. In *The Gladstonian Turn of Mind*, edited by B. Kinzer (ed.), 3–42.

Hilton, B., *The Age of Atonement: The Influence of Evangelicalism on Social and Economic Thought, 1785–1865* (Oxford University Press, Oxford, 1988).

Himmelfarb, G., 'Commitment and Ideology: The Case of the Second Reform Act', *Journal of British Studies* 9 (1969): 100–4.

———. 'The Politics of Democracy: the English Reform Act of 1867', *Journal of British Studies* 6 (1966): 97–138.

Hirst, F. W., *Gladstone as Economist and Financier* (Ernest Benn, London, 1931).

———. 'Notes and Memoranda: Mr. Gladstone. I.', *Economic Journal* 8 (1898): 395–402.

———. 'Notes and Memoranda: Mr. Gladstone. II.', *Economic Journal* 8 (1898): 533–43.

Hopkins, A. G., 'The Victorians and Africa: A Reconsideration of the Occupation of Egypt, 1882', *Journal of African History* 27 (1986): 363–91.

Hoppen, K. T., *The Mid-Victorian Generation 1846–1886* (Oxford University Press, Oxford, 1998).

———. 'Tories, Catholics, and the General Election of 1859', *Historical Journal* 13 (1970): 48–67.

Hurd, D. and Young, E., *Disraeli or The Two Lives* (Weidenfeld and Nicholson, London, 2013).

Jagger, P. J. (ed.), *Gladstone* (Hambledon Press, London, 1998).

Jenkins, R., *Gladstone* (Macmillan, London, 1995).

Jenkins, T. A., *Disraeli and Victorian Conservatism* (Palgrave Macmillan, London, 1996).

———. 'Gladstone, the Whigs and the Leadership of the Liberal Party, 1879–1880', *The Historical Journal* 27 (1984): 337–60.

———. *Gladstone, Whiggery and the Liberal Party 1874–1886* (Oxford University Press, Oxford, 1988).

———. *Parliament, Party and Politics in Victorian Britain* (Manchester University Press, Manchester, 1996).

Jennings, W. I., 'Disraeli and the Constitution', *Journal of Comparative Legislation and International Law*, Third Series, 13 (1931): 182–98.

Jones, A. W., 'Where "Governing is the use of Words"', *Historical Journal* 19 (1976): 251–56.

Jones, W. D., *Lord Derby and Victorian Conservatism* (Blackwell, Oxford, 1956).

Kalmar, I. D., 'Benjamin Disraeli, Romantic Orientalist', *Comparative Studies in Society and History* 47 (2005): 348–71.

Kebbel, T. E., *Lord Beaconsfield and Other Tory Memories* (Cassell and Company, London, 1907).

Kinzer, B. L. (ed.), *The Gladstonian Turn of Mind: Essays Presented to J. B. Conacher* (University of Toronto Press, Toronto, 1985).

Leonard, D., *The Great Rivalry: Gladstone and Disraeli* (I. B. Tauris, London, 2013).

Lewis, D. J., 'Theory and Expediency in the Policy of Disraeli', *Victorian Studies* 4, No. 3 (1961): 237–58.

Lyons, F. S. L., *Ireland Since the Famine* (Fontana Press, London, 1973 edn.).

———. 'Review of *Gladstone and Ireland* by John Vincent', *Irish Historical Studies* 22 (1979): 498–500

McCarthy, J., *A History of Our Own Times*, IV (Chatto and Windus, London, 1880).

———. *The Story of Gladstone's Life* (Adam and Charles Black, London, 1898).

Macaulay, T. B., 'Gladstone on Church and State' (1839). In *Lord Macaulay's Critical and Historical Essays*, II, edited by Montague, 329–88.

Machin, I., *Disraeli* (Longman, London, 1995).

Macintyre, A., 'Lord George Bentinck and the Protectionists: A Lost Cause?', *Transactions of the Royal Historical Society*, Fifth Series, 39 (1989): 141–65.

Magnus, P., *Gladstone: A Biography* (John Murray, London, 1954).

Marriott, J. A. R., *England Since Waterloo* (Methuen, London, 1913).

Marsh, P. T., *Joseph Chamberlain: Entrepreneur in Politics* (Yale University Press, New Haven, 1994).

Matthew, H. C. G., 'Disraeli, Gladstone, and the Politics of Mid-Victorian Budgets', *Historical Journal* 22 (1979): 615–43.

———. *Gladstone: 1809–1898* (Oxford University Press, Oxford, 1997).

Maurois, A., *Disraeli: A Picture of the Victorian Age* (Bodley Head, London, 1927).

Millar, M. S. and Wiebe, M. G., '"This Power so Vast…& so Generally Misunderstood": Disraeli and the Press in the 1840s', *Victorian Periodicals Review* 25 (1992): 79–85.

Milner, A., *England in Egypt* (Edward Arnold, London, 1892).

Montague, F. C. (ed.), *Lord Macaulay's Critical and Historical Essays* (Methuen, London, 1903).

Monypenny, W. F. and Buckle, G. E., *The Life of Benjamin Disraeli* (John Murray, London, 1929 edn).

Morley, J., *The Life of William Ewart Gladstone* (Macmillan, London, 1903).

Murray, D. L., *Disraeli* (Ernest Benn, London, 1927).

Nicholls, D., 'Gladstone on Liberty and Democracy', *Review of Politics* 23 (1961): 401–9.

O'Day, A., *Irish Home Rule 1867–1921* (Manchester University Press, Manchester, 1998).

Parry, J., *Benjamin Disraeli* (Oxford University Press, Oxford, 2007).

———. *Democracy and Religion: Gladstone and the Liberal Party, 1867–1875* (Cambridge University Press, Cambridge, 1986).

———. 'Disraeli and England', *Historical Journal* 43 (2000): 699–728.

———. *The Rise and Fall of Liberal Government in Victorian Britain* (Yale University Press, New Haven, 1993).

Partridge, M., 'Review of *Reading Gladstone* by R. Windscheffel', *Victorian Studies* 51 (2009): 581–2.

Pearson, H., *Dizzy: The Life and Personality of Benjamin Disraeli, Earl of Beaconsfield* (Methuen, London, 1951).

Porter, B., *Britannia's Burden: The Political Evolution of Modern Britain 1851–1990* (Hodder Education, London, 1994).

Quinault, R., 'Gladstone and War'. *William Gladstone*, edited by Quinault et al., 235–51.

Quinault, R., Swift, R., and Clayton Windscheffel, R. (eds.), *William Gladstone: New Studies and Perspectives* (Ashgate, Farnham, 2012).

Ramm, A., *William Ewart Gladstone* (University of Wales Press, Cardiff, 1989).

Raymond, E. T., *Disraeli: The Alien Patriot* (Hodder and Stoughton, London, 1925).

Richmond, C. and Smith, P. (eds.), *The Self-Fashioning of Disraeli 1818–1851* (Cambridge University Press, Cambridge, 1998).

Ridley, J., *The Young Disraeli: 1804–1846* (Sinclair-Stevenson, London, 1995).

Roberts, D., 'Tory Paternalism and Social Reform in Early Victorian England', *American Historical Review* 63 (1958): 323–37.

Robinson, R. and Gallagher, J., *Africa and the Victorians: The Official Mind of Imperialism* (Macmillan, London, Second ed., 1981).

Rodgers, N., 'The Abyssinian Expedition of 1867–1868: Disraeli's Imperialism or James Murray's War?', *Historical Journal* 27 (1984): 129–49.

Russell, G. W. E., *William Ewart Gladstone* (Sampson Low, Marston and Company, London, 1891).

Saab, A. P., 'Disraeli, Judaism, and the Eastern Question', *International History Review* 10 (1988): 559–78.

———. 'Foreign Affairs and New Tories: Disraeli, "The Press", and the Crimean War', *International History Review* 19 (1997): 286–311.

St John, I., *Disraeli and the Art of Victorian Politics* (Anthem Press, London, 2005).

———. *Gladstone and the Logic of Victorian Politics* (Anthem Press, London, 2010).

St John-Stevas, N. (ed.), *The Collected Works of Walter Bagehot* (Harvard University Press, Cambridge Massachusetts, 1968).

Saunders, R., 'The Politics of Reform and the Making of the Second Reform Act',

———. *Historical Journal* 50 (2007): 571–91.

Schreuder, D. M., 'Gladstone and Italian Unification, 1848–70: The Making of a Liberal?', *English Historical Review* 85 (1970): 475–501.

———. 'The Making of Mr Gladstone's Posthumous Career: The Role of Morley and Knaplund as "Monumental Masons" 1903–27'. In *The Gladstonian Turn of Mind*, edited by B. L. Kinzer, 197–243.

Seaman, L. C. B., *Victorian England: Aspects of English and Imperial History 1837–1901* (Routledge, London, 1973).

Seton-Watson, R. W., *Disraeli, Gladstone, and the Eastern Question* (W. W. Norton and Company, London, 1935).

Shannon, R., *The Age of Disraeli, 1868–1881: The Rise of Tory Democracy* (Longman, London, 1992).

———. *Gladstone Volume I: Peel's Inheritor* (Hamish Hamilton, London, 1982).

———. *Gladstone Volume II: Heroic Minister 1865–1898* (Allen Lane, London, 1999).

———. *Gladstone and the Bulgarian Agitation 1876* (Nelson, London, 1963).

———. *Gladstone: God and Politics* (Continuum, London, 2007).

Sichel, W., *Disraeli: A Study in Personality and Ideas* (Methuen, London, 1904).

———. *The Life of Lord Beaconsfield* (Methuen, London, 1904).

Smith, F. B., 'The "Dependence of License upon Faith": Miss Gertrude Himmelfarb on the Second Reform Act', *Journal of British Studies* 9 (1969): 96–9.

———. *The Making of the Second Reform Bill* (Cambridge University Press, Cambridge, 1966).

Smith, G., 'Mr. Morley's Life of Gladstone. II.', *North American Review* 178 (1904).

Smith, G. B., *The Life of the Right Honourable William Ewart Gladstone* (Cassell, Petter, Galpin and Company, London, 1880).

Smith, P., *Disraeli: A Brief Life* (Cambridge University Press, Cambridge, 1996).

———. *Disraelian Conservatism and Social Reform* (Routledge and Kegan Paul, London, 1967).

———. 'Disraeli's Politics', *Transactions of the Royal Historical Society*, Fifth Series, 37 (1987): 65–85.

Somervell, D. C., *Gladstone and Disraeli: A Duo-Biographical Sketch* (Faber and Faber, London, 1932).

Stansky, P., *Gladstone: A Progress in Politics* (W. W. Norton and Company, New York, 1979).

Stapledon, R. G., *Disraeli and the New Age* (Faber and Faber, London, 1943).

Steele, E. D., 'Gladstone and Ireland', *Irish Historical Studies* 17 (1970): 58–88.

Stembridge, S. R., 'Disraeli and the Millstones', *Journal of British Studies* 5 (1965): 122–39.

Temperley, H., 'Disraeli and Cyprus', *English Historical Review* 46 (1931): 274–79.

Thornton, A. P., *The Imperial Idea and Its Enemies* (Macmillan, London, 1959).

Trevelyan, G. M., *British History in the Nineteenth Century* (Longmans Green and Company, London, 1922).

Vidler, Alec R., *The Orb and the Cross: A Normative Study in the Relations of Church and State with reference to Gladstone's Early Writings* (London Society for Promoting Christian Knowledge, London, 1945).

Vincent, J., *Disraeli* (Oxford University Press, Oxford, 1990).

———. *The Formation of the British Liberal Party 1857–1868* (Penguin Books, Middlesex, 1972 edn).

———. 'Was Disraeli a Failure?', *History Today* (October, 1981).

Walker-Smith, D., *The Protectionist Case in the 1840s* (Basil Blackwell, Oxford, 1933).

Waller, P. J. (ed.), *Politics and Social Change in Modern Britain* (Harvester Wheatsheaf, Brighton, 1987).

Walton, J., *Disraeli* (Routledge, London, 1990).

Weeks, R. G., 'Disraeli as Political Egoist: A Literary and Historical Investigation', *Journal of British Studies* 28 (1989): 387–410.

Williamson, D., *William Ewart Gladstone: Statesman and Scholar* (Ward, Lock and Company, London, 1898).

Winstanley, M. J., *Gladstone and the Liberal Party* (Routledge, London, 1990).

Woodward, E. L., *The Age of Reform: 1815–1870* (Oxford University Press, Oxford, 1938).

INDEX

Lightning Source UK Ltd.
Milton Keynes UK
UKHW012042020719
345426UK00001B/40/P